Internet Law and Business

International Issues

Internet Law and Business
International Issues

Richard O Parry
California State University, USA

World Scientific

NEW JERSEY • LONDON • SINGAPORE • BEIJING • SHANGHAI • HONG KONG • TAIPEI • CHENNAI • TOKYO

Published by

World Scientific Publishing Co. Pte. Ltd.
5 Toh Tuck Link, Singapore 596224
USA office: 27 Warren Street, Suite 401-402, Hackensack, NJ 07601
UK office: 57 Shelton Street, Covent Garden, London WC2H 9HE

Library of Congress Control Number: 2023046851

British Library Cataloguing-in-Publication Data
A catalogue record for this book is available from the British Library.

INTERNET LAW AND BUSINESS
International Issues

ISBN 978-981-127-690-3 (hardcover)
ISBN 978-981-127-849-5 (paperback)
ISBN 978-981-127-691-0 (ebook for institutions)
ISBN 978-981-127-692-7 (ebook for individuals)

For any available supplementary material, please visit
https://www.worldscientific.com/worldscibooks/10.1142/13427#t=suppl

Desk Editors: Logeshwaran Arumugam/Nicole Ong

Typeset by Stallion Press
Email: enquiries@stallionpress.com

About the Author

Richard O. Parry is an Attorney and Professor at California State University, Fullerton, where he has taught a variety of courses, both undergraduate and graduate, for almost 30 years. Professor Parry earned his undergraduate degree at the University of Denver and his juris doctor at Loyola of Los Angeles Law School. He is the recipient of numerous awards including the prestigious Academy of Legal Studies in Business Distinguished Proceedings Award, Outstanding Business Honors Professor, as well as the Recipient of Recognition of Outstanding Scholarly Activity. He has served as an assistant Little League coach, a member of the board of directors of a charitable foundation and is AV rated by Martindale-Hubbell, their highest rating. His research interests include legal and ethical issues that affect business, such as ethical and constitutional issues related to business including the criminal prosecution of a business and its employees. He has authored or co-authored scholarly articles that have been published by the *Berkeley Business Law Journal*, the *Journal of Legal Studies in Business*, the *Drake Journal of Agricultural Law, the Journal of Business and Behavioral Sciences*, the *Houston Business and Tax Law Journal*, among others. Professor Parry may be reached via e-mail at rparry@fullerton.edu.

Contents

Chapter 1
Introduction

Abstract

Civil law traces its roots back at least 4,000 years ago to the Code of Hammurabi. Also playing a part in its development was the Roman Code. More recently, the Napoleonic Code played a significant role in the development of modern codes throughout the world. The common law system is a latecomer to this legal environment tracing its roots to the Battle of Hastings in 1066. Although both systems have notable differences, they also have some significant commonalities. And, although the United States is noted as a common law country it has a remarkable number of codes.

Globalization has presented challenges for countries as well as businesses. Among the significant challenges for both is the difference in legal systems. The two primary legal systems across the globe are common law and civil law.[1] Civil law is generally defined as codified, reducing laws to statutes, traditionally enacted by elected representatives, such as a legislature or its equivalent.[2] The common law, or judge-made law, on the other

[1] https://www.law.berkeley.edu/wp-content/uploads/2017/11/CommonLawCivilLawTraditions.pdf.

[2] https://www.law.cornell.edu/wex/civil_law#:~:text=Civil%20law%20refers%20either%20to,that%20originates%20from%20Roman%20Law.

hand, relies instead, on precedent or prior decisions by judges who were not elected.[3]

Codes are nothing new, possibly tracing their origin to the Code of Hammurabi, 282 laws inscribed into a stone by a Babylonian king, approximately 4,000 years ago.[4] In its more current form, civil law preceded the development of common law by centuries, tracing its roots to the sixth century and Emperor Justinian.[5] Civil law originated from the Latin *ius civile*, referring to the law that applied to Roman *cives* or citizens. As the World Bank notes, "Countries following a civil law system are typically those that were former French, Dutch, German, Spanish or Portuguese colonies or protectorates, including much of Central and South America. Most of the Central and Eastern European and East Asian countries also follow a civil law structure."[6]

The development of the common law is commonly associated with the Battle of Hastings in 1066. After William, Duke of Normandy defeated Harold Godwinson, he then set about unifying the country. One way that he did so was by way of a common law; law that was common throughout the land. Unsurprisingly, Emperor Justinian I (ruled 527–565 ce), faced the same challenge, although on a much larger scale.[7] In response, Justinian

> … formed a commission of jurists to compile all existing Roman law into one body, which would serve to convey the historical tradition, culture, and language of Roman law throughout the empire. This compilation is sometimes referred to as 'Justinian's Code,' but in fact the Code was only one element. The compilation … consisted of three different original parts: the Digest (Digesta), the Code (Codex), and the Institutes (Institutiones). The Digest (533 ce) collected and summarized all of the classical jurists' writings on law and justice. The Code (534 ce) outlined the actual laws of the empire, citing imperial constitutions, legislation, and pronouncements. The Institutes (535 ce) were a smaller work that summarized the Digest, intended as a textbook for students of

---

[3] https://www.law.berkeley.edu/wp-content/uploads/2017/11/CommonLawCivilLawTraditions.pdf.

[4] https://www.history.com/topics/ancient-history/hammurabi.

[5] https://onlinelaw.wustl.edu/blog/common-law-vs-civil-law/.

[6] https://ppp.worldbank.org/public-private-partnership/legislation-regulation/framework-assessment/legal-systems/common-vs-civil-law.

[7] https://www.law.berkeley.edu/wp-content/uploads/2019/08/romanlaw.pdf.

> law. A fourth work, the Novella (Novellae), was not a part of Justinian's project, but was created separately by legal scholars in 556 CE to update the Code with new laws created after 534 CE and summarize Justinian's own constitution. The compilation is widely considered to be the emperor's greatest contribution to the history of Western society.[8]

While commentators traditionally note that countries with a civil law system rely on codes rather than precedents[9] or *stare decisis*, the impact may be less significant. While common law systems are routinely found in countries where English is the predominant language, codes are also common. For instance, in the United States, the Federal Rules of Civil Procedure (FRCP) are just one of numerous federal "codes" that include the Federal Rules of Bankruptcy Procedure, the Federal Rules of Appellate Procedure, the Federal Rules of Criminal Procedure, and the Federal Rules of Evidence, among many others, which govern proceedings in federal courts. As the federal court notes,

> The FRCP governs civil proceedings in the United States district courts. Their purpose is to secure the just, speedy, and inexpensive determination of every action and proceeding. Fed. R. Civ. P. 1. The rules were first adopted by order of the Supreme Court on December 20, 1937, transmitted to Congress on January 3, 1938, and became effective September 16, 1938.[10]

In addition, there is the United States Code (U.S.C.). As govinfo.gov notes,

> The United States Code is the codification by subject matter of the general and permanent laws of the United States. It is divided by broad subjects into 53 titles and published by the Office of the Law Revision Counsel of the U.S. House of Representatives. The U.S. Code was first published in 1926 … Of the 54 titles, the following titles have been enacted into positive (statutory) law: 1, 3, 4, 5, 9, 10, 11, 13, 14, 17, 18, 23, 28, 31, 32, 35, 36, 37, 38, 39, 40, 41, 44, 46, 49, 51, and 54. When a title of the Code was enacted into positive law, the text of the title

---

[8] https://www.law.berkeley.edu/wp-content/uploads/2019/08/romanlaw.pdf.

[9] https://www.law.berkeley.edu/wp-content/uploads/2017/11/CommonLawCivilLawTraditions.pdf.

[10] https://www.uscourts.gov/rules-policies/current-rules-practice-procedure.

became legal evidence of the law. Titles that have not been enacted into positive law are only prima facie evidence of the law. In that case, the Statutes at Large still govern. For the current list of titles, see http://uscode.house.gov.

Likewise, state codes are also common. In California, there are currently 29 codes that cover a variety of subjects from Business & Professions to Welfare and Institutions. It should be clear that describing the two primary legal systems that exist as either civil or common law is simplistic.

Currently, French law has 78 different codes.[11] The codes that relate to private as well as commercial law, are numerous, including, but not limited to, the Civil Code, the Code of Commerce, as well as codes related to construction and habitation, intellectual property, insurance, consumers, as well as monetary and financial, all of which relate to the subjects covered in this textbook.

Some commentators opine that judges in common law countries wield an exceptional amount of power, shaping American and British law, to a greater degree than in a civil law country.[12] Indeed, France's Civil Code, Article 1, Section 5[13] specifically states, "It is forbidden for judges to pronounce by way of general and regulatory provision on the cases submitted to them." However, there are significant limitations on judges in common law jurisdictions. Particularly in the United States, with the separation of powers, the authority of a judge to shape a law enacted by the legislature is limited. The federal legislature, the Congress, is free to revise laws, interpreted by judges, to the extent that the Congress disagrees with a judge's interpretation. An example is the Americans with Disabilities Act of 1990. Originally enacted by Congress and signed into law by President Bush in 1990, it was amended in 2008 by way of the

---

[11] http://www.gip-recherche-justice.fr/conference-consensus/legifrance_subdomain/Traductions/en-English/ which notes, "Legifrance is the French government entity responsible for publishing legal texts online." The website also notes, "The section 'Translations of French legal texts' is for reference purposes only. The texts accessible there have no legal force." Unless otherwise noted, Google Translate was used to translate the French into English.

[12] https://www.law.berkeley.edu/wp-content/uploads/2017/11/CommonLawCivilLawTraditions.pdf.

[13] https://www.legifrance.gouv.fr/codes/section_lc/LEGITEXT000006070721/LEGISCTA000006089696?etatTexte=VIGUEUR&anchor=LEGIARTI000006419280#LEGIARTI000006419280. The version in force November 16, 2023.

ADA Amendments Act of 2008 (P.L. 110-325), which became effective on January 1, 2009. The law was amended by Congress in response to a decision by the United States Supreme Court that interpreted the original Americans with Disabilities Act. As ADA.gov notes,

> Congress passed the ADA Amendments Act (ADAAA) in response to several Supreme Court decisions that ... narrowly interpreted the Americans with Disabilities Act's (ADA) definition of disability .... The law made a number of significant changes to the ADA definition of 'disability' to ensure that it would be easier for individuals seeking the protection of the ADA to establish that they have a disability that falls within the meaning of the statute.

While similarities between the two systems are likely far more common than differences, in some areas the difference is significant. The difference in the availability of discovery as part of the litigation process is notable. Discovery in a civil law system is virtually non-existent.[14] Discovery in the United States is a relatively new development and greatly contributes to the significant expense in the conduct of litigation. Litigation in the United States is likely to be far more expensive than in a civil law country.

The presence, or absence of a jury is another significant difference.[15] In the United States a case may be decided by a jury who need not explain the reason for its decision. As part of that, a jury decides questions of fact, while the judge decides questions of law. However, the availability of a jury in a common law civil case in the United States is not absolute.[16] In addition, there are options available to a judge in a civil law jury case. Among the available options are a motion for new trial and a motion for judgment notwithstanding the verdict. And, although it is something that contributes to the cost of litigation in America, there is the availability of an appeal. Arguably the most significant issue in the United States is the

---

[14] Geoffrey C. Hazard, Discovery and the Role of the Judge in Civil Law Jurisdictions, 73 Notre Dame L. Review 1017 (1998).

[15] https://www.diffen.com/difference/Civil_Law_vs_Common_Law which notes, "Juries are present almost exclusively in criminal cases; virtually never involved in civil actions."

[16] In a criminal case the Sixth Amendment guarantees the right to a trial by a jury. In a civil case, the Seventh Amendment provides that "In suits at common law, where the value in controversy shall exceed twenty dollars, the right of trial by jury shall be preserved, and no fact tried by a jury, shall be otherwise reexamined in any court of the United States, than according to the rules of the common law."

availability of arbitration where the parties agree, by way of a contract, on a method to resolve a dispute. Binding arbitration, particularly in dealings between businesses, should likely be a part of any contract. An arbitration agreement may specify the individual, or individuals that are to decide the dispute, the location of the arbitration, the law to be applied, as well as the availability, if any, of discovery, among other issues.

Though the primary focus of this text is civil law, not criminal, in the case of a criminal prosecution, while a judge may decide the punishment that is appropriate, federal judges must detail the rationale for the decision, not unlike a civil law system, because of federal sentencing guidelines.

Although a code system relies on laws enacted by a legislature of elected individuals and requires that a judge only decide a case in conformity with the requirements of a code it therefore, at least theoretically, removes the element of discretion. However, *stare decisis* in a common law system is also intended to remove a judge's discretion.

The role of the judge is substantially different in the two systems. Litigation in a common law system is ordinarily adversarial, with attorneys the equivalent of the Old West's hired guns, presenting their case to a jury, with a judge as referee. In a civil law system, the judge, or a panel of judges, establish the facts of the case and then apply the rules of the controlling code. Although France is currently a civil law country, it was not always so and certainly not in 1066. Prior to the French Revolution, France was ruled by a monarch, the only person allowed to administer justice. France's civil law would not come into existence for close to 800 years. Therefore, it is unsurprising that William, Duke of Normandy, did not impose a civil law system on the English.

The Napoleonic Code, along with several other codes, has generally been credited with the basis for the current civil law system. However, the Napoleonic Code was not the first. As one scholarly article notes, "As civil law came into practice throughout Europe, the role of local custom as a source of law became increasingly important — particularly as growing European states sought to unify and organize their individual legal systems. Throughout the early modern period, this desire generated scholarly attempts to systematize scattered, disparate legal provisions and local customary laws and bring them into harmony with rational principles of civil law and natural law. Emblematic of these attempts is the Dutch jurist Hugo Grotius' 1631 work, *Introduction to Dutch Jurisprudence*, which synthesized Roman law and Dutch customary law into a cohesive whole. In the eighteenth century, the reforming aspirations of Enlightenment rulers aligned with jurists' desire to rationalize the law to produce comprehensive, systematic legal codes including Austria's 1786 *Code of Joseph II* and *Complete Civil Code of 1811*, Prussia's *Complete Territorial Code of 1794*, and France's *Civil Code* (known as the *Napoleonic Code*) of 1804. Such codes, shaped by the Roman law tradition, are the models of today's civil law systems."[17]

An effort to compare and contrast American law on the subject of the Internet with European law is difficult, if not impossible. While there are efforts underway to establish a European Code, at least at this point, one does not yet exist. Thus, just as there are 52 different court systems in the United States, so too there are numerous court systems throughout the European Union. And, just as the common law systems have their differences, so too do the civil law systems.

Because of the influence of the Napoleonic Code, and in an effort to address the different approaches, American law will generally be compared to French law as translated into English.[18,19] It should also be noted that English translations are not official and that they may not reflect recent changes in the law. As part of the effort to compare and contrast the legal systems, reference will also be made to various Restatements of the Law, prepared by the American Law Institute (ALI). The various Restatements prepared by ALI arguably represent a significant effort at codification of the common law. As the ALI notes,

> Restatements are primarily addressed to courts and aim at clear formulations of common law and its statutory elements, and reflect the law as it presently stands or might appropriately be stated by a court. Although Restatements aspire toward the precision of statutory language, they are also intended to reflect the flexibility and capacity for development and growth of the common law. However, the ALI also prepares model codes, such as the Model Penal Code which 'are addressed to legislatures with a view toward legislative enactment. They are written in prescriptive statutory language.'[20]

---

[17] https://www.law.berkeley.edu/wp-content/uploads/2017/11/CommonLawCivilLawTraditions.pdf.

[18] By Google Translate.

[19] The laws, as well as the translations, unless otherwise noted, were obtained from https://www.legifrance.gouv.fr/.

[20] www.ali.org/about-all/how-institute-works/. Accessed November 16, 2022.

Chapter 2

Jurisdiction

Abstract

"Jurisdiction" comes from "juris" meaning the law and "diction" meaning "to speak". Jurisdiction relates to a court's ability to speak the law. Arguably the most important issue with regard to jurisdiction, at least for courts in America, are the requirements established by the Constitution for due process, as interpreted by the courts. Courts in other countries, and countries that utilize the civil law system may not be bound by such considerations.

The Constitution, however, is not the only source of law in America. In addition to the Constitution, there are state constitutions, statutory laws passed by federal, state, and local legislatures, regulations created by administrative agencies, as well as the common law. To make matters even more complicated, there can be a conflict among the various laws. And, unfortunately, there may be more than one right answer to a particular question.

By setting forth the rights, obligations, and privileges of all in our society, the law allows individuals and companies to conduct themselves with confidence and at least some degree of predictability.

As part of that, the law sets forth enforceable rules that govern relationships among individuals, organizations, society, and government. A significant difficulty is that many different laws as well as agency regulations, both state, federal, and sometimes foreign and even international, may affect an action.

> The Internet knows no borders, which poses a fundamental problem for courts where jurisdiction may be based on artificial geographical borders.

Overview

One of the most essential functions of law, whether in a common or civil law system, may be the most important function, is to provide stability, predictability, and continuity so that individuals and companies can determine what is legally right (or wrong). If an individual or company commits a wrongful act, they must know what kind of sanction they face. Likewise, if an individual or a company suffers harm or pecuniary loss because of another's act, they must be able to recover compensation.

By setting forth the rights, obligations, and privileges of all in our society, the law allows individuals and companies to conduct themselves with confidence and at least some degree of predictability. In the United States this is done by way of the Constitution, both state and federal, statutory law, as well as judge-made, or common, law. In a civil law system, this is accomplished by way of codes. As the World Bank notes, "Only legislative enactments are considered binding for all. There is little scope for judge-made law in civil, criminal and commercial courts, although in practice judges tend to follow previous judicial decisions; constitutional and administrative courts can nullify laws and regulations and their decisions in such cases are binding for all."[1]

The law sets forth enforceable rules that govern relationships among individuals, organizations, society, and government. One of the difficulties that all of us face is that many different laws as well as agency regulations, both state, federal and sometimes foreign and even international, may affect a decision. Sources of law in America include the U.S. Constitution as well as state constitutions, statutory laws passed by federal, state, and local legislatures, regulations created by administrative agencies, and also the common law. To make matters even worse, there can be a conflict among the various laws. Consider marijuana, for example. While recreational marijuana is legal in some states, it is still illegal, as a Schedule 1 drug, by federal law.

[1] https://ppp.worldbank.org/public-private-partnership/legislation-regulation/framework-assessment/legal-systems/common-vs-civil-law.

Last, in the United States there may be more than one right answer to a particular issue! Consider, for example, the issue with the Americans with Disabilities Act as Amended, and previously noted. The United States Supreme Court's interpretation was far different from what Congress apparently intended. That may be less of an issue in a country with a civil law system.

The foregoing presents a challenge for business. And, an additional problem is that the borders of cyberspace do not map onto geography, which poses a fundamental problem for courts whose jurisdiction is based on geography.

Introduction to Jurisdiction

In the United States and many other countries, numerous government agencies, the courts, both domestic and foreign, as well as private organizations are involved with the Internet. Complicating the issue is the presence of 52 different court systems in the United States. In a civil law system, a single, nationwide court system is the general rule, although in Europe there are courts specific to the underlying codes.[2] The presence of multiple court systems and courts in the United States which, in many cases may have concurrent jurisdiction is virtually unheard of in a civil law system. In some situations, concurrent jurisdiction means that a lawsuit may properly be heard in either a federal or state court, or, in some situations, two or more state, or federal, courts.

In addition, unlike the U.S., civil law systems do not distinguish between personal jurisdiction and venue. In a country with a civil law system, where a lawsuit must be filed is specified in the relevant code. In a common law system, there is a complex system of laws that address the numerous legal issues that arise in a variety of areas including:

- Jurisdictional questions
- Criminal law
- Intellectual property law
- Contract law

---

[2]As the World Bank, *supra* notes, "... there are therefore usually separate constitutional court, administrative court and civil court systems that opine on consistency of legislation and administrative acts with and interpret that specific code."

- Tort law, and
- Admiralty

Business organizations, regardless of their location, are expected to be familiar with and comply with each and every law and regulation in every jurisdiction in which they do business.

Jurisdiction and the Internet

In the United States, because of constitutional requirements, courts, unlike courts in civil law systems, face limitations on the reach of their jurisdiction over defendants, whether civil or criminal. Jurisdiction and venue in the criminal context will be addressed in the chapter on criminal law.

The word "jurisdiction" comes from "juris" meaning the law, and "diction" meaning to speak. A court that has "jurisdiction" has the authority to speak the law. Thus, in a common law system, there are a variety of courts, both state and federal. In some situations, federal courts may have exclusive jurisdiction, while in others, state and federal courts may have concurrent jurisdiction. In the United States, federal courts have, for example, exclusive jurisdiction over patent infringement claims and bankruptcy matters. State courts have exclusive jurisdiction over, for example, probate and family law matters. In other situations, such as some breach of contract matters, personal injury, and wrongful death, a party may have the option of filing in either a federal or state court.

There are Different Kinds of Jurisdiction

Jurisdiction involves a number of issues that must be considered by a court. The court must determine whether it has the authority to address a lawsuit that involves a specific person or business, property, whether real or personal, as well as the subject matter of the lawsuit.

Subject Matter Jurisdiction

Subject matter jurisdiction is the authority of a court to hear a particular case. There are federal and state courts of general and limited jurisdiction.[3]

[3]At the state level there may be small claims courts, family and probate courts. At the federal level there are bankruptcy courts and the tax court, among others.

A court's jurisdiction over subject matter is usually defined in the statute or constitution that created the court. In both federal and state courts, a court's subject matter jurisdiction can be limited by any of the following:

1. The subject of the lawsuit (i.e., bankruptcy, probate);
2. The sum in controversy (small claims court);
3. Whether the case involves a felony or misdemeanor;
4. Whether the proceeding is a trial or an appeal.

Jurisdiction of the Federal Courts

Since the federal government is a government of limited power, the jurisdiction of the federal courts is also limited. Federal courts have subject matter jurisdiction in two situations:

1. When a federal question is involved;
2. When there is diversity of citizenship.

Federal Question Jurisdiction

Article II, Section 2 of the U.S. Constitution specifies that "the judicial power shall extend to all Cases, in Law and Equity, arising under this Constitution, the Laws of the United States, and Treaties made, or which shall be made, under their Authority." Whenever a plaintiff's claim is based, in whole or in part, on the federal Constitution, a treaty, or a federal law, a federal question arises. A "federal" question would include a person's rights under the federal Constitution. In that situation the court will apply federal law.

Diversity of Citizenship

Usually, diversity involves citizens of different states or a different country and requires both of the following:

1. The plaintiff and defendant must be residents of different states; and
2. The amount in controversy must be at least $75,000.00.

A court will usually apply the law of the state in which the court is located, although it may apply the "relevant" state law. Diversity may also exist in cases between:

1. A foreign country and citizens of a state or of different states; and
2. Citizens of a state and citizens or subjects of a foreign country.

A Corporation?

For purposes of diversity a corporation is a citizen of both the state in which it is incorporated and the state in which its principal place of business is located.

Jurisdiction over Real or Personal Property

In rem Jurisdiction

Jurisdiction over a "rem" or "thing" includes property both real and personal. A court has jurisdiction over property located within its boundaries. Examples of situations that may involve a court's *in rem* jurisdiction include probate courts, as well as courts involved with disputes over real property.

Personal (*in personam*) Jurisdiction

A court may exercise personal jurisdiction over a person or business that resides or is located, even if only temporarily, within a certain geographic area.

The Most Likely Source of Controversy Involving the Internet

When an issue arising out of the Internet exists, a court must initially determine if it has the power to exercise authority over a party, either a person or a business or both, in the event that a business, or an employee of a business, or both, have been sued.

Does a Court Have Jurisdiction Over a Person (Defendant)?

State "long-arm" statutes

All states have a "long-arm" statute that allows a court to exercise jurisdiction over non-resident defendants in certain situations. Whether a court can exercise jurisdiction over a non-resident defendant depends on whether jurisdiction in the forum state satisfies the constitutional requirements of due process.

Minimum contacts

Because businesses are considered legal "persons" courts use the same rules to determine whether it is fair to exercise jurisdiction over that business. However, a company that does business in multiple states may not necessarily be subject to jurisdiction in all of them. A business is subject to jurisdiction only in states where it does such substantial business that it is "'at home' in that state."[4]

To determine the answer to that question a court may compare the amount of business a company does within the state compared to the amount of business it does elsewhere.

Constitutional Protection of Due Process

The Fifth and Fourteenth Amendments limit a court's jurisdiction over a non-resident defendant.

The Fifth Amendment

Both the Fifth and Fourteenth Amendments specify that no person shall be deprived of life, liberty, or property without the due process of law.

---

[4] *Daimler AG v. Bauman*, 571 U.S. 117 (2014).

The Fourteenth Amendment's Due Process Clause

The Fourteenth Amendment extended the principle of due process to state and local governments, stating that "no state shall … deprive any person of life, liberty or property without the due process of law." The Due Process Clause has two aspects to it: procedural and substantive.

International Shoe Co. v. State of Wash., 326 U.S. 310 (1945)

The United States Supreme Court noted,

> The questions for decision are (1) whether, within the limitations of the due process clause of the Fourteenth Amendment, appellant, a Delaware corporation, has by its activities in the State of Washington rendered itself amenable to proceedings in the courts of that state to recover unpaid contributions to the state unemployment compensation fund exacted by state statutes … And (2) whether the state can exact those contributions consistently with the due process clause of the Fourteenth Amendment.

The Court noted that the

> Appellant has no office in Washington and makes no contracts either for sale or purchase of merchandise there. It maintains no stock of merchandise in that state and makes there no deliveries of goods in intrastate commerce. During the years from 1937 to 1940, now in question, appellant employed eleven to thirteen salesmen under direct supervision and control of sales managers located in St. Louis. These salesmen resided in Washington; their principal activities were confined to that state; and they were compensated by commissions based upon the amount of their sales. The commissions for each year totaled more than $31,000. Appellant supplies its salesmen with a line of samples, each consisting of one shoe of a pair, which they display to prospective purchasers. On occasion they rent permanent sample rooms, for exhibiting samples, in business buildings, or rent rooms in hotels or business buildings temporarily for that purpose. The cost of such rentals is reimbursed by appellant.
>
> The authority of the salesmen is limited to exhibiting their samples and soliciting orders from prospective buyers, at prices and on terms fixed by appellant. The salesmen transmit the orders to appellant's office in St. Louis for acceptance or rejection, and when accepted the

merchandise for filling the orders is shipped f.o.b. from points outside Washington to the purchasers within the state. All the merchandise shipped into Washington is invoiced at the place of shipment from which collections are made. No salesman has authority to enter into contracts or to make collections.

The Supreme Court of Washington was of the opinion that the regular and systematic solicitation of orders in the state by appellant's salesmen, resulting in a continuous flow of appellant's product into the state, was sufficient to constitute doing business in the state so as to make appellant amenable to suit in its courts. But it was also of opinion that there were sufficient additional activities shown to bring the case within the rule frequently stated, that solicitation within a state by the agents of a foreign corporation plus some additional activities there are sufficient to render the corporation amenable to suit brought in the courts of the state to enforce an obligation arising out of its activities there.

The court found such additional activities in the salesmen's display of samples sometimes in permanent display rooms, and the salesmen's residence within the state, continued over a period of years, all resulting in a substantial volume of merchandise regularly shipped by appellant to purchasers within the state. The court also held that the statute as applied did not invade the constitutional power of Congress to regulate interstate commerce and did not impose a prohibited burden on such commerce.

The Court went on to note, 'Historically the jurisdiction of courts to render judgment *in personam* is grounded on their *de facto* power over the defendant's person. Hence his presence within the territorial jurisdiction of court was prerequisite to its rendition of a judgment personally binding him. (Citation omitted). But now that the *capias ad respondendum* has given way to personal service of summons or other form of notice, due process requires only that in order to subject a defendant to a judgment *in personam*, if he be not present within the territory of the forum, he have certain minimum contacts with it such that the maintenance of the suit does not offend "traditional notions of fair play and substantial justice."'

Applying these standards, the activities carried on in behalf of appellant in the State of Washington were neither irregular nor casual. They were systematic and continuous throughout the years in question. They resulted in a large volume of interstate business, in the course of which appellant received the benefits and protection of the laws of the state, including the right to resort to the courts for the enforcement of its rights. The obligation which is here sued upon arose out of those very

> activities. It is evident that these operations establish sufficient contacts or ties with the state of the forum to make it reasonable and just according to our traditional conception of fair play and substantial justice to permit the state to enforce the obligations which appellant has incurred there. Hence we cannot say that the maintenance of the present suit in the State of Washington involves an unreasonable or undue procedure.
>
> Appellant having rendered itself amenable to suit upon obligations arising out of the activities of its salesmen in Washington, the state may maintain the present suit *in personam* to collect the tax laid upon the exercise of the privilege of employing appellant's salesmen within the state. For Washington has made one of those activities, which taken together establish appellant's 'presence' there for purposes of suit, the taxable event by which the state brings appellant within the reach of its taxing power. The state thus has constitutional power to lay the tax and to subject appellant to a suit to recover it. The activities which establish its 'presence' subject it alike to taxation by the state and to suit to recover the tax.

In its ruling, the United States Supreme Court affirmed the decision of the Supreme Court of Washington finding that the state had jurisdiction over a business located in another state because of the facts of the case.

How Should "Minimum Contacts," Formulated Prior to the Development of the Internet, be Interpreted?

"Minimum contacts" is a standard that depends on the facts of the case and may differ depending on the nature of the lawsuit, including whether it is an intentional tort such as defamation.

Keeton v. Hustler Magazine[5]

The "Continuous and Deliberate" Requirement

A resident of New York sued a publisher in Ohio, whose principal place of business was California, for libel, in a New Hampshire state court, taking advantage of the only statute of limitations that allowed a suit to go forward.

---

[5]465 U.S. 770 (1984).

The Court noted,

> Where, as in this case, *Hustler Magazine, Inc.*, has continuously and deliberately exploited the New Hampshire market, it must reasonably anticipate being haled into court there in a libel action based on the contents of its magazine.
>
> The district court found that "[t]he general course of conduct in circulating magazines throughout the state (10,000 to 15,000 copies per month) was purposefully directed at New Hampshire, and inevitably affected persons in the state.' Such regular monthly sales of thousands of magazines cannot by any stretch of the imagination be characterized as random, isolated, or fortuitous. It is, therefore, unquestionable that New Hampshire jurisdiction over a complaint based on those contacts would ordinarily satisfy the requirement of the Due Process Clause that a State's assertion of personal jurisdiction over a nonresident defendant be predicated on minimum contacts between the defendant and the State. And, as the Court of Appeals acknowledged, New Hampshire has adopted a "long-arm" statute authorizing service of process on nonresident corporations whenever permitted by the Due Process Clause. Thus, all the requisites for personal jurisdiction over Hustler Magazine, Inc., in New Hampshire are present.

The "Targeting" Requirement

Calder v. Jones[6]

In another libel case, the United States Supreme Court distinguished a tort based on negligence, from an intentional tort. The article, according to footnote 9 of the Court's opinion alleged that the respondent drank so heavily as to prevent her from fulfilling her professional obligations.

The Court noted,

> Respondent Shirley Jones brought suit in California Superior Court claiming that she had been libeled in an article written and edited by petitioners in Florida. The article was published in a national magazine with a large circulation in California. Petitioners were served with process by mail in Florida and caused special appearances to be entered on their behalf, moving to quash the service of process for lack of personal jurisdiction. The superior court granted the motion on the ground that First

[6] 465 U.S. 783 (1984).

Amendment concerns weighed against an assertion of jurisdiction otherwise proper under the Due Process Clause. The California Court of Appeal reversed, rejecting the suggestion that First Amendment considerations enter into the jurisdictional analysis. We now affirm.

Respondent lives and works in California. She and her husband brought this suit against the National Enquirer, Inc., its local distributing company, and petitioners for libel, invasion of privacy, and intentional infliction of emotional harm. The Enquirer is a Florida corporation with its principal place of business in Florida. It publishes a national weekly newspaper with a total circulation of over 5 million. About 600,000 of those copies, almost twice the level of the next highest State, are sold in California. Respondent's and her husband's claims were based on an article that appeared in the Enquirer's October 9, 1979 issue. Both the Enquirer and the distributing company answered the complaint and made no objection to the jurisdiction of the California court.

Petitioner South is a reporter employed by the Enquirer. He is a resident of Florida, though he frequently travels to California on business. South wrote the first draft of the challenged article, and his byline appeared on it. He did most of his research in Florida, relying on phone calls to sources in California for the information contained in the article. Shortly before publication, South called respondent's home and read to her husband a draft of the article so as to elicit his comments upon it. Aside from his frequent trips and phone calls, South has no other relevant contacts with California.

Petitioner Calder is also a Florida resident. He has been to California only twice — once, on a pleasure trip, prior to the publication of the article and once after to testify in an unrelated trial. Calder is president and editor of the Enquirer. He 'oversee[s] just about every function of the Enquirer.' He reviewed and approved the initial evaluation of the subject of the article and edited it in its final form. He also declined to print a retraction requested by respondent. Calder has no other relevant contacts with California.

In considering petitioners' motion to quash service of process, the superior court surmised that the actions of petitioners in Florida, causing injury to respondent in California, would ordinarily be sufficient to support an assertion of jurisdiction over them in California. But the court felt that special solicitude was necessary because of the potential 'chilling effect' on reporters and editors which would result from requiring them to appear in remote jurisdictions to answer for the content of articles upon which they worked. The court also noted that respondent's rights could be 'fully satisfied' in her suit against the publisher without requiring petitioners to appear as parties. The superior court, therefore, granted the motion.

The California Court of Appeal reversed ... The court agreed that neither petitioner's contacts with California would be sufficient for an assertion of jurisdiction on a cause of action unrelated to those contacts. (Citation omitted). But the court concluded that a valid basis for jurisdiction existed on the theory that petitioners intended to, and did, cause tortious injury to respondent in California. The fact that the actions causing the effects in California were performed outside the State did not prevent the State from asserting jurisdiction over a cause of action arising out of those effects. The court rejected the superior court's conclusion that First Amendment considerations must be weighed in the scale against jurisdiction.

The Due Process Clause of the Fourteenth Amendment to the United States Constitution permits personal jurisdiction over a defendant in any State with which the defendant has 'certain minimum contacts ... such that the maintenance of the suit does not offend 'traditional notions of fair play and substantial justice.' (Citations omitted). In judging minimum contacts, a court properly focuses on 'the relationship among the defendant, the forum, and the litigation.' (Citations omitted). The plaintiff's lack of 'contacts' will not defeat otherwise proper jurisdiction, see *Keeton v. Hustler Magazine, Inc.* (Citation omitted), but they may be so manifold as to permit jurisdiction when it would not exist in their absence. Here, the plaintiff is the focus of the activities of the defendants out of which the suit arises. (Citation omitted).

The allegedly libelous story concerned the California activities of a California resident. It impugned the professionalism of an entertainer whose television career was centered in California. The article was drawn from California sources, and the brunt of the harm, in terms both of respondent's emotional distress and the injury to her professional reputation, was suffered in California. In sum, California is the focal point both of the story and of the harm suffered. Jurisdiction over petitioners is therefore proper in California based on the 'effects' of their Florida conduct in California. (Citations omitted).

Petitioners argue that they are not responsible for the circulation of the article in California. A reporter and an editor, they claim, have no direct economic stake in their employer's sales in a distant State. Nor are ordinary employees able to control their employer's marketing activity. The mere fact that they can 'foresee' that the article will be circulated

> and have an effect in California is not sufficient for an assertion of jurisdiction. (Citations omitted). They do not 'in effect appoint the [article their] agent for service of process.' (Citation omitted). Petitioners liken themselves to a welder employed in Florida who works on a boiler which subsequently explodes in California. Cases which hold that jurisdiction will be proper over the manufacturer, (citations omitted), should not be applied to the welder who has no control over and derives no direct benefit from his employer's sales in that distant State.
>
> Petitioners' analogy does not wash. Whatever the status of their hypothetical welder, petitioners are not charged with mere untargeted negligence. Rather, their intentional, and allegedly tortious, actions were expressly aimed at California. Petitioner South wrote and petitioner Calder edited an article that they knew would have a potentially devastating impact upon respondent. And they knew that the brunt of that injury would be felt by respondent in the State in which she lives and works and in which the *National Enquirer* has its largest circulation. Under the circumstances, petitioners must 'reasonably anticipate being haled into court there' to answer for the truth of the statements made in their article. (Citations omitted). An individual injured in California need not go to Florida to seek redress from persons who, though remaining in Florida, knowingly cause the injury in California.
>
> Petitioners are correct that their contacts with California are not to be judged according to their employer's activities there. On the other hand, their status as employees does not somehow insulate them from jurisdiction. Each defendant's contacts with the forum State must be assessed individually … The requirements … must be met as to each defendant over whom a state court exercises jurisdiction. In this case, petitioners are primary participants in an alleged wrongdoing intentionally directed at a California resident, and jurisdiction over them is proper on that basis.

The differences in the Court's approach seen in Keeton and Calder are related to the differences in the facts. In Calder, the plaintiff was "targeted" by the defendant, whereas in Keeton, that was not the case.

Service of Process

Related to Personal Jurisdiction

Service of process involves the formal delivery of notice of the lawsuit, such as a summons and complaint, or other legal process and is specified by the rules of the specific court or jurisdiction where the lawsuit is filed. Federal as well as California's rules specify that anyone who is at least 18 years of age, not a party to the lawsuit, may act as a process server. Personal service may consist of handing the specified documents to the party at home, work, or virtually anywhere else. The process server then fills out a "proof of service" that is submitted to the court. Service by mail involves mailing the required documents to the other party. Several other forms of service may also be available.

Alternative Methods of Service

In certain situations, such as a party who is evading service of process, alternative methods may be available. "Substituted" service is one alternative. Service by publication involves publication of, for instance, the summons and complaint, in a newspaper of general circulation. This method may be limited to certain rare situations and may require approval by the court.

Social Media

In several situations, courts in the United States have allowed service by way of social media. In *WhosHere, Inc. v. Orun,*[7] a federal court allowed a plaintiff in a trademark infringement case to serve a defendant residing in Turkey by way of Facebook, LinkedIn, and e-mail. In *St. Francis of Assisi v. Kuwait Finance House,*[8] a federal judge in San Francisco allowed a plaintiff to use Twitter to serve several defendants in Kuwait who allegedly financed terrorism by way of their Twitter accounts. The critical issue for the court is likely to be whether such service meets the due process requirements that are noted above.[9]

The Internet has made the issue of doing business in another state or foreign country, and therefore the issue of a court's jurisdiction, far more complicated.

---

[7] 2014 WL 670817.

[8] 2016 WL 5725002.

[9] See, for example, *FTC v. PCCare247, Inc.*, 2013 WL 841037 and In re Adoption of K.P.M.A. 341 P.3d 38 (2014).

Zippo Manufacturing Company v. Zippo Dot Com, Inc.[10]

The manufacturer of Zippo lighters sued a computer news service that used the domain names "zippo.com," "zippo.net," "zipponews.com," alleging trademark dilution, infringement, and false designation under the Lanham Act and state law claims in Pennsylvania. The defendant moved to dismiss or transfer the action. In summary, the District Court held that: (1) the defendant purposefully availed itself of doing business in Pennsylvania and thus could be subject to personal jurisdiction there; (2) the action arose out of the defendant's forum-related conduct; (3) the exercise of jurisdiction in Pennsylvania is reasonable; and (4) venue was proper.

The court noted,

> Manufacturing is a Pennsylvania corporation with its principal place of business in Bradford, Pennsylvania. Manufacturing makes, among other things, well-known 'Zippo' lighters. Dot Com is a California corporation with its principal place of business in Sunnyvale, California. Dot Com operates an Internet website and an Internet news service and has obtained the exclusive right to use the domain names 'zippo.com,' 'zippo.net,' and 'zipponews.com' on the Internet.
>
> Dot Com's Web site contains information about the company, advertisements, and an application for its Internet news service. The news service itself consists of three levels of membership — public/free, 'Original' and 'Super.' Each successive level offers access to a greater number of Internet newsgroups. A customer who wants to subscribe to either the 'Original' or 'Super' level of service, fills out an on-line application that asks for a variety of information including the person's name and address. Payment is made by credit card over the Internet or the telephone. The application is then processed and the subscriber is assigned a password which permits the subscriber to view and/or download Internet newsgroup messages that are stored on the Defendant's server in California.
>
> Dot Com's contacts with Pennsylvania have occurred almost exclusively over the Internet. Dot Com's offices, employees and Internet servers are located in California. Dot Com maintains no offices, employees, or agents in Pennsylvania. Dot Com's advertising for its service to Pennsylvania residents involves posting information about its service

---

[10] 952 F.Supp. 1119 (1997).

on its Web page, which is accessible to Pennsylvania residents via the Internet. Defendant has approximately 140,000 paying subscribers worldwide. Approximately two percent (3,000) of those subscribers are Pennsylvania residents. These subscribers have contracted to receive Dot Com's service by visiting its Web site and filling out the application. Additionally, Dot Com has entered into agreements with seven Internet access providers in Pennsylvania to permit their subscribers to access Dot Com's news service. Two of these providers are located in the Western District of Pennsylvania.

The basis of the trademark claims is Dot Com's use of the word 'Zippo' in the domain names it holds, in numerous locations in its Web site and in the heading of Internet newsgroup messages that have been posted by Dot Com subscribers. When an Internet user views or downloads a newsgroup message posted by a Dot Com subscriber, the word 'Zippo' appears in the 'Message–Id' and 'Organization' sections of the heading. The news message itself, containing text and/or pictures, follows. Manufacturing points out that some of the messages contain adult oriented, sexually explicit subject matter.

Our authority to exercise personal jurisdiction in this case is conferred by state law. The extent to which we may exercise that authority is governed by the Due Process Clause of the Fourteenth Amendment to the Federal Constitution. The portion of Pennsylvania's long-arm statute authorizing us to exercise jurisdiction here permits the exercise of jurisdiction over non-resident defendants upon:

> (2) Contracting to supply services or things in this Commonwealth.

It is undisputed that Dot Com contracted to supply Internet news services to approximately 3,000 Pennsylvania residents and also entered into agreements with seven Internet access providers in Pennsylvania. Moreover, even if Dot Com's conduct did not satisfy a specific provision of the statute, we would nevertheless be authorized to exercise jurisdiction to the 'fullest extent allowed under the Constitution of the United States.'

The Constitutional limitations on the exercise of personal jurisdiction differ depending upon whether a court seeks to exercise general or specific jurisdiction over a non-resident defendant. General jurisdiction permits a court to exercise personal jurisdiction over a non-resident defendant for non-forum related activities when the defendant has engaged in 'systematic and continuous' activities in the forum state. In the absence of general jurisdiction, specific jurisdiction permits a court to exercise personal jurisdiction over a non-resident defendant for forum-related activities where the 'relationship between the defendant and the forum falls within the 'minimum contacts' framework' of International Shoe (noted above) … and its progeny. Manufacturing does not contend that we should exercise general personal jurisdiction over Dot Com. Manufacturing concedes that if personal jurisdiction exists in this case, it must be specific.

A three-pronged test has emerged for determining whether the exercise of specific personal jurisdiction over a non-resident defendant is appropriate: (1) the defendant must have sufficient 'minimum contacts' with the forum state, (2) the claim asserted against the defendant must arise out of those contacts, and (3) the exercise of jurisdiction must be reasonable. The 'Constitutional touchstone' of the minimum contacts analysis is embodied in the first prong, 'whether the defendant purposefully established' contacts with the forum state. Defendants who 'reach out beyond one state' and create continuing relationships and obligations with the citizens of another state are subject to regulation and sanctions in the other State for consequences of their actions.'

[T]he foreseeability that is critical to the due process analysis is … that the defendant's conduct and connection with the forum State are such that he should reasonably expect to be haled into court there. This protects defendants from being forced to answer for their actions in a foreign jurisdiction based on 'random, fortuitous or attenuated' contacts. Jurisdiction is proper, however, where contacts proximately result from actions by the defendant *himself* that create a 'substantial connection' with the forum State.

The 'reasonableness' prong exists to protect defendants against unfairly inconvenient litigation. Under this prong, the exercise of jurisdiction will be reasonable if it does not offend 'traditional notions of fair play and substantial justice.' When determining the reasonableness of a particular forum, the court must consider the burden on the defendant in light of other factors including: 'the forum state's interest in adjudicating the dispute; the plaintiff's interest in obtaining convenient and effective relief, at least when that interest is not adequately protected by the plaintiff's right to choose the forum; the interstate judicial system's interest in obtaining the most efficient resolution of controversies; and the shared interest of the several states in furthering fundamental substantive social policies.' (Citation omitted).

Enter the Internet, a global 'super-network' of over 15,000 computer networks used by over 30 million individuals, corporations, organizations, and educational institutions worldwide. In recent years, businesses have begun to use the Internet to provide information and products to consumers and other businesses. The Internet makes it possible to conduct business throughout the world entirely from a desktop. With this global revolution looming on the horizon, the development of the law concerning the permissible scope of personal jurisdiction based on Internet use is in its infant stages. The cases are scant. Nevertheless, our review of the available cases and materials reveals that the likelihood that personal jurisdiction can be constitutionally exercised is directly proportionate to the nature and quality of commercial activity that an entity conducts over the Internet. This sliding scale is consistent with well developed personal jurisdiction principles. At one end of the spectrum are situations where a defendant clearly does business over the Internet. If the defendant enters into contracts with residents of a foreign jurisdiction that involve the knowing and repeated transmission of computer files over the Internet, personal jurisdiction is proper. At the opposite end are situations where a defendant has simply posted information on an Internet Web site which is accessible to users in foreign jurisdictions. A passive Web site that does little more than make information available to those who are interested in it is not grounds for the exercise of personal jurisdiction. The middle ground is occupied by interactive Web sites where a user can exchange information with the host computer. In these cases, the exercise of jurisdiction is determined by examining the level of interactivity and commercial nature of the exchange of information that occurs on the Web site.

Traditionally, when an entity intentionally reaches beyond its boundaries to conduct business with foreign residents, the exercise of specific jurisdiction is proper. Different results should not be reached simply because business is conducted over the Internet.

First, we note that this is not an Internet advertising case ... Dot Com has not just posted information on a Web site that is accessible to Pennsylvania residents who are connected to the Internet. This is not even an interactivity case ... Dot Com has done more than create an interactive Web site through which it exchanges information with Pennsylvania residents in hopes of using that information for commercial gain later. We are being asked to determine whether Dot Com's

> conducting of electronic commerce with Pennsylvania residents constitutes the purposeful availment of doing business in Pennsylvania. We conclude that it does. Dot Com has contracted with approximately 3,000 individuals and seven Internet access providers in Pennsylvania. The intended object of these transactions has been the downloading of the electronic messages that form the basis of this suit in Pennsylvania.

In conclusion, the court held that "We find Dot Com's efforts to characterize its conduct as falling short of purposeful availment of doing business in Pennsylvania wholly unpersuasive. We conclude that this Court may appropriately exercise personal jurisdiction over the Defendant and that venue is proper in this judicial district."

The "Sliding Scale"

The court in the Zippo case referred to the sliding scale that is used to determine whether a website has minimum contacts with a forum state to justify jurisdiction over a non-resident defendant. The sliding scale considers three issues:

1. Does the defendant conduct substantial business over the Internet, such as sales and the making of contracts?
2. Is there some interactivity? If so, a court will determine if there is sufficient "minimum contacts".
3. Is it strictly passive advertising?

Is a Website Interactive?

As the court in the Zippo case noted, "If the defendant enters into contracts with residents of a foreign jurisdiction that involve the knowing and repeated transmission of computer files over the Internet, personal jurisdiction is proper." At the other end of the sliding scale is the situation where a non-resident's website is limited to advertising, in which case it may be considered passive and that is generally insufficient to establish minimum contacts.

While jurisdictional issues in the United States are guided by constitutional requirements, the issue becomes far more complicated when litigation crosses international boundaries.

International Jurisdictional Issues

Convention on the Service Abroad of Judicial and Extrajudicial Documents in Civil and Commercial matters (The Hague Service Convention)[11]

Overall, the Convention seeks to simplify, standardize, and generally improve the process of serving documents abroad, specifying certain approved methods of service and preempting inconsistent methods of service wherever it applies.[12] One of the significant issues is whether the Convention allows service of process by mail. The issue caused a split in federal appellate courts that eventually resulted in a decision by the Supreme Court resolving the question. In *Water Splash, Inc. v. Menon,*[13] the Court referred to Article 10 of the Convention, '... the English text of which reads as follows: Provided the State of destination does not object, the present Convention shall not interfere with —

> (a) the freedom to send judicial documents, by postal channels, directly to persons abroad ...'
>
> The Court went on to conclude '... in cases governed by the Hague Service Convention, service by mail is permissible if two conditions are met: first, the receiving state has not objected to service by mail; and second, service by mail is authorized under otherwise applicable law. (Citation omitted).'

Yahoo! Inc., v. La Ligue Contre Le Racisme Et L'Antisimiste, a French association; L'Union Des Etudiants Juifs De France, a French association, Defendants–Appellants.[14]

"Yahoo! is a Delaware corporation with its principal place of business in California. Through its United States-based website yahoo.com, Yahoo! makes available a variety of Internet services, including a search engine, e-mail, web page hosting, instant messaging, auctions, and chat rooms. While some of these services rely on content created by Yahoo!, others are forums and platforms for user-generated content."

---

[11] T.I.A.S. No. 6638, 20 U.S.T. 361.

[12] *Volkswagenwerk Aktiengesellschaft v. Schlunk*, 486 U.S. 694, 699 (1988).

[13] 581 U.S. 271 (2017).

[14] 433 F.3d 1199 (2006).

The court noted,

Sometime in early April 2000, LICRA's chairman sent by mail and fax a cease and desist letter, dated April 5, 2000, to Yahoo!'s headquarters in Santa Clara, California. The letter, written in English, stated in part:

'[W]e are particularly choked [sic] to see that your Company keeps on presenting every day hundreds of nazi symbols or objects for sale on the Web. This practice is illegal according to French legislation and it is incumbent upon you to stop it, at least on the French Territory. Unless you cease presenting nazi objects for sale within 8 days, we shall size [sic] the competent jurisdiction to force your company to abide by the law.' On April 10, five (rather than eight) days after the date on the letter, LICRA filed suit against Yahoo! and Yahoo! France in the Tribunal de Grande Instance de Paris. On April 20, UEJF joined LICRA's suit in the French court. LICRA and UEJF used United States Marshals to serve process on Yahoo! in California. After a hearing on May 15, 2000, the French court issued an 'interim' order on May 22 requiring Yahoo! to '*take all necessary measures to dissuade and render impossible* any access [from French territory] via Yahoo.com to the Nazi artifact auction service and to any other site or service that may be construed as constituting an apology for Nazism or a contesting of Nazi crimes.'

In a second interim order, issued on November 20, 2000, the French court reaffirmed its May 22 order and directed Yahoo! to comply within three months, 'subject to a penalty of 100,000 Francs per day of delay effective from the first day following expiry of the 3 month period.' (The May 22 order had specified a penalty of 100,000 Euros rather than 100,000 Francs.)

First Amendment issues arising out of international Internet use are new, important and difficult. We should not rush to decide such issues based on an inadequate, incomplete or unclear record. We should proceed carefully, with awareness of the limitations of our judicial competence, in this undeveloped area of the law. Precisely because of the novelty, importance and difficulty of the First Amendment issues Yahoo! seeks to litigate, we should scrupulously observe the prudential limitations on the exercise of our power.

There was a live dispute when Yahoo! first filed suit in federal district court, but Yahoo! soon thereafter voluntarily changed its policy to

> comply, at least in part, with the commands of the French court's interim orders. This change in policy may or may not have mooted Yahoo!'s federal suit, but it has at least come close. Unless and until Yahoo! changes its policy again, and thereby more clearly violates the French court's orders, it is unclear how much is now actually in dispute.
>
> It is possible that because of Yahoo!'s voluntary change of policy it has now complied 'in large measure' with the French court's orders. It is also possible that Yahoo! has not yet complied 'in large measure'. If further compliance is required, Yahoo! will have to impose further restrictions on access by French users. The necessary consequence of such further restrictions on French users may or may not be that Yahoo! will have to impose restrictions on access by American users. Until we know whether further restrictions on access by French, and possibly American, users are required, we cannot decide whether or to what degree the First Amendment might be violated by enforcement of the French court's orders, and whether such enforcement would be repugnant to California public policy. We do not know whether further restrictions are required, and what they might be, because Yahoo! has chosen not to ask the French court. Instead, it has chosen to come home to ask for a declaratory judgment that the French court's orders — whatever they may or may not require, and whatever First Amendment questions they may or may not present — are unenforceable in the United States.

The court concluded, "When the votes of the three judges who conclude that the suit is unripe are combined with the votes of the three dissenting judges who conclude that there is no personal jurisdiction over LICRA and UEJF, there are six votes to dismiss Yahoo!'s suit." A majority of the *en banc* court having voted therefor, the judgment of the district court was reversed and the case remanded with directions to dismiss the action without prejudice.

International Jurisdictional Issues

Although courts in America seem to have adopted an expansive view of jurisdiction over foreign defendants, whether out-of-state or out-of-country, the Supreme Court recently showed an inclination to limit the reach of American courts' jurisdiction.

Daimler AG v. Bauman[15]

This case concerns the authority of a court in the United States to entertain a claim brought by foreign plaintiffs against a foreign defendant based on events occurring entirely outside the United States. The litigation commenced in 2004, when 22 Argentinian residents filed a complaint in the United States District Court for the Northern District of California against DaimlerChrysler Aktiengesellschaft (Daimler), a German public stock company, headquartered in Stuttgart, which manufactures Mercedes-Benz vehicles in Germany. The complaint alleged that during Argentina's 1976–1983 "Dirty War," Daimler's Argentinian subsidiary, Mercedes-Benz Argentina (MB Argentina) collaborated with state security forces to kidnap, detain, torture, and kill certain MB Argentina workers, among them, plaintiffs or persons closely related to plaintiffs. Damages for the alleged human-rights violations were sought from Daimler under the laws of the United States, California, and Argentina. Jurisdiction over the lawsuit was predicated on the California contacts of Mercedes-Benz USA, LLC (MBUSA), a subsidiary of Daimler incorporated in Delaware with its principal place of business in New Jersey. MBUSA distributes Daimler-manufactured vehicles to independent dealerships throughout the United States, including California.

The Court noted,

> The question presented is whether the Due Process Clause of the Fourteenth Amendment precludes the District Court from exercising jurisdiction over Daimler in this case, given the absence of any California connection to the atrocities, perpetrators, or victims described in the complaint. Plaintiffs invoked the court's general or all-purpose jurisdiction. California, they urge, is a place where Daimler may be sued on any and all claims against it, wherever in the world the claims may arise.
>
> After allowing jurisdictional discovery on plaintiffs' agency allegations, the District Court granted Daimler's motion to dismiss. Daimler's own affiliations with California, the court first determined, were insufficient to support the exercise of all-purpose jurisdiction over the corporation. Next, the court declined to attribute MBUSA's California contacts to Daimler on an agency theory, concluding that plaintiffs failed

[15]471 U.S. 117 (2014).

to demonstrate that MBUSA acted as Daimler's agent. The Ninth Circuit at first affirmed the District Court's judgment. Addressing solely the question of agency, the Court of Appeals held that plaintiffs had not shown the existence of an agency relationship of the kind that might warrant attribution of MBUSA's contacts to Daimler. Judge Reinhardt dissented. In his view, the agency test was satisfied and considerations of 'reasonableness' did not bar the exercise of jurisdiction. Granting plaintiffs' petition for rehearing, the panel withdrew its initial opinion and replaced it with one authored by Judge Reinhardt, which elaborated on reasoning he initially expressed in dissent.

The canonical opinion in this area remains *International Shoe* ..., in which we held that a State may authorize its courts to exercise personal jurisdiction over an out-of-state defendant if the defendant has 'certain minimum contacts with [the State] such that the maintenance of the suit does not offend traditional notions of fair play and substantial justice.'

Following *International Shoe*, 'the relationship among the defendant, the forum, and the litigation, rather than the mutually exclusive sovereignty of the States on which the rules of *Pennoyer* rest, became the central concern of the inquiry into personal jurisdiction.

This Court has not yet addressed whether a foreign corporation may be subjected to a court's general jurisdiction based on the contacts of its in-state subsidiary.

Even if we were to assume that MBUSA is at home in California, and further to assume MBUSA's contacts are imputable to Daimler, there would still be no basis to subject Daimler to general jurisdiction in California, for Daimler's slim contacts with the State hardly render it at home there.

Here, neither Daimler nor MBUSA is incorporated in California, nor does either entity have its principal place of business there. If Daimler's California activities sufficed to allow adjudication of this Argentina-rooted case in California, the same global reach would presumably be available in every other State in which MBUSA's sales are sizable. Such exorbitant exercises of all-purpose jurisdiction would scarcely permit out-of-state defendants 'to structure their primary conduct with some minimum assurance as to where that conduct will and will not render them liable to suit.'

It was therefore error for the Ninth Circuit to conclude that Daimler, even with MBUSA's contacts attributed to it, was at home in California, and

> hence subject to suit there on claims by foreign plaintiffs having nothing to do with anything that occurred or had its principal impact in California.
>
> Finally, the transnational context of this dispute bears attention.
>
> The Ninth Circuit, moreover, paid little heed to the risks to international comity its expansive view of general jurisdiction posed. Other nations do not share the uninhibited approach to personal jurisdiction advanced by the Court of Appeals in this case. In the European Union, for example, a corporation may generally be sued in the nation in which it is 'domiciled,' a term defined to refer only to the location of the corporation's 'statutory seat,' 'central administration,' or 'principal place of business.' European Parliament and Council Reg. 1215/2012, Arts. 4(1), and 63(1), 2012 O.J. (L. 351) 7, 18. See also *id.,* Art. 7(5), 2012 O.J. 7 (as to 'a dispute *arising out of the operations of a branch, agency or other establishment,*' a corporation may be sued 'in the courts for the place where the branch, agency or other establishment is situated' (emphasis added)). The Solicitor General informs us, in this regard, that 'foreign governments' objections to some domestic courts' expansive views of general jurisdiction have in the past impeded negotiations of international agreements on the reciprocal recognition and enforcement of judgments.' … Considerations of international rapport thus reinforce our determination that subjecting Daimler to the general jurisdiction of courts in California would not accord with the 'fair play and substantial justice' due process demands.

The Court concluded, "For the reasons stated, the judgment of the United States Court of Appeals for the Ninth Circuit is *Reversed.*"

Contractual Issues in Jurisdiction

Choice-of-Law Provision

Which jurisdiction's law should govern?

While the laws of the various American states, as well as European countries may be similar, they are unlikely to be identical. Even the Uniform Commercial Code, discussed in the chapter on commercial law, is hardly "uniform". Therefore, once jurisdiction has been established, the next question that must be addressed by a court is the law that governs the dispute.

A choice-of-law provision in a contract (and addressed also in the chapter on contract creation) specifies the law of a specific jurisdiction that is used to analyze a dispute and determine the outcome. A choice-of-law clause may determine a variety of issues, including:

1. The damages to be awarded, if any, and the method of calculation;
2. The causes of action that are available pursuant to state law;
3. The interpretation of a contract.

Such clauses may be critical in contracts that involve companies in more than one country. Without such a clause, litigation may be more complicated or uncertain. Litigation may occur in more than one state or country, with each court applying its relevant law to the circumstances of the case. An additional factor to consider is whether a court of a different country will enforce the judgment.

While a choice-of-law clause may be controlling, a party is free to challenge such a clause and a court may consider other issues. In the absence of a contract, a court is free to decide the law that should apply to a dispute.

The Restatement (Second) Choice-of-Law specifies the factors that a court should consider when confronted with the issue, whether a contract contains a choice-of-law clause or not.

Section 6 Choice-of-Law Principles

1. A court, subject to constitutional restrictions, will follow a statutory directive of its own state on choice of law.
2. When there is no such directive, the factors relevant to the choice of the applicable rule of law include:
   (a) The needs of the interstate and international systems;
   (b) The relevant policies of the forum;
   (c) The relevant policies of other interested states and the relative interests of those states in the determination of the particular issue;
   (d) The protection of justified expectations;
   (e) The basic policies underlying the particular field of law;
   (f) Certainty, predictability and uniformity of result; and
   (g) Ease in the determination and application of the law to be applied.

Section 187. Law of the State Chosen by the Parties

1. The law of the state chosen by the parties to govern their contractual rights and duties will be applied if the particular issue is one which the parties could have resolved by an explicit provision in their agreement directed to that issue.
2. The law of the state chosen by the parties to govern their contractual rights and duties will be applied, even if the particular issue is one which the parties could not have resolved by an explicit provision in their agreement directed to that issue, unless either
   (a) the chosen state has no substantial relationship to the parties or the transaction and there is no other reasonable basis for the parties' choice, or
   (b) application of the law of the chosen state would be contrary to a fundamental policy of a state which has a materially greater interest than the chosen state in the determination of the particular issue and which, under the rule of Section 188, would be the state of the applicable law in the absence of an effective choice of law by the parties.
3. In the absence of a contrary indication of intention, the reference is to the local law of the state of the chosen law.

Section 188. Law Governing in Absence of Effective Choice by the Parties

1. The rights and duties of the parties with respect to an issue in contract are determined by the local law of the state which, with respect to that issue, has the most significant relationship to the transaction and the parties under the principles stated in Section 6.
2. In the absence of an effective choice of law by the parties (see Section 187), the contacts to be taken into account in applying the principles of Section 6 to determine the law applicable to the issue include:
   (a) The place of contracting;
   (b) The place of negotiation of the contract;
   (c) The place of performance;
   (d) The location of the subject matter of the contract; and
   (e) The domicil, residence, nationality, place of incorporation and place of business of the parties.

   These contacts are to be evaluated according to their relative importance with respect to the particular issue.

3. If the place of negotiating the contract and the place of performance are in the same state, the local law of this state will usually be applied, except as otherwise provided in Sections 189–199 and 203.

However, a choice-of-law clause is not the only issue to be considered. In the absence of a choice-of-forum clause, it is possible for a court in another state to apply the law of a foreign jurisdiction, whether American, European, or other, to a dispute.

Venue

The most appropriate location for a trial

In the United States venue in a civil case typically is where the defendant resides, or, if a business, where it does business. Venue may also be specified by way of a contract. Venue in a criminal case is normally where the crime occurred. The Constitution specifies that a criminal defendant be tried in the state and district where the crime occurred.

Federal Rules of Criminal Procedure Rule 18

> Unless a statute or these rules permit otherwise, the government must prosecute an offense in a district where the offense was committed. The court must set the place of trial within the district with due regard for the convenience of the defendant and the witnesses, and the prompt administration of justice.

In the context of cybercrime, neither the Constitution nor the Federal Rules of Criminal Procedure specify where such an offense was committed nor how to deal with crimes committed in multiple states and/or countries. In addition, where a criminal defendant is charged with more than one count, venue must be proper with respect to all of the counts. If no single district has a proper venue for all of the counts, a prosecutor must either charge the defendant in multiple districts and then seek a transfer to a specific district, or bring all charges in one district and seek a waiver from the defendant.

Determining where a crime was committed may also be a challenge. As one court noted, "… in today's wired world of telecommunications and technology, it is often difficult to determine exactly where a crime was committed, since different elements may be widely scattered in both time and space, and those elements may not coincide with the accused's actual presence."[16]

Forum Selection Clause

A contractual requirement by which the parties establish the location, whether a specific court, state, or country, for litigation or alternative forms of dispute resolution, such as arbitration. In the absence of a contract, venue refers to the most appropriate location for a trial and may be an issue that is resolved by a court.

Tests for Validity

As with a choice-of-law clause, a forum-selection clause may also be the subject of a dispute. In such a situation a court is likely to consider two issues:

1. Reasonableness under all the circumstances;
2. Fundamental fairness.

When a court considers those factors, it may decide that a forum-selection clause is unenforceable if a party, usually the defendant, did not have sufficient notice of the forum-selection clause prior to entering the contract. This subject may be determined by an analysis of contract formation issues relating to offer and acceptance and may be of particular importance in a contract that involves a consumer.

---

[16] *U.S. v. Saavedra*, 223 F.3d 85 (2000). The court noted, "The question before us is where venue should lie for this criminal prosecution. Venue ordinarily lies only in the state and district where the offense was committed. That rule, derived from two constitutional guarantees, is intended to afford an accused the protection of being tried in the place where he was physically present when the crime was committed. Under it, venue appears to be well and wisely fixed. But, in today's wired world of telecommunication and technology, it is often difficult to determine exactly where a crime was committed, since different elements may be widely scattered in both time and space, and those elements may not coincide with the accused's actual presence. Such is the circumstance in the present case where venue was laid for the prosecution of the instant case in a district where defendant was not physically present at the time of the charged offense."

Other Constitutional Issues

Full Faith and Credit Clause

The Full Faith and Credit Clause comes into play when a plaintiff seeks to enforce a judgment that was entered by a court in another state, or, as in Yahoo!, noted earlier, another country.

Article IV of the Constitution

> Full faith and credit shall be given in each state to the public acts, records, and judicial proceedings of every other state. And the Congress may by general laws prescribe the manner in which such acts, records, and proceedings shall be proved, and the effect thereof.

The Full Faith and Credit Clause requires that each state give effect to the official acts of another state. Thus, a judgment entered in one state must generally be respected in another, although there are limitations. Among the issues that a court must decide would be whether the original court had jurisdiction over the parties and the subject matter. In addition, states are only required to give the same force to judgments as would be given by the courts of the state in which the judgment was rendered.

International Jurisdictional Issues

Generally, what is considered subject matter jurisdiction in the United States corresponds to "competence" in a civil law system.[17] While the United States considers the Constitutional standard of "minimum contacts" to be of prime importance, many other countries consider the issue of "effect" to be of primary importance.

Jurisdictional Issues in the European Union

Unlike the United States, civil law systems do not distinguish between personal jurisdiction and venue. Where a lawsuit must be filed is generally specified by the relevant code in that country. The Brussels

[17] See, for instance, The French Code of Civil Procedure Section 42, noted below.

Convention on Jurisdiction and the Enforcement of Judgments in Civil and Commercial Matters,[18] applicable to the European Economic Community, notes in Title I "Scope" Article 1 that it is controlling "… in civil and commercial matters whatever the nature of the court or tribunal. It shall not extend, in particular, to revenue, customs or administrative matters." It goes on to note, "Subject to the provisions of this Convention, persons domiciled in a Contracting State shall, whatever their nationality, be sued in the courts of that State." Section 2, "Special Jurisdiction" Article 5 goes on to note:

'A person domiciled in a Contracting State may, in another Contracting State, be sued:

> In matters relating to a contract, in the courts for the place of performance of the obligation in question …
>
> In matters relating to tort, delict, or quasi-delict, in the courts for the place where the harmful event occurred …'

Article 6 goes on to note:

"A person domiciled in a Contracting State may also be sued:

> Where he is one of a number of defendants, in the courts for the place where any one of them is domiciled …

Section 3 covers "Jurisdiction in matters relating to insurance."

Section 4 covers "Jurisdiction over consumer contracts" and Section 5, "Exclusive jurisdiction" specifies the courts that "… shall have exclusive jurisdiction, regardless of domicile."

Section 5, "Prorogation of jurisdiction" addresses those situations where, "… the parties, one or more of whom is domiciled in a Contracting State, have agreed that a court or the courts of a Contracting State are to have jurisdiction to settle any disputes which have arisen or which may arise in connection with a particular legal relationship, that court or those courts shall have exclusive jurisdiction …"

And, in recognition of the possibility that litigation involving the same claim may be filed in more than one jurisdiction, Section 8, "*Lis pendens*-related actions" goes on to note, where proceedings

---

[18] https://curia.europa.eu/common/recdoc/convention/en/c-textes/brux.htm.

involving the same cause of action and between the same parties are brought in the courts of different Contracting States, any court other than the court first seised shall of its own motion stay its proceedings until such time as the jurisdiction of the court first seised is established.

> Where the jurisdiction of the court first seised is established, any court other than the court first seised shall decline jurisdiction in favour of that court.

In Europe, the "domicile" of the defendant is likely to be the controlling factor. Title III, Section 102 of the French Civil Code is illustrative:

> The domicile of every French person, with regards to the exercise of his civil rights, is in the place where he has his principal establishment.[19]

As a result, the American concept of "doing business" as a test for jurisdiction is virtually unheard of in a civil law system. In addition, in a civil law system it is unlikely that anything that even vaguely resembles an American "long-arm" statute exists and *forum nonconveniens* is unheard of.

The Brussels Convention on Jurisdiction and the Enforcement of Judgments in Civil and Commercial Matters distinguishes between consumers and business. Article 13 defines a "consumer" as well as the kind of contract that is covered, and Article 14 specifies that "A consumer may bring proceedings against the other party to a contract either in the courts of the Contracting State in which that party is domiciled or in the courts of the Contracting State in which he is himself domiciled." If the consumer is a defendant, "[p]roceedings may be brought against a consumer by the other party to the contract only in the courts of the Contracting State in which the consumer is domiciled."

The French Code of Civil Procedure Section 42 is similar and specifies:

> The territorially competent jurisdiction is, unless otherwise provided, that of the place where the defendant lives.

---

[19]Taken from Google Translate of the French Civil Code, Section 102, version in force since March 27, 2014.

If there are several defendants, the plaintiff seises, at his option, the jurisdiction of the place where one of them lives.

If the defendant has no known domicile or residence, the plaintiff may seise the jurisdiction of the place where he lives or that of his choice if he lives abroad.

Persons domiciled in a contracting state shall, whatever their nationality, be sued in the courts of that state.

Section 43 of the French Code of Civil Procedure goes on to note:

The defendant's place of residence means:

> if it is a natural person, the place where he has his domicile or, failing that, his residence;
>
> if it is a legal person, the place where it is established.

To determine if a party is domiciled in a contracting state a court applies its internal law

> In the case of a company, the headquarters of the company shall be considered its domicile.

Exceptions

Contract performance

In the event of a dispute over contract performance in France, two options are provided. Litigation may commence either in:

1. The place of performance; or
2. The domicile of the defendant, if different.

Litigation Involving a Consumer

The consumer as a plaintiff has an option and may …

1. Sue in the consumer's country of domicile; or
2. Sue in the seller's country of domicile.

The parties may specify the particular jurisdiction however, a contract that specifies a particular jurisdiction will only be enforced if:

1. The agreement is in writing or evidenced by a writing; or
2. In a form which accords with practices established between the parties; or
3. In the case of international commerce, in a form that accords with established custom.

In a section that reflects the Constitutional Full Faith and Credit Clause, noted earlier, the Brussel's Convention includes, under Title II, "Recognition and Enforcement" Section 1 "Recognition" Article 26 that, "A judgment given in a Contracting State shall be recognized in the other Contracting States without any special procedure being required ..."

Just as there are limitations to the Full Faith and Credit Clause in the United States, Article 27 also establishes limitations and goes on to note, "A judgment shall not be recognized":

1. If such recognition is contrary to the public policy in the State in which recognition is sought;
2. Where it was given in default of appearance, if the defendant was not duly served with the document which instituted the proceedings or with an equivalent document in sufficient time to enable him to arrange for his defense;
3. If the judgment is irreconcilable with a judgment given in a dispute between the same parties in the State in which recognition is sought;
4. If the court of the State of origin, in order to arrive at its judgment, has decided a preliminary question concerning the status or legal capacity of natural persons, rights in property arising out of a matrimonial relationship, wills or succession in a way that conflicts with a rule of the private international law of the State in which the recognition is sought, unless the same result would have been reached by the application of the rules of private international law of that State;
5. If the judgment is irreconcilable with an earlier judgment given in a non-contracting State involving the same cause of action and between the same parties, provided that this latter judgment fulfills the conditions necessary for its recognition in the state addressed.

Articles 28–30 go on to specify other issues with regard to the enforcement of a judgment.

The Rome Convention

Generally, the jurisdiction chosen by the parties is controlling. While the agreement need not be in writing, it must be reasonably certain by either the terms of the agreement or the circumstances. In the absence of an agreement by the parties:

> The law of the country most closely connected with the agreement shall control. It is presumed that a contract is most closely connected to the party who is to perform, its residence or its central administration.

When there is a contract with a consumer, while the parties are free to agree, the consumer may not be deprived of protection provided by his country of residence.

Other Issues

Juries

The use of a jury is generally limited to the United States and some Canadian provinces.[20]

In England, there is a limited right to a jury in a case alleging an intentional tort. Civil law countries ordinarily do not allow complicated business-related lawsuits, or any other lawsuit for that matter, to be decided by a jury. As one commentator noted, having a complicated matter decided by a jury that is not required to explain the reason for its decision, and that may be swayed by emotional appeals is appalling to many individuals from a country with a civil law system.

---

[20]For instance, the Sixth Amendment states that in all criminal prosecutions the accused has the right to a trial by an impartial jury. The Seventh Amendment states that for suits in common law, if the "value in controversy exceeds twenty dollars, the right of trial by jury shall be preserved." The Supreme Court has excluded petty offenses for purposes of the right to a trial by jury and there is no right to a trial by a jury in juvenile proceedings.

Punitive Damages

Punitive damages are generally unavailable in countries with a civil law system, although the chapter on torts and product liability discusses the issue of punitive damages in France. In the United States punitive damages may be available in situations involving intentional torts although a number of U.S. states have abolished punitive damages.[21]

Judges

Federal

Article III judges

Judges that are appointed pursuant to Article III of the Constitution are nominated by the president and confirmed by the Senate.

Article I judges

Congress created certain courts, such as bankruptcy, tax, and military. Judges in those courts are appointed by Congress and serve for 10 years, after which they may be reappointed.

State

The states use several different methods. Generally, judges in state courts are chosen by way of:

> Appointment by the governor or legislature;
>
> Merit selection by a legislative committee; such judges may be subject to a retention or confirmation election;
>
> Partisan elections where a judge is voted on by the electorate;
>
> Non-partisan elections where judges are named on a ballot without an indication of their party affiliation;
>
> A combination of the foregoing.

---

[21] Gregory F. Hauser Representing Clients from Civil Law Legal Systems in U.S. Litigation: Understanding how Clients from Civil Law Nations View Civil Litigation and Helping them Understand U.S. Lawsuit. 17-AUT Int'l L. Practicum 129 (2004).

Europe

As with American states, the countries of Europe use a variety of methods to appoint judges.

France

Judicial appointments in France are determined by the country's High Council of the Judiciary. This is composed of 12 members, but given the specific features of the French system of government, the nation's president has the majority of votes in the council. The president of France is himself part of the High Council of the Judiciary, and he also appoints three of its members. The other members are the heads of the National Assembly and the Senate (both usually come from political parties allied with the head of state); the justice minister (usually politically close to the president); a prosecutor; a representative of the country's constitutional court; and five judges. This inevitably means that the president — a politician — has the majority of votes in the High Council of the Judiciary.[22]

In civil law country judges are career civil servants and play a much more active role in the conduct of litigation than a judge in the U.S.

Litigation

One of the significant differences between litigation in the United States and Europe is the absence of pre-trial discovery in a civil law system. Evidence is generally produced during the trial phase, either voluntarily or as ordered by a judge.

In a Civil Law System:

> The judge decides questions of law as well as fact.
>
> There is no equivalent of a motion for summary judgment.
>
> The hearings that occur as part of the civil litigation process may or may not be public and may, or may not, include verbal testimony from witnesses.

---

[22] http://archiwum.thenews.pl/1/10/Artykul/317562, How-judges-are-selected-across-Europe. Accessed November 16, 2023.

Particularly in a commercial case, the lawsuit is likely determined strictly on the basis of documentary evidence.

The testimony of witnesses is likely to occur by way of written witness statements.

The actual trial may consist solely of the attorneys and judge or judges exchanging views on the evidence.

The only questions for a witness are likely to come from the judge, although attorneys may suggest questions.[23]

Summary

Jurisdiction in the United States is a complicated subject that involves constitutional issues, issues regarding the subject matter of the dispute and the location of the parties, among others. Jurisdiction, or competence, in France, as well as other civil law countries, is a matter of statute and far less complicated.

[23] Gregory F. Hauser. *op. cit.*

Chapter 3

Freedom of Expression

Abstract

The First Amendment personifies one of America's and Americans' most cherished freedom: to freely express oneself. However, neither First Amendment rights, nor any other constitutional rights, are unlimited. For that reason, the First Amendment is a source of confusion for many Americans and most foreigners. "Freedom of expression" does not mean "unlimited" freedom of expression. While there are few words that will get an American sent to jail, there are a few. Yelling "FIRE!" in a crowded theater is criminal. Sexual harassment, defamation, obscenity, and fighting words are some of the other examples of expression that may lead to civil, not criminal, litigation. Arguably defamation is the most significant issue when it comes to the Internet. Even when it is clear that a statement is defamatory, there are defenses, or other issues, which may make civil litigation difficult if not impossible.

Introduction

While current state, national, and international laws pronouncements as well as constitutional protections that promote freedom of expression are numerous, the right is a fairly recent development and one that is subject to numerous, sometimes vague, limitations. Whether in the United States or Europe, in general, individuals have a right to express their opinions, subject to certain restrictions as noted below. Business has a duty to respect that right. Government has a duty to protect that right.

The United States

An analysis of free speech or, more accurately, freedom of expression is difficult and complicated.

The First Amendment

"Congress shall make no law respecting an establishment of religion, or prohibiting the free exercise thereof; or abridging the freedom of speech, or of the press, or the right of the people peaceably to assemble, and to petition the government for a redress of grievances."

Although the First Amendment refers specifically to speech, its application is far broader. Freedom of expression in the United States is protected both by the First Amendment, as well as state constitutions. In addition, while the First Amendment refers specifically to "Congress," the Due Process Clause of the Fourteenth Amendment extends the protection enunciated in the First Amendment to states.

The Road to the First Amendment

Criminal Prosecution of Speech

While it is rare for speech to result in a criminal prosecution, it is not unheard of. Twenty-four states have laws that allow for criminal prosecution of certain speech.[1] The Montana Criminal Code provides an example:

45-8-212. Criminal defamation. (1) Defamatory matter is anything that exposes a person or a group, class, or association to hatred, contempt, ridicule, degradation, or disgrace in society or injury to the person's or its business or occupation.

(2) Whoever, with knowledge of its defamatory character, orally, in writing, or by any other means, including by electronic communication, as defined in 45-8-213, communicates any defamatory matter to a third

---

[1] https://www.aclu.org/issues/free-speech/map-states-criminal-laws-against-defamation. The figure may be inaccurate. Another publication notes that 15 states and U.S. territories have criminal libel statutes. https://www.mtsu.edu/first-amendment/article/941/criminal-libel.

person without the consent of the person defamed commits the offense of criminal defamation and may be sentenced to imprisonment for not more than 6 months in the county jail or a fine of not more than $500, or both.

(3) Violation of Subsection (2) is justified if:
- (a) The defamatory matter is true;
- (b) The communication is absolutely privileged;
- (c) The communication consists of fair comment made in good faith with respect to persons participating in matters of public concern;
- (d) The communication consists of a fair and true report or a fair summary of any judicial, legislative, or other public or official proceedings; or
- (e) The communication is between persons each having an interest or duty with respect to the subject matter of the communication and is made with the purpose to further the interest or duty.

(4) A person may not be convicted on the basis of an oral communication of defamatory matter except upon the testimony of at least two other persons that they heard and understood the oral statement as defamatory or upon a plea of guilty or *nolo contendere*.

In some ways, this law seems to mirror issues related to hate speech as noted below.

The history of criminal libel, at least in America, traces its roots to England, and the infamous English Star Chamber.[2]

Arguably the first case of criminal libel in America involved John Peter Zenger, who criticized the colonial governor of New York. In 1735, Zenger was tried for the crime of "seditious libel." Seditious libel was defined as the intentional publication, without lawful excuse or justification, of written blame of any public man or the law, or any institution established by law.[3] Of particular note is that truth was not a defense.

Fortunately for Mr. Zenger, his attorney, Andrew Hamilton, convinced the jury that, contrary to the judge's instructions, truth was, in fact, relevant. Currently, such a defense would be referred to as jury nullification. However, that was not the end of criminal prosecutions pursuant to similar laws.

---

[2] https://www.mtsu.edu/first-amendment/article/941/criminal-libel.

[3] https://history.nycourts.gov/case/crown-v-zenger/.

The Alien and Sedition Acts of 1798

"In 1798, the United States stood on the brink of war with France. The Federalist Party, which advocated for a strong central government, believed that Democratic-Republican criticism of Federalist policies was disloyal and feared that 'aliens,' or non-citizens, living the United States would sympathize with the French during war."

"As a result, a Federalist-controlled Congress passed four laws, known collectively as the Alien and Sedition Acts. These laws raised the residence requirements for citizenship from 5 to 14 years, authorized the president to deport 'aliens,' and permitted their arrest, imprisonment, and deportation during wartime. The Sedition Act made it a crime for American citizens to 'print, utter, or publish … any false, scandalous, and malicious writing' about the government."

"The laws were directed against Democratic-Republicans, the party typically favored by new citizens. The only journalists prosecuted under the Sedition Act were editors of Democratic-Republican newspapers."

"Sedition Act trials, along with the Senate's use of its contempt powers to suppress dissent, set off a firestorm of criticism against the Federalists and contributed to their defeat in the election of 1800, after which the acts were repealed or allowed to expire. The controversies surrounding them, however, provided for some of the first tests of the limits of freedom of speech and press."[4]

Fortunately, by 1805 the legislature of New York adopted truth as a qualified defense to criminal libel and incorporated it into the state constitution of 1821.[5] Article 1, Section 8:

> Every citizen may freely speak, write and publish his or her sentiments on all subjects, being responsible for the abuse of that right; and no law shall be passed to restrain or abridge the liberty of speech or of the press. In all criminal prosecutions or indictments for libels, the truth may be given in evidence to the jury; and if it shall appear to the jury that the matter charged as libelous is true, and was published with good motives and for justifiable ends, the party shall be acquitted; and the jury shall have the right to determine the law and the fact.

---

[4] https://www.archives.gov/milestone-documents/alien-and-sedition-acts.

[5] https://www.mtsu.edu/first-amendment/article/941/criminal-libel.

Although cases involving criminal libel continued for decades, support gradually eroded. In 1964 the Supreme Court decided *New York Times v. Sullivan*.[6] Although civil, not criminal litigation, the case established the principle that to recover, a public figure must demonstrate that a defendant acted with "actual malice". The Court defined actual malice as "... knowledge ..." that a statement "... was false or with reckless disregard of whether it was false or not." The Supreme Court noted, in part, "For good reason, 'no court of last resort in this country has ever held, or even suggested, that prosecutions for libel on government have any place in the American system of jurisprudence.' (Citations omitted). The present proposition would sidestep this obstacle by transmuting criticism of government, however impersonal it may seem on its face, into personal criticism, and hence potential libel, of the officials of whom the government is composed. There is no legal alchemy by which a State may thus create the cause of action that would otherwise be denied for a publication which, as respondent himself said of the advertisement, 'reflects not only on me but on the other Commissioners and the community.' Raising as it does the possibility that a good-faith critic of government will be penalized for his criticism, the proposition relied on by the Alabama courts strikes at the very center of the constitutionally protected area of free expression. We hold that such a proposition may not constitutionally be utilized to establish that an otherwise impersonal attack on governmental operations was a libel of an official responsible for those operations. Since it was relied on exclusively here, and there was no other evidence to connect the statements with respondent, the evidence was constitutionally insufficient to support a finding that the statements referred to respondent."[7]

Later that year, in *Garrison v. State of Louisiana*,[8] the Court held that the actual malice requirement established in the *New York Times v. Sullivan* applied to criminal libel prosecutions arising from statements about public officials and that truth was an absolute defense. As the Court noted, "Applying the principles of the *New York Times* case, we hold that the Louisiana statute, as authoritatively interpreted by the Supreme Court of Louisiana, incorporates constitutionally invalid standards in the context of criticism of the official conduct of public officials. For, contrary to the

---

[6]376 U.S. 254.

[7]376 U.S. 254, 291–292.

[8]379 U.S. 64.

New York Times rule, which absolutely prohibits punishment of truthful criticism, the statute directs punishment for true statements made with 'actual malice,' (citations omitted), handed down after the *New York Times* decision. (Citations omitted). And 'actual malice' is defined in the decisions below to mean 'hatred, ill will or enmity or a wanton desire to injure ***.' (Citation omitted). The statute is also unconstitutional as interpreted to cover false statements against public officials. The *New York Times* standard forbids the punishment of false statements, unless made with knowledge of their falsity or in reckless disregard of whether they are true or false. But the Louisiana statute punishes false statements without regard to that test if made with ill-will; even if ill-will is not established, a false statement concerning public officials can be punished if not made in the reasonable belief of its truth. 'The Louisiana Supreme Court affirmed the conviction solely on the ground that the evidence sufficed to support the trial court's finding of ill-will, enmity, or a wanton desire to injure. But the trial court also rested the conviction on additional findings that the statement was false and not made in the reasonable belief of its truth.'"[9]

Needless to say, no one is free to express whatever they please whenever and wherever they like. Restrictions are a necessary and important part of all societies. An analysis of First Amendment protection in the United States is far from easy. The subject involves the consideration of a variety of different issues.

Protected or Unprotected Expression?

The Supreme Court has interpreted the First Amendment to restrict governmental regulation of certain areas of "protected" speech (that includes some forms of expressive conduct) while allowing the government greater discretion to regulate other kinds of speech, including a few categories that may be "unprotected" by the First Amendment.

Speech or Conduct?

A court may have to consider whether a law is directed at speech or conduct. If the law is directed at conduct, is the conduct expressive?

---

[9]379 U.S. 64, 77–78.

If so, expressive conduct may be protected by the First Amendment. Regardless, as part of this analysis, a court may have to determine if a law is "content neutral," for example, does the law establish reasonable restrictions on the time, place, or manner of expression?[10] Or, does the law regulate speech on the basis of its content or the speaker's viewpoint?[11]

Laws that apply to particular speech because of the topic discussed or the idea or message to be expressed, in other words, a restriction based on "content" are presumptively unconstitutional and subject to strict scrutiny by the court.[12]

Categories

A court may also have to determine the "category" of speech that is at issue. There are a number of categories. For instance, it has long been recognized that "commercial" speech, usually advertising, is subject to reasonable restrictions. Truth-in-advertising laws are an obvious example. Obscenity is another category. Determining the category of speech may determine the First Amendment standards, including the level of judicial scrutiny, that the court will apply to the law. The court has various levels of "scrutiny" that it will apply when analyzing a case. Laws that affect protected speech are subject to a rigorous analysis by the court. Laws that affect unprotected speech are subject to a much less rigorous analysis by the court.

Protected Expression

Protected speech is that which relates to "... pursuit of a wide variety of political, social, economic, educational, religious and cultural ends."[13] This exceedingly broad and vague definition extends First Amendment protection to a wide variety of expressions aside from those that fall within one of the narrow categories of unprotected speech.

---

[10] *Hill v. Colorado*, 530 U.S. 703 (2000).

[11] *Reed v. Town of Gilbert*, Ariz., 576 U.S. 155 (2015).

[12] *Reed*, 576 U.S. 155, 163.

[13] *Roberts v. U.S. Jaycees*, 468 U.S. 609, 622 (1984).

What Level of Scrutiny Will a Court Apply?

Whether a court will apply "strict scrutiny" or a lower form of scrutiny depends on the character and context of the speech.

Political and Ideological Speech

Any laws that affect this area receive the strictest level of scrutiny by a court because they are considered to be the forms of expression that are the heart of the First Amendment and have been broadly described as any speech that relates to "politics, nationalism, religion, or other matters of opinion."[14] Political speech may take other forms beyond the written or spoken word, such as money[15] or symbolic acts.[16] When a court employs a strict scrutiny analysis the government must demonstrate that the law is narrowly tailored to achieve a compelling government interest. Any law that fails to meet that standard will be struck down by a court.

Strict Scrutiny

The court uses strict scrutiny, the most rigorous standard that is applied by a court in cases involving a "suspect classification," such as a government classification that is based on race,[17] or in situations involving a "fundamental right". As Justice Souter observed in a dissenting opinion, "Strict scrutiny leaves few survivors".[18] The most rigorous standard used by a court to evaluate the constitutionality of a law passed by a legislative body involves the analysis of three issues that are vaguely reminiscent of the standards applied by the French court in the Avia law case, noted below. Under this standard[19] a challenged law must:

1. Promote a compelling governmental interest;
2. Be narrowly tailored to achieve the goal or interest; and
3. Be the least restrictive means to achieve that interest.

---

[14] *W. Va. State Bd. of Educ. v. Barnette*, 319 U.S. 624, 642 (1943).

[15] *Buckley v. Valeo*, 424 U.S. 1 (1976) (*per curiam*).

[16] *Texas v. Johnson*, 491 U.S. 397 (1989).

[17] *Adarand Constructors v. Pena*, 515 U.S. 200 (1995), overruling *Metro Broadcasting, Inc. v. FCC*, 497 U.S. 547 (1990).

[18] *City of Los Angeles v. Alameda Books, Inc.*, 535 U.S. 425 (2002).

[19] *Sable Communications of California, Inc. v. F.C.C.*, 492 U.S. 115 (1989).

Commercial Speech

Historically, courts generally considered commercial speech, or speech that merely proposed a commercial transaction or relates solely to the speaker and audience's economic interests, to be less deserving of First Amendment protection than political speech. As noted in the Bad Frog Brewery case below, that changed with the Court's 1976 decision in *Virginia State Board of Pharmacy v. Virginia Citizens Consumer Council, Inc.*[20]

Bad Frog Brewery, Inc. v. New York State Liquor Authority, 134 F.3d 87 (1998)

The Bad Frog Brewery made alcoholic beverages, some of which featured a label with a frog making an obscene gesture. Since state law required approval for the label by the New York State Liquor Authority prior to sale, the brewery submitted an initial application that included the statement that "he's mean, green and obscene." The application was rejected by the NYSLA. Bad Frog filed a subsequent application in August, resubmitting the prior labels and slogans, but omitting the label with the slogan "He's mean, green and obscene," a slogan the Authority had previously found rendered the entire label obscene. That slogan was replaced with a new slogan, "Turning bad into good." The second application, like the first, included promotional material making the extravagant claim that the frog's gesture, whatever its past meaning in other contexts, now means "I want a Bad Frog beer," and that the company's goal was to claim the gesture as its own and as a symbol of peace, solidarity, and good will.

The NYSLA denied Bad Frog's second application, finding Bad Frog's contention as to the meaning of the frog's gesture "ludicrous and disingenuous." Explaining its rationale for the rejection, the Authority found that the label "encourages combative behavior" and that the gesture and the slogan, "He just don't care," placed close to and in larger type than a warning concerning potential health problems, fostered a defiance to the health warning on the label, enticed underage drinkers, and invited the public not to heed conventional wisdom and to disobey standards of decorum. In addition, the Authority said that it considered that approval of this label meant that the label could appear in grocery and convenience stores, with obvious exposure on the shelf to children of tender age and that it is

---

[20] 425 U.S. 748 (1976).

sensitive to and has concern as to the label's adverse effects on such a youthful audience. Finally, the Authority said that it considered that within the state of New York, the gesture of "giving the finger" to someone, has the insulting meaning of "F*** You," or "Up Yours," … a confrontational, obscene gesture, known to lead to fights, shootings and homicides … and concluded that the encouraged use of this gesture in licensed premises is akin to yelling "fire" in a crowded theater, … [and] finds that to approve this admittedly obscene, provocative confrontational gesture, would not be conducive to proper regulation and control and would tend to adversely affect the health, safety and welfare of the People of the State of New York. Upon receiving the rejection, the brewery sued the Authority in federal district court. The District Court for the Northern District of New York rejected Bad Frog's commercial free speech challenge to the Authority's decision and granted summary judgment in favor of NYSLA and its three Commissioners.

The court noted,

> In 1942, the Court was 'clear that the Constitution imposes no [First Amendment] restraint on government as respects purely commercial advertising.' (Citation omitted) … In *Chrestensen*, the Court sustained the validity of an ordinance banning the distribution on public streets of handbills advertising a tour of a submarine. Twenty-two years later, in *New York Times Co. v. Sullivan* (citation omitted), the Court characterized *Chrestensen* as resting on 'the factual conclusion … that the handbill was "purely commercial advertising,"' and noted that *Chrestensen* itself had 'reaffirmed the constitutional protection for "the freedom of communicating *information* and disseminating opinion."' (Citation omitted). The famously protected advertisement for the Committee to Defend Martin Luther King was distinguished from the unprotected *Chrestensen* handbill:
>
> The publication here was not a 'commercial' advertisement in the sense in which the word was used in *Chrestensen.* It communicated *information,* expressed opinion, recited grievances, protested claimed abuses, and sought financial support on behalf of a movement whose existence and objectives are matters of the highest public interest and concern.
>
> The implication of this distinction between the King Committee advertisement and the submarine tour handbill was that the handbill's solicitation of customers for the tour was not 'information' entitled to First Amendment protection.

In 1973, the Court referred to *Chrestensen* as supporting the argument that 'commercial speech [is] unprotected by the First Amendment.' (Citation omitted). (The case) … also endeavored to give content to the then 'unprotected' category of 'commercial speech' by noting that '[t]he critical feature of the advertisement in *Valentine v. Chrestensen* was that, in the Court's view, it did no more than propose a commercial transaction.' (Citation omitted). Similarly, the gender-separate help-wanted ads in *Pittsburgh Press* were regarded as 'no more than a proposal of possible employment,' which rendered them 'classic examples of commercial speech.' … The Court rejected the newspaper's argument that commercial speech should receive some degree of First Amendment protection, concluding that the contention was unpersuasive where the commercial activity was illegal …

Just two years later, *Chrestensen* was relegated to a decision upholding only the '*manner* in which commercial advertising could be distributed.' (Citation omitted). (That case) … somewhat generously read *Pittsburgh Press* as 'indicat[ing] that the advertisements would have received some degree of First Amendment protection if the commercial proposal had been legal.' (Citation omitted). However, in according protection to a newspaper advertisement for out-of-state abortion services, the Court was careful to note that the protected ad 'did more than simply propose a commercial transaction.' (Citation omitted). Though it was now clear that some forms of commercial speech enjoyed some degree of First Amendment protection, it remained uncertain whether protection would be available for an ad that only 'propose[d] a commercial transaction.'

That uncertainty was resolved just one year later in *Virginia State Board of Pharmacy v. Virginia Citizens Consumer Council.* (Citation omitted). Framing the question as 'whether speech which does "no more than propose a commercial transaction" … is so removed from [categories of expression enjoying First Amendment protection] that it lacks all protection,' the Court said, 'Our answer is that it is not.' Though *Virginia State Board* interred the notion that 'commercial speech' enjoyed no First Amendment protection, it arguably kept alive the idea that protection was available only for commercial speech that conveyed information:

Advertising, however tasteless and excessive it sometimes may seem, is nonetheless dissemination of information as to who is producing and selling what product, for what reason, and at what price … (emphasizing the 'consumer's interest in the free flow of commercial information').

Supreme Court commercial speech cases upholding First Amendment protection since *Virginia State Board* have all involved the dissemination of information. (Citations omitted). In the one case since *Virginia State Board* where First Amendment protection was sought for commercial speech that contained minimal information — the trade name of an optometry business — the Court sustained a governmental prohibition. (Citation omitted). Acknowledging that a trade name 'is used as part of a proposal of a commercial transaction,' … and 'is a form of commercial speech,' … the Court pointed out '[a] trade name conveys no information about the price and nature of the services offered by an optometrist until it acquires meaning over a period of time …' … Moreover, the Court noted, 'the factual information associated with trade names may be communicated freely and explicitly to the public,' (citation omitted) presumably through the type of informational advertising protected in *Virginia State Board.* The trade name prohibition was ultimately upheld because use of the trade name had permitted misleading practices, such as claiming standardized care, … but the Court added that the prohibition was sustainable just because of the 'opportunity' for misleading practices …

Prior to *Friedman,* it was arguable from language in *Virginia State Board* that a trademark would enjoy commercial speech protection since, 'however tasteless,' its use is the 'dissemination of information as to who is producing and selling what product …' (Citation omitted). But the prohibition against trademark use in *Friedman* puts the matter in considerable doubt, unless *Friedman* is to be limited to trademarks that either have been used to mislead or have a clear potential to mislead. Since *Friedman*, the Supreme Court has not explicitly clarified whether commercial speech, such as a logo or a slogan that conveys no information, other than identifying the source of the product, but that serves, to some degree, to 'propose a commercial transaction,' enjoys any First Amendment protection. The Court's opinion in *Posadas*, however, points in favor of protection. Adjudicating a prohibition on some forms of casino advertising, the Court did not pause to inquire whether the advertising conveyed information. Instead, viewing the case as involving 'the restriction of pure commercial speech which does "no more than propose a commercial transaction,"' (citations omitted) … the Court applied the standards set forth in *Central Hudson.*

Bad Frog's label attempts to function, like a trademark, to identify the source of the product. The picture on a beer bottle of a frog behaving badly is reasonably to be understood as attempting to identify to consumers a product of the Bad Frog Brewery. In addition, the label serves to propose a commercial transaction. Though the label communicates no information beyond the source of the product, we think that minimal information, conveyed in the context of a proposal of a commercial transaction, suffices to invoke the protections for commercial speech, articulated in *Central Hudson*.

The 'core notion' of commercial speech includes 'speech which does no more than propose a commercial transaction.' (Citation omitted). Outside this so-called 'core' lie various forms of speech that combine commercial and non-commercial elements. Whether a communication *combining* those elements is to be treated as commercial speech depends on factors such as whether the communication is an advertisement, whether the communication makes reference to a specific product, and whether the speaker has an economic motivation for the communication … *Bolger* explained that while none of these factors alone would render the speech in question commercial, the presence of all three factors provides 'strong support' for such a determination …

We are unpersuaded by Bad Frog's attempt to separate the purported social commentary in the labels from the hawking of beer. Bad Frog's labels meet the three criteria identified in *Bolger*: the labels are a form of advertising, identify a specific product, and serve the economic interest of the speaker. Moreover, the purported non-commercial message is not so 'inextricably intertwined' with the commercial speech as to require a finding that the entire label must be treated as 'pure' speech. (Citation omitted). Even viewed generously, Bad Frog's labels at most 'link a product to a current debate,' (citation omitted) which is not enough to convert a proposal for a commercial transaction into 'pure' noncommercial speech. Indeed, the Supreme Court considered and rejected a similar argument in *Fox*, when it determined that the discussion of the non-commercial topics of 'how to be financially responsible and how to run an efficient home' in the course of a Tupperware demonstration did not take the demonstration out of the domain of commercial speech. (Citation omitted).

We thus assess the prohibition of Bad Frog's labels under the commercial speech standards outlined in *Central Hudson*.

The *Central Hudson* Test

Central Hudson sets forth the analytical framework for assessing governmental restrictions on commercial speech:

At the outset, we must determine whether the expression is protected by the First Amendment. For commercial speech to come within that provision, it at least must concern lawful activity and not be misleading. Next, we ask whether the asserted government interest is substantial. If both inquiries yield positive answers, we must determine whether the regulation directly advances the government interest asserted, and whether it is not more extensive than is necessary to serve that interest.

We agree with the District Court that Bad Frog's labels pass *Central Hudson*'s threshold requirement that the speech 'must concern lawful activity and not be misleading.' The consumption of beer (at least by adults) is legal in New York, and the labels cannot be said to be deceptive, even if they are offensive. Indeed, although NYSLA argues that the labels convey no useful information, it concedes that 'the commercial speech at issue … may not be characterized as misleading or related to illegal activity.'

NYSLA advances two interests to support its asserted power to ban Bad Frog's labels: (i) the State's interest in 'protecting children from vulgar and profane advertising,' and (ii) the State's interest 'in acting consistently to promote temperance, i.e., the moderate and responsible use of alcohol among those above the legal drinking age and abstention among those below the legal drinking age.'

Both of the asserted interests are 'substantial' within the meaning of *Central Hudson.* States have 'a compelling interest in protecting the physical and psychological well-being of minors,' and '[t]his interest extends to shielding minors from the influence of literature that is not obscene by adult standards.' (Citations omitted). ('[W]e have repeatedly recognized the governmental interest in protecting children from harmful materials.').

The Supreme Court also has recognized that states have a substantial interest in regulating alcohol consumption. (Citation omitted). We agree with the District Court that New York's asserted concern for 'temperance' is also a substantial state interest.

To meet the 'direct advancement' requirement, a state must demonstrate that 'the harms it recites are real and that its restriction will in fact alleviate them *to a material degree.*' (Citation omitted) … A restriction will fail this third part of the *Central Hudson* test if it 'provides only ineffective or remote support for the government's purpose.' (Citation omitted).

In the pending case, NYSLA endeavors to advance the state interest in preventing exposure of children to vulgar displays by taking only the limited step of barring such displays from the labels of alcoholic beverages. In view of the wide currency of vulgar displays throughout contemporary society, including comic books targeted directly at children, barring such displays from labels for alcoholic beverages cannot realistically be expected to reduce children's exposure to such displays to any significant degree.

The District Court ruled that the third criterion was met because the prohibition of Bad Frog's labels indisputably achieved the result of keeping these labels from being seen by children. That approach takes too narrow a view of the third criterion. Under that approach, any regulation that makes *any* contribution to achieving a state objective would pass muster. *Edenfield,* however, requires that the regulation advance the state interest 'in a material way.' The prohibition of 'For Sale' signs in *Linmark* succeeded in keeping those signs from public view, but that limited prohibition was held not to advance the asserted interest in reducing public awareness of realty sales. The prohibition of alcoholic strength on labels in *Rubin* succeeded in keeping that information off of beer labels, but that limited prohibition was held not to advance the asserted interest in preventing strength wars since the information appeared on labels for other alcoholic beverages. The valid state interest here is not insulating children from these labels, or even insulating them from vulgar displays on labels for alcoholic beverages; it is insulating children from displays of vulgarity.

NYSLA maintains that the raised finger gesture and the slogan 'He just don't care' urge consumers generally to defy authority and particularly to disregard the Surgeon General's warning, which appears on the label next to the gesturing frog. NYSLA also contends that the frog appeals to youngsters and promotes underage drinking.

The truth of these propositions is not so self-evident as to relieve the state of the burden of marshalling some empirical evidence to support its assumptions. All that is clear is that the gesture of 'giving the finger' is offensive. Whether viewing that gesture on a beer label will encourage disregard of health warnings or encourage underage drinking remain matters of speculation.

NYSLA has not shown that its denial of Bad Frog's application directly and materially advances either of its asserted state interests.

Central Hudson's fourth criterion, sometimes referred to as 'narrow tailoring,' (citation omitted) requires consideration of whether the prohibition is more extensive than necessary to serve the asserted state interest. Since NYSLA's prohibition of Bad Frog's labels has not been shown to make even an arguable advancement of the state interest in temperance, we consider here only whether the prohibition is more extensive than necessary to serve the asserted interest in insulating children from vulgarity.

In its most recent commercial speech decisions, the Supreme Court has placed renewed emphasis on the need for narrow tailoring of restrictions on commercial speech.

Even if we were to assume that the state materially advances its asserted interest by shielding children from viewing the Bad Frog labels, it is plainly excessive to prohibit the labels from all use, including placement on bottles displayed in bars and taverns where parental supervision of children is to be expected. Moreover, to whatever extent NYSLA is concerned that children will be harmfully exposed to the Bad Frog labels when wandering without parental supervision around grocery and convenience stores where beer is sold, that concern could be less intrusively dealt with by placing restrictions on the permissible locations where the appellant's products may be displayed within such stores. Or, with the labels permitted, restrictions might be imposed on placement of the frog illustration on the outside of six-packs or cases, sold in such stores.

NYSLA's complete statewide ban on the use of Bad Frog's labels lacks a 'reasonable fit' with the state's asserted interest in shielding minors from vulgarity, and NYSLA gave inadequate consideration to alternatives to this blanket suppression of commercial speech. (Citation omitted).

In the Bad Frog case the Court referred to *Central Hudson Gas & Elec. Corp. v. Public Service Commission of New York.* In December 1973, the Commission ordered electric utilities in New York State to cease all advertising that 'promot[es] the use of electricity.' The order was based on the Commission's finding that "the interconnected utility system in New York State does not have sufficient fuel stocks or sources of supply to continue furnishing all customer demands for the 1973–1974 winter.

Three years later, when the fuel shortage had eased, the Commission requested comments from the public on its proposal to continue the ban on promotional advertising. Central Hudson Gas & Electric Corp., the appellant in this case, opposed the ban on First Amendment grounds. After reviewing the public comments, the Commission extended the prohibition in a Policy Statement issued on February 25, 1977.

The Policy Statement divided advertising expenses 'into two broad categories: promotional — advertising intended to stimulate the purchase of utility services — and institutional and informational, a broad category inclusive of all advertising not clearly intended to promote sales.' The Commission declared all promotional advertising contrary to the national policy of conserving energy. It acknowledged that the ban is not a perfect vehicle for conserving energy. For example, the Commission's order prohibits promotional advertising to develop consumption during periods when demand for electricity is low. By limiting growth in 'off-peak' consumption, the ban limits the 'beneficial side effects' of such growth in terms of more efficient use of existing power-plants. And since oil dealers are not under the Commission's jurisdiction and thus remain free to advertise, it was recognized that the ban can achieve only 'piecemeal conservationism.' Still, the Commission adopted the restriction because it was deemed likely to 'result in some dampening of unnecessary growth' in energy consumption.

Our decision today in no way disparages the national interest in energy conservation. We accept without reservation the argument that conservation, as well as the development of alternative energy sources, is an imperative national goal. Administrative bodies empowered to regulate electric utilities have the authority — and indeed the duty — to take appropriate action to further this goal. When, however, such action involves the suppression of speech, the First and Fourteenth Amendments require that the restriction be no more extensive than is necessary to serve the state interest. In this case, the record before us fails to show that the total ban on promotional advertising meets this requirement.

The court noted 'The judgment of the District Court is reversed, and the case is remanded for entry of judgment in favor of Bad Frog on its claim for injunctive relief; the injunction shall prohibit NYSLA from rejecting Bad Frog's label application, without prejudice to such further consideration and possible modification of Bad Frog's authority to use its labels as New York may deem appropriate, consistent with this opinion...'

As the court in the Bad Frog case notes, the analysis is far from easy and requires consideration of the kind of expression, whether commercial or not, among other considerations, and tends to be addressed on a case-by-case basis.

Even then the analysis is less than straightforward with several standards of review. Restrictions on commercial speech generally receive at least an intermediate level of scrutiny as long as the restrictions are directed at non-misleading speech concerning a lawful activity. Again, as noted in the Bad Frog Brewery case, *Central Hudson Gas & Electric Corp. v. Public Service Commission of New York*[21] established that such laws are constitutional only if they:

1. directly advance a substantial government interest; and
2. are not broader than necessary to serve that interest.

Recently, the Court has signaled that it may apply a heightened level of scrutiny to certain commercial regulations that single out commercial speakers for less favorable treatment based on the content of their speech.[22]

Unprotected Expression

The court has identified certain categories of speech that the government may regulate simply because of its content. However, even in this situation a limitation exists: the Supreme Court recognized limited categories of speech that the government may regulate because of their content, as long as it does so evenhandedly.[23]

The kind of speech that the government may regulate generally falls into one or more of the following categories:

- obscenity,
- defamation,

---

[21] 447 U.S. 557 (1980).

[22] See, e.g., *Sorrell v. IMS Health Inc.*, 564 U.S. 552 (2011). Cf *Zauderer v. Office of Disciplinary Counsel*, 471 U.S. 626 (1985) where the court applied a less stringent standard than intermediate scrutiny to a law that required the disclosure of factual, uncontroversial information.

[23] See, e.g., *R.A.V. v. St. Paul*, 505 U.S. 377, 382–386 (1992).

- fraud,
- incitement,
- fighting words,
- true threats,
- speech integral to criminal conduct
- child pornography, and
- obscenity

A workable definition of obscenity has proved to be elusive and Congress has struggled to pass legislation on the subject that meets constitutional requirements. Marvin Miller, a publisher based in California was referred to as the "King of Smut". He was prosecuted for mailing advertisements for books, along with a movie. Miller was convicted and he appealed his case to the Supreme Court. In *Miller v. California*[24] the Court, in a 5-4 decision, affirmed his conviction and defined obscenity as material that, on the whole, must

> appeal to the prurient interest in sex (as judged by contemporary community standards),
>
> depict or describe sexual conduct (as specifically defined by state law) in a patently offensive way, and
>
> lacks 'serious literary, artistic, political, or scientific value.'

The Miller case was decided long before the Internet was a twinkle in anyone's eye. And, although Miller remains the dominant test for obscenity prosecutions, it is, and always will be, subject to criticism, involving, for instance, application of the "… contemporary community standards." As the court noted in *United States v. Kilbride*,[25] "… a national community standard must be applied in regulating obscene speech on the Internet, including obscenity disseminated via e-mail." In doing so the court disagreed with the late Chief Justice Burger who rejected the notion that the First Amendment required a national community standard and observed, "It is neither realistic nor constitutionally sound to read the First Amendment as requiring that the people of Maine or Mississippi

[24] 413 U.S. 15, 24 (1973).
[25] 584 F.3d 1240 (2009).

accept public depiction of conduct found tolerable in Las Vegas, or New York City."

Defamation

As noted in Chapter 5, defamation is not a protected speech. However, in certain situations the First Amendment may require the plaintiff in a defamation lawsuit to demonstrate that the speaker acted with a specific intent (actual malice), generally involving a public figure, which has proven to be virtually impossible to meet.[26]

Fraud

In a somewhat surprising recognition that "some false statements are inevitable if there is to be an open and vigorous expression of views in public and private conversation," that may have implications for "false news" (as noted below) the Court rejected a categorical First Amendment exception for false statements.[27] Therefore, the government may regulate fraudulent speech in order to prevent public or consumer deception, generally referred to as truth-in-advertising laws.[28] But, any such regulations may not be overbroad or unduly burdensome "prophylactic" rules for this purpose.[29]

Incitement

Perhaps surprisingly, the Court has held that the First Amendment protects advocating the use of force or lawbreaking "... except where such advocacy is directed to inciting or producing imminent lawless action and is likely to incite or produce such action."[30]

---

[26] *Gertz v. Robert Welch*, 418 U.S. 323 (1974); *New York Times Co. v. Sullivan*, 376 U.S. 254 (1964).

[27] *United States v. Alvarez*, 567 U.S. 709, 718–719 (2012) (plurality opinion).

[28] *Illinois ex rel. Madigan v. Telemarketing Assocs.*, 538 U.S. 600, 612 (2003).

[29] *Riley v. Nat'l Fed'n of the Blind*, 487 U.S. 781, 798 (1988); *Zauderer v. Office of Disciplinary Counsel of Supreme Court of Ohio*, 471 U.S. 626 (1985).

[30] *Brandenburg v. Ohio*, 395 U.S. 444, 447–448 (1969).

Fighting Words

In *Chaplinsky v. New Hampshire*,[31] the Court stated that "fighting words," defined as those "... likely to provoke the average person to retaliation and thereby cause a breach of the peace" are not protected by the First Amendment, although in a later case the Court clarified that "... speech cannot be restricted simply because it is upsetting or arouses contempt."[32]

True Threats

A threat that "encompass those statements where the speaker means to communicate a serious expression of an intent to commit an act of unlawful violence to a particular individual or group of individuals ... Intimidation in the constitutionally proscribable sense of the word is a type of true threat, where a speaker directs a threat to a person or group of persons with the intent of placing the victim in fear of bodily harm or death."[33] However, this category does not include "political hyperbole" nor statements uttered in jest.[34]

Speech Integral to Criminal Conduct

Under this exception to the First Amendment, the government may proscribe, among other actions, conspiracy or solicitation to commit a crime, offer or request to obtain illegal material, or impersonating a government officer.[35]

Child Pornography

Separate from obscenity, the advertising and sale of child pornography is not protected by the First Amendment since it is integral to the criminal conduct that is directly related to its creation.[36]

---

[31] 315 U.S. 568, 574 (1942).

[32] *Snyder v. Phelps*, 562 U.S. 443, 458 (2011).

[33] *Virginia v. Black*, 538 U.S. 343, 359 (2003).

[34] *Watts v. United States*, 394 U.S. 705, 708 (1969) (*per curiam*) where the Court overturned the conviction of an individual that threatened to shoot the president during a political rally in opposition to the war in Vietnam.

[35] *U.S. v. Williams*, 553 U.S. 285, 297–298 (2008); *U.S. v. Alvarez* 567 U.S. 709, 721 (2012).

[36] *New York v. Ferber*, 458 U.S. 747, 764 (1982).

Other Limitations on Freedom of Expression

Freedom of expression is never absolute and most, if not all societies, as well as the various pronouncements on the freedom of expression contain specific limitations on the right.

Other Limitations in the United States

Among other limitations, the First Amendment does not protect the right:

To incite imminent lawless action[37];

To make or distribute obscene materials[38] including child pornography[39];

To burn draft cards at an anti-war protest[40];

To permit students to print articles in a school newspaper over the objections of the school administration[41];

Of students to make an obscene speech at a school-sponsored event[42];

Of students to advocate illegal drug use at a school-sponsored event.[43]

Other limitations on the freedom of expression include a prohibition on:

Assault;

Defamatory statements;

Infliction of emotional distress, all of which are discussed in Chapter 5; and

Sexual harassment.

---

[37] *Brandenburg v. Ohio*, 395 U.S. 444 (1969).
[38] *Roth v. United States*, 354 U.S. 476 (1957).
[39] *United States v. Williams*, 553 U.S. 285 (2008).
[40] *United States v. O'Brien*, 391 U.S. 367 (1968).
[41] *Hazelwood School District v. Kuhlmeier*, 484 U.S. 260 (1988).
[42] *Bethel School District #43 v. Fraser*, 478 U.S. 675 (1986).
[43] *Morse v. Frederick*, 551 U.S. 393 (2007).

The Internet and Freedom of Expression

The Internet presents a special challenge to freedom of expression. Although defamation is likely the primary concern (and as covered in Chapter 5), hate speech also presents a special challenge. A court's analysis of a criminal prosecution involving alleged hate speech is likely to involve many of the considerations aforementioned with regard to incitement, fighting words, and true threats as well as speech integral to criminal conduct, and will be difficult and complicated. The subject is further complicated by Section 230 of the Communications Decency Act (CDA) (also addressed in Chapter 5).

As noted in Chapter 5, prior to the enactment of Section 230 of the CDA, courts ruled that Internet Service Providers (ISPs) that passively hosted third-party content were not liable as a publisher for any of the content that was defamatory[44] (although the author of the defamatory comment could be liable), but that an ISP would be liable as a publisher for all of the third-party content if it exercised discretion to remove third-party material.[45] ISPs faced an impossible choice: moderate third-party content and risk being held liable for content posted by third parties, or fail to moderate and be flooded with obscene or other inappropriate or even illegal content and material.

There are two parts of Section 230 that provide virtual immunity to ISPs. Section 230 (c)(1) states: "No provider or user of an interactive computer service shall be treated as the publisher or speaker of any information provided by another information content provider."

Section 230(c)(2) goes on to note:

"No provider or user of an interactive computer service shall be held liable on account of

(A) any action voluntarily taken in good faith to restrict access to or availability of material that the provider or user considers to be obscene, lewd, lascivious, filthy, excessively violent, harassing, or otherwise objectionable, whether or not such material is constitutionally protected; or

[44] *Cubby, Inc. v. CompuServe*, Inc., 776 F.Supp. 135 (S.D.N.Y. 1991).

[45] *Stratton Oakmont, Inc. v. Prodigy Servs. Co.*, 1995 WL 323710 (N.Y.Sup. Ct. 1995).

(B) any action taken to enable or make available to information content providers or others the technical means to restrict access to material described in paragraph (1)."

Section 230(c), referred to as "Protection for 'Good Samaritan' blocking and screening of offensive material," though arguably well-intentioned, has been interpreted by courts so broadly, as to provide virtual immunity to ISPs that rivals the immunity for newspapers, television, and radio provided by the Supreme Court's ruling in *New York Times v. Sullivan.*

In particular, the use of the phrase "... otherwise objectionable ..." gives ISPs unfettered discretion to remove content arbitrarily or in ways that are inconsistent with its terms of service simply by deeming it "objectionable". As a result, ISPs have little incentive to address illicit material, while censoring lawful content without transparency or accountability.[46]

While the immunity provided by Section 230 is broad, it is not without limits. Section 230(e) requires providers to remove material that violates, among others, laws on

- Intellectual property;
- Obscenity;
- The sexual exploitation of children; or
- Sex trafficking.

The exceptions are limited and while society has benefited from the explosion of legal goods and services that are available online, criminals have also benefited with a resulting increase in the sale of illegal drugs, cyberstalking, human trafficking, as well as terrorism.[47] Section 230 immunizes not only the Good Samaritan but also the criminal element (bad Samaritans) that take advantage of the immunity provided ISPs that intentionally facilitate or solicit content and activities that violate federal criminal laws.[48]

In addition, there is a serious concern that the avenues for engaging in online commerce as well as speech have become concentrated in

[46] https://www.justice.gov/archives/ag/department-justice-s-review-section-230-communications-decency-act-1996.

[47] *Ibid.*

[48] *Ibid.*

the hands of a few key players that are immune from antitrust laws where liability is based on harm to competition and not third-party speech.[49]

Freedom of Expression at the International Level

The United Nations

The United Nations has a number of pronouncements that repeat, in large part, many of the protections that are specified in the Bill of Rights. Among them is the Universal Declaration of Human Rights[50] (1948). The Preamble notes, in part, "Whereas disregard and contempt for human rights have resulted in barbarous acts which have outraged the conscience of mankind, and the advent of a world in which human beings shall enjoy freedom of speech and belief and freedom from fear and want has been proclaimed as the highest aspiration of the common people ..."

Article 19 goes on to note, "Everyone has the right to freedom of opinion and expression; this right includes freedom to hold opinions without interference and to seek, receive and impart information and ideas through any media and regardless of frontiers."

Article 29 contains restrictions on the various noted rights and states, in part:

> In the exercise of his rights and freedoms, everyone shall be subject only to such limitations as are determined by law solely for the purpose of securing due recognition and respect for the rights and freedoms of others and of meeting the just requirements of morality, public order and the general welfare in a democratic society.
>
> These rights and freedoms may in no case be exercised contrary to the purposes and principles of the United Nations.

---

[49] *Ibid.*

[50] https://www.un.org/en/about-us/universal-declaration-of-human-rights.

The International Covenant on Civil and Political Rights (ICCPR)[51] also addresses the subject.

Article 19 notes:

> (1) Everyone shall have the right to hold opinions without interference.
> (2) Everyone shall have the right to freedom of expression; this right shall include freedom to seek, receive and impart information and ideas of all kinds, regardless of frontiers, either orally, in writing or in print, in the form of art, or through any other media of his choice.

Freedom of Expression in the European Union

The European Union, as well as various countries of Europe, has a variety of pronouncements on the subject of freedom of expression. For example, the European Convention on Human Rights[52] Article 10 notes:

> (1) Everyone has the right to freedom of expression. This right shall include freedom to hold opinions and to receive and impart information and ideas without interference by public authority and regardless of frontiers. This Article shall not prevent States from requiring the licensing of broadcasting, television or cinema.

Article 11 of the Charter of Fundamental Rights of the European Union[53] (2000) is intended to protect freedom of expression and provides:

> Everyone has the right to freedom of expression. This right shall include freedom to hold opinions and to receive and impart information and ideas without interference by public authority and regardless of frontiers.
>
> The freedom and pluralism of the media shall be respected.

---

[51] https://www.ohchr.org/en/instruments-mechanisms/instruments/international-covenant-civil-and-political-rights.

[52] https://www.echr.coe.int/european-convention-on-human-rights.

[53] https://eur-lex.europa.eu/legal-content/EN/TXT/?uri=CELEX:12012P/TXT.

Various national constitutions of member states of the European Union may also contain provisions that address freedom of expression.[54]

Freedom of Expression in France

Article 4 of the Declaration of the Rights of Man and of the Citizen in 1789 states:

> Liberty consists in the freedom to do everything which injures no one else; hence the exercise of the natural rights of each man has no limits except those which assure to the other members of the society the enjoyment of the same rights. These limits can only be determined by law.[55]

Limitations on Freedom of Expression

International Limitations on Freedom of Expression

The ICCPR (aforementioned), Article 19(3) provides guidance on evaluating restrictions on freedom of expression and notes:

The exercise of the rights provided for in paragraph 2 of this Article carries with it special duties and responsibilities. It may therefore be subject to certain restrictions, but these shall only be such as are provided by law and are necessary:

(a) For respect of the rights or reputations of others;
(b) For the protection of national security or of public order or of public health or morals.

Article 20 goes on to note:

1. Any propaganda for war shall be prohibited by law.
2. Any advocacy of national, racial or religious hatred that constitutes incitement to discrimination, hostility or violence shall be prohibited by law.

---

[54] https://www.ivir.nl/publicaties/download/TWG_Freedom_of_Expression.pdf.

[55] https://avalon.law.yale.edu/18th_century/rightsof.asp#:~:text=Liberty%20consists%20in%20the%20freedom,5.

Limitations in Europe

As noted above, Article 10, Section (1) of the 1950 European Convention on Human Rights (ECHR), provides protection for freedom of expression. Section (2) notes the restrictions:

> The exercise of these freedoms, since it carries with it duties and responsibilities, may be subject to such formalities, conditions, restrictions or penalties as are prescribed by law and are necessary in a democratic society, in the interests of national security, territorial integrity or public safety, for the prevention of disorder or crime, for the protection of health or morals, for the protection of the reputation or rights of others, for preventing the disclosure of information received in confidence, or for maintaining the authority and impartiality of the judiciary.

Perhaps surprisingly, Russia ratified the Convention in May of 1998.[56] Unfortunately, in part a reflection of the weakness of the Convention, Russian citizens bring some of the highest number of claims of violations to the European Court of Human Rights (ECtHR).[57]

Limitations in France

Originally, the law of 1881 established a number of press offenses, including:

> Provocation to crimes or misdemeanors;
>
> Provocation to a certain number of serious crimes, in particular to attacks on the authority of the State;
>
> Seditious shouting or singing;
>
> Publication of false news that has disturbed the public peace;
>
> Offense and contempt toward heads of State or foreign diplomatic agents.

---

[56] https://scholarlycommons.law.emory.edu/cgi/viewcontent.cgi?article=1089&context=eilr.

[57] *Ibid.*

Some of the offenses that were a part of the original law of 1881 were removed or incorporated elsewhere:

> Provocation to members of the military to turn away from their duties was incorporated into the French penal code;
>
> Offense to the President of the Republic;
>
> Offense to public decency (incorporated into the French penal code);
>
> Defamation and insult (incorporated into the French penal code);
>
> Offense and contempt toward heads of State or foreign diplomatic agents was revised to, 'contempt towards foreign diplomatic agents.'

While certain offenses from the initial list have been removed, others have been added:

> The apology of war crimes or crimes against humanity,
>
> The incitement of discrimination, hatred, or violence on the basis of origin, ethnicity, nationality, race, or religion (Pleven Law, 1972),
>
> Sex, sexual orientation or identity, or handicap (Law n°2004-1486 of 30 December 2004).

Following the Gayssot Law (1990), the denial of crimes against humanity was added to the list of press offenses.

Hate Speech

The United States

As with "obscenity," a specific definition of "hate" speech does not appear to exist, although various states have enacted laws on the subject. California for example, distinguishes between a hate "crime" and a hate "incident". A hate crime in California is defined as:

A crime against a person, group, or property motivated by the victim's real or perceived protected social group. A hate crime may occur if a person has been targeted because of an actual or perceived:

(1) disability,
(2) gender,

(3) nationality,
(4) race or ethnicity,
(5) religion,
(6) sexual orientation, and
(7) association with a person or group with one or more of these actual or perceived characteristics.

In California a hate crime may result in imprisonment. A hate "incident" is defined as an action or behavior motivated by hate but which, for one or more reasons, is not a crime. Examples of hate incidents include:

- Name-calling;
- Insults;
- Displaying hate material on your own property;
- Posting hate material that does not result in property damage;
- Distribution of materials with hate messages in public places.

The U.S. Constitution allows hate speech as long as it does not interfere with the civil rights of others and thus do not rise to the level of criminal violations that may be prosecuted.[58] However, an important distinction is in order. While a hate "incident" may not result in criminal prosecution, it may still result in civil litigation involving an allegation of assault or infliction of emotional distress, possibly among other causes of action.

California Civil Code Section 51.7 notes that a person's civil rights may be violated in the event of hate violence or the threat of violence, even if the incident does not rise to the level of a hate crime and may be otherwise constitutionally protected from prosecution by the government, as long as the incident occurred because of a person's actual or perceived: sex, race, color, religion, ancestry, national origin, disability, medical condition, genetic information, marital status, sexual orientation, citizenship, primary language, immigration status, political affiliation, and position in a labor dispute. A civil violation may result in restraining orders, injunctive and/or equitable relief, damages, a civil penalty of $25,000, and attorneys' fees.

---

[58] https://oag.ca.gov/hatecrimes.

International Law

While international law does not appear to address the issue of hate speech specifically, limitations exist that might arguably apply.

The United Nations

Article 19, and specifically Subsection (3) (as noted above) of the ICCPR (1976) states that:

3. The exercise of the rights provided for in paragraph 2 of this Article carries with it special duties and responsibilities. It may therefore be subject to certain restrictions, but these shall only be such as are provided by law and are necessary:
   (a) For respect of the rights or reputations of others;
   (b) For the protection of national security or of public order or of public health or morals.

Article 20 and specifically Subsection (2) states that:

1. Any propaganda for war shall be prohibited by law.
2. Any advocacy of national, racial, or religious hatred that constitutes incitement to discrimination, hostility or violence shall be prohibited by law.

Europe

As with America, a consistent definition, as well as a consistent approach to the subject of hate speech in Europe does not appear to exist.[59] However, the European Commission Against Racism and Intolerance notes, "Hate speech covers many forms of expressions which advocate, incite, promote or justify hatred, violence and discrimination against a person or group of persons for a variety of reasons."[60]

---

[59] See, e.g., Article 19, Responding to 'hate speech': Comparative overview of six EU countries, 2018. https://www.article19.org/wp-content/uploads/2018/03/ECA-hate-speech-compilation-report_March-2018.pdf.

[60] https://www.coe.int/en/web/european-commission-against-racism-and-intolerance/hate-speech-and-violence.

The Council Framework Decision 2008/913/JHA of 28 November 2008 on combating certain forms of expressions of racism and xenophobia by means of criminal law addresses the subject.

Art. 1 (1) Offences concerning racism and xenophobia

1. Each Member State shall take the measures necessary to ensure that the following intentional conduct is punishable:
   (a) publicly inciting to violence or hatred directed against a group of persons or a member of such a group defined by reference to race, color, religion, descent, or national or ethnic origin;
   (b) the commission of an act referred to in point (a) by public dissemination or distribution of tracts, pictures, or other material;
   (c) publicly condoning, denying or grossly trivializing crimes of genocide, crimes against humanity and war crimes as defined in Articles 6–8 of the Statute of the International Criminal Court, directed against a group of persons or a member of such a group defined by reference to race, color, religion, descent, or national or ethnic origin when the conduct is carried out in a manner likely to incite to violence or hatred against such a group or a member of such a group;
   (d) publicly condoning, denying or grossly trivializing the crimes defined in Article 6 of the Charter of the International Military Tribunal appended to the London Agreement of 8 August 1945, directed against a group of persons or a member of such a group defined by reference to race, color, religion, descent, or national or ethnic origin when the conduct is carried out in a manner likely to incite to violence or hatred against such a group or a member of such a group.

By way of a limitation, paragraph 2 goes on to note that, "For the purpose of paragraph 1, Member States may choose to punish only conduct which is either carried out in a manner likely to disturb public order or which is threatening, abusive or insulting."

France

The Law on the Freedom of the Press of 1881 (as noted above).

The First Amendment protects far more than simply the right of free speech as well as the freedom of the press. However, tort law, among others, establishes limits on freedom of expression, as noted above and elsewhere. Just as the First Amendment protects far more than the right of free speech and the freedom of the press, French Law on the Freedom of the Press of 29 July 1881 protects far more than simply the freedom of the press. And, just as there is no absolute constitutional right, the Law on the Freedom of the Press also established limits by way of "press offences" that were excluded from protection.

Both the First Amendment, as well as the Law on the Freedom of the Press were written at a time when newspapers, the press, was the only form of mass communication. The protection that had been established was extended to the electronic communication that was to follow.

Press Offenses

In its initial form, the law of 1881 established the following nine press offenses[61]:

1. Provocation to crimes or misdemeanors;
2. Provocation to a certain number of serious crimes, in particular to attacks on the authority of the State;
3. Seditious shouting or singing;
4. Provocation to members of the military to turn away from their duties;
5. Offense to the President of the Republic;
6. Publication of false news that has disturbed the public peace;
7. Offense to public decency;
8. Defamation and insult;
9. Offense and contempt toward heads of State or foreign diplomatic agents.

Several of the original offenses have since been modified, eliminated, or deleted or incorporated into the French penal code as previously noted.

In 2020, the French National Assembly attempted to address an online hate speech law by way of the Avia Law, a draconian measure that

---

[61] https://www.fondationdescartes.org/en/2021/07/the-law-on-the-freedom-of-the-press-of-29-july-1881-a-text-that-both-guarantees-and-restricts-freedom-of-expression/.

specified "... operators of online platforms ... offering an online public communication service ... shall be required (given the general interest attached to respecting human dignity and combating content published on the internet that condones crimes against humanity, incites acts of terrorism, advocates such acts or incites hatred, violence or discrimination, or insults a person or group of persons on the grounds of origin, race, religion, ethnicity, nationality, sex, sexual orientation, gender identity or disability, whether true or alleged, to render inaccessible, within 24 hours of notification by one or more persons of any content manifestly constituting one of the offences mentioned in paragraph 3 of Article 6(I)(7) of this law and Article 33(3 and 4) of the Law of 29 July 1881 on freedom of the press, or to cease referencing this content, within the same period."[62]

The law went on to amend the French Code of Criminal Procedure and referred to, "... The offence of refusing to remove a manifestly illegal message ..."[63]

The penalties for a violation were severe.

A failure to remove content within 24 hours, one hour in the case of child pornography or promotion of terrorism when notified by the government, would result in a fine of up to €200,000.[64] In addition, the law gave an independent government agency the power to impose fines of up to €20 million or 4% of the company's global annual revenue, whichever was higher, for specified violations.[65]

The French Constitutional Council, the constitutional authority in France, in a scenario remarkably similar to legal procedures in the United States, struck down key parts of the law. In an English translation of its opinion,[66] the court noted, among other issues, "The dissemination of pornographic images representing minors, on the one hand, and the provocation to acts of terrorism or the glorification of such acts, on the other hand, constitute abuses of the freedom of expression and communication. which seriously undermine public order and the rights of third parties ..."

"However, on the one hand, the determination of the unlawful nature of the content in question is not based on its manifest nature. It is subject to the sole assessment of the administration. On the other hand, the

[62] https://ecnl.org/sites/default/files/files/Text-of-Avia-Bill-EN.pdf.

[63] *Ibid.*

[64] *Ibid.*

[65] *Ibid.*

[66] https://www.conseil-constitutionnel.fr/decision/2020/2020801DC.htm.

initiation of an appeal against the withdrawal request is not suspensive and the one-hour period given to the publisher or the host to withdraw or make inaccessible the content concerned does not allow him to obtain a decision from the judge before being forced to withdraw it. Finally, the host or publisher who does not comply with this request within this period may be sentenced to one year's imprisonment and a fine of 250,000 euros."

"Consequently, the legislator has made an attack on the freedom of expression and communication which is not appropriate, necessary and proportionate to the aim pursued."

In summary, and in language that is vaguely reminiscent of the standards established by the United States Supreme Court when evaluating government restrictions on freedom of expression, the French court noted, "While reaffirming that the Constitution allows the legislator to repress abuses of the freedom of expression and communication, the Constitutional Council censures provisions affecting this freedom that are not appropriate, necessary and proportionate."[67] As part of that, the court noted that the law did not allow for a meaningful appeal. The requirement to withdraw material that was allegedly child pornography or promotion of terrorism was only one hour. Even in situations where an appeal was taken from notice by an "administrative authority," the one-hour time limitation remained and a failure to remove the allegedly offending material within that time required one year in prison and a fine of €250,000, regardless of the outcome of an appeal.

The French court's reference to a lack of a "meaningful appeal" is vaguely reminiscent of the American constitutional requirement of due process: notice and an opportunity to be heard, by a fair and neutral decision-maker before being deprived of life, liberty, or property.

Protection for Online Expression

The United States

The online environment presents a unique challenge, particularly for ISPs. Under tort law, anyone who repeats or republishes a defamatory statement may be sued for defamation. Thus, newspapers, television, and radio

---

[67] https://www.conseil-constitutionnel.fr/actualites/communique/decision-n-2020-801-dc-du-18-juin-2020-communique-de-presse.

stations face potential liability, as determined by the standard established in *New York Times v. Sullivan*, as noted elsewhere. And, ISPs, or what the CDA refers to as an "interactive computer service" that publishes information provided by third-party users face the same potential liability.

To address that issue, the CDA Section 230 provides that "No provider or user of an interactive computer service shall be treated as the publisher or speaker of any information provided by another information content provider."

Although discussed in detail in Chapter 5, in summary, the CDA provides a safe harbor for ISPs for the speech of others except in the area of intellectual property and federal criminal offenses and provides protection for ISPs that filter or remove posts.

The Digital Millennium Copyright Act (DMCA)

Passed by Congress in 1998 this law amended U.S. copyright law to address important parts of the relationship between copyright and the Internet. The three main updates were:

(1) Establishing protections for online service providers in certain situations if their users engage in copyright infringement, including the notice-and-takedown system, which allows copyright owners to inform online service providers about infringing material so it can be taken down;
(2) Encouraging copyright owners to give greater access to their works in digital formats by providing them with legal protections against unauthorized access to their works, such as hacking passwords or circumventing encryption; and
(3) Making it unlawful to provide false copyright management information, such as names of authors and copyright owners as well as titles of works, or to remove or alter that type of information in specified circumstances.

The European Union

Article 12-15 of the e-commerce Directive (ECD):

As with the CDA, it provides for safe harbors but with significant exceptions:

> Article 15 prohibits states from imposing general duties on intermediaries to monitor "illegal" content. However, once an online intermediary is aware of illegal content it has potential liability.

Misinformation/Disinformation

Distinguishing between the two in most situations is virtually impossible, the exception being truth-in-advertising laws.

The United States

The issue is related to the First Amendment and is exceedingly complex. "This Court has struggled for nearly a decade to define the proper accommodation between the law of defamation and the freedoms of speech and press protected by the First Amendment ..."[68] The Court then went on to note, "We begin with the common ground. Under the First Amendment there is no such thing as a false idea. However pernicious an opinion may seem, we depend for its correction not on the conscience of judges and juries but on the competition of other ideas. But there is no constitutional value in false statements of fact. Neither the intentional lie nor the careless error materially advances society's interest in 'uninhibited, robust, and wide-open' debate on public issues. (Citation omitted). They belong to that category of utterances which 'are no essential part of any exposition of ideas, and are of such slight social value as a step to truth that any benefit that may be derived from them is clearly outweighed by the social interest in order and morality.' (Citation omitted)."[69]

"Although the erroneous statement of fact is not worthy of constitutional protection, it is nevertheless inevitable in free debate. As James Madison pointed out in the Report on the Virginia Resolutions of 1798: 'Some degree of abuse is inseparable from the proper use of every thing; and in no instance is this more true than in that of the press.' 4 J. Elliot, Debates on the Federal Constitution of 1787, p. 571 (1876). And punishment of error runs the risk of inducing a cautious and restrictive exercise

[68] *Gertz v. Robert Welch*, Inc., 418 U.S. 323, 325 (1973).

[69] *Ibid.* at 339, 340.

of the constitutionally guaranteed freedoms of speech and press. Our decisions recognize that a rule of strict liability that compels a publisher or broadcaster to guarantee the accuracy of his factual assertions may lead to intolerable self-censorship. Allowing the media to avoid liability only by proving the truth of all injurious statements does not accord adequate protection to First Amendment liberties. As the Court stated in *New York Times Co. v. Sullivan* … 'Allowance of the defense of truth, with the burden of proving it on the defendant, does not mean that only false speech will be deterred.' The First Amendment requires that we protect some falsehood in order to protect speech that matters."[70]

"With that caveat we have no difficulty in distinguishing among defamation plaintiffs. The first remedy of any victim of defamation is self-help — using available opportunities to contradict the lie or correct the error and thereby to minimize its adverse impact on reputation. Public officials and public figures usually enjoy significantly greater access to the channels of effective communication and hence have a more realistic opportunity to counteract false statements than private individuals normally enjoy. Private individuals are therefore more vulnerable to injury, and the state interest in protecting them is correspondingly greater."[71]

"We hold that, so long as they do not impose liability without fault, the States may define for themselves the appropriate standard of liability for a publisher or broadcaster of defamatory falsehood injurious to a private individual. This approach provides a more equitable boundary between the competing concerns involved here. It recognizes the strength of the legitimate state interest in compensating private individuals for wrongful injury to reputation, yet shields the press and broadcast media from the rigors of strict liability for defamation. At least this conclusion obtains where, as here, the substance of the defamatory statement 'makes substantial danger to reputation apparent.' This phrase places in perspective the conclusion we announce today. Our inquiry would involve considerations somewhat different from those discussed above if a State purported to condition civil liability on a factual misstatement whose content did not warn a reasonably prudent editor or broadcaster of its defamatory potential. (Citation omitted). Such a case is not now before us, and we intimate no view as to its proper resolution."[72]

---

[70] *Ibid.* at 340, 341.

[71] *Ibid.* at 344.

[72] *Ibid.* at 347, 348.

The European Union

The European Union faces the same challenges. And, in a case from 1986, the ECtHR distinguished between facts and value judgments.[73] A political figure sued for defamation pursuant to Article 111 of the Austrian Criminal Code. Article 112 specified that the only defense was the truth. Inasmuch as the statements that gave rise to the action included allegations of immorality, undignified behavior, and basest opportunism, and, as such, constituted value judgments, requiring proof that the statements were true was impossible. The Vienna Regional Court found the defendant guilty of defamation. The conviction was upheld by the Vienna Court of Appeal on 29 October 1981. The matter finally ended up in front of the ECtHR. The defendant claimed that the court decision infringed his freedom of expression to a degree incompatible with the fundamental principles of a democratic society and, in particular, whether there was "interference by public authority" with the exercise of the applicant's freedom of expression. At issue was Article 10 of the European Convention for the Protection of Human Rights that states in Section 1, "Everyone has the right to freedom of expression. This right shall include freedom to hold opinions and to receive and impart information and ideas without interference by public authority and regardless of frontiers ..."

The court concluded that there was a breach of Article 10 of the Convention and noted in paragraph 46 of its judgment, "A careful distinction needs to be made between facts and value-judgments. The existence of facts can be demonstrated, whereas the truth of value-judgments is not susceptible of proof."

Commercial Speech

Europe

As previously noted, Article 10 of the European Convention for the Protection of Human Rights states:

1. Everyone has the right to freedom of expression. This right shall include freedom to hold opinions and to receive and impart information and ideas without interference by public authority and regardless

[73] *Lingens v. Austria* (1986) 8 EHRR 407.

of frontiers. This Article shall not prevent States from requiring the licensing of broadcasting, television or cinema enterprises.

As noted previously, Section 2 allows for certain restrictions.

Article 11 (Freedom of expression and information) of the European Union Charter of Fundamental Rights:

1. Everyone has the right to freedom of expression. This right shall include freedom to hold opinions and to receive and impart information and ideas without interference by public authority and regardless of frontiers.
2. The freedom and pluralism of the media shall be respected.

Article 11 corresponds to Article 10 of the European Convention on Human Rights. The Article goes on to note that the limitations that may be imposed may not exceed those provided for in Article 10(2) of the Convention. Because the Article refers to commercial enterprises, such as broadcasting, television and cinema, it would appear to allow states to regular commercial advertising, as in the United States by, for example, truth-in-advertising laws.

Chapter 4

Privacy

Abstract

The common law recognized a right of privacy, by way of the tort of invasion of privacy, more than 100 years ago. Surprisingly, the United States Supreme Court did not recognize a right of privacy until 1965 in *Griswold v. Connecticut*. The law of privacy therefore encompasses not only the federal Constitution, as well as state constitutions, but state common law, as well as federal and state statutory law. The issue of privacy encompasses not only civil issues, but criminal matters as well. The issue is complicated because the right of privacy depends, at least in part, on a "reasonable expectation" of privacy. What is "reasonable" may depend, at least in part, on where we are. For instance, a home is treated differently than a vehicle. In addition, a reasonable expectation of privacy at work is considerably different from a reasonable expectation of privacy at home. A reasonable expectation of privacy in a civil matter may be different from an expectation of privacy in a criminal matter. The Fourth Amendment requires a search warrant only in the case of an "unreasonable" search. If the search is "reasonable" a search warrant may not be necessary. Further complicating the issue is the constitutional requirement of "probable cause" to justify the issuance of a search warrant.

Introduction

Currently, privacy in America is a combination of Constitutional law, both federal and state, statutory law, both federal and state, as well as common law. Although arguments in favor of a right to privacy are nothing new,[1] a right of privacy has not always been recognized and, in some cases, was outright rejected.[2] The legislature responded to the rejection, although the earliest response provided only a limited right to privacy. As the Court in *Lohan v. Take-Two Interactive Software, Inc.*[3] noted, "In response to *Roberson*..." a case from 1902, "... the legislature codified 'a limited statutory right of privacy' in article 5 of the Civil Rights Law (citations omitted). Civil Rights Law Section 50 makes it a misdemeanor to use a living person's 'name, portrait or picture' for advertising or trade purposes without having first obtained the written consent of such person, or if a minor of his or her parent or guardian' (citations omitted) and 'makes a violation of section 50 actionable in a civil suit' (citations omitted)."

As relevant here, Civil Rights Law Section 51 specifically provides that

> [a]ny person whose name, portrait, picture or voice is used within this state for advertising purposes or for the purposes of trade without the written consent first obtained as ... provided [in Civil Rights Law Section 50 may maintain an equitable action ... to prevent and restrain the use thereof; and may also sue and recover damages for any injuries sustained by reason of such use....

A constitutional right to privacy in the United States was not recognized by the Supreme Court until 1965.[4] Since that time, federal and state laws, agency regulations on the subject of privacy, as well as courts' interpretations of those laws and regulations have multiplied to the point where there is a confusing patchwork of laws, agency regulations, and court decisions that represents a challenge to companies in their efforts to comply. The situation is far more complicated for companies that conduct

---

[1] Samuel D. Warren and Louis D. Brandeis, The Right to Privacy, 4 *Harv. L. Rev.*, 193 (1890).

[2] *Roberson v. Rochester Folding Box Co.*, 171 N.Y. 538 (1902). Superseded by statute as stated in *Lohan v. Take-Two Interactive Software, Inc.* 31 N.Y.3d 111 (2018).

[3] 31 N.Y.3d 111 (2018).

[4] *Griswold v. Connecticut*, 381 U.S. 479 (1965).

international business operations. In addition, any discussion of privacy necessarily entails issues regarding criminal law and is addressed in this chapter as well.

The Federal Constitution

Privacy under the federal Constitution depends, at least in part, on what the Supreme Court has referred to as a reasonable expectation of privacy[5] and involves a discussion of two factors that are discussed in additional detail in Chapter 6. In the United States the concept of privacy was first noted by the Supreme Court in Griswold, *supra.*, where the Court referred to a variety of constitutional Amendments "…creating a right of privacy, no less important than any other right carefully and particularly reserved to the people."[6] Although Griswold involved a criminal prosecution, the case provides guidance on the subject of privacy in the United States.

Griswold v. Connecticut

Appellant Griswold is Executive Director of the Planned Parenthood League of Connecticut. Appellant Buxton is a licensed physician and a professor at the Yale Medical School who served as Medical Director for the League at its Center in New Haven — a center open and operating from November 1 to November 10, 1961, when appellants were arrested.

They gave information, instruction, and medical advice to married persons as to the means of preventing conception. They examined the wife and prescribed the best contraceptive device or material for her use. Fees were usually charged, although some couples were serviced free.

There are several statutes that are involved (including) one that provides:

> Any person who uses any drug, medicinal article or instrument for the purpose of preventing conception shall be fined not less than fifty dollars or imprisoned not less than sixty days nor more than one year or be both fined and imprisoned. (Another section) provides: 'Any person who assists, abets, counsels, causes, hires or commands another to

[5] *California v. Greenwood,* 486 U.S. 35, 39 (1988).

[6] *Griswold v. Connecticut,* 381 U.S. 479 (1965). *Op. cit.*, at 484–485.

> commit any offense may be prosecuted and punished as if he were the principal offender.'

The appellants were found guilty as accessories and fined $100 each, against the claim that the accessory statute as so applied violated the Fourteenth Amendment. The Appellate Division of the Circuit Court affirmed. The Supreme Court of Errors affirmed that judgment. We noted probable jurisdiction.

Coming to the merits, we are met with a wide range of questions that implicate the Due Process Clause of the Fourteenth Amendment. We do not sit as a super-legislature to determine the wisdom, need, and propriety of laws that touch economic problems, business affairs, or social conditions. This law, however, operates directly on an intimate relation of husband and wife and their physician's role in one aspect of that relation. The association of people is not mentioned in the Constitution nor in the Bill of Rights. The right to educate a child in a school of the parents' choice — whether public or private or parochial — is also not mentioned. Nor is the right to study any particular subject or any foreign language. Yet the First Amendment has been construed to include certain of those rights.

By *Pierce v. Society of Sisters*, *supra*, the right to educate one's children as one chooses is made applicable to the States by the force of the First and Fourteenth Amendments. By *Meyer v. State of Nebraska*, *supra*, the same dignity is given the right to study the German language in a private school. In other words, "the State may not, consistently with the spirit of the First Amendment, contract the spectrum of available knowledge. The right of freedom of speech and press includes not only the right to utter or to print, but the right to distribute, the right to receive, the right to read … and freedom of inquiry, freedom of thought, and freedom to teach … — indeed the freedom of the entire university community. Without those peripheral rights the specific rights would be less secure…"

In *NAACP v. State of Alabama*, "we protected the 'freedom to associate and privacy in one's associations,' noting that freedom of association was a peripheral First Amendment right. Disclosure of membership lists of a constitutionally valid association, we held, was invalid 'as entailing the likelihood of a substantial restraint upon the exercise by petitioner's members of their right to freedom of association.' *Ibid.* In other words, the First Amendment has a penumbra where privacy is protected from governmental intrusion. In like context, we have protected forms of 'association' that are not political in the customary sense but pertain to the social, legal, and economic benefit of the members. In *Schware v. Board of Bar Examiners*...we held it not permissible to bar a lawyer from practice, because he had once been a member of the Communist Party. The man's 'association with that Party' was not shown to be 'anything more than a political faith in a political party' and was not action of a kind proving bad moral character.

Those cases involved more than the 'right of assembly' — a right that extends to all irrespective of their race or ideology ... The right of 'association,' like the right of belief ... is more than the right to attend a meeting; it includes the right to express one's attitudes or philosophies by membership in a group or by affiliation with it or by other lawful means. Association in that context is a form of expression of opinion; and while it is not expressly included in the First Amendment its existence is necessary in making the express guarantees fully meaningful.

The foregoing cases suggest that specific guarantees in the Bill of Rights have penumbras, formed by emanations from those guarantees that help give them life and substance. Various guarantees create zones of privacy. The right of association contained in the penumbra of the First Amendment is one, as we have seen ... The Fourth Amendment explicitly affirms the 'right of the people to be secure in their persons, houses, papers, and effects, against unreasonable searches and seizures.' The Fifth Amendment in its Self-Incrimination Clause enables the citizen to create a zone of privacy which government may not force him to surrender to his detriment. The Ninth Amendment provides: 'The enumeration in the Constitution, of certain rights, shall not be construed to deny or disparage others retained by the people.'

"The Fourth and Fifth Amendments were described in *Boyd v. United States*, as protection against all governmental invasions 'of the sanctity of a man's home and the privacies of life.' We recently referred in *Mapp v. Ohio*...to the Fourth Amendment as creating a 'right to privacy, no less important than any other right carefully and particularly reserved to the people.' We have had many controversies over these penumbral rights of 'privacy and repose.' ... These cases bear witness that the right of privacy which presses for recognition here is a legitimate one. The present case, then, concerns a relationship lying within the zone of privacy created by several fundamental constitutional guarantees. And it concerns a law which, in forbidding the use of contraceptives rather than regulating their manufacture or sale, seeks to achieve its goals by means having a maximum destructive impact upon that relationship. Such a law cannot stand in light of the familiar principle, so often applied by this Court, that a 'governmental purpose to control or prevent activities constitutionally subject to state regulation may not be achieved by means which sweep unnecessarily broadly and thereby invade the area of protected freedoms.' Would we allow the police to search the sacred precincts of marital bedrooms for telltale signs of the use of contraceptives? The very idea is repulsive to the notions of privacy surrounding the marriage relationship.

We deal with a right of privacy older than the Bill of Rights — older than our political parties, older than our school system. Marriage is a coming together for better or for worse, hopefully enduring, and intimate to the degree of being sacred. It is an association that promotes a way of life, not causes; a harmony in living, not political faiths; a bilateral loyalty, not commercial or social projects. Yet it is an association for as noble a purpose as any involved in our prior decisions."

The Court reversed the conviction. In overruling the state court, the Court found a right to privacy in the penumbras of the First, Third, Fourth, Fifth and Ninth Amendments in a marital relationship.

Two years later, in *Katz v. United States*[7] (also a criminal prosecution and discussed in Chapter 6) the Supreme Court was called upon to address the concept of an "unreasonable" search and seizure. The Fourth Amendment to the Constitution states, "The right of the people to be secure in their persons, houses, papers, and effects, against unreasonable searches and seizures, shall not be violated, and no warrants shall issue, but upon probable cause, supported by oath or affirmation, and particularly describing the place to be searched, and the persons or things to be seized."

The Fourth Amendment does not protect Americans from all searches and seizures, only "unreasonable" searches and seizures. If the search is considered "unreasonable," law enforcement is generally required to obtain a search warrant, although there are exceptions. Whether a search is unreasonable or not depends on several issues. A court when faced with determining whether a search was "unreasonable" or not must consider:

1. The individual's Fourth Amendment rights; and
2. Legitimate law enforcement issues, such as, public safety.[8]

---

[7] *Katz v. United States*, 389 U.S. 347 (1967).

[8] *Minnesota v. Carter*, 525 U.S. 83 (1998).

However, that is not the end of the inquiry, the court must also consider the place.

The Court has had to consider the issue of reasonableness with regard to searches of persons, home, schools, and vehicles, among other locations, as noted in the cases below. Generally, the courts consider a search of a home without a warrant as "presumptively" unreasonable[9] although there are exceptions, such as in the case of consent, as discussed in Chapter 6.

Katz v. U.S. 389 U.S. 347 (1967)

The petitioner was convicted of transmitting wagering information by telephone from Los Angeles to Miami and Boston in violation of a federal statute. At trial the Government was permitted, over the petitioner's objection, to introduce evidence of the petitioner's end of telephone conversation, overheard by FBI agents who had attached an electronic listening and recording device to the outside of the public telephone booth from which he had placed his calls. In affirming his conviction, the Court of Appeals rejected the contention that the recordings had been obtained in violation of the Fourth Amendment, because "(t)here was no physical entrance into the area occupied by, (the petitioner)." We granted *certiorari* in order to consider the constitutional questions thus presented.

The Court noted,

> … the correct solution of Fourth Amendment problems is not necessarily promoted by incantation of the phrase 'constitutionally protected area.' Secondly, the Fourth Amendment cannot be translated into a general constitutional 'right to privacy.' That Amendment protects individual privacy against certain kinds of governmental intrusion, but its protections go further, and often have nothing to do with privacy at all. Other provisions of the Constitution protect personal privacy from other forms of governmental invasion. But the protection of a person's general right to privacy — his right to be let alone by other people — is, like the protection of his property and of his very life, left largely to the law of the individual States.[7]

---

[9] *Payton v. New York*, 445 U.S. 573 (1980).

… the parties have attached great significance to the characterization of the telephone booth from which the petitioner placed his calls. The petitioner has strenuously argued that the booth was a 'constitutionally protected area.' The Government has maintained with equal vigor that it was not. But this effort to decide whether or not a given 'area,' viewed in the abstract, is 'constitutionally protected' deflects attention from the problem presented by this case. For the Fourth Amendment protects people, not places. What a person knowingly exposes to the public, even in his own home or office, is not a subject of Fourth Amendment protection. But what he seeks to preserve as private, even in an area accessible to the public, may be constitutionally protected.

The Government stresses the fact that the telephone booth from which the petitioner made his calls was constructed partly of glass, so that he was as visible after he entered it as he would have been if he had remained outside. But what he sought to exclude when he entered the booth was not the intruding eye — it was the uninvited ear. He did not shed his right to do so simply because he made his calls from a place where he might be seen. No less than an individual in a business office, in a friend's apartment, or in a taxicab, a person in a telephone booth may rely upon the protection of the Fourth Amendment. One who occupies it, shuts the door behind him, and pays the toll that permits him to place a call is surely entitled to assume that the words he utters into the mouthpiece will not be broadcast to the world. To read the Constitution more narrowly is to ignore the vital role that the public telephone has come to play in private communication.

The Government's activities in electronically listening to and recording the petitioner's words violated the privacy upon which he justifiably relied while using the telephone booth and thus constituted a 'search and seizure' within the meaning of the Fourth Amendment. The fact that the electronic device employed to achieve that end did not happen to penetrate the wall of the booth can have no constitutional significance. The question remaining for decision, then, is whether the search and seizure conducted in this case complied with constitutional standards. In that regard, the Government's position is that its agents acted in an entirely defensible manner: They did not begin their electronic surveillance until investigation of the petitioner's activities had established a strong probability that he was using the telephone in question to transmit gambling information to persons in other States, in violation of federal law. Moreover, the surveillance was limited, both in scope and in duration, to the specific purpose of establishing the contents of the petitioner's unlawful telephonic communications. The agents confined their surveillance to the brief periods during which he used the telephone booth, and they took great care to overhear only the conversations of the petitioner himself.

The Government urges that, because its agents relied upon the decisions in (... prior cases), and because they did no more here than they might properly have done with prior judicial sanction, we should retroactively validate their conduct. That we cannot do. It is apparent that the agents in this case acted with restraint. Yet the inescapable fact is that this restraint was imposed by the agents themselves, not by a judicial officer. They were not required, before commencing the search, to present their estimate of probable cause for detached scrutiny by a neutral magistrate.

They were not compelled, during the conduct of the search itself, to observe precise limits established in advance by a specific court order. Nor were they directed, after the search had been completed, to notify the authorizing magistrate in detail of all that had been seized. In the absence of such safeguards, this Court has never sustained a search upon the sole ground that officers reasonably expected to find evidence of a particular crime and voluntarily confined their activities to the least intrusive means consistent with that end. Searches conducted without warrants have been held unlawful 'notwithstanding facts unquestionably showing probable cause,' ... for the Constitution requires 'that the deliberate, impartial judgment of a judicial officer * * * be interposed between the citizen and the police * * *.' 'Over and again this Court has emphasized that the mandate of the (Fourth) Amendment requires adherence to judicial processes,' ... and that searches conducted outside the judicial process, without prior approval by judge or magistrate, are *per se* unreasonable under the Fourth Amendment — subject only to a few specifically established and well-delineated exceptions.

It is difficult to imagine how any of those exceptions could ever apply to the sort of search and seizure involved in this case. Even electronic surveillance substantially contemporaneous with an individual's arrest could hardly be deemed an 'incident' of that arrest. Nor could the use of electronic surveillance without prior authorization be justified on grounds of 'hot pursuit'. And, of course, the very nature of electronic surveillance precludes its use pursuant to the suspect's consent.

The Government does not question these basic principles. Rather, it urges the creation of a new exception to cover this case. It argues that surveillance of a telephone booth should be exempted from the usual requirement of advance authorization by a magistrate upon a showing of

> probable cause. We cannot agree. Omission of such authorization 'bypasses the safeguards provided by an objective predetermination of probable cause, and substitutes instead the far less reliable procedure of an after-the-event justification for the * * * search, too likely to be subtly influenced by the familiar shortcomings of hindsight judgment' and bypassing a neutral predetermination of the scope of a search leaves individuals secure from Fourth Amendment violations 'only in the discretion of the police.' These considerations do not vanish when the search in question is transferred from the setting of a home, an office, or a hotel room to that of a telephone booth. Wherever a man may be, he is entitled to know that he will remain free from unreasonable searches and seizures. Held: The government agents here ignored 'the procedure of antecedent justification * * * that is central to the Fourth Amendment, a procedure that we hold to be a constitutional precondition of the kind of electronic surveillance involved in this case. Because the surveillance here failed to meet that condition, and because it led to the petitioner's conviction, the judgment must be reversed.

Justice White, concurring: In joining the Court's opinion, I note the Court's acknowledgment that there are circumstance in which it is reasonable to search without a warrant. In this connection, in footnote 23 the Court points out that today's decision does not reach national security cases. Wiretapping to protect the security of the Nation has been authorized by successive Presidents. The present Administration would apparently save national security cases from restrictions against wiretapping … We should not require the warrant procedure and the magistrate's judgment if the President of the United States or his chief legal officer, the Attorney General, has considered the requirements of national security and authorized electronic surveillance as reasonable."

However, it was the late Justice Harlan's concurring opinion that established the standard that is followed when analyzing a situation that encompasses the Fourth Amendment. In that concurring opinion, Justice Harlan noted:

> As the Court's opinion states, 'the Fourth Amendment protects people, not places.' The question, however, is what protection it affords to those people. Generally, as here, the answer to that question requires reference to a 'place.' My understanding of the rule that has emerged from prior decisions is that there is a twofold requirement, first that a person have exhibited an actual (subjective) expectation of privacy and, second, that

> the expectation be one that society is prepared to recognize as 'reasonable.' Thus, a man's home is, for most purposes, a place where he expects privacy, but objects, activities, or statements that he exposes to the "plain view" of outsiders are not 'protected,' because no intention to keep them to himself has been exhibited. On the other hand, conversations in the open would not be protected against being overheard, for the expectation of privacy under the circumstances would be unreasonable.

In Fourth Amendment cases a court will use a two-step analysis. First, did the person exhibit an actual (subjective) expectation of privacy? After all, that which a person exposes to the "plain view" of outsiders is not protected. If the answer is "yes," then the court will move to the second step: Is that expectation one that society is prepared to recognize as reasonable? Only if the answer to both questions is in the affirmative would a court find a reasonable expectation of privacy that is due Fourth Amendment protection.

While a search of a home, for instance, appears rather clear-cut in terms of a reasonable expectation of privacy, other situations may not be so obvious. Although another criminal prosecution, and also noted in Chapter 6, the Court had to decide the issue of privacy with regard to trash.

California v. Greenwood 486 U.S. 35 (1988)

> The Laguna Beach Police Department received information that respondent Greenwood might be engaged in narcotics trafficking. A criminal suspect informed a federal drug enforcement agent that a truck filled with illegal drugs was en route to the Laguna Beach address at which Greenwood resided. In addition, a neighbor complained of heavy vehicular traffic late at night in front of Greenwood's single-family home. The neighbor reported that the vehicles remained at Greenwood's house for only a few minutes.
>
> ...the Laguna Beach Police Department conducted a surveillance of Greenwood's home. She observed several vehicles make brief stops at the house during the late-night and early morning hours, and she followed a truck from the house to a residence that had previously been under investigation as a narcotics-trafficking location. An investigator from the police department asked the neighborhood's regular trash collector to pick up the plastic garbage bags that Greenwood had left on the curb in front of his house and to turn the bags over to her without mixing their contents with garbage from other houses. The trash collector

cleaned his truck bin of other refuse, collected the garbage bags from the street in front of Greenwood's house, and turned the bags over to the investigator. The officer searched through the rubbish and found items indicative of narcotics use. She recited the information that she had gleaned from the trash search in an affidavit in support of a warrant to search Greenwood's home.

Police officers encountered both respondents at the house later that day when they arrived to execute the warrant. The police discovered quantities of cocaine and hashish during their search of the house. Respondents were arrested on felony narcotics charges. They subsequently posted bail.

The police continued to receive reports of many late-night visitors to the Greenwood house. Subsequently, another investigator obtained Greenwood's garbage from the regular trash collector in the same manner as had been done previously and again, the garbage contained evidence of narcotics use. The investigator secured another search warrant for Greenwood's home based on the information from the second trash search. The police found more narcotics and evidence of narcotics trafficking when they executed the warrant. Greenwood was again arrested.

Finding that probable cause to search the house would not have existed without the evidence obtained from the trash searches, the State Superior Court dismissed the charges pursuant to a California state court case holding that warrantless trash searches violate the Fourth Amendment and the California Constitution. Although noting a state constitutional amendment eliminating the exclusionary rule for evidence seized in violation of state, but not federal, law, the State Court of Appeal affirmed on the ground that the California state court decision was based on federal, as well as state, law. The prosecution filed a *writ of certiorari* with the United States Supreme Court that was granted.

The Court noted,

The warrantless search and seizure of the garbage bags left at the curb outside the Greenwood house would violate the Fourth Amendment only if respondents manifested a subjective expectation of privacy in their garbage that society accepts as objectively reasonable (citing *Katz v. United States*).

They assert, however, that they had, and exhibited, an expectation of privacy with respect to the trash that was searched by the police: The trash, which was placed on the street for collection at a fixed time, was contained in opaque plastic bags, which the garbage collector was expected to pick up, mingle with the trash of others, and deposit at the garbage dump. The trash was only temporarily on the street, and there was little likelihood that it would be inspected by anyone. It may well be that respondents did not expect that the contents of their garbage bags would become known to the police or other members of the public. An expectation of privacy does not give rise to Fourth Amendment protection, however, unless society is prepared to accept that expectation as objectively reasonable.

Here, we conclude that respondents exposed their garbage to the public sufficiently to defeat their claim to Fourth Amendment protection. It is common knowledge that plastic garbage bags left on or at the side of a public street are readily accessible to animals, children, scavengers, snoops, and other members of the public (citing the same case that the court in California referenced in dismissing the case). Moreover, respondents placed their refuse at the curb for the express purpose of conveying it to a third party, the trash collector, who might himself have sorted through respondents' trash or permitted others, such as the police, to do so. Accordingly, having deposited their garbage 'in an area particularly suited for public inspection and, in a manner of speaking, public consumption, for the express purpose of having strangers take it,'.... respondents could have had no reasonable expectation of privacy in the inculpatory items that they discarded.

Furthermore, as we have held, the police cannot reasonably be expected to avert their eyes from evidence of criminal activity that could have been observed by any member of the public. Hence, '[w]hat a person knowingly exposes to the public, even in his own home or office, is not a subject of Fourth Amendment protection.'

Similarly, we held in *California v. Ciraolo,* that the police were not required by the Fourth Amendment to obtain a warrant before conducting surveillance of the respondent's fenced backyard from a private plane flying at an altitude of 1,000 feet. We concluded that the respondent's expectation that his yard was protected from such surveillance was unreasonable because '[a]ny member of the public flying in this airspace who glanced down could have seen everything that these officers observed.'

California could amend its Constitution to negate the holding in *Krivda* that state law forbids warrantless searches of trash. We are convinced that the State may likewise eliminate the exclusionary rule as a remedy for violations of that right. At the federal level, we have not

> required that evidence obtained in violation of the Fourth Amendment be suppressed in all circumstances … Rather, our decisions concerning the scope of the Fourth Amendment exclusionary rule have balanced the benefits of deterring police misconduct against the costs of excluding reliable evidence of criminal activity. We have declined to apply the exclusionary rule indiscriminately 'when law enforcement officers have acted in objective good faith or their transgressions have been minor,' because 'the magnitude of the benefit conferred on … guilty defendants [in such circumstances] offends basic concepts of the criminal justice system.'
>
> The States are not foreclosed by the Due Process Clause from using a similar balancing approach to delineate the scope of their own exclusionary rules. Hence, the people of California could permissibly conclude that the benefits of excluding relevant evidence of criminal activity do not outweigh the costs when the police conduct at issue does not violate federal law.

The Court concluded, "The judgment of the California Court of Appeal is therefore reversed, and this case is remanded for further proceedings not inconsistent with this opinion."

Changes in technology, such as electronic communication, present a significant challenge for the courts, and specifically, what constitutes a reasonable expectation of privacy. In 2010, the Court was called upon to address the issue of government monitoring of electronic communication, in that case a pager. Fortunately, a discussion of privacy is not limited to cases involving a criminal prosecution although this case is also discussed in Chapter 6.

City of Ontario v. Quon, 560 U.S. 746 (2010)

The case arose out of incidents in 2001 and 2002 when respondent Jeff Quon was employed by the Ontario Police Department (OPD). He was a police sergeant and member of OPD's Special Weapons and Tactics (SWAT) Team … In October 2001, the City acquired 20 alphanumeric pagers capable of sending and receiving text messages. Arch Wireless Operating Company provided wireless service for the pagers. Under the City's service contract with Arch Wireless, each pager was allotted a limited number of characters sent or received each month. Usage in excess of that amount would result in an additional fee. The City issued pagers to Quon and other SWAT Team members in order to help the SWAT Team mobilize and respond to emergency situations. Before acquiring the pagers, the City announced a "Computer Usage, Internet and E-Mail Policy" (Computer Policy) that applied to all employees. Among other provisions, it specified that the City "reserves the right to monitor and log all network activity including e-mail and Internet use, with or without notice. Users should have no expectation of privacy or confidentiality when using these resources." In March 2000, Quon signed a statement acknowledging that he had read and understood the Computer Policy. The Computer Policy did not apply, on its face, to text messaging. Text messages share similarities with e-mails, but the two differ in an important way. In this case, for instance, an e-mail sent on a City computer was transmitted through the City's own data servers, but a text message sent on one of the City's pagers was transmitted using wireless radio frequencies from an individual pager to a receiving station owned by Arch Wireless. It was routed through Arch Wireless' computer network, where it remained until the recipient's pager or cellular telephone was ready to receive the message, at which point Arch Wireless transmitted the message from the transmitting station nearest to the recipient. After delivery, Arch Wireless retained a copy on its computer servers. The message did not pass through computers owned by the City. Although the Computer Policy did not cover text messages by its explicit terms, the City made clear to employees, including Quon, that the City would treat text messages the same way as it treated e-mails. At an April 18, 2002, staff meeting at which Quon was present, Lieutenant Steven Duke, the OPD officer responsible for the City's contract with Arch Wireless, told officers that messages sent on the pagers "are considered e-mail messages. This means that [text] messages would fall under the City's policy as public information and [would be] eligible for auditing." Duke's comments were put in writing in a memorandum sent on April 29, 2002, by Chief Scharf to Quon and other City personnel.

Within the first or second billing cycle after the pagers were distributed, Quon exceeded his monthly text message character allotment. Duke told Quon about the overage, and reminded him that messages sent on the pagers were 'considered e-mail and could be audited.' Duke said, however, that 'it was not his intent to audit [an] employee's text messages to see if the overage [was] due to work related transmissions.' Duke suggested that Quon could reimburse the City for the overage fee rather than have Duke audit the messages. Quon wrote a check to the City for the overage. Duke offered the same arrangement to other employees who incurred overage fees. Over the next few months, Quon exceeded his character limit three or four times. Each time he reimbursed the City.

Quon and another officer again incurred overage fees for their pager usage in August 2002. At a meeting in October, Duke told Scharf that he had become 'tired of being a bill collector.' Scharf decided to determine whether the existing character limit was too low — that is, whether officers such as Quon were having to pay fees for sending work-related messages — or if the overages were for personal messages. Scharf told Duke to request transcripts of text messages sent in August and September by Quon and the other employee who had exceeded the character allowance. At Duke's request, an administrative assistant employed by OPD contacted Arch Wireless. After verifying that the City was the subscriber on the accounts, Arch Wireless provided the desired transcripts. Duke reviewed the transcripts and discovered that many of the messages sent and received on Quon's pager were not work related, and some were sexually explicit. Duke reported his findings to Scharf, who, along with Quon's immediate supervisor, reviewed the transcripts himself. After his review, Scharf referred the matter to OPD's internal affairs division for an investigation into whether Quon was violating OPD rules by pursuing personal matters while on duty ...

The Court noted,

> 'Raising claims under Rev. Stat. Section 1979, 42 U.S.C. Section 1983; 18 U.S.C. Section 2701 *et seq.*, popularly known as the Stored Communications Act (SCA); and California law, Quon filed suit against petitioners in the United States District Court for the Central District of California ... Quon was joined in his suit by another plaintiff who is not a party before this Court and by the other respondents, each of whom exchanged text messages with Quon during August and September 2002: Jerilyn Quon, Jeff Quon's then-wife, from whom he was separated; April Florio, an OPD employee with whom Jeff Quon was romantically involved; and Steve Trujillo, another member of the OPD SWAT Team. Among the allegations in the complaint was that petitioners violated respondents' Fourth Amendment rights and the SCA by obtaining and reviewing the transcript of Jeff Quon's pager messages and that Arch Wireless had violated the SCA by turning over the transcript to the City. The parties filed cross-motions for summary judgment.
>
> The District Court granted Arch Wireless' motion for summary judgment on the SCA claim but denied petitioners' motion for summary judgment on the Fourth Amendment claims....the District Court

determined that Quon had a reasonable expectation of privacy in the content of his text messages. Whether the audit of the text messages was nonetheless reasonable, the District Court concluded, turned on Chief Scharf's intent: '[I]f the purpose for the audit was to determine if Quon was using his pager to 'play games' and 'waste time,' then the audit was not constitutionally reasonable'; but if the audit's purpose 'was to determine the efficacy of the existing character limits to ensure that officers were not paying hidden workrelated costs, … no constitutional violation occurred.' The District Court held a jury trial to determine the purpose of the audit. The jury concluded that Scharf ordered the audit to determine the efficacy of the character limits. The District Court accordingly held that petitioners did not violate the Fourth Amendment. It entered judgment in their favor. The United States Court of Appeals for the Ninth Circuit reversed in part. The panel agreed with the District Court that Jeff Quon had a reasonable expectation of privacy in his text messages but disagreed with the District Court about whether the search was reasonable. Even though the search was conducted for 'a legitimate work-related rationale,' the Court of Appeals concluded, it 'was not reasonable in scope.' The panel disagreed with the District Court's observation that 'there were no less-intrusive means' that Chief Scharf could have used 'to verify the efficacy of the 25,000-character limit … without intruding on [respondents'] Fourth Amendment rights.' The opinion pointed to a 'host of simple ways' that the chief could have used instead of the audit, such as warning Quon at the beginning of the month that his future messages would be audited, or asking Quon himself to redact the transcript of his messages. The Court of Appeals further concluded that Arch Wireless had violated the SCA by turning over the transcript to the City.

Before turning to the reasonableness of the search, it is instructive to note the parties' disagreement over whether Quon had a reasonable expectation of privacy. The record does establish that OPD, at the outset, made it clear that pager messages were not considered private. The City's Computer Policy stated that '[u]sers should have no expectation of privacy or confidentiality when using' City computers. Chief Scharf's memo and Duke's statements made clear that this official policy extended to text messaging. The disagreement, at least as respondents see the case, is over whether Duke's later statements overrode the official policy. Respondents contend that because Duke told Quon that an audit would be unnecessary if Quon paid for the overage, Quon reasonably could expect that the contents of his messages would remain private.

The Court must proceed with care when considering the whole concept of privacy expectations in communications made on electronic equipment owned by a government employer. The judiciary risks error by elaborating too fully on the Fourth Amendment implications of emerging technology before its role in society has become clear. In Katz, the Court relied on its own knowledge and experience to conclude that there is a reasonable expectation of privacy in a telephone booth. It is not so clear that courts at present are on so sure a ground. Prudence counsels caution before the facts in the instant case are used to establish far-reaching premises that define the existence, and extent, of privacy expectations enjoyed by employees when using employer-provided communication devices.

Rapid changes in the dynamics of communication and information transmission are evident not just in the technology itself but in what society accepts as proper behavior. As one *amici* brief notes, many employers expect or at least tolerate personal use of such equipment by employees because it often increases worker efficiency….Another amicus points out that the law is beginning to respond to these developments, as some States have recently passed statutes requiring employers to notify employees when monitoring their electronic communications….At present, it is uncertain how workplace norms, and the law's treatment of them, will evolve.

Cell phone and text message communications are so pervasive that some persons may consider them to be essential means or necessary instruments for self-expression, even self-identification. That might strengthen the case for an expectation of privacy. On the other hand, the ubiquity of those devices has made them generally affordable, so one could counter that employees who need cell phones or similar devices for personal matters can purchase and pay for their own. And employer policies concerning communications will of course shape the reasonable expectations of their employees, especially to the extent that such policies are clearly communicated.

Even if Quon had a reasonable expectation of privacy in his text messages, petitioners did not necessarily violate the Fourth Amendment by obtaining and reviewing the transcripts. Although as a general matter, warrantless searches 'are per se unreasonable under the Fourth Amendment,' there are 'a few specifically established and well-delineated exceptions' to that general rule (quoting Katz). The Court has held that the 'special needs' of the workplace justify one such exception…

The search was justified at its inception because there were 'reasonable grounds for suspecting that the search [was] necessary for a noninvestigatory work-related purpose.' As a jury found, Chief Scharf ordered the search in order to determine whether the character limit on the City's contract with Arch Wireless was sufficient to meet the City's needs. This was, as the Ninth Circuit noted, a 'legitimate work-related rationale.' The City and OPD had a legitimate interest in ensuring that employees were not being forced to pay out of their own pockets for work-related expenses, or on the other hand that the City was not paying for extensive personal communications. As for the scope of the search, reviewing the transcripts was reasonable because it was an efficient and expedient way to determine whether Quon's overages were the result of work-related messaging or personal use. The review was also not 'excessively intrusive.'…. Although Quon had gone over his monthly allotment a number of times, OPD requested transcripts for only the months of August and September 2002. While it may have been reasonable as well for OPD to review transcripts of all the months in which Quon exceeded his allowance, it was certainly reasonable for OPD to review messages for just two months in order to obtain a large enough sample to decide whether the character limits were efficacious. And it is worth noting that during his internal affairs investigation, McMahon redacted all messages Quon sent while off duty, a measure which reduced the intrusiveness of any further review of the transcripts. Furthermore, and again on the assumption that Quon had a reasonable expectation of privacy in the contents of his messages, the extent of an expectation is relevant to assessing whether the search was too intrusive….Even if he could assume some level of privacy would inhere in his messages, it would not have been reasonable for Quon to conclude that his messages were in all circumstances immune from scrutiny. Quon was told that his messages were subject to auditing. As a law enforcement officer, he would or should have known that his actions were likely to come under legal scrutiny, and that this might entail an analysis of his on-the-job communications. Under the circumstances, a reasonable employee would be aware that sound management principles might require the audit of messages to determine whether the pager was being appropriately used. Given that the City issued the pagers to Quon and other SWAT Team members in order to help them more quickly respond to crises — and given that

> Quon had received no assurances of privacy — Quon could have anticipated that it might be necessary for the City to audit pager messages to assess the SWAT Team's performance in particular emergency situations.
>
> Because the search was motivated by a legitimate work-related purpose, and because it was not excessive in scope, the search was reasonable … For these same reasons — that the employer had a legitimate reason for the search, and that the search was not excessively intrusive in light of that justification — the Court also concludes that the search would be 'regarded as reasonable and normal in the private-employer context' … The search was reasonable, and the Court of Appeals erred by holding to the contrary. Petitioners did not violate Quon's Fourth Amendment rights.
>
> Finally, the Court must consider whether the search violated the Fourth Amendment rights of Jerilyn Quon, Florio, and Trujillo, the respondents who sent text messages to Jeff Quon….In light of this litigating position and the Court's conclusion that the search was reasonable as to Jeff Quon, it necessarily follows that these other respondents cannot prevail. Because the search was reasonable, petitioners did not violate respondents' Fourth Amendment rights, and the court below erred by concluding otherwise. The judgment of the Court of Appeals for the Ninth Circuit is reversed, and the case is remanded for further proceedings consistent with this opinion.

However, a reasonable expectation of privacy is not limited to intrusion by the government, even when the government is the employer, as in Quon. The courts are also called upon to decide what constitutes an employee's reasonable expectation of privacy in the work environment *vis-a-vis* his private employer.

Smyth v. the Pillsbury Company, 914 F.Supp. 97 (1996)

> Defendant maintained an electronic mail communication system (e-mail) in order to promote internal corporate communications between its employees. Defendant repeatedly assured its employees, including plaintiff, that all e-mail communications would remain confidential and privileged. Defendant further assured its employees, including plaintiff, that e-mail communications could not be intercepted and used by defendant against its employees as grounds for termination or reprimand … plaintiff received certain e-mail communications from his supervisor

over defendant's e-mail system on his computer at home. In reliance on defendant's assurances regarding defendant's e-mail system, plaintiff responded and exchanged e-mails with his supervisor. At some later date, contrary to the assurances of confidentiality made by defendant, defendant, acting through its agents, servants and employees, intercepted plaintiff's private e-mail messages....Several months later, defendant notified plaintiff that it was terminating his employment effective the following month, for transmitting what it deemed to be inappropriate and unprofessional comments over defendant's e-mail system.... plaintiff, an at-will employee, claims he was wrongfully discharged from his position as a regional operations manager by the defendant. Presently before the court is the motion of the defendant to dismiss.... 'For the reasons which follow, the motion is granted.'

A claim may be dismissed....only if the plaintiff can prove no set of facts in support of the claim that would entitle him to relief. The reviewing court must consider only those facts alleged in the Complaint and accept all of the allegations as true. Applying this standard, we find that plaintiff has failed to state a claim upon which relief can be granted.

The plaintiff sued his former employer, claiming that his termination was in violation of 'public policy which precludes an employer from terminating an employee in violation of the employee's right to privacy as embodied in Pennsylvania common law.'

As a general rule, Pennsylvania law does not provide a common law cause of action for the wrongful discharge of an at-will employee such as plaintiff. Pennsylvania is an employment at-will jurisdiction and an employer 'may discharge an employee with or without cause, at pleasure, unless restrained by some contract.' However, in the most limited of circumstances, exceptions have been recognized where discharge of an at-will employee threatens or violates a clear mandate of public policy.

The court concluded, noting that,

... we find that plaintiff has failed to state a claim upon which relief can be granted. In the first instance, unlike urinalysis and personal property searches, we do not find a reasonable expectation of privacy in e-mail communications voluntarily made by an employee to his supervisor over the company e-mail system notwithstanding any assurances that such communications would not be intercepted by management. Once plaintiff communicated the alleged unprofessional comments to a second person (his supervisor) over an e-mail system which was apparently utilized by the entire company, any reasonable expectation of privacy was lost. Significantly, the defendant did not require plaintiff, as in the case of an urinalysis or personal property search to disclose any personal information about himself. Rather, plaintiff voluntarily communicated the alleged unprofessional comments over the company e-mail system. We find no privacy interests in such communications.

In the second instance, even if we found that an employee had a reasonable expectation of privacy in the contents of his e-mail communications over the company e-mail system, we do not find that a reasonable person would consider the defendant's interception of these communications to be a substantial and highly offensive invasion of his privacy. Again, we note that by intercepting such communications, the company is not, as in the case of urinalysis or personal property searches, requiring the employee to disclose any personal information about himself or invading the employee's person or personal effects. Moreover, the company's interest in preventing inappropriate and unprofessional comments or even illegal activity over its e-mail system outweighs any privacy interest the employee may have in those comments. In sum, we find that the defendant's actions did not tortiously invade the plaintiff's privacy and, therefore, did not violate public policy. As a result, the motion to dismiss is granted. In a footnote, the court went on to note, 'Defendant alleges in its motion to dismiss that the e-mails concerned sales management and contained threats to "kill the backstabbing bastards" and referred to the planned holiday party as the "Jim Jones Koolaid affair."'

State Constitutions

A number of state constitutions expressly state a right to privacy. California's right of privacy is not limited to protection from the government. In 1972, by way of initiative, voters in California added "privacy" to the "inalienable rights" that are guaranteed by Article 1, Section 1 of the California Constitution.

Article 1, Section 1:

> All people are by nature free and independent and have inalienable rights. Among these are enjoying and defending life and liberty, acquiring, possessing, and protecting property, and pursuing and obtaining safety, happiness, and privacy.

The protection provided by California's constitution may sometimes be broader than that provided by the federal Constitution.[10]

Statutory Protection of Privacy

Numerous federal and state laws specifically address the subject of privacy. Among the federal laws on the subject is the Federal Trade Commission (FTC) Act[11] that, arguably, may be the most significant. The FTC Act covers a variety of subjects including consumer protection. In general, the FTC Act gives the Federal Trade Commission the authority to, among other things:

a. Prevent unfair methods of competition and unfair or deceptive acts or practices in or affecting commerce;
b. Seek monetary redress and other relief for conduct injurious to consumers;
c. Prescribe rules defining with specificity acts or practices that are unfair or deceptive, and establishing requirements designed to prevent such acts or practices;
d. Gather and compile information and conduct investigations relating to the organization, business, practices, and management of entities engaged in commerce; and
e. Make reports and legislative recommendations to Congress and the public.

Section 5(a) of the FTC Act provides that "unfair or deceptive acts or practices in or affecting commerce … are … declared unlawful." The U.S. Safe Web Act, which amended the FTC Act, clarified that unfair or deceptive acts or practices in Section 5(a) include such acts or practices involving foreign commerce that cause or are likely to cause reasonably foreseeable injury within the United States or involve material conduct occurring within the United States.

In the event of a violation, fines may be substantial. While "unfair or deceptive acts or practices" may appear to be unrelated to the issue of privacy, that is hardly the case. Twitter agreed with the federal Department

---

[10] See J. Clark Kelso, *California's Constitutional Right to Privacy*, 19 Pepp. L. Rev. 2 (1992).

[11] 15 U.S.C. Sections 41–58, as amended.

of Justice and the Federal Trade Commission to pay a $150 million civil penalty and to implement a comprehensive compliance program to resolve privacy violations. From May 2013 to September 2019, Twitter represented to its users that it was collecting their telephone numbers and e-mail addresses for account-security purposes. Twitter failed to disclose that it also would use that information to allow companies, their advertisers, the primary source of Twitter's revenue, to send targeted advertisements to consumers.

The government's lawsuit also stated that Twitter knowingly violated the terms of the European Union-U.S. and Swiss-U.S. Privacy Shield Frameworks, an agreement that prohibits companies from processing user information in ways that are not compatible with the purposes that were authorized by the users. That was not Twitter's first run-in with the FTC. More than a decade ago, Twitter told its users that users could control who had access to their tweets and that their private messages could be viewed only by recipients. However, Twitter did not have reasonable safeguards to ensure users' choices were honored resulting in multiple instances where Twitter's actions – and inactions – led to unauthorized access of users' personal information. To settle that case, the company agreed to an order in 2011 that would impose substantial financial penalties if it further misrepresented "the extent to which [Twitter] maintains and protects the security, privacy, confidentiality, or integrity of any nonpublic consumer information."

"Deceptive" practices are defined in the Commission's Policy Statement on Deception and include a material misrepresentation, omission or practice that is likely to mislead a consumer acting reasonably in the circumstances.

In addition, the FTC Act goes on to note that an act or practice is "unfair" if it causes or is likely to cause substantial injury to consumers that is not reasonably avoidable by consumers themselves, and not outweighed by countervailing benefits to consumers or to competition.[12]

Additional sections of the FTC address other issues. Section 5 of the FTC Act declares unfair or deceptive acts or practices unlawful. Section 12 specifically prohibits false ads likely to induce the purchase of food, drugs, devices, or cosmetics. Section 15 defines a false ad for purposes of

---

[12] 15 U.S.C. Section 45(n).

Section 12 as one that is misleading in a material respect. Although courts and the Federal Trade Commission itself provide guidance there is no one definitive statement that explains the phrase "deceptive acts or practices" under both Sections 5 and 12.

Nonetheless, the FTC notes that certain elements are common in cases that involve deception:

1. There must be a representation, omission, or practice that is likely to mislead the consumer.
   a. Practices that have been found misleading or deceptive in specific cases include:
      i. false oral or written representations,
      ii. misleading price claims,
      iii. sales of hazardous or systematically defective products or services without adequate disclosures,
      iv. failure to disclose information regarding pyramid sales,
      v. use of bait and switch techniques,
      vi. failure to perform promised services, and
      vii. failure to meet warranty obligations.

In these aforementioned situations, the FTC will examine the practice from the perspective of a consumer acting reasonably in the circumstances. If the representation or practice affects or is directed primarily to a particular group, the Commission examines reasonableness from the perspective of that group.

In order to rise to the level of actionable, the FTC also requires that the representation, omission, or practice must be a "material" one. This inquiry determines whether the act or practice is likely to affect the consumer's conduct or decision with regard to a product or service. If so, the practice is material, and consumer injury is likely, because consumers are likely to have chosen differently but for the deception. In many instances, materiality, and hence injury, can be presumed from the nature of the practice. In other situations, evidence of materiality may be necessary.

The FTC is likely to find deception if there is a representation, omission or practice, that is likely to mislead the consumer acting reasonably in the circumstances, to the consumer's detriment.

Almost needless to say, the FTC has determined that most deception involves:

1. written or oral misrepresentations, or
2. omissions of material information.

However, deception may also occur in other forms of conduct associated with a sales transaction. As part of that the entire advertisement, transaction or course of dealing will be considered. It is not necessary that the advertisement cause actual deception, although that may also warrant an investigation. Instead, the issue is whether the act or practice is likely to mislead. The topic is discussed in additional detail in Chapter 7.

Health Privacy

Health Insurance Portability and Accountability Act (HIPAA)

HIPAA attempted to protect the confidentiality of health information as it is transmitted through and collected by electronic portals.

Electronic Health Records (EHR)

The law established standards for privacy and security of "personal health information" and addressed conflicting state privacy laws relating to health information and regulated protected health information (PHI) held by covered entities defined as:

1. Health plans;
2. Healthcare clearinghouses;
3. Health care providers who transmit health information electronically in certain information transactions.

HIPAA originally excluded significant entities involved in electronic health information exchanges. HIPAA was then amended by the Health Information Technology for Economic and Clinical Health Act (HITECH) to extend HIPAA to outside vendors who also have access to personal health information and extended the regulations to additional "business associates."

A "business associate" is defined as a person or entity who performs certain functions or activities that involve the use or disclosure of PHI, including claims processing, data analysis, among others. In order to disclose PHI to business associates, a covered entity must assure that the associate has adequate security as required by the law.

As the Centers for Disease Control and Protection note, the Health Insurance Portability and Accountability Act of 1996 (HIPAA) required the creation of national standards to protect sensitive patient health information from being disclosed without the patient's consent or knowledge. A significant part of HIPAA is the HIPAA Privacy Rule, as well as the HIPAA Security Rule that is intended to protect a subset of information covered by the Privacy Rule.

The HIPAA Privacy Rule

The Privacy Rule standards address the use and disclosure of individuals' health information (known as "protected health information") by entities subject to the Privacy Rule known as "covered entities." "The Privacy Rule also contains standards for individuals' rights to understand and control how their health information is used. A major goal of the Privacy Rule is to ensure that individuals' health information is properly protected while allowing the flow of health information needed to provide and promote high quality health care and to protect the public's health and well-being. The Privacy Rule strikes a balance that permits important uses of information while protecting the privacy of people who seek care and healing."

The HIPAA Security Rule

The HIPAA Privacy Rule safeguards PHI. The Security Rule protects "...all individually identifiable health information a covered entity creates, receives, maintains, or transmits in electronic form" also known as "electronic protected health information" (e-PHI), although it does not apply to PHI transmitted orally or in writing.

Credit Reporting

The Fair Credit Reporting Act (FCRA)

The Federal Trade Commission notes that the FCRA protects information collected by a variety of consumer reporting agencies. The Act contains a variety of restrictions, such as restricting the information that is available in a consumer report to only those who have a purpose that is specified in the Act. To address issues involving disputes about the accuracy of information, those companies that are affected by the law are required to conduct an investigation. And recipients of the information for specified purposes must notify consumers when there is an adverse action on the basis of such reports. The FCRA has been supplemented by, for instance, The Fair and Accurate Credit Transactions Act that addressed, among other issues, identity theft.

Data security

FTC rules require many companies that keep sensitive personal information about customers or employees in their files or on their network to have a security plan to collect only what is needed, keep it safe, and dispose of it securely. Among the agency requirements governing data security are the FTC Act and the Fair Credit Reporting Act discussed above, and the Gramm–Leach–Bliley Act.

Gramm–Leach–Bliley Act[13]

This Act requires financial institutions, any company that offers consumers financial products or services such as loans, financial or investment advice, or insurance, to explain their information-sharing practices to their customers and to safeguard sensitive data.

Red flags rule[14]

Sometimes referred to as the Fair Credit Reporting Act's Identity Theft Rules, this rule requires many businesses and organizations to implement a written identity theft prevention program that detects the warning signs — red flags — of identity theft, in their day-to-day operations.

[13]Public Law 106–102—12 November 1999.

[14]FTC.Gov/business-guideance/privacy-security/red-flags-rule

Privacy Shield (Also Addressed in the Section on Privacy in the European Union)

The EU-U.S.[15] and Swiss-U.S. Privacy Shield[16] Frameworks were intended by the U.S. Department of Commerce, and the European Commission (EC) and Swiss Administration, respectively, to provide companies on both sides of the Atlantic with guidance on compliance with data protection requirements governing the transfer of personal data from the European Union and Switzerland to the United States. Both Frameworks were deemed adequate by the EC and the Swiss Government. However, the European Court of Justice declared the EC's Decision approving the EU-U.S. Privacy Shield Framework to be invalid in 2020. Regardless, the FTC urges companies to continue to:

1. Comply with their ongoing obligations with respect to transfers that are made pursuant to the Privacy Shield Framework;
2. Continue to follow robust privacy principles, such as those underlying the Privacy Shield Framework; and
3. Review their privacy policies to ensure that they accurately describe their privacy practices accurately, including those related to international data transfers.

The U.S.-EU Safe Harbor Framework[17]

In 2015, the European Court of Justice declared invalid the EC's 25 July 2000, decision on the legal adequacy of the U.S.-EU Safe Harbor Framework. The Framework replaced the Safe Harbor program and specified the mechanism by which companies may transfer personal data from the EU to the United States. Nonetheless, the FTC continues to enforce the Privacy Shield Framework and companies should continue to comply with requirements for data transfers under the Safe Harbor Framework.

---

[15] https://www.privacyshield.gov/ps/eu-us-framework.

[16] *Ibid.*

[17] https://www.ftc.gov/business-guidance/privacy-security/us-eu-safe-harbor-framework.

The Privacy Act of 1974 as Amended, 5 U.S.C. Section 552a (2018)

Overview

In significant part, the development of the Privacy Act was a recognition that society was seeing a fundamental shift from paper to computers, electronic storage and the information that was contained in electronic storage. The Privacy Act protects certain federal government records pertaining to individuals. In particular, the Act covers systems of records that an agency maintains and retrieves by an individual's name or other personal identifier, such as a social security number. In general, the Privacy Act prohibits the unauthorized disclosure of the records it protects. It also gives individuals the right to

a. review records about themselves,
b. find out if these records have been disclosed, and
c. request corrections or amendments of these records unless the records are legally exempt.

Federal agencies have 10 days to either make the correction or to notify the requestor that the correction will not be made. The Privacy Act went into effect in 1975 and became the principal law that governed the handling of personal information by the federal government.

The Privacy Act seeks to balance the government's need to maintain information about individuals with the right of individuals to be protected against unwarranted invasions of their privacy stemming from federal agencies' collection, maintenance, use, and disclosure of personal information about them.

The Act has four basic objectives:

1. To restrict disclosure of personally identifiable records maintained by agencies.
2. To grant individuals increased rights of access to agency records maintained on them.
3. To grant individuals the right to seek amendment of agency records maintained on themselves upon a showing that the records are not accurate, relevant, timely, or complete.

4. To establish a code of fair information practices that requires agencies to comply with statutory norms for collection, maintenance, and dissemination of records.

The Act requires agencies to keep an accurate accounting of information disclosures, except when the disclosure is made within the agency for routine administrative use or made under the Freedom of Information Act. The Act also requires each agency that maintains a system of records to restrict the collection of information to only the information relevant to the purpose, to ensure the information remains accurate, to collect information directly from the subject whenever possible, and to tell the subject the purpose for which the information is being collected and the authority under which it is being collected.[18]

To address these concerns the government developed "Fair Information Practice Principles" or FIPPs. FIPPs allow individuals to determine what records pertaining to them:

> are collected, maintained, used, or disseminated by an agency;
>
> require agencies to obtain consent before records pertaining to an individual collected for one purpose could be used for other incompatible purposes;
>
> afford individuals a right of access to records pertaining to them and to have them corrected if inaccurate; and
>
> require agencies to collect such records only for lawful and authorized purposes and safeguard them appropriately.

FIPPs are central to the Privacy Act and have been the basis for almost every other privacy law and treaty. There are some limited exceptions to these principles.

The Privacy Act was amended by the Computer Matching and Privacy Act of 1988 followed by the Computer Matching and Privacy Protection Amendments of 1990.

---

[18] 5 U.S.C. Section 552a(e).

The Freedom of Information Act as Amended[19]

Even before the Privacy Act of 1974, there was concern about information on private citizens that was collected by the government. To address that concern, since 1967, the Freedom of Information Act has provided citizens the right to request access to records that are maintained by any federal agency. The FOIA does not apply to records held by Congress, the courts, or by state or local government agencies. Each state has its own public access laws for access to state and local records.

Federal agencies are required to disclose any information that is requested pursuant to the FOIA unless it falls under one of nine exemptions that protect interests such as personal privacy, national security, and law enforcement. The FOIA also requires agencies to proactively post online certain categories of information, including frequently requested records.

The Presumption of Openness

When processing a request, agencies should withhold information only if they reasonably foresee that disclosure would:

1. harm an interest protected by an exemption, or
2. if disclosure is prohibited by law.

There are a variety of exemptions that exist, for example, in the case of national security, among others.

The Electronic Freedom of Information Act (E-FOIA)[20]

The Freedom of Information Act was amended by the Electronic Freedom of Information Act Amendments of 1996 to expand the scope of the FOIA to encompass electronic records and require the creation of electronic reading rooms to make records readily available to the public.

---

[19]The Freedom of Information Act, 5 U.S.C. Section 552 as Amended by Public Law No. 110-175, 121 Stat. 2524.

[20]Public Law 104-231 — Oct. 2, 1996.

The Electronic Communications Privacy Act[21] (ECPA) and the Stored Wire Electronic Communications Act

Overview

These two laws are generally referred to as the Electronic Communications Privacy Act (ECPA) of 1986. The ECPA updated the Federal Wiretap Act of 1968, that addressed interception of conversations using hard (or land-line) telephone lines, but did not apply to the interception of computer and other digital and electronic communications.

Subsequent legislation, including the USA Patriot Act clarified and updated the ECPA to keep pace with the evolution of new communications technologies and methods, including easing restrictions on law enforcement access to stored communications in some cases. The ECPA, as amended, protects wire, oral, and electronic communications while those communications are being made, are in transit, and when they are stored on computers. The Act applies to email, telephone conversations, and data stored electronically. The structure of the SCA reflects a series of classifications about what kinds of information implicate greater or lesser privacy interests. For instance, the law gives greater privacy interests in the content of stored emails than in subscriber account information. In addition, the law notes that computing services available to the public required stricter regulation than services that are not available to the public. In addition, the Act offers different degrees of legal protection depending on the perceived importance of the privacy interest involved. Some information may be obtained from providers by way of:

A subpoena;

A special court order; and

A search warrant.

Some forms of legal process require notice to the subscriber, while others do not.

The ECPA prohibits unauthorized access to computers such as through false pretenses or hacking, as well as providing privacy protection for mobile communications such as the contents of text messages,

[21] 18 U.S.C. Sections 2510–2523.

voice-mail messages, and live mobile phone conversations. The ECPA was significantly amended by the Communications Assistance to Law Enforcement Act (CALEA) in 1994, the USA PATRIOT Act[22] in 2001, the USA PATRIOT Improvement and Reauthorization Act in 2005,[23] as well as the Foreign Intelligence Surveillance Act Amendments Act of 2008.[24] Other acts have made specific amendments of lesser significance.

These laws protect the privacy of wire, oral, and electronic communications from unlawful wiretapping, eavesdropping, and other forms of unauthorized access and disclosure by private business, law enforcement, and the government. A violation is subject to both civil and criminal liability. The laws prohibit both the:

1. intentional "interception" of electronic communications, as well as
2. accessing electronically stored communications.

Family Educational Rights and Privacy Act

The Family Educational Rights and Privacy Act (FERPA) protects the privacy of student education records. The law applies to all schools that receive funds under an applicable program of the U.S. Department of Education. FERPA gives parents certain rights with respect to their children's education records. These rights transfer to the student when he or she reaches the age of 18 or attends a school beyond the high school level.

The law gives parents or eligible students the right to inspect and review the student's education records maintained by the school as well as to request that a school correct records which they believe to be inaccurate or misleading. If the school decides not to amend the record, the parent or eligible student then has the right to a formal hearing. After the hearing, if the school still decides not to amend the record, the parent or eligible student has the right to place a statement with the record setting forth his or her view about the contested information.

---

[22] Public Law 107–156.

[23] Public Law 109–177.

[24] https://www.govinfo.gov/content/pkg/BILLS-110hr6304pcs/pdf/BILLS-110hr6304pcs.pdf.

Generally, schools must have written permission from the parent or eligible student in order to release any information from a student's education record.

Exceptions

FERPA allows schools to disclose those records, without consent, to the following parties or under the following conditions:

1. School officials with legitimate educational interest;
2. Other schools to which a student is transferring;
3. Specified officials for audit or evaluation purposes;
4. Appropriate parties in connection with financial aid to a student;
5. Organizations conducting certain studies for or on behalf of the school;
6. Accrediting organizations;
7. To comply with a judicial order or lawfully issued subpoena;
8. Appropriate officials in cases of health and safety emergencies; and

State and local authorities, within a juvenile justice system, pursuant to specific State law.

In addition, schools may disclose, without consent, "directory" information such as a Student's name, address, telephone number, date and place of birth, honors and awards, and dates of attendance. However, schools must tell parents and eligible students about directory information and allow parents and eligible students a reasonable amount of time to request that the school not disclose directory information about them.

Schools must notify parents and eligible students annually of their rights under FERPA although the method of notification, such as a letter, inclusion in a PTA bulletin, student handbook, or newspaper article is left to the discretion of each school.

Children's Online Privacy Protection Act of 1998 (COPPA)[25]

As the Federal Trade Commission notes, the Children's Online Privacy Protection Act, "… imposes certain requirements on operators of

[25] 15 U.S.C. Sections 6501–6505.

websites or online services directed to children under 13 years of age, and on operators of other websites or online services that have actual knowledge that they are collecting personal information online from a child under 13 years of age.

The Primary Goal of COPPA is to put parents in control over what information is collected from their young children online. The Rule was designed to protect children under age 13 and applies to operators of commercial websites and online services, including mobile apps and the Internet of Things (IoT) devices, such as smart toys directed to children under the age of 13 that collect, use, or disclose personal information from children, or on whose behalf such information is collected or maintained, such as when personal information is collected by an ad network to serve targeted advertising.

The IoT includes a wide variety of companies that design, manufacture, market, or support Internet-connected devices — everything from light bulbs to smart TVs to wearable fitness trackers. If a connected device is unsecured it may give malicious actors access not just to the confidential information transmitted by the device, but to everything else to which the device is connected.

The Rule also applies to operators of general audience websites or online services with actual knowledge that they are collecting, using, or disclosing personal information from children under 13, and to websites or online services that have actual knowledge that they are collecting personal information directly from users of another website or online service directed to children.

Operators covered by the Rule must:

1. Post a clear and comprehensive online privacy policy describing their information practices for personal information collected online from children;
2. Provide direct notice to parents and obtain verifiable parental consent, with limited exceptions, before collecting personal information online from children;
3. Give parents the choice of consenting to the operator's collection and internal use of a child's information, but prohibiting the operator from disclosing that information to third parties (unless disclosure is integral to the site or service, in which case, this must be made clear to parents);
4. Provide parents access to their child's personal information to review and/or have the information deleted;

5. Give parents the opportunity to prevent further use or online collection of a child's personal information;
6. Maintain the confidentiality, security, and integrity of information they collect from children, including by taking reasonable steps to release such information only to parties capable of maintaining its confidentiality and security;
7. Retain personal information collected online from a child for only as long as is necessary to fulfill the purpose for which it was collected and delete the information using reasonable measures to protect against its unauthorized access or use; and
8. Not condition a child's participation in an online activity on the child providing more information than is reasonably necessary to participate in that activity.

The COPPA Rule Summarized

Websites and online services covered by COPPA must post privacy policies, provide parents with direct notice of their information practices, and get verifiable consent from a parent or guardian before collecting personal information from children. A violation of the Rule may be expensive. Google LLC and its subsidiary YouTube, LLC paid $170 million to settle allegations by the FTC and the New York Attorney General that YouTube illegally collected personal information from children without parental consent. By using the identifiers, known as "cookies," YouTube earned millions of dollars in advertising fees.

The FTC and New York Attorney General sued, alleging that YouTube violated the COPPA Rule by collecting personal information from viewers of "child-directed" channels. The complaint noted that while YouTube claimed to be a general-audience site, some of YouTube's individual channels, including those operated by toy manufacturers, are child-directed and therefore subject to the COPPA Rule.

The lawsuit alleged that the defendants knew that YouTube had numerous child-directed channels, along with general-audience sites, and marketed itself as a significant destination for kids in presentations to Mattel, among other, noting that "YouTube is today's leader in reaching children age 6–11 against top TV channels." YouTube told Hasbro that YouTube is the "#1 website regularly visited by kids."

As part of its approach YouTube allowed Google account holders, including commercial entities, to create "channels" to display content.

The complaint alleged that eligible channel owners could monetize their channel by allowing YouTube to direct targeted advertisements, generating revenue for both the commercial entity as well as YouTube.

Personal Liability

Violations of federal laws on privacy may even involve civil liability for individuals at a company. Washington, D.C.'s attorney general sued Facebook CEO Mark Zuckerberg over the company's allegedly misleading privacy policies and failure to protect user data. The Washington Examiner noted:

> This lawsuit is not only warranted, but necessary, D.C.'s attorney general Racine noted, 'Misleading consumers, exposing their data, and violating the law comes with consequences, not only for companies that breach that trust, but also corporate executives.' The lawsuit stems from an investigation that occurred when whistleblower Christopher Wylie reveal that Cambridge Analytica, an electioneering firm that is based in London, gained the personal data of more than seventy million Facebook users in an alleged effort to influence the 2016 presidential election. Racine sued Cambridge Analytica because of the incident several years ago, but is not seeking to hold CEO Mark Zuckerberg personally liable. Documents that were allegedly obtained as a result of the prior lawsuit reportedly provide '...extensive evidence that Zuckerberg was personally involved in the failures that led to the Cambridge Analytica incident,' according to Racine. As part of that Racine noted Zuckerberg's 'unparalleled level of control over the operations of Facebook,' stating he 'is personally involved in nearly every major decision the company makes' according to the complaint.

Privacy in the European Union (EU)

The EU has a variety of laws and regulations on the subject of privacy. In addition to the European laws noted in the prior chapter, the 1950 European Convention on Human Rights notes a stated goal to "… protect, on an international level, human rights from violations by a state and to provide collective international enforcement of these rights."

The Convention went on to note that, "Everyone has the right to respect for his private and family life, his home and his correspondence." The Council of Europe enforced the Convention.

Directive 95/46/EC (1995)

This directive was intended to require "... member states to protect the fundamental rights and freedoms of natural persons and in particular their right to privacy with respect to the processing of personal data" and also required that the data be "... adequate, relevant, and not excessive in relation to the purposes for which they are collected" as well as "up to date." The directive is repealed with effect from May 25, 2018.

The EU General Data Protection Regulation (GDPR) (2018)

The GDPR governs how personal data of individuals in the EU may be processed and transferred. Personal data is broadly defined as anything that relates to an identified or identifiable living individual, including name, e-mail address, tax identification number, online identifier, etc. "Processing" data is also broadly defined to include collecting, recording, storing, and transferring data.

The Right-To-Be Forgotten (RTBF)

Recitals 65 and 66 and Article 17 of the GDPR note that:

1. The data subject shall have the right to obtain from the controller the erasure of personal data concerning him or her without undue delay and the controller shall have the obligation to erase personal data without undue delay where one of the following grounds applies:
   a. The personal data are no longer necessary in relation to the purposes for which they were collected or otherwise processed;
   b. The data subject withdraws consent on which the processing is based according to point (a) of Article 6(1), or point (a) of Article 9(2), and where there is no other legal ground for the processing;
   c. The data subject objects to the processing pursuant to Article 21(1) and there are no overriding legitimate grounds for the

processing, or the data subject objects to the processing pursuant to Article 21(2);

d. The personal data have been unlawfully processed;

e. The personal data have to be erased for compliance with a legal obligation in Union or Member State law to which the controller is subject;

f. The personal data have been collected in relation to the offer of information society services referred to in Article 8(1).

2. Where the controller has made the personal data public and is obliged pursuant to paragraph 1 to erase the personal data, the controller, taking account of available technology and the cost of implementation, shall take reasonable steps, including technical measures, to inform controllers which are processing the personal data that the data subject has requested the erasure by such controllers of any links to, or copy or replication of, those personal data.

3. Paragraphs 1 and 2 shall not apply to the extent that processing is necessary:

   a. for exercising the right of freedom of expression and information;
   b. for compliance with a legal obligation which requires processing by Union or Member State law to which the controller is subject or for the performance of a task carried out in the public interest or in the exercise of official authority vested in the controller;
   c. for reasons of public interest in the area of public health in accordance with points (h) and (i) of Article 9(2) as well as Article (3);
   d. for archiving purposes in the public interest, scientific or historical research purposes or statistical purposes in accordance with Article 89(1) in so far as the right referred to in paragraph 1 is likely to render impossible or seriously impair the achievement of the objectives of that processing; or
   e. for the establishment, exercise, or defense of legal claims.

The right to be forgotten dovetails with people's right to access their personal information in Article 15. The right to control one's data is meaningless if people cannot take action when they no longer consent to processing, when there are significant errors within the data, or if they believe information is being stored unnecessarily. In these cases, an individual can request that the data be erased. But this is not an absolute right. If it were, the critics who argue that the right to be forgotten amounts to nothing more than a rewriting of history would be correct. Thus, the GDPR walks a fine line on data erasure.

Coverage

Even a company that is not located in the EU may be obligated to comply with the regulation when processing personal data of EU and the European Economic Area (EEA) residents (EEA countries are Norway, Lichtenstein, and Switzerland).[26] Accessibility of a company's website to residents of the EU is not sufficient to require compliance, but simply tracking and analyzing EU visitors to a website is likely sufficient to require compliance.[27] The EC assesses whether a country outside the EU has sufficient legal protection for the EC to issue an "adequacy finding" to that country. The U.S. has not sought such a finding and the U.S. companies may only receive personal data from the EU if they:

1. Join the EU-U.S. Privacy Shield program; or
2. Provide appropriate safeguards such as contractual requirements and binding business rules; or
3. Refer to one of the GDPR's derogations.

The EU-U.S. and Swiss-U.S. Privacy Shield (www.privacyshield.gov)

As noted previously, the EU-U.S. and Swiss-U.S. Privacy Shield Frameworks were formulated by the U.S. Department of Commerce, and the EC and Swiss Administration, respectively, to provide companies on both sides of the Atlantic with a mechanism to comply with data protection requirements when transferring personal data from the European Union and Switzerland to the United States in support of transatlantic commerce. On July 12, 2016, the EC deemed the EU-U.S. Privacy Shield Framework adequate to enable data transfers under EU law. Subsequently, the Swiss Government announced the approval of the Swiss-U.S. Privacy Shield Framework as a valid legal mechanism to comply with Swiss

---

[26] https://gdpr.eu/companies-outside-of-europe/.

[27] *Ibid.*

requirements when transferring personal data from Switzerland to the United States.

On July 16, 2020, the Court of Justice of the European Union issued a judgment declaring as "invalid" the EC's Decision (EU) 2016/1250 of 12 July 2016 on the adequacy of the protection provided by the EU-U.S. Privacy Shield. As a result of that decision, the EU-U.S. Privacy Shield Framework is no longer a valid mechanism to comply with EU data protection requirements when transferring personal data from the European Union to the United States. Unfortunately, that decision does not relieve participants in the EU-U.S. Privacy Shield of their obligations under the EU-U.S. Privacy Shield Framework. On September 8, 2020, the Federal Data Protection and Information Commissioner (FDPIC) of Switzerland issued an opinion concluding that the Swiss-U.S. Privacy Shield Framework does not provide an adequate level of protection for data transfers from Switzerland to the United States pursuant to Switzerland's Federal Act on Data Protection (FADP). As a result of that opinion, organizations wishing to rely on the Swiss-U.S. Privacy Shield to transfer personal data from Switzerland to the United States should seek guidance from the FDPIC or legal counsel. That opinion does not relieve participants in the Swiss-U.S. Privacy Shield of their obligations under the Swiss-U.S. Privacy Shield Framework.

The U.S. Department of Commerce continues to administer the Privacy Shield program, including processing submissions for self-certification and re-certification to the Privacy Shield Frameworks and maintaining the Privacy Shield List.

Although much has been stated about the differences between civil law and common law, the differences may not always be significant. The Court of Justice of the European Union had occasion to address a lawsuit regarding an individual's right to privacy in Spain. In doing so, the court utilized a balancing test that is reminiscent of the approach used by the United States Supreme Court in *Katz*, *supra*.

Google Inc. v Agencia Española de Protección de Datos (AEPD), Mario Costeja González, May 13, 2014 C-131/12

On March 5, 2010, Mr Costeja González, a Spanish national resident in Spain, lodged with the AEPD a complaint against La Vanguardia Ediciones SL, which publishes a daily newspaper with a large circulation, in particular in Catalonia (Spain) ('La Vanguardia'), and against Google Spain and Google Inc. The complaint was based on the fact that, when an internet user entered Mr Costeja González's name in the search engine of the Google group ('Google Search'), he would obtain links to two pages of La Vanguardia's newspaper, of January 19 and March 9, 1998 respectively, on which an announcement mentioning Mr Costeja González's name appeared for a real-estate auction connected with attachment proceedings for the recovery of social security debts. By that complaint, Mr Costeja González requested, first, that La Vanguardia be required either to remove or alter those pages so that the personal data relating to him no longer appeared or to use certain tools made available by search engines in order to protect the data. Second, he requested that Google Spain or Google Inc. be required to remove or conceal the personal data relating to him so that they ceased to be included in the search results and no longer appeared in the links to La Vanguardia. Mr Costeja González stated in this context that the attachment proceedings concerning him had been fully resolved for a number of years and that reference to them was now entirely irrelevant.

By decision of 30 July 2010, the AEPD rejected the complaint in so far as it related to La Vanguardia, taking the view that the publication by it of the information in question was legally justified as it took place upon order of the Ministry of Labour and Social Affairs and was intended to give maximum publicity to the auction in order to secure as many bidders as possible. On the other hand, the complaint was upheld in so far as it was directed against Google Spain and Google Inc. The AEPD considered in this regard that operators of search engines are subject to data protection legislation given that they carry out data processing for which they are responsible and act as intermediaries in the information society. The AEPD took the view that it has the power to require the withdrawal of data and the prohibition of access to certain data by the operators of search engines when it considers that the locating and dissemination of the data are liable to compromise the fundamental right to data protection and the dignity of persons in the broad sense, and this would also encompass the mere wish of the person concerned that such data not be known to third parties. The AEPD considered that that obligation may be owed directly by operators of search engines, without it being necessary to erase the data or information from the website where they appear, including when retention of the information on that site is justified by a statutory provision.

Google Spain and Google Inc. brought separate actions against that decision before the Audiencia Nacional (National High Court). The Audiencia Nacional joined the actions.

That court states in the order for reference that the actions raise the question of what obligations are owed by operators of search engines to protect personal data of persons concerned who do not wish that certain information, which is published on third parties' websites and contains personal data relating to them that enable that information to be linked to them, be located, indexed and made available to internet users indefinitely. The answer to that question depends on the way in which Directive 95/46 must be interpreted in the context of these technologies, which appeared after the directive's publication.

… first, the referring court asks, in essence, whether Article 2(b) of Directive 95/46 is to be interpreted as meaning that the activity of a search engine as a provider of content which consists in finding information published or placed on the internet by third parties, indexing it automatically, storing it temporarily and, finally, making it available to internet users according to a particular order of preference must be classified as 'processing of personal data' within the meaning of that provision when that information contains personal data. If the answer is in the affirmative, the referring court seeks to ascertain furthermore whether Article 2(d) of Directive 95/46 is to be interpreted as meaning that the operator of a search engine must be regarded as the 'controller' in respect of that processing of the personal data, within the meaning of that provision. According to Google Spain and Google Inc., the activity of search engines cannot be regarded as processing of the data which appear on third parties' web pages displayed in the list of search results, given that search engines process all the information available on the internet without effecting a selection between personal data and other information. Furthermore, even if that activity must be classified as 'data processing,' the operator of a search engine cannot be regarded as a 'controller' in respect of that processing since it has no knowledge of those data and does not exercise control over the data.

On the other hand, Mr Costeja González, the Spanish, Italian, Austrian and Polish Governments and the European Commission consider that that activity quite clearly involves 'data processing' within the meaning of Directive 95/46, which is distinct from the data processing by the publishers of websites and pursues different objectives from such processing. The operator of a search engine is the 'controller' in respect of the data processing carried out by it since it is the operator that determines the purposes and means of that processing. Article 2(b) of Directive 95/46 defines 'processing of personal data' as 'any operation or set of operations which is performed upon personal data, whether or not by automatic means, such as collection, recording, organization, storage, adaptation or alteration, retrieval, consultation, use, disclosure by transmission, dissemination or otherwise making available, alignment or combination, blocking, erasure or destruction.'

As regards in particular the internet, the Court has already had occasion to state that the operation of loading personal data on an internet page must be considered to be such 'processing' within the meaning of Article 2(b) of Directive 95/46 (see Case C-101/01 *Lindqvist* EU:C:2003:596, paragraph 25).

So far as concerns the activity at issue in the main proceedings, it is not contested that the data found, indexed and stored by search engines and made available to their users include information relating to identified or identifiable natural persons and thus 'personal data' within the meaning of Article 2(a) of that directive.

Therefore, it must be found that, in exploring the internet automatically, constantly and systematically in search of the information which is published there, the operator of a search engine 'collects' such data which it subsequently 'retrieves,' 'records' and 'organises' within the framework of its indexing programmes, 'stores' on its servers and, as the case may be, 'discloses' and 'makes available' to its users in the form of lists of search results. As those operations are referred to expressly and unconditionally in Article 2(b) of Directive 95/46, they must be classified as 'processing' within the meaning of that provision, regardless of the fact that the operator of the search engine also carries out the same operations in respect of other types of information and does not distinguish between the latter and the personal data.

Nor is the foregoing finding affected by the fact that those data have already been published on the internet and are not altered by the search engine. Furthermore, it would be contrary not only to the clear wording of that provision but also to its objective — which is to ensure, through a broad definition of the concept of 'controller,' effective and complete protection of data subjects — to exclude the operator of a search engine from that definition on the ground that it does not exercise control over the personal data published on the web pages of third parties.

In this connection, it should be pointed out that the processing of personal data carried out in the context of the activity of a search engine can be distinguished from and is additional to that carried out by publishers of websites, consisting in loading those data on an internet page. Moreover, it is undisputed that that activity of search engines plays a decisive role in the overall dissemination of those data in that it renders the latter accessible to any internet user making a search on the basis of the data subject's name, including to internet users who otherwise would not have found the web page on which those data are published.

Also, the organization and aggregation of information published on the internet that are effected by search engines with the aim of facilitating their users' access to that information may, when users carry out their search on the basis of an individual's name, result in them obtaining through the list of results a structured overview of the information relating to that individual that can be found on the internet enabling them to establish a more or less detailed profile of the data subject. Inasmuch as the activity of a search engine is therefore liable to affect significantly, and additionally compared with that of the publishers of websites, the fundamental rights to privacy and to the protection of personal data, the operator of the search engine as the person determining the purposes and means of that activity must ensure, within the framework of its responsibilities, powers and capabilities, that the activity meets the requirements of Directive 95/46 in order that the guarantees laid down by the directive may have full effect and that effective and complete protection of data subjects, in particular of their right to privacy, may actually be achieved. Finally, the fact that publishers of websites have the option of indicating to operators of search engines, by means in particular of exclusion protocols such as 'robot.txt' or codes such as 'noindex' or 'noarchive,' that they wish specific information published on their site to be wholly or partially excluded from the search engines' automatic indexes does not mean that, if publishers of websites do not so indicate, the operator of a search engine is released from its responsibility for the processing of personal data that it carries out in the context of the engine's activity. It follows from all the foregoing considerations that the activity of a search engine consisting in finding information published or placed on the internet by third parties, indexing it automatically, storing it temporarily and, finally, making it available to internet users according to a particular order of preference must be classified as 'processing of personal data' within the meaning of Article 2(b) when that information contains personal data and, second, the operator of the search engine must be regarded as the 'controller' in respect of that processing, within the meaning of Article 2(d).

In the light of that objective of Directive 95/46 and of the wording of Article 4(1)(a), it must be held that the processing of personal data for the purposes of the service of a search engine such as Google Search, which is operated by an undertaking that has its seat in a third State but has an establishment in a Member State, is carried out 'in the context of the activities' of that establishment if the latter is intended to promote and sell, in that Member State, advertising space offered by the search engine which serves to make the service offered by that engine profitable. In such circumstances, the activities of the operator of the search engine and those of its establishment situated in the Member State concerned are inextricably linked since the activities relating to the advertising space constitute the means of rendering the search engine at issue economically profitable and that engine is, at the same time, the means enabling those activities to be performed.

As has been stated in paragraphs 26 to 28 of the present judgment, the very display of personal data on a search results page constitutes processing of such data. Since that display of results is accompanied, on the same page, by the display of advertising linked to the search terms, it is clear that the processing of personal data in question is carried out in the context of the commercial and advertising activity of the controller's establishment on the territory of a Member State, in this instance Spanish territory.

That being so, it cannot be accepted that the processing of personal data carried out for the purposes of the operation of the search engine should escape the obligations and guarantees laid down by Directive 95/46, which would compromise the directive's effectiveness and the effective and complete protection of the fundamental rights and freedoms of natural persons which the directive seeks to ensure …, in particular their right to privacy, with respect to the processing of personal data, a right to which the directive accords special importance as is confirmed in particular by Article 1(1) thereof and recitals 2 and 10 in its preamble …

In light of all the foregoing considerations … In order to comply with the rights laid down in those provisions and in so far as the conditions laid down by those provisions are in fact satisfied, the operator of a search engine is obliged to remove from the list of results displayed

> following a search made on the basis of a person's name links to web pages, published by third parties and containing information relating to that person, also in a case where that name or information is not erased beforehand or simultaneously from those web pages, and even, as the case may be, when its publication in itself on those pages is lawful.

The court's decision is notable for several reasons. First, although a civil law system, the court was called upon to interpret statutory language, just as courts in the United States are oftentimes called upon to do. Second, the court utilized a balancing test that compared the interest of the individual, referred to as the "data subject" with the economic interests of the operator of the search engine, as well as the "... interest of the general public in having, on account of its inclusion in the list of results, access to the information in question."

In the context of a right of privacy, the consideration of the economic interests of the operator of the search engine is surprising.

Summary

For any business, compliance with the various laws and regulations, issued by various countries as well as the European Union, on the subject of privacy is challenging. This is particularly so for companies that do business internationally. But it is not limited to companies that do business internationally, as in the case of the EU General Data Protection Regulation, that applies to any business that collects data from individuals located within the EU. And, with advances in technology, including virtual and augmented reality, the legal environment will only continue to grow more complicated.

Chapter 5

Torts and Product Liability

Abstract

Tort law compensates those who suffered a loss, injury, or death, due to another person's intentional or negligent act. Intentional torts result from the intentional violation of the rights of a person or their property. An unintentional or negligent tort results from the breach of a duty to act reasonably. In other words, the tortfeasor, the person committing the tort is negligent but there is no intent, as there is in the case of an "intentional" tort. Torts committed over the Internet are primarily intentional torts, most likely defamation, with few exceptions. An intentional tort requires a person to have a specific intent to commit a wrong. A harmful or evil motive is NOT required in order to commit an intentional tort. Those with a harmful or evil motive have crossed over into the area of criminal law that will be discussed in another chapter. Both negligent and intentional torts may be committed against a person, personal or real property, or a business. For the Internet, the most likely situation involves a person or business. The major difference between negligent and intentional torts, aside from the intent element, is the potential for punitive damages.

Social media made y'all way too comfortable with disrespecting people and not getting punched in the face for it — Mike Tyson

Introduction

Tort Law

A tort is an unreasonable interference with the interests of another.[1] The unreasonable interference may be either negligent or intentional. As part of that, tort law recognizes that individuals as well as businesses have a right to be free from:

1. Personal injury, including both physical and emotional injuries;
2. Wrongful death;
3. Invasion of privacy;
4. Harm to reputation;
5. Loss or damage to property, personal or real;
6. Improper business activities.

Therefore, tort law provides compensation for individuals and businesses who suffer an injury or death, property damage, or economic loss, as a result of another's wrongful, possibly criminal act.

Thus, intentional torts may provide a basis for both criminal prosecution as well as a civil lawsuit.

Tort Law Falls into Three General Categories

The brilliant jurist Oliver Wendell Holmes categorized torts into three categories[2]:

1. Intentional torts;
2. Torts based on negligence; and
3. Strict liability torts.

The vast majority of torts that result in a lawsuit are likely to be negligent, or unintentional torts. However, when it comes to the Internet, it is likely that most torts are intentional. An intentional tort is one where

---

[1] *Werner v. Plater-Zyberk*, 799 A.2d 776 (2002).

[2] In re Samgja. 2022 WL 987421 (U.S. Bankruptcy Court, C.D. California).

the tortfeasor, the one who commits the tort, has an intent. While "intent" is something that is also discussed in Chapters 6 and 8, the intent that is required for an intentional tort is a bit different. The intent that is required for a criminal act may involve the intent to commit an evil or harmful act. An intentional tort does not require an evil or harmful motive. The perpetrator may not intend for someone to be harmed, injured, or killed, but harm, injury, or death is the end result.

As related to the Internet, intentional torts, primarily defamation and intentional infliction of emotional distress, are far more likely than negligent torts. Nonetheless, it is likely that a lawsuit based on an intentional tort will also include allegations of negligence. As far as negligent torts, a company that sells products over the Internet may likely face a lawsuit in the event that the product causes injury or death.

"Tort" Defined

Restatement (Second) of Torts Section 6:

Conduct, whether an act or omission, that is of such a character as to subject an actor to liability under the principles of the law of torts.

In addition to what was previously noted, tort law serves to:

1. Deter conduct that causes harm by providing compensation for persons injured by such conduct.[3]
2. Place an injured party in the same position, as nearly as possible, that they would have occupied had the tort not occurred.

Generally, compensation is intended to put the plaintiff, whether a person or business in the same position that they would have occupied had the wrongful act not occurred. To accomplish this, tort law provides a variety of remedies. The Restatement distinguishes between "injury" and "harm."

[3] *Reyno v. Piper Aircraft Co.*, 630 F.2d 149 (#d Cir. 1980) judgment rev-d on other grounds, 454 U.S. 235 (1981).

Injury

The Restatement (Second) of Torts Section 7(1) defines a tort as an invasion of any legally protected interest of another.

Harm

The Restatement (Second) of Torts, Section 7(2) defines "harm" as a loss or detriment in fact of any kind, resulting from any cause to a person. The definition of "physical harm" found in Section 7(3) is, "the physical impairment of the human body or of land or chattels." A chattel is an item of personal property. Comment (e) goes on to note that "bodily harm" refers to impairment of the body.

However, as noted previously, tort law is not limited to individuals. Businesses have a right, among others, to be free from:

1. Unfair competition; as well as
2. Harm to reputation.

Tort law provides compensation for a wrongful act that causes a loss, injury, death, or other harm or damage, either to a person or business, due to the improper actions of another, whether a person or business.

Determining Negligence

The Restatement (Second) of Torts Section 299 states that an act may be negligent if it is done without the competence that a reasonable person in the position of the actor would recognize as necessary to prevent it from creating an unreasonable risk of harm to another. Section 298 Comment (a) goes on to note that competence is to be distinguished from care, competence being a matter of the ability or capacity of the individual to use care, and care being the attention and caution exercised in the use made of that competence.

Section 299 comment (c) goes on to note that a person who voluntarily does an act which, as a reasonable person, they should recognize as involving an unreasonable risk of harm to others unless the person has sufficient competence to do it properly, may be negligent if the person does not have and exercise such competence, and their lack of it causes harm to another. On the other hand, if the actor in fact possesses greater competence than that which the normal reasonable person would have, the actor must exercise that superior competence with reasonable attention and care.

Section 281 notes that a defendant may be liable for an invasion of an interest of another if:

1. The interest invaded is protected against unintentional invasion;
2. The conduct of the actor is negligent with respect to the other, or a class of persons within which the actor is included;
3. The actor's conduct is a legal cause of the invasion; and
4. The other has not so conducted itself as to disable itself from bringing an action for such invasion.

Section 293 specifies the factors that are to be evaluated to determine whether a party was negligent:

1. The social value which the law attaches to the interests which are imperiled;
2. The extent of the chance that the actor's conduct will cause an invasion of any interest of the other or one of a class of which the other is a member;
3. The extent of the harm likely to be caused to the interests imperiled; and
4. The number of persons whose interests are likely to be invaded if the risk takes effect in harm.

Section 299 provides additional guidance and notes that,

An act may be negligent if it is done without the competence that a reasonable person in the position of the actor would recognize as necessary to prevent it from creating an unreasonable risk of harm to another.

French Law

The French Civil Code covers most, if not all of the issues that are addressed by the American tort law. However, unlike the United States, where court decisions are consulted for guidance, France is virtually the opposite. The Civil Code, Preliminary Title: Of the Publication, Effects and Application of Laws in General, Section 5 specifically states,[4] "It is forbidden for judges to pronounce by way of general and regulatory provision on the cases submitted to them." And, this requirement is not limited to the subject of torts but applies to all areas of the law.

The French Civil Code, Book III, Title III, Subtitle II on "extra-contractual liability" (tort) sections one through six, specifies those who are liable in the event of damage to another:

> Item 1240:
>
> Any act whatever of man, which causes damage to another, obliges the one by whose fault it happened to repair it.
>
> Item 1241:
>
> Everyone is responsible for the damage he has caused not only by his act, but also by his negligence or imprudence.
>
> Item 1242:
>
> One is responsible not only for the damage which one causes by one's own act, but also for that which is caused by the act of the persons for whom one must answer, or of the things which one has in one's custody.
>
> However, whoever owns, in any capacity whatsoever, all or part of the building or movable property in which a fire started will only be liable to third parties for damage caused by this fire if it is proved that it must be attributed to his fault or to the fault of the persons for whom he is responsible.
>
> This provision does not apply to relations between owners and tenants, which remain governed by articles 1733 and 1734 of the Civil Code.
>
> The father and the mother, insofar as they exercise parental authority, are jointly and severally liable for the damage caused by their minor children living with them.

---

[4] https://www.legifrance.gouv.fr/codes/section_lc/LEGITEXT000006070721/LEGISCTA000032021488?etatTexte=VIGUEUR&anchor=LEGISCTA000032021488#LEGISCTA000032021488.

Masters and principals, for damage caused by their servants and servants in the functions for which they have employed them;

Teachers and craftsmen, from the damage caused by their pupils and apprentices during the time they are under their supervision.

The above liability takes place, unless the father and mother and the craftsmen prove that they could not prevent the fact which gives rise to this liability.

With regard to the teachers, the faults, imprudence, or negligence invoked against them as having caused the harmful event, must be proven, in accordance with common law, by the plaintiff, at the instance.

Intentional Torts

An "intentional" tort requires an element of intent. And, although the issue of intent is also discussed in Chapter 6, as well as Chapter 7, the intent that is required for an intentional tort is different from the intent that is required for a crime. The Restatement (Second) of Torts Section 8A, comments "a" and "b" specify the requirements for an intentional tort:

> 8 a. 'Intent,' as it is used throughout the Restatement of Torts, has reference to the consequences of an act rather than the act itself. When an actor fires a gun in the midst of the Mojave Desert, he intends to pull the trigger; but when the bullet hits a person who is present in the desert without the actor's knowledge, he does not intend that result. 'Intent' is limited, wherever it is used, to the consequences of the act.
>
> b. All consequences which the actor desires to bring about are intended, as the word is used in this Restatement. Intent is not, however, limited to consequences which are desired. If the actor knows that the consequences are certain, or substantially certain, to result from his act, and still goes ahead, he is treated by the law as if he had in fact desired to produce the result. As the probability that the consequences will follow decreases, and becomes less than substantial certainty, the actor's conduct loses the character of intent, and becomes mere recklessness, as defined in Section 500. As the probability decreases further, and amounts only to a risk that the result will follow it becomes ordinary negligence, as defined in Section 282. All three have their important place in the law of torts, but the liability attached to them will differ.

Therefore, according to the Restatement, a tort is "intentional" if the tortfeasor:

a. intended the consequences of the act; or

b. knew that the consequences were substantially certain to occur.

Intentional Torts against Persons

Defamation

In defamation actions there are three recognized classes of plaintiffs:

1. general public figures, i.e., public officials or persons whose conduct is generally a matter of interest to the public;
2. limited public figures, i.e., persons whose conduct is of interest to certain portions of the public as to a limited range of issues; and
3. private figures.[5]

The Restatement (Second) of Torts Section 558 notes that the elements of defamation are:

a. a false and defamatory statement concerning another;
b. an unprivileged publication to a third party;
c. fault amounting at least to negligence on the part of the publisher; and
d. either actionability of the statement irrespective of special harm or the existence of special harm caused by the publication.

The Restatement (Second) of Torts Section 558(a) notes that the first element is

> 'a false and defamatory statement concerning another.'

By way of explanation, The Restatement, Section 559 goes on to note that a statement is defamatory only if

> 'it tends so to harm the reputation of another as to lower him in the estimation of the community or to deter third persons from associating or dealing with him.'

---

[5] *Enigma Software Grp. USA, LLC v. Bleeping Computer LLC*, 194 F.Supp.3d 263 at 287.

Defamation requires an untrue statement of a material fact that harms the reputation of another, along with publication.

Requirements for defamation

1. A false statement of fact
   The false statement of fact may be further broken down into two categories:
   Slander is spoken;
   Libel is written or contained in some other permanent record.
2. The statement was understood to be about the plaintiff and damaged the plaintiff's reputation;
3. The statement was published;

The First Amendment and Opinion

Defamation requires an untrue statement of a material fact that harms the reputation of another, along with publication.

The publication requirement

Restatement Section 557 makes clear that in order to be defamatory, a statement must be communicated to a third person and notes that it is the communication, intentionally or by negligent act, to one other than the person defamed. In other words, the defamatory statement must be communicated to a person or persons other than the defamed party. This also means that anyone who repeats or republishes a defamatory statement normally is also liable for defamation.

Categories of Defamation

Slander *per se*[6]:
Accusing someone of

1. Having a loathsome disease (STDs, mental illness);
2. Committing improprieties in a profession or trade;
3. Having committed or been imprisoned for a serious crime;
4. Being unchaste.

---

[6]https://www.law.cornell.edu/wex/libel_per_se.

Defenses to Defamation

Truth

If a statement is true, it does not meet the definition of defamation, which requires an untrue statement of a material fact.

Privilege

The Restatement specifies two kinds of "privileges" that may protect an alleged defamatory statement. The first privilege is "absolute" as noted in Restatement Sections 583–592(A). The second kind of privilege is much more limited and is conditional as noted in Restatement Sections 593–598.

The Difference Between an Absolute and Conditional Privilege

The Restatement (Second), Torts Sections 585, 587, and 488 (1977), note generally that the absolute privilege affords absolute protection upon a showing that the statements were issued as part of a judicial proceeding and the alleged defamation is relevant to a matter at issue in the proceeding. Absolute privilege provides complete immunity, regardless of the purpose or motive of the individual, to assure free and open expression in judicial and governmental areas.[7]

Restatement Section 598A, comment (c) notes, "The conditional privilege stated in this Section is to be contrasted with the absolute privilege stated in Section 591. The absolute privilege applies to any executive or administrative officer of the United States, to a superior executive officer of a State and, in some States, to executive officers of lesser rank. This privilege applies to all other executive and administrative officers of a State or of any of its subdivisions."

A conditional privilege exists where a communication is:

1. Made in good faith; and
2. On a subject in which the person making it has a legitimate interest; or
3. In reference to which he has a duty; and
4. Where the communication is limited to:

[7] *McGrew v. Heinold Commodities, Inc.*, 145 Ill. App. 3d 104, 115 (1986).

   a. The scope of the interest; and
   b. The recipient is entitled to receive it;
5. Even though the communication contains matter which, without the privilege, would be an invasion of privacy.[8]

Limitation on a Privilege

In certain circumstances, Restatement Sections 599–605A note that if a privilege is abused the privilege may be lost, thus exposing the speaker to potential litigation. Section 599 notes that a person who publishes false and defamatory matter upon an occasion giving rise to a conditional privilege abuses the privilege if she:

(a) knows the matter to be false, or
(b) acts in reckless disregard as to its truth or falsity (Section 600).

A conditional privilege typically arises in a business situation, such as an evaluation by a supervisor.

Public Figures and Officials

Public officials such as politicians, as well as public figures, such as individuals who "have thrust themselves to the forefront of particular public controversies in order to influence the resolution of the issues involved"[9] must meet a much higher standard, specifically "actual malice" in order to recover damages for defamation.

Actual Malice

In 1964, the United States Supreme Court held that the public official must prove "actual malice" in order to recover in a lawsuit for defamation.[10] And, a few years later the Court extended the requirement of actual malice to a situation involving a public figure. Three years later, the Court extended

---

[8] *Hines v. Arkansas Louisiana Gas Co.*, 613 So. 2d 646, 658 (La. Ct. App. 2d Cir. 1993, writ denied, 617 So. 2d 932 (La. 1993).

[9] *Curtis Publ'g v. Butts*, 388 U.S. 130, 345 (1967).

[10] *New York Times v. Sullivan*, 376 U.S. 254 (1964).

the actual malice ruling to public figures.[11] Then, in *Gertz v. Robert Welch, Inc.*,[12] the Court drew a distinction between limited purpose and involuntary public figures and ruled that private figures, although not held to the requirement of "actual malice" must prove a breach of a duty, at least negligence, although the states were free to require an elevated standard of fault.[13]

Defamation and the Internet

The Communications Decency Act (1996)

Section 230

The Internet presents a challenge for the traditional view of defamation. As noted previously, defamation is the publication of an untrue statement of fact that harms the reputation of another. Thus, anyone who repeats a defamatory statement is potentially liable for defamation. Traditionally, newspapers, television, and radio stations faced potential liability should they repeat a defamatory statement unless they were protected by the virtually insurmountable standard set forth in *New York Times v. Sullivan*. With the development of the Internet the question then arose whether Internet service providers (ISPs) or what the Communications Decency Act Section 230(c)(1) refers to as an "interactive computer service" should face the same liability as newspapers, television, and radio stations for repeating a defamatory statement.

The history of Section 230

Court decisions created a quandary for ISPs. Although courts had held that

[11] *Curtis Publ'g v. Butts*, 388 U.S. 130 (1967).
[12] 418 U.S. 323 (1974).
[13] *Ibid.*, at 342–348.

1. ISPs that passively hosted third-party content were not liable as a publisher if any of that content was defamatory. The courts went on to note
2. that a platform would be liable as a publisher for all its third-party content if it exercised discretion to remove any third-party material.

Thus, any ISP that moderated third-party content risked being held liable for content posted by third parties. The alternative was to avoid moderating the content but be overwhelmed with content that was obscene or unlawful. To protect ISPs that were trapped between Scylla and Charybdis, Congress enacted Section 230 to, at least in part, resolve this dilemma by providing immunity to online platforms both for third-party content on their services or for removal of certain categories of content. Using a carrot-and-stick approach, the statute attempted to nurture emerging Internet businesses while encouraging them to regulate obscene or otherwise inappropriate or illegal online content.

Section 230(c) provides protection for "Good Samaritan" blocking and screening of offensive material and states that:

1. No provider or user of an interactive computer service shall be treated as the publisher or speaker of any information provided by another information content provider.

Section 230(c)(2) goes on to note:
No provider or user of an interactive computer service shall be held liable on account of

A. Any action voluntarily taken in good faith to restrict access to or availability of material that the provider or user considers to be obscene, lewd, lascivious, filthy, excessively violent, harassing, or otherwise objectionable, whether or not such material is constitutionally protected; or
B. Any action taken to enable or make available to information content providers or others the technical means to restrict access to material described in paragraph (1).

However, 230(e) currently provides for a variety of exceptions:

1. No effect on criminal law: Nothing in this section shall be construed to impair the enforcement of … obscenity … sexual exploitation of children … or any other Federal criminal statute.
2. No effect on intellectual property law: Nothing in this section shall be construed to limit or expand any law pertaining to intellectual property.
3. State law: Nothing in this section shall be construed to prevent any State from enforcing any State law that is consistent with this section.
4. No effect on communications privacy law: Nothing in this section shall be construed to limit the application of the Electronic Communications Privacy Act of 1986 or any of the amendments made by such Act, or any similar State law.
5. No effect on sex trafficking law.

Section 230 is subject to significant criticism. As with the virtually insurmountable barrier to litigation that is provided to traditional news media by the standard established in *New York Times v. Sullivan*, courts have interpreted the protection provided by Section 230 so broadly that ISPs have virtually unfettered discretion with the content that is available. As a result, ISPs are no longer motivated to address illicit material on their services and are free to moderate lawful content without transparency or accountability.[14]

Thus, while Section 230, much like the standard in *New York Times v. Sullivan*, has presented an insurmountable barrier to successful lawsuits against ISPs, cracks are beginning to appear. In addition to potential legislative changes, plaintiffs are now suing on a theory of negligent design, rather than third-party content.[15] In analyzing the lawsuit the court noted that in order "To determine whether Section 230(c)(1) applies here — and thus immunizes Snap from the Parents' claim — we apply the three-prong test set forth in *Barnes v. Yahoo!, Inc*., (citation omitted). Snap thus enjoys

---

[14] https://www.justice.gov/archives/ag/department-justice-s-review-section-230-communications-decency-act-1996.

[15] *Lemmon v. Snap, Inc*., doing business in California as Snapchat, Inc. 995 F.3d 1085 (2022).

CDA immunity only if it is '(1) a provider or user of an interactive computer service (2) whom a plaintiff seeks to treat, under a state law cause of action, as a publisher or speaker (3) of information provided by another information content provider.'" (Citation omitted).[16] The court noted, "Here, the Parents seek to hold Snap liable for its allegedly 'unreasonable and negligent' design decisions regarding Snapchat. They allege that Snap created: (1) Snapchat; (2) Snapchat's Speed Filter; and (3) an incentive system within Snapchat that encouraged its users to pursue certain unknown achievements and rewards. The Speed Filter and the incentive system then supposedly worked in tandem to entice young Snapchat users to drive at speeds exceeding 100 MPH." The court then noted that, "It is thus apparent that the Parents' amended complaint does not seek to hold Snap liable for its conduct as a publisher or speaker. Their negligent design lawsuit treats Snap as a products manufacturer, accusing it of negligently designing a product (Snapchat) with a defect (the interplay between Snapchat's reward system and the Speed Filter). Thus, the duty that Snap allegedly violated "springs from" its distinct capacity as a product designer…" The court concluded, "Because the Parents' claim does not seek to hold Snap responsible as a publisher or speaker, but merely 'seek[s] to hold Snapchat liable for its own conduct, principally for *the creation* of the Speed Filter,'" Section 230(c)(1) immunity is unavailable.

Intentional Infliction of Emotional Distress (Outrageous Conduct)

The Restatement (Second) of Torts Section 46(1)

One who by extreme and outrageous conduct intentionally or recklessly causes severe emotional distress to another is subject to liability for such emotional distress, and if bodily harm to the other results from it, for such bodily harm.

Outrageous conduct

The Restatement (Second) of Torts Section 46, comment (e) notes that

---

[16]*Ibid.*, at 1091.

The extreme and outrageous character of the conduct may arise from an abuse by the actor of a position, or relation with the other, which gives him actual or apparent authority over the other, or power to affect his interests.

Section 46 comment (f) goes on to note that

The extreme and outrageous character of the conduct may arise from the actor's knowledge that the other is peculiarly susceptible to emotional distress, by reason of some physical or mental condition or peculiarity.

A court went on to note that the principle applies only to unprivileged, intentional, or reckless conduct of an extreme and outrageous nature, and only that which causes severe emotional distress.[17] "By extreme we refer to conduct so outrageous in character and so extreme in degree as to go beyond all possible bounds of decency, and to be regarded as atrocious and utterly intolerable in a civilized society."[18]

Claims of intentional infliction of emotional distress are usually coupled with a claim of negligent infliction of emotional distress since a claim of intentional infliction of emotion distress requires proof of an intentional act that is much more difficult to prove. Unlike negligent infliction of emotional distress, intentional infliction of emotional distress may result in an award of punitive damages.

Limitations Based on the First Amendment

When speech about a public figure is involved, in addition to the heightened requirement of "actual malice," there may also be a First Amendment issue.

As the Court noted in *Snyder v. Phelps*,[19]

'The Free Speech Clause of the First Amendment can serve as a defense in state tort suits, including suits for intentional infliction of emotional distress. (Citation omitted). Whether the First Amendment prohibits holding (the defendant) liable for its speech in this case turns largely on

---

[17] *American Road Service Co. v. Inmon*, 394 So. 2d 361 (Ala. 1980).
[18] *Ibid.*
[19] 562 U.S. 443 (2011).

whether that speech is of public or private concern, as determined by all the circumstances of the case.' '[S]peech on public issues occupies the "highest rung of the hierarchy of First Amendment values" and is entitled to special protection. (Citation omitted). Although the boundaries of what constitutes speech on matters of public concern are not well defined, this Court has said that speech is of public concern when it can "be fairly considered as relating to any matter of political, social, or other concern to the community," (citation omitted) or when it "is a subject of general interest and of value and concern to the public" (citation omitted). A statemen's arguably "inappropriate or controversial character ... is irrelevant to the question whether it deals with a matter of public concern." (Citation omitted). To determine whether speech is of public or private concern, this Court must independently examine the "content, form, and context" of the speech "as revealed by the whole record." (citation omitted). In considering content, form, and context, no factor is dispositive, and it is necessary to evaluate all aspects of the speech.'

Parody

Although parody traditionally implicates fair use, a subject that is covered in Chapter 10, it may also provide a defense to a lawsuit based on defamation.

As the Court noted in *Campbell v. Acuff-Rose Music, Inc.*,[20] 'Like less ostensibly humorous forms of criticism, it can provide social benefit, by shedding light on an earlier work, and, in the process, creating a new one. We thus line up with the courts that have held that parody, like other comment or criticism, may claim fair use ...' (citations omitted).

'... Modern dictionaries ... describe a parody as a 'literary or artistic work that imitates the characteristic style of an author or a work for comic effect or ridicule,' or as a 'composition in prose or verse in which the characteristic turns of thought and phrase in an author or class of authors are imitated in such a way as to make them appear ridiculous.'

[20] 510 U.S. 569 (1994).

> For the purposes of copyright law, the nub of the definitions, and the heart of any parodist's claim to quote from existing material, is the use of some elements of a prior author's composition to create a new one that, at least in part, comments on that author's works. (Citation omitted). If, on the contrary, the commentary has no critical bearing on the substance or style of the original composition, which the alleged infringer merely uses to get attention or to avoid the drudgery in working up something fresh, the claim to fairness in borrowing from another's work diminishes accordingly (if it does not vanish), and other factors, like the extent of its commerciality, loom larger. Parody needs to mimic an original to make its point, and so has some claim to use the creation of its victim's (or collective victims') imagination, whereas satire can stand on its own two feet and so requires justification for the very act of borrowing. (Citation omitted).

Assault

While we typically refer to assault and battery, that is not accurate. An assault may occur without a battery and a battery may occur without an assault. The Restatement (Second) of Torts Section 21 notes that an assault occurs where a person

a. acts intending to cause a harmful or offensive contact with the person of another or a third person, or an imminent apprehension of such contact; and
b. the other is thereby put in such imminent apprehension. A battery goes one step beyond an assault in that harmful contact usually occurs.

A claim of assault is likely to be combined with a claim of intentional or negligent infliction of emotional distress and may include allegations regarding both statements as well as conduct. The elements of assault include consideration of the following factors:

1. Would a reasonable person believe that harmful or offensive contact will occur?
2. Would a reasonable person want to avoid the contact?

Although unlikely in the case of the Internet, the completion of the act that caused the apprehension, is a battery. The Restatement (Second) of Torts Section 13 defines a battery as:

> An act with the intent to cause a harmful or offensive contact with another or a third person, or an imminent apprehension of such a contact, and a harmful contact with the person of the other individual directly or indirectly results. Section 19 goes on to note that a bodily contact is offensive if it offends a reasonable sense of personal dignity.

Section 19 comment "a" explains that such offense is one that would offend the ordinary person — it is a contact that is unwarranted by the social usages prevalent at the time and place at which it is inflicted. Section 16(1) notes that if an act is done with the intention of inflicting upon another an offensive but not a harmful bodily contact, or of putting another in apprehension of either a harmful or offensive bodily contact, and that act causes a bodily contact to the other, the actor is liable for a battery, even though the act was not done with the intention of bringing about the resulting bodily harm.

The reasonable (or "ordinary") person standard determines whether contact is offensive. In other words, would the contact be considered offensive to a reasonable or ordinary person?

Defenses

Provocation: For a lawsuit that alleges assault, provocation may be a partial defense, although generally, mere words alone, may be insufficient to justify the defense.[21] If the words are coupled with other acts or other circumstances that create a reasonable apprehension or fear of an imminent harmful or offensive contact, it may be sufficient to establish a defense of provocation.[22]

Battery: As with assault, the defense of provocation may arise in situations where more than mere words are involved.

---

[21] *Brower v. Ackerley*, 88 Wash. App. 87 (Div. 1 1997).

[22] *Martin v. Bigner*, 665 So. 2d 709 (La. Ct. App. 2d Cir. 1995).

Self-defense: Self-defense is commonly asserted as a defense to a claim of battery, along with the claim of adequate provocation. Generally, an individual is allowed to use that force reasonably necessary under the circumstances. The Restatement (Second) distinguishes between deadly force in Section 65 and nondeadly force in Section 63.

Defense of others: As with self-defense, individuals are permitted to go to the aid of others that are threatened. However, a party, again, may only use that force that is reasonably necessary under the circumstances.

Defense of property: Ordinarily, force that is likely to cause death or great bodily injury normally cannot be used in the case of defense of property. In the case of a trespasser, reasonable force may be used to remove trespassers from a home or business. Or a trespasser may be detained for a reasonable amount of time and in a reasonable manner.

Invasion of privacy

This area of tort law is separate and distinct from the right of privacy that was first recognized by the United States Supreme Court in *Griswold v. Connecticut* as noted in Chapter 4. The constitutional right of privacy restricts actions by the government, traditionally law enforcement, while tort law protects the personal rights of individuals from others, other than the government.

The Common Law

The Restatement (Second) of Torts (1977) recognizes four distinct offenses.

1. Intrusion on an individual's solitude or seclusion;
2. Publicity which violates the ordinary decencies;
3. Putting the plaintiff in a false, but not necessarily defamatory, position in the public eye;
4. The appropriation of some element of the plaintiff's personality for a commercial use.

Invasion of privacy is distinct from defamation.[23] Invasion of privacy may involve the unjustified disclosure of the truthful, but intimate details, of an individual's private life. Thus, even though the information is accurate, its disclosure is a violation of an individual's right of privacy. So, while truth is a defense to a claim of defamation, it is not a defense to a claim for invasion of privacy. In addition, defamation requires "publication," that may involve only one individual while the invasion of privacy does not require publication or communication, although a claim of "false light" does require publicity, but to a far greater number of individuals than defamation. Last, invasion of privacy involves private matters and not matters that are public or of a legitimate interest to the public.

A lawsuit alleging an invasion of the right of privacy generally must establish each of the following:

1. A legally protected privacy interest;
2. A reasonable expectation of privacy in the circumstances; and
3. Conduct by defendant constituting a serious invasion of privacy.[24]

However, that is not the end of the inquiry. Assuming that a claimant has met all of those requirements, that interest must then be measured against other competing or countervailing interests in a balancing test.[25]

Intrusion on Individual's Affairs or Seclusion

The Restatement of the law, Second, Torts Section 652 defines it as:

> One who intentionally intrudes, physically or otherwise, upon the solitude or seclusion of another or his private affairs or concerns, is subject

---

[23] In some situations, a lawsuit based on the right of privacy may also include an allegation of "libel *per quod.*" See, e.g., *Time, Inc. v. Hill*, 385 U.S. 374 (1967). Libel *per quod* is different from libel *per se*.

[24] *Alexiadis v. Cambridge Systematics, Inc.*, 2022 WL 3137458 (United States District Court, C.D. California).

[25] *Pioneer Elecs. (USA), Inc. v. Superior*, Ct. 40 Cal. 4th 360, 371 (2007).

> to liability to the other for invasion of his privacy, if the intrusion would be highly offensive to a reasonable person.

Section 652B goes on to note:

> The invasion may be a physical intrusion into a place in which the plaintiff has secluded himself, as when the defendant forces his way into the plaintiff's room in a hotel or insists over the plaintiff's objection in entering his home. It may also be use of the defendant's senses, with or without mechanical aids, to oversee or overhear the plaintiff's private affairs, as by looking into his upstairs window with binoculars or tapping his telephone wires. It may be by some other form of investigation or examination into his private concerns.

This area may also involve a violation of the Electronic Communications Privacy Act as noted in Chapter 4 as well as the Computer Fraud and Abuse Act in the event that there was wrongful access to a protected computer (Section 1030(a)(2)(c).

Intentional prying

May occur physically or electronically. The Restatement of the Law, Second, Torts Section 652(B) notes:

The form of invasion of privacy covered by this section consists solely of an intentional interference with his interest in solitude or seclusion, either as to his person or as to his private affairs or concerns, of a kind that would be highly offensive to a reasonable person.

The Restatement goes on to note that the offense may also occur by:

1. Opening his private and personal mail
2. Searching his safe or his wallet
3. Examining his private bank account
4. Or compelling him by a forged court order to permit an inspection of his personal documents.

The intrusion itself makes the defendant subject to liability, even though there is no publication or other use of any kind of the photograph or information outlined.

Publicity Which Violates the Ordinary Decencies

The Restatement of Torts (Second) Section 652D states, "One who gives publicity to a matter concerning the private life of another is subject to liability to the other for invasion of his privacy, if the matter publicized is of a kind that

a. would be highly offensive to a reasonable person, and that
b. is not of legitimate concern to the public."

The Restatement goes on to note, "Thus it is not an invasion of the right of privacy, within the rule stated in this Section, to communicate a fact concerning the plaintiff's private life to a single person or even to a small group of persons. On the other hand, any publication in a newspaper or a magazine, even of small circulation, or in a handbill distributed to a large number of persons, or any broadcast over the radio, or statement made in an address to a large audience, is sufficient to give publicity within the meaning of the term …" Note that "publication" and "publicity" are not the same concepts.

Section 652(D) goes on to note:

> This section provides for tort liability involving a judgment for damages for publicity given to true statements of fact. It has not been established with certainty that liability of this nature is consistent with the free-speech and free-press provisions of the First Amendment....
>
> Under the First Amendment there can be no recovery for disclosure of and publicity to facts that are a matter of public record.

False Light

Restatement (Second) of the law, Torts, Section 652(e) states that this tort may occur if a defendant:

1. Gives publicity to a matter concerning another;
2. That places the other before the public in a false light;
3. That the false light would be highly offensive to a reasonable person; and

4. That the defendant knew of or acted in reckless disregard as to the falsity of the publicized matter and the false light in which the other would be placed.

A claim based on "false light" does not require that the information be private, but it does require that the information be false, as in the case of defamation. Unlike defamation however, truth is not an affirmative defense.

The Restatement (Second) Torts, Section 652E, comment (a) notes that "'Publicity,' as it is used in this Section, differs from 'publication,' as that term is used in Section 577 in connection with liability for defamation. 'Publication,' in that sense, is a word of art, which includes any communication by the defendant to a third person. 'Publicity,' on the other hand, means that the matter is made public, by communicating it to the public at large, or to so many persons that the matter must be regarded as substantially certain to become one of public knowledge. The difference is not one of the means of communication, which may be oral, written or by any other means. It is one of a communication that reaches, or is sure to reach, the public…"

The "publicity" in this case would be to make the matter public, or to communicate it to the public at large. Misleading implications that the average person would find highly offensive may be sufficient.

The Appropriation of Some Element of the Plaintiff's Personality for Commercial Use

This right of privacy is similar to, but different from the right of publicity. The former is intended to protect an individual's interest in privacy, which involve psychological interests, while the latter is intended to protect economic or financial interests.

The right of privacy includes the right to the exclusive use of a person's identity.

The Restatement notes that the common form of misappropriation is the use of the plaintiff's name or likeness to advertise the defendant's business or product or for some other commercial use. However, it is not limited to commercial situations and may include situations where a defendant makes use of the plaintiff's name or likeness for his own purposes and benefit, even though the use is not a commercial one, and even though the benefit sought to obtained is not a pecuniary one.

Fraudulent Misrepresentation — Intentional Deceit for Personal Gain

Also discussed in Chapter 7, the elements of fraud are:

1. A representation;
2. Its falsity;
3. Its materiality;
4. The speaker's knowledge of its falsity or ignorance of its truth;
5. Intent to induce reliance on the misrepresentation;
6. The recipient's ignorance of its falsity;
7. Justifiable reliance;
8. Damages;
9. Causation.[26]

A Statement of Fact or an Opinion?

Fraud requires more than mere puffery, or seller's talk and normally requires a statement of fact, not opinion. However, there may be an exception in the case of a statement by an expert or someone with superior knowledge.

What is a "Material" Fact?

The Restatement (Second), Torts Section 538 (1977) notes, "The matter is material if a reasonable person would attach importance to its existence in making a decision as to a transaction, or one who makes a representation knows or has reason to know the recipient is likely to regard the matter as important, although a reasonable person would not."

---

[26] See, e.g., *Watson Laboratories, Inc. v. State of Mississippi*, 241 So. 3d 573 (2018).

Non-disclosure may Constitute Fraud

The Restatement (Second) Torts Section 551(2)(e) and comments "j" to "l" note that the duty to disclose may arise regarding facts basic to a transaction, where one party knows the other is about to enter the transaction under a mistake of fact, and the other, because of the relationship between them, the customs of the trade, or other objective circumstances, would reasonably expect disclosure of those facts.

Concealment

The Restatement (Second) Torts, Section 550 notes that a party who successfully prevents another from an investigation which would have disclosed material facts, or who frustrates an investigation, is liable for fraudulent concealment. In addition, comment (b) notes that a false denial of knowledge or information by one party to a transaction, who is in possession of the facts, may subject him to liability as fully as if he had expressly misstated the facts, if its effect upon the other leads him to believe that the facts do not exist or cannot be discovered.

Negligent Misrepresentation

A claim of negligent, as opposed to intentional or fraudulent misrepresentation may arise in situations where the misrepresentation was not intentional but was made without a reasonable basis for its truthfulness. In that situation, the only element that is missing from the definition of fraudulent misrepresentation is "intent".

Sexual Harassment

There are two kinds of sexual harassment[27]:

Quid Pro Quo

Hostile Environment

---

[27]Meritor Sav. Bank FSB v. Vinson, 477 U.S. 57 (1986).

Quid pro Quo Harassment

To establish a prima facie case a plaintiff must show all of the following:

1. That plaintiff was a member of a protected class;
2. That the plaintiff was subject to unwelcome sexual advances or requests for sexual favors;
3. That the harassment complained of was based on sex;
4. That submission to unwelcome advances was an express or implied condition for receiving benefits or that a refusal to submit to the sexual demands resulted in adverse consequences; and
5. That *respondent superior* liability exists.

Note that if a plaintiff is able to produce direct evidence, he may prevail without proving all the elements of a prima facie case.[28]

Hostile Environment Harassment

The elements of a hostile work environment claim are:

1. The plaintiff is a member of a protected group;
2. The plaintiff was subjected to unwelcome harassment;
3. The harassment was based on the protected characteristic; and
4. The harassment was sufficiently severe or pervasive to alter a term, condition, or privilege of the plaintiff's employment and created an abusive working environment.[29]

Business Torts

Wrongful Interference
Two kinds:

1. With a contractual relationship;
2. With a business relationship.

---

[28] *Figueroa v. Pompeo*, 923 F.3d 1078, 1086 (2019).

[29] *Bobelu-Boone v. Wilkie*, 526 F.Supp.3d 971, 983 (2021).

Wrongful Interference With a Contractual Relationship

The Restatement (Third) of Torts Sections 16 and 17 specify the elements that are necessary in order for a violation to occur:

1. A valid contract;
2. Defendant engaged in wrongful conduct;
3. Defendant intended to cause a breach or disruption of its performance;
4. Defendant's conduct caused a breach or disruption of performance;

Note that this lawsuit may also involve a claim for breach of contract. The Restatement states that the following are examples of conduct that is wrongful:

1. Defendant acted for the purpose of appropriating the benefits of the plaintiff's contract; or
2. The defendant's conduct constituted an independent and intentional legal wrong; or
3. The defendant engaged in the conduct for the sole purpose of injuring the plaintiff.

Wrongful Interference With a Business Relationship

The Restatement (Third) of torts Section 17 goes further than the prior section and notes that:

A defendant is subject to liability for interference with economic expectation if

a. The plaintiff had a reasonable expectation of an economic benefit from a relationship with a third party;
b. The defendant committed an independent and intentional legal wrong;
c. The defendant intended to interfere with the plaintiff's expectation; and
d. The defendant's wrongful conduct caused the expectation to fail.

In this situation, "wrongful conduct" means conduct wrongful in some way recognized elsewhere by the law. Under this definition, vigorous competition is different from actionable wrongful conduct. Examples of vigorous, and legal competition, include:

1. Effective advertising;
2. A superior product.

Intentional Torts against Property

Trespass to Personal Property (Chattels/Personalty)

Trespass to personal property occurs where there is an intentional interference with the owner or possessor's possession of personal property that has proximately caused an injury. A claim of trespass to personal property may also give rise to a claim for conversion.

The elements of a claim for conversion are:

1. The plaintiff's ownership or right to possession of the property;
2. The defendant's conversion by a wrongful act or disposition of property rights; and
3. Damages.[30]

Therefore, conversion is the wrongful exercise of dominion over the property of another and may consist of the unauthorized taking, damage or interference with the property. Stated another way, conversion is the civil equivalent of theft and involves depriving an owner of personal property or the use of the property without:

1. authorization; or
2. good cause

Conversion may extend to the taking of electronic records and data, which may also constitute trespass.

Failure to Return Goods

In situations where the original taking was a trespass, for instance where it occurred by mistake, retention may rise to the level of conversion. If the initial taking was a trespass, retention may constitute conversion. If the initial taking was proper, such as checking a book out of a library, a failure to return the property may constitute conversion.

Defenses

In some cases, a defendant may successfully argue that the trespass was warranted, for instance in the case where an automobile repair facility

[30] *Welco Electronics, Inc. v. Mora*, 223 Cal. App. 4th 202, 208 (2014).

retains possession of an automobile pending payment for the cost of repairs (a "mechanic's lien").

The Intent Element

Conversion may occur intentionally, or by mistake. Thus, anyone in possession of stolen property is presumed to know that it is stolen and even good intentions would not constitute a defense. So, someone who purchases stolen property, whether by mistake or not, has committed the tort of conversion. Likewise, an employee's unauthorized use of a company credit card may constitute conversion.

Disparagement of Property

Disparagement of property generally constitutes untrue statements of fact about another's product or personal property. There are two kinds of disparagement of property:

Slander of quality

The elements of slander of quality, which is also known as trade libel are:

1. a false publication,
2. which induces others not to deal with the party, and
3. special damages.[31]

In other words, it is the intentional disparagement of the quality of property or a product, which results in pecuniary damage.[32]

Note that such an allegation also defames the character of a person that would sell such a product and may constitute slander *per se* as well as an unfair or deceptive trade practice or act.

Slander of title

The other form of disparagement calls into question the legal ownership of property, generally implying that property is stolen. Generally, the

---

[31] *Aetna Cas. & Surety Co. v. Centennial Ins. Co.*, 838 F.2d 346, 351 (9th Cir. 1988).
[32] *Erlich v. Etner*, 224 Cal. App. 2d 69, 73 (1964).

elements for the slander of title are publication of a false statement that is derogatory to the plaintiff's title, with malice, causing special damages as a result of diminished value in the eyes of third parties.[33]

In summary, slander of title denies or questions the legal ownership of property with the intent to cause a monetary loss and, as with slander of quality, may also be defamatory as well as an unfair or deceptive trade practice or act.

Intentional Torts and Punitive Damages

Punitive damages may be recoverable in certain cases that involve an intentional tort. Punitive damages are intended to punish a party for a particularly reprehensible intentional tort.

State Limitations on the Recovery of Punitive Damages

As is common in Europe, many states limit or ban punitive damages. In certain situations there may also be a constitutional issue with punitive damages. The Eighth Amendment notes, "Excessive bail shall not be required, nor excessive fines imposed, nor cruel and unusual punishments inflicted." However, the Court has not yet addressed the issue of punitive damages as a potential violation of the Eighth Amendment. Regardless, the Court has held that punitive damages may be controlled by the Fourteenth Amendment requirement of Due Process.[34]

Punitive Damages in France

The French Code of Civil Procedure Rule 32-1[35] provides that:

---

[33] TXO Production Corp. 419 S.E.2d 870 (1992).

[34] *State Farm Mut. Auto. Ins. Co. v. Campbell*, 538 U.S. 408 (2003). The Court held that the award of $145 million in punitive damages, where the compensatory damages were $1 million, violated due process. See also *BMW of North America, Inc. v. Gore*, 517 U.S. 559 (1996).

[35] However, as one commentator noted, "Currently, the French equivalent of punitive damages is "*amende civile*," or civil fine. This civil fine, provided for in Article 32-1 of the French Civil Procedure Code, applies in case of abusive or dilatory proceedings. It is not much of a deterrent since its maximum amount is €10,000 and it is seldom applied. In addition, when judges impose such fines, they set them at limited amounts.

Recently, since the Trade Secrets Act of 30 July 2018, the amount of the civil fine has been increased as the judge can now order a civil fine representing 20% of the claim for

Anyone who acts in court in a dilatory or abusive manner may be sentenced to a civil fine of a maximum of 10,000 euros,[36] without prejudice to any damages that may be claimed.

Unintentional Torts (Negligence)

The Restatement (Second) of Torts Section 295A notes that in determining whether conduct is negligent, the customs of the community, or of others under like circumstances, are factors to be considered, but are not controlling where a reasonable man would not follow them.

The Restatement (Third) of Torts Liability for Physical and Emotional Harm Section 13 goes on to note:

a. An actor's compliance with the custom of the community, or of others in like circumstances, is evidence that the actor's conduct is not negligent but does not preclude a finding of negligence.
b. An actor's departure from the custom of the community, or of others in like circumstances, in a way that increases risk is evidence of the actor's negligence but does not require a finding of negligence.

---

damages or, failing such a claim, €60,000 to penalize the initiator of an abusive procedure (intended, for instance, to silence an investigating journalist) or dilatory procedure introduced pursuant to the new legislative provisions protecting trade secrets.

Finally, punitive damages, as found in other legal systems, starting with common law, are currently recognized in French law only in the context of the enforcement of a foreign judgment that ordered punitive damages. However, this recognition is controlled as a French judge has the option to limit the authorization to recover punitive damages ordered abroad, in case of disproportion, on the jurisprudential grounds that "[…] if the award of punitive damages is not, as a matter of principle, contrary to public policy [Editor's note: international, French], the situation is different where the allocated amount is disproportionate compared to the loss suffered and the breaches of the debtor's contractual obligations".*Citation omitted). https://www.morganlewis.com/pubs/2018/11/coming-soon-punitive-damages-the-french-way. Accessed November 17, 2023.

[36] Currently about $10,000.00.

The Restatement (Second) of Torts Section 290 states that in determining whether an actor should recognize that his or her conduct involves a risk, the actor is required to know:

1. The qualities and habits of human beings and animals and the qualities, characteristics, and capacities of things and forces insofar as they are matters of common knowledge at the time and in the community; and
2. The common law, legislative enactments, and general customs insofar as they are likely to affect the conduct of the other or third persons.

Section 290 comment "e" goes on to note that in general the actor is required to know everything with respect to the risk of harm that is a matter of common knowledge in the community in which the actor's conduct occurs.

While most torts that are committed over the Internet are likely to be intentional, any lawsuit may also include a claim for negligence. Thus, any tort that lacks the element of intent, but that causes damage, injury, or death will likely result in a lawsuit.

The requirements for a lawsuit based on negligence are:

1. Duty of care;
2. Breach of the duty;
3. Damages;
4. Causation.

The Duty of Care and Its Breach

The duty of care includes an obligation to always act in a reasonably prudent manner. Thus, negligence may consist of an act of commission or omission.

Determining the Standard of Care

The Reasonable Person Standard

The reasonable person standard is society's judgment of how an ordinary, prudent person should act in the same or similar circumstances. Thus, the degree of care that is demanded may vary depending on the circumstances.

Duty of Professionals

A professional, or another person with a greater degree of knowledge than the average person, whether a result of training, education, or experience may be held to a higher standard. If an individual has:

1. knowledge; or
2. skill;
3. superior to that of an ordinary person, the individual's conduct must be consistent with that status.

Therefore, a person with knowledge or skill that is superior to an ordinary person is expected to act in conformity with superior knowledge or skill. Thus, a medical doctor is expected to act as a "reasonable" medical doctor would act under the same or similar circumstances. The same rule applies to engineers, accountants, attorneys, and other professionals.

Causation

Courts traditionally require that, to recover damages for a defendant's negligent conduct, a plaintiff must establish both:

1. that the defendant's conduct was one of the causes of the plaintiff's injury (sometimes referred to as "factual causation," "but-for causation," or "cause-in-fact"), and
2. that the defendant's conduct has been so significant and important a cause of the plaintiff's injury that the defendant should be legally responsible ("proximate" or "legal" cause).

Causation-in-Fact and Proximate Cause

There are two tests to determine if there is causation:

1. Is there causation in fact?

   The "but for" test. But for the actions of the defendant, the tort would not have occurred.

2. Is there a proximate cause? (Legal cause)

When the connection between the act and injury is strong enough to impose liability. Did the defendant's actions create a foreseeable risk of injury? There must be both causation in fact and proximate cause for there to be liability in tort.

Foreseeability

Palsgraf v. Long Island Railroad Co.[37]

The plaintiff was standing on a platform of defendant's railroad after buying a ticket to go to Rockaway Beach. A train stopped at the station, bound for another place. Two men ran forward to catch it. One of the men reached the platform of the car without mishap, though the train was already moving. The other man, carrying a package, jumped aboard the car, but seemed unsteady as if about to fall. A guard on the car, who had held the door open, reached forward to help him in, and another guard on the platform pushed him from behind. In this act, the package was dislodged, and fell upon the rails. It was a package of small size, about fifteen inches long, and was covered by a newspaper. In fact it contained fireworks, but there was nothing in its appearance to give notice of its contents. The fireworks when they fell exploded. The shock of the explosion threw down some scales at the other end of the platform many feet away. The scales struck the plaintiff, causing injuries for which she sues. A jury found in favor of Mrs. Palsgraf and the appellate court affirmed. The defendant appealed.

The Court noted, The conduct of the defendant's guard, if a wrong in its relation to the holder of the package, was not a wrong in its relation to the plaintiff, standing far away. Relatively to her it was not negligence at all. Nothing in the situation gave notice that the falling package had in it the potency of peril to persons thus removed. Negligence is not actionable unless it involves the invasion of a legally protected interest, the violation of a right. 'Proof of negligence in the air, so to speak, will not do.'...'Negligence is the absence of care, according to the circumstances.'...The plaintiff, as she stood upon the platform of the station, might claim to be protected against intentional invasion of her bodily

[37] 248 N.Y. 339 (1928).

security. Such invasion is not charged. She might claim to be protected against unintentional invasion by conduct involving in the thought of reasonable men an unreasonable hazard that such invasion would ensue. These, from the point of view of the law, were the bounds of her immunity, with perhaps some rare exceptions, survivals for the most part of ancient forms of liability, where conduct is held to be at the peril of the actor....If no hazard was apparent to the eye of ordinary vigilance, an act innocent and harmless, at least to outward seeming, with reference to her, did not take to itself the quality of a tort because it happened to be a wrong, though apparently not one involving the risk of bodily insecurity, with reference to someone else. 'In every instance, before negligence can be predicated of a given act, back of the act must be sought and found a duty to the individual complaining, the observance of which would have averted or avoided the injury.'...'The ideas of negligence and duty are strictly correlative.' ...The plaintiff sues in her own right for a wrong personal to her, and not as the vicarious beneficiary of a breach of duty to another.

The conduct of the railroad's guard was not a wrong as to the plaintiff, standing far away. If the harm was not willful, plaintiff must show that the act as to him had possibilities of danger so many and apparent as to entitle him to be protected against the doing of it though the harm was unintended. To rule otherwise would entail liability for any and all consequences, however novel or extraordinary.

The Injury Requirement and Damages

In order to recover in tort, a plaintiff must demonstrate a legally recognizable injury. If there is no injury, there is no tort since the purpose of tort law is to compensate, not punish.

Defenses to Negligence

Superseding cause

A superseding cause is an unforeseeable intervening event. This is related to the proximate cause test that is previously noted. If an intervening event is unforeseen, and unforeseeable, it may break the chain of causation between the wrongful act and injury.

Contributory and comparative negligence

Did the plaintiff contribute to his injuries in some way? The Restatement (Second) of Torts, Section 463 notes that contributory negligence is conduct on the part of the plaintiff which falls below the standard to which he should conform for his own protection, and which is a legally contributing cause cooperating with the negligence of the defendant in bringing about the plaintiff's harm. Section 467 goes on to note that except where the defendant has the last clear chance, the plaintiff's contributory negligence bars recovery against a defendant whose negligent conduct would otherwise make him liable to the plaintiff for the harm sustained by him.

Many jurisdictions have replaced contributory negligence with comparative negligence where the trier of fact compares the negligence of the plaintiff, if any, to the negligence of the defendant, if any, and assigns a percentage to each.

Some jurisdictions utilize "pure" comparative negligence, in which case a plaintiff may recover even if his fault is greater than that of the defendant. Other jurisdictions utilize a form of comparative negligence where, if the plaintiff's negligence equals or exceeds the defendants, the plaintiff is barred from recovery. This concept is discussed further below.

Product Liability

The Restatement (Second) of Torts Section 402(A)(1) states:

One who sells any product in a defective condition unreasonably dangerous to the user or consumer or to his property is subject to liability for physical harm thereby caused to the ultimate user or consumer, or to his property, if

a. the seller is engaged in the business of selling such a product, and
b. it is expected to and does reach the end user or consumer without substantial change in the condition in which it was sold.

As one court observed, "[t]he liability imposed by section 402A is special liability limited to manufacturers and distributors engaged in the business of selling the product in question."[38]

[38] *Griffin Indus. v. Jones*, 975 S.W.2d 100, 102 (Ky. 1998).

Public Policy

The policy underpinnings supporting imposition of strict liability on product manufacturers and suppliers include:

i. Placing the cost of injuries caused by defective products on the manufacturer who is in a better position to pass the true product cost on to all distributors, retailers, and consumers of the product;
ii. Relieving the injured plaintiff of the onerous burden of establishing the manufacturer's negligence;
iii. Providing a full chain of supply protection; and
iv. In the interest of fairness, providing relief against the manufacturer who — while perhaps innocent of negligence — cast the defective product into the stream of commerce and profited thereby.[39]

The Restatement (Third) of Torts, Section 1 (1998)

The Restatement (Third) of Torts, unlike the Restatement (Second), recognizes the difference between manufacturing, design, or warning cases.

Section 1 notes "One engaged in the business of selling or otherwise distributing products who sells or distributes a defective product is subject to liability for harm to persons or property caused by the defect."

Section 2 Categories of Product Defect

A product is defective when, at the time of sale or distribution, it contains a manufacturing defect, is defective in design, or is defective because of inadequate instructions or warnings. A product:

a. Contains a manufacturing defect when the product departs from its intended design even though all possible care was exercised in the preparation and marketing of the product;
b. Is defective in design when the foreseeable risks of harm posed by the product could have been reduced or avoided by the adoption of a reasonable alternative design by the seller or other distributor, or a predecessor in the commercial chain of distribution, and the omission of the alternative design renders the product not *reasonably* safe;

[39] *Brooks v. Beech Aircraft Corp.*, 902 P.2d 54, 57–58 (1995).

c. Is defective because of inadequate instructions or warnings when the foreseeable risks of harm posed by the product could have been reduced or avoided by the provision of reasonable instructions or warnings by the seller or other distributor, or a predecessor in the commercial chain of distribution, and the omission of the instructions or warnings renders the product not *reasonably* safe.

Generally, a manufacturer, seller, or lessor of goods may be held liable for harm or damage if a product was defective. Any such lawsuit may be based on a variety of theories, including:

1. Negligence;
2. Misrepresentation;
3. Strict Liability;
4. Breach of Warranty.

Product Liability Based on Negligence

As noted previously, negligence involves:

1. A duty owed;
2. A breach of that duty;
3. Causation; and
4. Injury or death.

If a manufacturer breaches their duty in the creation or marketing of a product and the product causes an injury, death, or damage, the basis of product liability is negligence. The duty of due care extends to every facet of the creation of a product including the:

1. Design;
2. Materials selected;
3. Production;
4. Assembly;
5. Testing;
6. Adequacy of the instructions and warnings;
7. Quality of materials and components from outside suppliers; and
8. Marketing of its products.

Product Liability Based on Misrepresentation

The misrepresentation may be either intentional or fraudulent, or negligent. When a misrepresentation has been made to a user or consumer, whether intentional or not, and that misrepresentation results in an injury or death, the basis of liability may be the tort of fraud. Examples of misrepresentation include intentional mislabeling; or intentional concealment of a defect, danger, or hazard. However, in order to rise to the level of a misrepresentation, as noted previously, the misrepresentation must be:

1. Of a material fact;
2. With an intent to induce the buyer's reliance; and
3. The buyer's justifiable reliance on the misrepresentation.

And, in the case of fraudulent misrepresentation, it must include an intent on the part of the defendant.

The Requirements for Product Liability

The Restatement Section 388 Chattel Known to Be Dangerous for Intended Use states, "One who supplies directly or through a third person a chattel for another to use is subject to liability to those whom the supplier should expect to use the chattel with the consent of the other or to be endangered by its probable use, for physical harm caused by the use of the chattel in the manner for which and by a person for whose use it is supplied, if the supplier

a. knows or has reason to know that the chattel is or is likely to be dangerous for the use for which it is supplied, and
b. has no reason to believe that those for whose use the chattel is supplied will realize its dangerous condition, and
c. fails to exercise reasonable care to inform them of its dangerous condition or of the facts which make it likely to be dangerous."

Comment C notes that "suppliers," as used in Section 388, is intended to be broad in scope and seems to extend to any who had possession or control over the chattel.

Even broader is the protection specified by Restatement Section 324A, that states,

> One who undertakes, gratuitously or for consideration, to render services to another which he should recognize as necessary for the protection of a third person or his things, is subject to liability to the third person for physical harm resulting from his failure to exercise reasonable care to protect his undertaking, if
>
> (a) his failure to exercise reasonable care increases the risk of such harm, or
>
> (b) he has undertaken to perform a duty owed by the other to the third person, or
>
> (c) the harm is suffered because of reliance of the other or the third person upon the undertaking.

Generally, if a product was sold without a defect and subsequently altered or modified, creating a defect, the manufacturer, seller, or lessor may not be strictly liable. However, courts have severely restricted this defense and it may not be available at all if a plaintiff is able to demonstrate foreseeability. If a product was modified or altered in a way that is foreseeable to a reasonable manufacturer, thus creating a dangerous condition, the manufacturer has two options:

1. Design out the risk of modification;
2. Provide a warning about the risk of modification.

The first option is usually far superior since warnings may not make it to the original purchaser, may not be read by the purchaser and may not be provided by the original purchaser to subsequent purchasers or users.[40]

Unreasonably Dangerous Products

The Restatement (Second) of Torts Section 388 imposes a duty to warn of dangers that are known or that should reasonably be known. Section 402A imposes liability for unreasonably dangerous products. In addition, there is a difference in approach depending on whether the lawsuit is based on

---

[40] See, for example, *Johnson v. Medtronic, Inc.*, 365 S.W.3d 226 (2012), where a court noted that "...a manufacturer may be held liable where it chooses to warn of the danger... rather than preclude the danger by design." In the case a physician used a defibrillator improperly because he failed to read the instructions.

negligence of the manufacturer, or strict liability. In a lawsuit based on strict liability the critical issue is the product itself. In a negligence case the critical issue is the conduct of the manufacturer.[41]

Section 388 established a three-part test that must be met to impose liability on the part of the manufacturer. Section 388(a) specifies that the plaintiff must first establish that the supplier knew or had reason to know that the product was likely to be dangerous for its intended uses, including reasonably foreseeable misuses.

While the section does not expressly cover the subject of misuses, comment (e) appears to equate the intended use of a product with a use that the manufacturer should *reasonably expect.* Therefore, it appears to establish a manufacturer's duty to warn that includes reasonably foreseeable misuse of a product.

Section 388(b) requires a finding that the manufacturer had no reason to know that expected users of the product will realize its dangerous condition. Therefore, where a danger is obvious or where the user of a product has knowledge of a product's characteristics that is equal to or superior to that of the manufacturer or seller, a manufacturer may escape liability. The last part of the test is Section 388(c) that requires a manufacturer to exercise reasonable care to inform users of product dangers. To determine whether a manufacturer has used reasonable care, comment (n) sets forth a balancing test that relies on a number of factors. The factors are:

1. The dangerous condition of the product;
2. The purpose for which the product is used;
3. The form of any warnings given;
4. The reliability of the third parties as conduits of necessary information about the product;
5. The magnitude of the risk involved; and
6. The burdens imposed on the supplier by requiring that he directly warn all users.

The Restatement (Second) of Torts, Section 402A provides that:

1. One who sells any product in a defective condition unreasonably dangerous to the user or consumer or to his property is subject to liability

[41] *Lance v. Wyeth*, 85 A.3d 434, 458 (2014).

for physical harm thereby caused to the ultimate user or consumer, or his property if:

a. The seller is engaged in the business of selling such a product, and
b. It is expected to and does reach the user or consumer without substantial change in the condition in which it is sold.

Thus, a product may be defective in one of three ways:

1. Its design;
2. Its manufacture; and/or
3. Its lack of an adequate warning.

To recover under Section 402(A), a plaintiff must establish that:

1. The product was defective;
2. The defect was a proximate cause of the plaintiff's injuries; and
3. The defect causing the injury existed at the time the product left the seller's hands.[42]

A product may be unreasonably dangerous as a result of

1. a manufacturing defect — that is, a physical defect in the individual product itself,
2. a defect in the product's design, or
3. the manufacturer's failure to warn of a known danger associated with the product or to instruct the consumer on the proper use of the product.

A manufacturing defect occurs when one unit in a product line is defective, whereas a design defect occurs when the specific unit conforms to the intended design but the intended design itself renders the product unreasonably dangerous.

A court may use two different approaches to determine whether a product is unreasonably dangerous:

1. The consumer expectations test; or
2. The risk-utility test.

---

[42] *McPeak v. Direct Outdoor Products, LLC.*, 2022 WL 4369966.

The consumer expectations test asks whether the product is dangerous to an extent beyond that which would be contemplated by the ordinary consumer who purchases it, with the ordinary knowledge common to the community as to its characteristics. The risk-utility test balances the magnitude of the danger against the utility of the product, as designed.[43]

Under the risk-utility test, a product may be defective if a reasonable person would conclude that the probability and seriousness of the harm caused by the product outweigh the burden or costs of taking precautions.[44] Factors to consider as part of the risk-utility test are:

1. The usefulness and desirability of the product — its utility to the user and to the public as a whole.
2. The safety aspects of the product — the likelihood that it will cause injury, and the probable seriousness of the injury.
3. The availability of a substitute product which would meet the same need and not be as unsafe.
4. The manufacturer's ability to eliminate the unsafe character of the product without impairing its usefulness or making it too expensive to maintain its utility.
5. The user's ability to avoid danger by the exercise of care in the use of the product.[45]
6. The user's anticipated awareness of the dangers inherent in the product and their availability, because of general public knowledge of the obvious condition of the product, or of the existence of suitable warnings or instructions.
7. The feasibility, on the part of the manufacturer, of spreading the loss by setting the price of the product or carrying liability insurance.

Under the consumer expectation standard, the product is in a defective condition if the danger is unknowable and unacceptable to the average or ordinary consumer.[46]

---

[43] *Ibid.*, at 407.

[44] *Igwe v. Skaggs*, 258 F.Supp.3d 596 (2017).

[45] *Ibid.*

[46] *Ibid.*

Inadequate Warnings

Comment (j) to Section 402A notes that where a warning is given, the seller may reasonably assume that it will be read and heeded; and a product bearing such a warning, which is safe for use if it is followed, is not in a defective condition, nor is it unreasonably dangerous.

Generally, a manufacturer is required to provide an adequate warning of any danger inherent in the normal use of its product which is not within the knowledge of or obvious to the ordinary user. In assessing what hazards are foreseeable, a manufacture is held to a higher standard, that of an expert. If the trier of fact determines that the inherent danger in the product is not obvious, and that the consumer is not trained to know or is not aware of the danger, then the warning, or lack thereof, must be scrutinized.[47]

Thus, where a manufacturer has reason to anticipate that danger may result from a particular use of his product, but fails to provide an adequate warning of such a danger, the product is considered defective. Even where a product is designed and manufactured without fault or danger, it is unreasonably dangerous to place it in commerce without adequate warnings concerning its safe and proper use.[48]

Therefore, when a duty to warn arises, an adequate warning must, at a minimum,

1. be designed to reasonably catch the consumer's attention,
2. be comprehensible and give a fair indication of the specific risks attendant to the use of the product, and
3. be of sufficient intensity justified by the magnitude of the risk. The warnings must communicate adequately any dangers that may result from the product's use or foreseeable misuse. This presents a challenge to manufacturers that manufacture products marketed to minors, although the product itself may be purchased by an adult. It also presents a challenge to manufacturers in other situations.

---

[47] *Hix v. Zimmer Biomet Holdings, Inc.*, 2022 WL 946914.

[48] *Ibid.*

Defenses

The Learned Intermediary

Perhaps most commonly arising in a lawsuit that alleges a lack of an adequate warning involving medication prescribed by a physician, a drug manufacturer may be immune from liability to a patient taking the manufacturer's drug so long as the manufacturer has provided the patient's doctor with all relevant safety information for that drug. The learned intermediary doctrine recognizes that the physician is in the best position to warn the consumer of a given medication's risks.[49]

Unavoidably Unsafe Products

Some products, such as gasoline, are unavoidably unsafe and cannot be made safe. For example, California Civil Code Section 1714.45 states, in part:

a. In a product liability action, a manufacturer or seller shall not be liable if both of the following apply:
    1. The product is inherently unsafe and the product is known to be unsafe by the ordinary consumer who consumes the product with the ordinary knowledge common to the community.
    2. The product is a common consumer product intended for personal consumption, such as sugar, castor oil, alcohol, and butter, as identified in comment (i) to Section 402A of the Restatement (Second) of Torts.

b. This section does not exempt the manufacture or sale of tobacco products by tobacco manufacturers and their successors in interest from product liability actions, but does exempt the sale or distribution of tobacco products by any other person, including, but not limited to, retailers or distributors.

According to comment (g) to Section 402A, a defective condition is one not contemplated by the ultimate consumer, which will be unreasonably dangerous to him. Comment (i), defining "unreasonably dangerous," states "'The article sold must be dangerous to an extent beyond that which would be contemplated by the ordinary consumer who

---

[49] *Ibid.*

purchases it, with the ordinary knowledge common to the community as to its characteristics." Examples given in comment (i) note that innocuous products such as sugar and butter, unless contaminated, do not give rise to a strict liability claim merely because the former may be harmful to a diabetic or the latter may aggravate the blood cholesterol level of a person with heart disease. Presumably, such dangers are squarely within the contemplation of the ordinary consumer. The "unreasonably dangerous" qualification was added to foreclose the possibility that the manufacturer of a product with inherent possibilities for harm, such as, but not limited to, butter, drugs, whiskey, and automobiles, would become automatically responsible for all the harm that such things do in the world.[50]

Section 402A comment (k) also addresses unavoidably unsafe products and notes:

> There are some products which, in the present state of human knowledge, are quite incapable of being made safe for their intended and ordinary use. These are especially common in the field of drugs. An outstanding example is the vaccine for the Pasteur treatment of rabies, which not uncommonly leads to very serious and damaging consequences when it is injected. Since the disease itself invariably leads to a dreadful death, both the marketing and the use of the vaccine are fully justified, notwithstanding the unavoidable high degree of risk which they involve. Such a product, properly prepared, and accompanied by proper directions and warning, is not defective, nor is it unreasonably dangerous. The same is true of many other drugs, vaccines, and the like, many of which for this very reason cannot legally be sold except to physicians, or under the prescription of a physician. It is also true in particular of many new or experimental drugs as to which, because of lack of time and opportunity for sufficient medical experience, there can be no assurance of safety, or perhaps even of purity of ingredients, but such experience as there is justifies the marketing and use of the drug notwithstanding a medically recognizable risk. The seller of such products, again with the qualification that they are properly prepared and marketed, and proper warning is given, where the situation calls for it, is not to be held to strict liability for unfortunate consequences attending their use, merely because he has

[50] Prosser, Strict Liability to the Consumer in California (1966) 18 Hastings L.J. 9, 23.

> undertaken to supply the public with an apparently useful and desirable product, attended with a known but apparently reasonable risk.

Section 402A establishes strict liability for anyone who sells any product in a defective condition unreasonably dangerous to the user or consumer, and comment (k) provides an exception for unavoidably unsafe products even where a product is inherently dangerous by nature but is still desirable because of its public benefit. However, all of the requirements of Section 402A must be met in order for the exemption from strict liability to apply.[51] And, as comment (k) notes, the exemption is not available to a manufacturer who fails to provide an adequate warning.

French Law

In France, as well as the European Union, the source of law on the subject of product liability is found in the European Union's directive, 85/374/EEC, as found in the French Civil Code, Book II, Title III, Subtitle II, Chapter II: Liability for Defective Products (Articles 1245–1245-17). Section 1245-2 has a broad definition of a "product" and notes that a product, "Is… any movable property, even if it is incorporated in a building, including the products of the soil, breeding, hunting and fishing. Electricity is considered a product." And, the Ministry of Justice, in response to a question submitted by a Member of Parliament, advised that software also qualifies as a "product." The relevant portions of the French Civil Code go on to note:

> Item 1245:
>
> The producer is liable for damage caused by a defect in his product, whether or not he is bound by a contract with the victim.
>
> Section 1245-3:
>
> A product is defective within the meaning of this chapter when it does not offer the security that can legitimately be expected. In assessing the safety that can legitimately be expected, account must be taken of all the

[51] *Taylor v. Intuitive Surgical, Inc.*, 187 Wash.2d 743, 760–761 (2017).

circumstances and in particular the presentation of the product, the use that can reasonably be expected of it and the time of its use.

A product cannot be considered defective by the mere fact that another, more perfected one, has subsequently been put into circulation.

Section 1245-4:

A product is put into circulation when the producer voluntarily disposes of it.

A product is only put into circulation once.

Section 1245-5:

A producer, when acting in a professional capacity, is the manufacturer of a finished product, the producer of a raw material, the manufacturer of a component part. Any person acting in a professional capacity is assimilated to a producer for the purposes of this chapter.

1. Who presents himself as a producer by affixing his name, trademark, or other distinctive sign to the product;
2. Who imports a product into the European Community with a view to sale, rental, with or without promise of sale, or any other form of distribution.

Thus, under French law, the producer of the finished product, the provider of the raw materials or the provider of a component part may be liable, depending on the nature of the claimed defect. Section 1245-5 also provides for certain exceptions to the noted rules as specified in articles 1702 to 1792-6 and 1646-1.

Section 1245-6:

If the producer cannot be identified, the seller, the lessor, with the exception of the financial lessor or the lessor assimilated to the financial lessor, or any other professional supplier, is responsible for the lack of safety of the product, under the same conditions, than the producer, unless he designates his own supplier or the producer, within three months from the date on which the victim's request was notified to him.

The recourse of the supplier against the producer obeys the same rules as the claim emanating from the direct victim of the defect. However, he must act within one year of the date of his summons.

Section 1245-7:

In the event of damage caused by the defect of a product incorporate into another, the producer of the component part and the person who carried out the incorporation are jointly and severally liable.

Section 1245-8:

The plaintiff must prove the damage, the defect and the causal link between the defect and the damage.

Section 1245-9:

The producer may be liable for the defect even though the product has been manufactured in accordance with the rules of the art or existing standards or has been the subject of an administrative authorization.

Section 1245-10 specifies five defenses that are available, noting, The producer is fully liable unless he proves:

1. That he had not put the product into circulation;
2. That, taking into account the circumstances, it is necessary to consider that the defect having caused the damage did not exist at the time when the product was put into circulation by him or that this defect arose subsequently;
3. That the product was not intended for sale or any other form of distribution;
4. That the state of scientific and technical knowledge, at the time when he put the product into circulation, did not allow the existence of the defect to be detected;
5. Or that the defect is due to the conformity of the product with mandatory rules of a legislative or regulatory nature.

The producer of the component part is also not liable if he establishes that the defect is attributable to the design of the product in which this part has been incorporated or to the instructions given by the producer of this product.

Section 1245-11:

> The producer cannot invoke the cause of exemption provided for in 4. of article 1245-10 when the damage was caused by an element of the human body or by products derived from it.

Articles 1245-15 and 1245-16 establish a statute of limitations, as well as a statute of repose. Article 1245-15 provides, "Save for fault on the part of the producer, the latter's liability, based on the provisions of this chapter, is extinguished ten years after the marketing of the very product which caused the damage unless, during this period, the victim has initiated legal action."

Article 1245-16 specifies that, "The action for compensation based on the provisions of this chapter is prescribed within a period of three years from the date on which the plaintiff had or should have had knowledge of the damage, the defect and the identity of the producer." Therefore, an action must be brought within three years of the date the injured party knew, or should have known of the defect, the identity of the producer and the existence of the lawsuit. Any action must be brought within ten years after the product was placed on the market.

Pursuant to Section 1231-1 of the French Civil Code, a party to a contract is also obligated to deliver a product that is free of defects and may face liability for a breach of that obligation. And, pursuant to Item 1641 a seller is liable for a defect, although not apparent at the time of sale, if it renders a product unfit for its intended purposes, or reduces its usefulness to such an extent that the buyer either:

1. Would not have acquired it; or
2. Would not have paid the same price had the buyer been aware of the defect.

Defenses to Product Liability

Many of the defenses that are aforementioned are also available in the case of a lawsuit based on product liability. In addition, and as noted earlier, a plaintiff is expected to meet certain requirements, for example, those established by the Restatement. A plaintiff that is unable to meet all of the requirements may be unable to proceed with a lawsuit. Thus, if a lawsuit is based on a claim of negligence, the plaintiff must be all the requirements that were noted previously. That is, the plaintiff must establish that he was owed a duty, the manufacturer breached the duty, that as a result of the breach there was causation and injury. If the plaintiff is unable to prove any one of those elements that plaintiff's lawsuit may fail.

Assumption of Risk

This defense takes several forms. Generally, the most common form, at least with regard to sporting events or activities[52] where the risk of injury is inherent in the event, is primary assumption of the risk where a defendant must establish that:

1. The plaintiff had actual knowledge of the danger; and
2. Voluntarily proceeded knowing the danger.[53]

The result is that the defendant is relieved of legal duty to the plaintiff; and being under no duty, he cannot be charged with negligence.[54] Primary assumption of risk is a complete bar to recovery.[55] Other forms include express assumption of the risk which arises where an injured party expressly agreed (either verbally, in writing, or by action) to a known risk and secondary assumption of the risk where a defendant owes a duty of care to the plaintiff but the plaintiff proceeds to encounter a known risk created by the defendant's breach of duty.

Assumption of the risk may arise in a variety of ways. For instance, when an individual signs an express waiver of liability, he promises not to exercise the right to sue for harm caused in the future by the wrongful behavior of a potential defendant, eliminating a remedy for wrongdoing.[56] Thus, the potential plaintiff agrees not to expect the potential defendant to act carefully, thus eliminating the potential defendant's duty of care, and acknowledging the possibility of negligent wrongdoing. Such agreements

[52] *Wattenbarger v. Cincinnati Reds, Inc.*, 28 Cal. App. 4th 746 (1994).

[53] *Knight v. Jewett*, 3 Cal. 4th 296, 301 (1992).

[54] Prosser & Keeton on Torts [(5th ed. 1984)] Section 68, pp. 480–481, fn. omitted, second italics added.) (*Knight v. Jewett*, 3 Cal. 4th 296, 338 (1992).

[55] *Ibid.*, at 314–315.

[56] *Coates v. Newhall Land & Farming, Inc.*, 191 Cal. App, 3d 1,7 (1987)

permit behavior that normally would be actionable as tortious, although an express assumption of risk goes further, more clearly authorizing this behavior.[57]

There are, however, limitations. For example, an agreement made in the context of sports or recreational programs or services may only serve as a bar to liability based on negligence. A release that attempts to release liability for future gross negligence or intentional conduct generally is unenforceable as a matter of public policy.[58]

French Law

French law, Civil Code Section 1245-14 places a restriction on the use of such limitations and notes, "Clauses that aim to exclude or limit liability for defective products are prohibited and deemed unwritten. However, for damage caused to goods which are not used by the victim mainly for his private use or consumption, the clauses stipulated between professionals are valid."

Another principle that may reduce a plaintiff's recovery is comparative negligence, as previously noted. Comparative negligence in America compares the negligence, or fault, of the defendant, if any, to the negligence of the plaintiff, if any, and reduces the award to the plaintiff by the percentage of fault that is attributable to the plaintiff. There are two basic kinds of comparative negligence in America: "Pure" comparative negligence that apportions liability in direct proportion to fault in all cases, and another that applies apportionment based on fault up to the point at which the plaintiff's negligence is equal to or greater than that of the defendant — when that point is reached, plaintiff is barred from recovery.[59]

French Law, Civil Code Section 1245-12 is similar to American comparative negligence and states, "The producer's liability may be reduced or eliminated, taking into account all the circumstances, when the damage is caused jointly by a defect in the product and by the fault of the victim or of a person for whom the victim is responsible." Thus, if an injury is due to the actions of a third-party under the claimant's control, such as employees, the producer's liability may be reduced or eliminated. For third parties that are not under the claimant's control that cause

[57] *Ibid.*, at 7–8.

[58] *City of Santa Barbara v. Superior Court*, 41 Cal. 4th at 751 (2007).

[59] *Li v. Yellow Cab Co.*, 13 Cal. 3d 804, 827 (1975).

or contribute to an injury, Section 1245-13 specifies that the producer retains liability, although the producer may seek indemnity from the third-party.

Other Defenses

Statute of Limitation

A statute of limitations establishes a time frame within which a lawsuit must be filed. In the United States, the statute of limitations for a personal injury or death may be established by statute. For example, in California, the statute of limitations for "an action assault, battery, or injury to, or for the death of, an individual caused by the wrongful act or neglect of another" is two years.[60]

French Law, Civil Code Section 1245-16 specifies, "The action for compensation based on the provisions of this chapter is prescribed within a period of three years from the date on which the plaintiff had or should have had knowledge of the damage, the defect and the identity of the producer."

Statute of Repose

A statute of repose places a time limit on claims from the date of sale or manufacture of a product.

As previously noted, French Law, Civil Code Section 1245-15 establishes a statute of repose and notes, "Save for fault on the part of the producer, the latter's liability, based on the provisions of this chapter, is extinguished ten years after the marketing of the very product which caused the damage unless, during this period, the victim has initiated legal action." Section 1245-17 goes on to note, "The provisions of this chapter do not affect the rights which the victim of damage may claim under the law of contractual or extra-contractual liability or under a special liability regime. The producer remains responsible for the consequences of his fault and that of the persons for whom he answers."

---

[60]California Code of Civil Procedure Section 335.1.

European Tort Law

The United States has 52 separate court systems. And, while those legal systems are generally based on the common law, there are still differences among those court systems. The differences in Europe may be even more pronounced than those in America. There is a significant difference between the common law of England and Ireland, and continental civil law systems. Although at least partly based on Roman law, the countries of the European Union have been independent for centuries and their legal systems reflect that independence.

There are a variety of agreements in place that address a variety of subjects. For instance, The Hague Convention on the Law Applicable to Traffic Accidents[61] specifies that where two or more vehicles are involved the law of the place of the accident must be applied.[62] Whether family members may be entitled to recover for the death of a relative in a traffic accident, generally referred to as emotional distress in the United States, may depend on the particular country in which they reside.[63]

The European Group on Tort Law[64] created the Principles on European Tort Law.[65]

The group meets regularly to discuss fundamental issues of tort law liability as well as recent developments and the future directions of the law of tort. The Group has drafted a collection of *Principles of European Tort Law* (PETL) similar to the Principles of European Contract Law drafted by the European Contract Law Commission (Lando Commission). The Group cooperates with the European Centre of Tort and Insurance Law in Vienna. Within the framework of this cooperation, the Group presented the Principles in a public conference on May 19 and 20, 2005, in Vienna. Additionally, the Group is supported by the Institute for European Tort Law (also established in Vienna).

---

[61] Convention of 4 May 1971 on the Law Applicable to Traffic Accidents.

[62] Article 3. https://www.hcch.net/en/instruments/conventions/full-text/?cid=81.

[63] *Ibid.*, Article 8.

[64] http://www.egtl.org/index.html.

[65] http://www.egtl.org/petl.html.

The American Law Institute[66] notes it was created to, among other goals, "... promote the clarification and simplification of the law and its better adaptation to social needs, to secure the better administration of justice and to encourage and carry on scholarly and scientific legal work." One of the Committee's suggestions was for a Restatement of the Law that "should not only be to help make certain much that is now uncertain and to simplify unnecessary complexities, but also to promote those changes which will tend better to adapt the laws to the needs of life." A Restatement should be critical and constructive, and although largely based on statutes and decisions, "it should not be confined to examining and setting forth the law applicable to those situations which have been the subject of court action or statutory regulation, but should also take account of situations not yet discussed by courts or dealt with by legislatures...."[67]

[66] https://www.ali.org/about-ali/faq/.

[67] https://www.ali.org/about-ali/story-line/.

Chapter 6

Criminal Law

Abstract

Criminal law exists to protect both individuals and businesses. For every crime there is probably a corresponding tort. The reverse is not necessarily true, depending on whether the tort is intentional or not. Although intentional torts may rise to the level of a crime, negligent torts ordinarily do not. Our legal system offers numerous constitutional protections for those accused of a crime. The Fourth Amendment governs the issue of search warrants. The Fifth Amendment allows a criminal defendant protection from self-incrimination. Although that applies to individuals and maybe sole proprietorships, but not other forms of business, such as a corporation. A defendant in a civil matter has no such protection. Our criminal justice system may require a unanimous jury as well as a higher standard of proof, beyond a reasonable doubt, in order to convict a defendant of a crime. In many situations a prosecutor must also prove that a criminal defendant had both a guilty mind (*mens rea*) as well as a guilty act (*actus reus*), and they may need to occur concurrently in order for a crime to be committed. A business may be held liable for crimes committed by their employees "in the course and scope of their employment." For a conviction, the prosecution must ordinarily prove that the business could have prevented the crime, or that a supervisor approved or knew of the criminal act. That is why it is important that a business do a "reasonable" background check before hiring an employee, and adequately monitor their employees.

Introduction

Unlike Europe, criminal law in the United States did not arise from criminal codes. This resulted in a significant departure from the existing thought. As one commentator noted,

> Rather than concern themselves with the threat of punishment, American reformers pragmatically proceeded directly to reform the punishment itself. In the new field of corrections ... As a French resident of Philadelphia noted admiringly in 1796, 'the attempt at an almost entire abolition of the punishment of death, and the substitution of a system of reason and justice, to that of bonds, ill-treatment, and arbitrary punishment, was never made but in America.' As early as 1776, Thomas Jefferson had drafted a bill for the Virginia legislature that called for punishment based on the theory of prevention outlined by Cesare Beccaria and developed by Jeremy Bentham. The final two decades of the eighteenth century brought the establishment of solitary confinement prisons in Philadelphia and then in New York and other states, including Virginia. 1823 saw the opening of the prison in Auburn, New York, to which visitors flocked from around the world, including Alexis de Tocqueville.[1]

The Constitution

The U.S. Constitution gives the primary responsibility to impose criminal sanctions to the states under their "police" power that is far broader than simply criminal prosecution and that derives, in part, from the Tenth Amendment.[2] The federal government's jurisdiction over criminal matters is generally limited to offenses especially related to federal interests, such as crimes that are committed on property that is exclusively within the jurisdiction of the federal government, such as military bases, crimes against certain federal officers, and crimes that involve conduct in more than one state that is difficult for a single state to effectively prosecute, such as drug and organized crime offenses.[3]

---

[1] Paul H. Robinson and Markus D. Dubber, The American Model Penal Code: A Brief Overview, 10 *New Crim. L. Rev*., 319 (2007) 319, 320 (footnotes omitted).

[2] See e.g., *United States v. Lopez*, 514 U.S. 549 (1995). The federal government has no police power and must rely on, for instance, Article I, Section 8 of the Constitution, commonly referred to as the Commerce Clause to regulate criminal law.

[3] *Ibid.*

As a result, most crimes are addressed by the laws of the 50 states or the District of Columbia.[4]

The States

With 50 different states, the District of Columbia as well as the federal government, the United States has 52 criminal codes. While there are differences, there are also common elements, at least in part thanks to the American Law Institute's Model Penal Code (MPC or "the code") that was issued in 1962.

The Model Penal Code

As one scholarly article noted, The Model Penal Code "…was specifically designed to wrest the criminal law out of the hands of the judiciary which, after centuries of common-law making, had left the criminal law an unprincipled mess."[5]

Following the issuance of the MPC, a considerable number of states' criminal codes underwent significant reforms and are based on the MPC.[6] While the MPC represented a notable change, not all aspects of the MPC have been adopted by the states. For instance, the code allowed far greater sentencing discretion within each offense grade, allowing a judge broad discretion to craft the punishment something that French law seeks to avoid and for good reason. While the code sought to remove judicial discretion in some areas, it encouraged it in others.

---

[4] *Ibid.*, at 320.

[5] *Ibid.*, at 332.

[6] As noted by Markus and Dubber, *id.* at 326, new codes were enacted in Illinois, effective in 1962; Minnesota and New Mexico in 1963; New York in 1967; Georgia in 1969; Kansas in 1970; Connecticut in 1971; Colorado and Oregon in 1972; Delaware, Hawaii, New Hampshire, Pennsylvania, and Utah in 1973; Montana, Ohio, and Texas in 1974; Florida, Kentucky, North Dakota, and Virginia in 1975; Arkansas, Maine, and Washington in 1976; South Dakota and Indiana in 1977; Arizona and Iowa in 1978; Missouri, Nebraska, and New Jersey in 1979; Alabama and Alaska in 1980; and Wyoming in 1983. All of these 34 enactments were influenced in some part by the Model Penal Code. Draft criminal codes produced in other states, such as California, Massachusetts, Michigan, Oklahoma, Rhode Island, Tennessee, Vermont, and West Virginia, did not pass legislative review and may yet be revived.

The federal United States Sentencing Commission is a result of the significant disparities that resulted from the exercise of discretion by judges.[7] As the commission's website notes, it "... was created by Congress in 1984 to reduce sentencing disparities and promote transparency and proportionality in sentencing." In addition, as noted by one commentator,

> discretion increases the potential for abuse by a biased decision-maker. Discretion undercuts predictability, which is important for both effective deterrence and fair notice. Finally, discretion shifts the criminalization and punishment decisions away from the legislative branch and to the less democratic judicial and executive branches of government...[8]

Where Criminal Law and Civil Law Intersect

For every crime there is likely to be a civil equivalent, a tort, although the reverse may not be true. This is particularly true for intentional, not negligent, torts. And the MPC recognizes that civil remedies are unaffected. Thus, Section 3.01 notes that although justification may be an affirmative defense for someone charged with a crime. However, "... conduct [that] is justifiable under this Article does not abolish or impair any remedy for such conduct that is available in any civil action."

For business this raises a significant issue. The potential for criminal prosecution and civil lawsuits based on tort are, arguably, the most important reason a company must:

1. Do an adequate background check before hiring an employee;
2. Properly supervise and monitor employees;
3. Monitor and prevent unlawful, dangerous, or negligent actions in the workplace.

Categories of Crimes

Similar to French law, the MPC, Section 1.04(1) has several categories of crimes and notes, "An offense defined by this Code or by any other

[7] www.ussc.gov.
[8] *Ibid.*, at 328.

statute of this State, for which a sentence of [death or of] imprisonment is authorized, constitutes a crime. Crimes are classified as felonies, misdemeanors, petty misdemeanors."

Felonies

The MPC, Section 1.04(2) notes that a crime is a felony if it is so designated in this Code or if persons convicted thereof may be sentenced [to death or] to imprisonment for a term that, apart from an extended term, is in excess of one year.

Misdemeanors

MPC Section 1.04(3) notes that a crime is a misdemeanor if it is so designated in this Code or in a statute other than this Code enacted subsequent thereto.

MPC Section 1.04(4) notes that a crime is a petty misdemeanor if it is so designated in this Code or in a statute other than this Code enacted subsequent thereto or if it is defined by a statute other than this Code that now provides that persons convicted thereof may be sentenced to imprisonment for a term of which the maximum is less than one year.

MPC Sections 1.04(5) and 2.05 also note an "offense," called a "violation," that is referred to as "absolute liability," and that arises "…if no other sentence than a fine, or fine and forfeiture or other civil penalty is authorized…"

The French Penal Code

Article 111-1

> Criminal offenses are classified, according to their seriousness, into crimes, misdemeanors and contraventions.

Criminal Liability of a Business Entity

Section 2.07 of the MPC notes the situations where a business incurs criminal liability:

> (1) A corporation may be convicted of the commission of an offense if:
>
> (a) the offense is a violation or the offense is defined by a statute other than the Code in which a legislative purpose to impose liability on corporations plainly appears and the conduct is performed by an agent of the corporation acting in behalf of the corporation within the scope of his office or employment, except that if the law defining the offense designates the agents for whose conduct the corporation is accountable or the circumstances under which it is accountable, such provisions shall apply; or
>
> (b) the offense consists of an omission to discharge a specific duty of affirmative performance imposed on corporations by law; or
>
> (c) the commission of the offense was authorized, requested, commanded, performed or recklessly tolerated by the board of directors or by a high managerial agent acting on behalf of the corporation within the scope of his office or employment.

An "agent" is defined broadly in the MPC to refer to "…any director, officer, servant, employee or other person authorized to act in behalf of the corporation or association and, in the case of an unincorporated association, a member of such association." And a "high managerial agent" refers to "…an officer of a corporation or an unincorporated association, or, in the case of a partnership, a partner, or any other agent of a corporation or association having duties of such responsibility that his conduct may fairly be assumed to represent the policy of the corporation or association."

In summary, a business may be liable for crimes committed by its agents and employees within the course and scope of their employment if the prosecutor can demonstrate that the business:

1. Could have prevented the act; or
2. That a supervisor authorized, knew, or should have known about the act.

Related to situations where a business may incur criminal liability is liability for the act of another. MPC Section 2.06 addresses this area and notes that:

1. A person is guilty of an offense if it is committed by his own conduct or by the conduct of another person for which he is legally accountable, or both.

2. A person is legally accountable for the conduct of another person when:
   a. acting with the kind of culpability that is sufficient for the commission of the offense, he causes an innocent or irresponsible person to engage in such conduct; or
   b. he is made accountable for the conduct of such other person by the Code or by the law defining the offense; or
   c. he is an accomplice of such other person in the commission of the offense.
3. A person is an accomplice of another person in the commission of an offense if:
   a. with the purpose of promoting or facilitating the commission of the offense, he
      i. solicits such other person to commit it, or
      ii. aids or agrees or attempts to aid such other person in planning or committing it, or
      iii. having a legal duty to prevent the commission of the offense, fails to make proper effort so to do; or
   b. his conduct is expressly declared by law to establish his complicity.
4. When causing a particular result is an element of an offense, an accomplice in the conduct causing such result is an accomplice in the commission of that offense if he acts with the kind of culpability, if any, with respect to that result that is sufficient for the commission of the offense.
5. A person who is legally incapable of committing a particular offense himself may be guilty thereof if it is committed by the conduct of another person for which he is legally accountable, unless such liability is inconsistent with the purpose of the provision establishing his incapacity.
6. Unless otherwise provided by the Code or by the law defining the offense, a person is not an accomplice in an offense committed by another person if:
   a. he is a victim of that offense; or
   b. the offense is so defined that his conduct is inevitably incident to its commission; or
   c. he terminates his complicity prior to the commission of the offense and
      i. wholly deprives it of effectiveness in the commission of the offense; or

   ii. gives timely warning to the law enforcement authorities or otherwise makes proper effort to prevent the commission of the offense.

7. An accomplice may be convicted on proof of the commission of the offense and of his complicity therein, though the person claimed to have committed the offense has not been prosecuted or convicted or has been convicted of a different offense or degree of offense or has an immunity to prosecution or conviction or has been acquitted.

French law is similar. While Article 121-1 notes, “No one is criminally responsible except for his own act” unsurprisingly, an exception exists. Section 121-2 goes on to note that legal persons, to the exclusion of the State, are criminally liable, according to the distinctions in Articles 121-4–121-7, for offenses committed on their behalf, by their bodies or representatives. The French Penal Code distinguishes between “natural” and “legal” persons, as does American law.

Territoriality

Although Section 1.03(1) of the MPC contains limitations, it notes that a person may be convicted in a wide variety of situations:

> … a person may be convicted under the law of this State of an offense committed by his own conduct or the conduct of another for which he is legally accountable if:
>
> (a) either the conduct that is an element of the offense or the result that is such an element occurs within this State; or
>
> (b) conduct occurring outside the State is sufficient under the law of this State to constitute an attempt to commit an offense within the State; or
>
> (c) conduct occurring outside the State is sufficient under the law of this State to constitute a conspiracy to commit an offense within the State and an overt act in furtherance of such conspiracy occurs within the State; or
>
> (d) conduct occurring within the State establishes complicity in the commission of, or an attempt, solicitation or conspiracy to commit, an offense in another jurisdiction that also is an offense under the law of this State; or

(e) the offense consists of the omission to perform a legal duty imposed by the law of this State with respect to domicile, residence or a relationship to a person, thing or transaction in the State; or

(f) the offense is based on a statute of this State that expressly prohibits conduct outside the State, when the conduct bears a reasonable relation to a legitimate interest of this State and the actor knows or should know that his conduct is likely to affect that interest.

French Law

Section 113-2:

French criminal law is applicable to offenses committed on the territory of the Republic.

The offense is deemed to have been committed on the territory of the Republic when one of its constitutive acts has taken place on this territory.

Section 113-2-1:

Any crime or misdemeanor carried out by means of an electronic communication network, when it is attempted or committed to the detriment of a natural person residing on the territory of the Republic or of a legal person whose head office is located on the territory of the Republic, is deemed to have been committed in the territory of the Republic.

Section 113-5:

French criminal law is applicable to anyone who is guilty on the territory of the Republic, as an accomplice, of a crime or misdemeanor committed abroad if the crime or misdemeanor is punished both by French law and by foreign law and if it has been established by a final decision of the foreign jurisdiction.

It is also applicable to the acts of complicity provided for in the second paragraph of Article 121-7 committed on the territory of the Republic and concerning, when they are committed abroad, the crimes provided for in Book II.

The Requirements for Criminal Liability

Most, but not all crimes require an act as well as a specific intent.

1. The *actus reus* (the guilty act): Section 2.01(1) of the MPC notes, "A person is not guilty of an offense unless his liability is based on conduct that includes a voluntary act or the omission to perform an act of which he is physically capable."
2. The *mens rea* (The guilty mind): Generally, this is referred to as the "intent" element. While the two requirements are perhaps outwardly simplistic, as the Supreme Court explained,[9] "Few areas of criminal law pose more difficulty than the proper definition of the *mens rea* required for any particular crime ... [a]t common law, crimes generally were classified as requiring either "general intent" or "specific intent." This venerable distinction, however, has been the source of a good deal of confusion. As one treatise explained:

"Sometimes 'general intent' is used in the same way as 'criminal intent' to mean the general notion of *mens rea,* while 'specific intent' is taken to mean the mental state required for a particular crime. Or, 'general intent' may be used to encompass all forms of the mental state requirement, while 'specific intent' is limited to the one mental state of intent. Another possibility is that 'general intent' will be used to characterize an intent to do something on an undetermined occasion, and 'specific intent' to denote an intent to do that thing at a particular time and place. (Citation omitted)."

This ambiguity has led to a movement away from the traditional dichotomy of intent and toward an alternative analysis of *mens rea.* (Citation omitted). This new approach, exemplified in the American Law Institute's Model Penal Code is based on two principles. First, the ambiguous and elastic term "intent" is replaced with a hierarchy of culpable states of mind. The different levels in this hierarchy are commonly identified, in descending order of culpability, as purpose, knowledge, recklessness, and negligence. (Citations omitted). Perhaps the most significant, and most esoteric, distinction drawn by this analysis is that between the mental states of "purpose" and "knowledge." As we pointed out, "a person who causes a particular result is said to act purposefully if 'he consciously

[9] *U.S. v. Bailey*, 444 U.S. 394, 403–404 (1979).

desires that result, whatever the likelihood of that result happening from his conduct,' while he is said to act knowingly if he is aware 'that that result is practically certain to follow from his conduct, whatever his desire may be as to that result.'"

In its opinion, the Supreme Court in Bailey referred to Section 2.02 of the MPC that notes:

> (1) … Except as provided in Section 2.05, a person is not guilty of an offense unless he acted purposely, knowingly, recklessly or negligently, as the law may require, with respect to each material element of the offense.
>
> (2) Kinds of Culpability Defined.
>
> (a) Purposely. A person acts purposely with respect to a material element of an offense when:
>
> (i) if the element involves the nature of his conduct or a result thereof, it is his conscious object to engage in conduct of that nature or to cause such a result; and
>
> (ii) if the element involves the attendant circumstances, he is aware of the existence of such circumstances or he believes or hopes that they exist.
>
> (b) Knowingly. A person acts knowingly with respect to a material element of an offense when:
>
> (i) if the element involves the nature of his conduct or the attendant circumstances, he is aware that his conduct is of that nature or that such circumstances exist; and
>
> (ii) if the element involves a result of his conduct, he is aware that it is practically certain that his conduct will cause such a result.
>
> (c) Recklessly. A person acts recklessly with respect to a material element of an offense when he consciously disregards a substantial and unjustifiable risk that the material element exists or will result from his conduct. The risk must be of such a nature and degree that, considering the nature and purpose of the actor's conduct and the circumstances known to him, its disregard involves a gross deviation from the standard of conduct that a law-abiding person would observe in the actor's situation.

(d) Negligently. A person acts negligently with respect to a material element of an offense when he should be aware of a substantial and unjustifiable risk that the material element exists or will result from his conduct. The risk must be of such a nature and degree that the actor's failure to perceive it, considering the nature and purpose of his conduct and the circumstances known to him, involves a gross deviation from the standard of care that a reasonable person would observe in the actor's situation.

The first two categories, "purpose," and "knowledge" are generally considered to be intentional. The latter two, "recklessness" and "carelessness' are generally considered to be negligent.

French Law

Section 121-1:

No one is criminally responsible except for his own act.

Section 121-3:

There is no crime or misdemeanor without the intention of committing it. However, when the law provides for it, there is an offense in the event of deliberate endangerment of the person of others.

There is also an offence, when the law so provides, in the event of a fault or imprudence, negligence or breach of an obligation of prudence or safety provided for by law or regulation, if it is established that the author of the facts has not carried out the normal diligence taking into account, where applicable, the nature of his missions or functions, his skills as well as the power and means at his disposal.

In the case provided for in the preceding paragraph, natural persons who have not directly caused the damage, but who have created or contributed to creating the situation which has allowed the damage to occur or who did not take the steps enabling it to be avoided, are criminally liable if it is established that they either violated in a manifestly deliberate manner a particular obligation of prudence or safety provided for by law or regulation, or committed a serious fault and which exposed others to a particularly serious risk that they could not ignore.

'There is no contravention in case of *force majeure*.'

While generally, to convict someone of a crime, there must be both the *actus reus* and the *mens rea*, there are exceptions. The first exception to the requirement of an act relates to what the MPC refers to as "inchoate crimes."

Criminal Attempt

MPC Section 5.01(1) notes, "A person is guilty of an attempt to commit a crime if, acting with the kind of culpability otherwise required for commission of the crime, he:

a. Purposely engages in conduct that would constitute the crime if the attendant circumstances were as he believes them to be; or
b. When causing a particular result is an element of the crime, does or omits to do anything with the purpose of causing or with the belief that it will cause such result without further conduct on his part; or
c. Purposely does or omits to do anything that, under the circumstances as he believes them to be, is an act or omission constituting a substantial step in a course of conduct planned to culminate in his commission of the crime."

MPC Section 5.01(2) specifies the conduct that may be a substantial step under Subsection (1)(c), above:

> Conduct shall not be held to constitute a substantial step under Subsection (1)(c) of this Section unless it is strongly corroborative of the actor's criminal purpose. Without negativing the sufficiency of other conduct, the following, if strongly corroborative of the actor's criminal purpose, shall not be held insufficient as a matter of law:
>
> (a) lying in wait, searching for or following the contemplated victim of the crime;
>
> (b) enticing or seeking to entice the contemplated victim of the crime to go to the place contemplated for its commission;
>
> (c) reconnoitering the place contemplated for the commission of the crime;
>
> (d) unlawful entry of a structure, vehicle or enclosure in which it is contemplated that the crime will be committed;

(e) possession of materials to be employed in the commission of the crime, that are specially designed for such unlawful use or that can serve no lawful purpose of the actor under the circumstances;

(f) possession, collection or fabrication of materials to be employed in the commission of the crime, at or near the place contemplated for its commission, if such possession, collection or fabrication serves no lawful purpose of the actor under the circumstances;

(g) soliciting an innocent agent to engage in conduct constituting an element of the crime.

French Law

Section 121-4:

The person committing the offense is the person who:

1. Commits the incriminated acts;
2. Attempts to commit a crime or, in cases provided for by law, an offence.

Section 121-5:

The attempt is established when, manifested by a commencement of execution, it has been suspended or has failed in its effect only due to circumstances beyond the control of its author.

Accomplice

MPC Section 2.06(3)(ii) addresses the subject and notes, "A person is an accomplice of another person in the commission of an offense if:

a. with the purpose of promoting or facilitating the commission of the offense, he
   i. solicits such other person to commit it, or
   ii. aids or agrees or attempts to aid such other person in planning or committing it, or
   iii. having a legal duty to prevent the commission of the offense, fails to make proper effort so to do, or
b. his conduct is expressly declared by law to establish his complicity. French law is similar.

Section 121-7:
A person is an accomplice to a crime or misdemeanor who knowingly, by aiding or abetting, facilitated the preparation or consumption thereof.

A person is also an accomplice who, by gift, promise, threat, order, abuse of authority or power, provokes an offense or gives instructions to commit it.

Aiding and Abetting

The MPC addresses aiding and abetting, as well as attempt in Section 5.01(3):

> A person who engages in conduct designed to aid another to commit a crime that would establish his complicity under Section 2.06 if the crime were committed by such other person, is guilty of an attempt to commit the crime, although the crime is not committed or attempted by such other person.

French law is similar.

Section 121-2:
Legal persons, to the exclusion of the State, are criminally liable, according to the distinctions in Articles 121-4–121-7, for offenses committed, on their behalf, by their bodies or representatives.

However, local authorities and their groupings are only criminally liable for offenses committed in the exercise of activities likely to be the subject of public service delegation agreements.

The criminal liability of legal persons does not exclude that of natural persons who are perpetrators or accomplices in the same acts, subject to the provisions of the fourth paragraph of Article 121-3.

As previously noted, Section 121-3 states, "There is no crime or misdemeanor without the intention of committing it."

However, when the law so provides, it is an offense in the event of deliberate endangerment of the person of others.

There is also an offence, when the law so provides, in the event of a fault of imprudence, negligence or breach of an obligation of prudence or safety provided for by law or regulation, if it is established that the author of the facts did not carry out the normal diligence taking into account, where applicable, the nature of his missions or his functions, his skills as well as the power and means at his disposal.

In the case provided for in the preceding paragraph, natural persons who did not directly cause the damage, but who created or contributed to creating the situation which allowed the damage to occur or who did not take the steps to avoid it, are criminally liable if it is established that they either violated in a manifestly deliberate manner a particular obligation of prudence or safety provided for by law or regulation, or committed a serious fault and which exposed others to a particularly serious risk that they could not ignore.

There is no contravention in case of force majeure.

Exceptions

As noted previously, some crimes, involving an "attempt" may be prosecuted even without an "act." In addition, in some situations a specific intent, or *mens rea*, is not necessary in order for the prosecution to secure a criminal conviction. Such offenses may be referred to as strict or "absolute" liability. MPC Section 2.05 notes that,

1. The requirements of culpability prescribed by Sections 2.01 and 2.02 do not apply to:
   a. offenses that constitute violations, unless the requirement involved is included in the definition of the offense or the Court determines that its application is consistent with effective enforcement of the law defining the offense; or
   b. offenses defined by statutes other than the Code, insofar as a legislative purpose to impose absolute liability for such offenses or with respect to any material element thereof plainly appears.
2. Notwithstanding any other provision of existing law and unless a subsequent statute otherwise provides:
   a. when absolute liability is imposed with respect to any material element of an offense defined by a statute other than the Code and a conviction is based upon such liability, the offense constitutes a violation; and
   b. although absolute liability is imposed by law with respect to one or more of the material elements of an offense defined by a statute other than the Code, the culpable commission of the offense may

be charged and proved, in which event negligence with respect to such elements constitutes sufficient culpability and the classification of the offense and the sentence that may be imposed therefor upon conviction are determined by Section 1.04 and Article 6 of the Code.

As the Supreme Court explained, there are situations where "...criminal liability is imposed in the absence of any *mens rea* whatsoever. Such 'strict liability' crimes are exceptions to the general rule that criminal liability requires an "evil-meaning mind." (Citations omitted). Under the Model Penal Code, the only offenses based on strict liability are "violations," actions punishable by a fine, forfeiture, or other civil penalty rather than imprisonment" citing the Model Penal Code Section 2.05.[10]

Ignorance of the Law

While ignorance of the law is generally not a defense, MPC Section 2.04(1) notes,

"(1) Ignorance or mistake as to a matter of fact or law is a defense if:

a. the ignorance or mistake negatives the purpose, knowledge, belief, recklessness, or negligence required to establish a material element of the offense; or
b. the law provides that the state of mind established by such ignorance or mistake constitutes a defense.

2. Although ignorance or mistake would otherwise afford a defense to the offense charged, the defense is not available if the defendant would be guilty of another offense had the situation been as he supposed. In such case, however, the ignorance or mistake of the defendant shall reduce the grade and degree of the offense of which he may be convicted to those of the offense of which he would be guilty had the situation been as he supposed.
3. A belief that conduct does not legally constitute an offense is a defense to a prosecution for that offense based upon such conduct when:

---

[10] *United States v. Lopez*, 514 U.S. 549 (1995). *Op. cit.*, at 320.

a. the statute or other enactment defining the offense is not known to the actor and has not been published or otherwise reasonably made available prior to the conduct alleged; or
b. he acts in reasonable reliance upon an official statement of the law, afterward determined to be invalid or erroneous, contained in
   i. a statute or other enactment;
   ii. a judicial decision, opinion or judgment;
   iii. an administrative order or grant of permission; or
   iv. an official interpretation of the public officer or body charged by law with responsibility for the interpretation, administration or enforcement of the law defining the offense.

4. The defendant must prove a defense arising under Subsection (3) of this Section by a preponderance of evidence."

French Law Section 122-3

A person is not criminally liable if he justifies having believed, through an error in the law that he was unable to avoid, to be able to legitimately perform the act. In other words, a person is not criminally liable if he establishes that he believed he could legitimately perform the action because of a mistake of law, that he was not in a position to avoid.

Jurisdiction

The United States

When a crime is committed, a significant issue is whether the federal, or a state government will have jurisdiction.

Federal Jurisdiction

Although the power of Congress to enact criminal laws is extensive, it is not without limitation. For purposes of this textbook the relevant Constitutional authority giving Congress the power to enact criminal law is Article I, Section 8 of the Constitution. As the Supreme Court noted in *United States v. Lopez*,[11] *United States v. Morrison*,[12] and *Gonzales v.*

[11] 514 U.S. 549 (1995).
[12] 529 U.S. 598 (2000).

Raich[13] the Clause grants Congress authority to enact three classes of statutes. "First, Congress may regulate the use of the channels of interstate commerce…."[14] "Second, Congress is empowered to regulate and protect the instrumentalities of interstate commerce, or persons or things in interstate commerce, even though the threat may come only from intrastate activities…."[15] "Finally, Congress' commerce authority includes the power to regulate those activities having a substantial relation to interstate commerce…."[16] as it has done when it outlaws cultivation and possession of controlled substances.

Federal Law and the Internet

Introduction

The 1980s arguably was the dawn of the computer age, at least in respect to widespread use of computers. At that time law enforcement lacked the means to address the burgeoning computer crimes. The laws on mail and wire fraud were limited in their reach and did not address these new crimes.[17]

While numerous federal laws apply to criminal activity involving the Internet, the main federal laws associated with crimes committed over the Internet are:

1. The Counterfeit Access Device and Computer Fraud and Abuse Act is popularly known as the Computer Fraud and Abuse Act (CFAA) as amended, 18 U.S.C. Section 1030.

In 1986 Congress enacted the CFAA, in an attempt to strike an "appropriate balance between the federal government's interest in computer crime and the interests and abilities of the states to proscribe and punish such offenses."[18] Because of Constitutional requirements Congress

---

[13] 545 U.S. 1 (2005).

[14] *United States v. Lopez*, 514 U.S. at 558; *United States v. Morrison*, 529 U.S. at 609; *Gonzales v. Raich*, 545 U.S. at 16.

[15] *United States v. Lopez*, at 558; *United States v. Morrison*, 529 U.S. at 609; *Gonzales v. Raich*, 545 U.S. at 16–17.

[16] *United States v. Lopez*, at 558–559; *United States v. Morrison*, 529 U.S. at 609; *Gonzales v. Raich*, 545 U.S. at 17.

[17] See H.R. Rep. No. 98–894, at 6 (1984), reprinted in 1984 U.S.C.C.A.N. 3689, 3692.

[18] See S. Rep. No. 99–432, at 4 (1986), reprinted in 1986 U.S.C.C.A.N. 2479, 2482.

limited federal jurisdiction to situations where there was a compelling federal interest, such as computers of the federal government, the banking industry as well as computers that are used in or affecting interstate or foreign commerce.[19] As part of that the CFAA is intended to address situations where those computers are subject to trespassing, threats, damage, espionage, or are used to commit fraud.

Among the provisions of the CFAA are:

1. Criminalizing additional computer-related acts such as penalizing the theft of property by computer that occurs as a part of a scheme to defraud; and
2. Criminalizing the intentional altering, damaging, or destruction of data that belongs to others.

The second category was intended to address the distribution of malicious code and denial of service attacks.

Key Provisions of the CFAA

A "protected" computer

A violation of the CFAA requires access of a "protected" computer. This provision is quite broad and applies to a computer that is used in, or affects, interstate or foreign commerce, as well as computers used by the federal government and financial institutions. As long as a computer is connected to the Internet it is likely to satisfy this requirement.

Prior to 2008 this definition did not cover computers that were not connected to the Internet and that were not used by the federal government or financial institutions, but, because some state-operated utilities have computers that are not connected to the Internet for security purposes, Congress was forced to remedy this issue by way of the Identity Theft Enforcement and Restitution Act of 2008 by broadening the definition of a protected computer to include computers that simply "affect' interstate or foreign commerce or communications.

Then, by way of the USA PATRIOT Act, Congress again revised the definition of a protected computer to include computers outside of the

---

[19] *Ibid.*

United States as long as they affect interstate or foreign commerce or communication of the United States.

"Without authorization"

Although not defined, this requirement addresses situations involving outsiders, such as hackers as well as certain "insiders" but only if they clearly lack authorization. Thus, a party who, for instance, exceeds the authority of their authorization may not be prosecuted under this section, although courts in several civil cases ruled that defendants lacked authorization when they breached a duty of loyalty.[20]

"Exceeds authorization"

This phrase means "...to access a computer with authorization and to use such access to obtain or alter information in the computer that the accessor is not entitled so to obtain or alter."[21] This phrase is directed at insiders, such as employees who utilize a company's network for an improper purpose where access was limited by documented restrictions in, for example, an employment agreement, computer access policy, or a website's terms of service, among others.

In summary, one who accesses a computer online, without authority, to obtain classified, restricted, or protected data, or attempts to do so, is subject to criminal prosecution. The kind of data that is protected may include financial and credit records, medical records, legal files, military, and national security information as well as other confidential

---

[20] See, e.g., *Int'l Airport Ctrs., LLC v. Citrin*, 1 440 F.3d 418, 420–421 (7th Cir. 2006); *Shurgard Storage Ctrs., Inc. v. Safeguard Self Storage, Inc.*, 119 F.Supp.2d 1121, 1125 (W.D. Wash. 2000); *Ervin & Smith Advertising and Public Relations, Inc. v. Ervin*, 2009 WL 249998 (D. Neb. 2009). Some of these cases further suggest that such a breach can occur when the user decides to access the computer for a purpose that is contrary to the interests of the authorizing party. See, e.g., Citrin, 440 F.3d at 420 (defendant's authorization to access computer terminated when he resolved to destroy employer's files); *ViChip Corp. v. Lee*, 438 F.Supp.2d 1087, 1100 (N.D. Cal. 2006) (same); *NCMIC Finance Corp. v. Artino*, 638 F.Supp.2d 1042, 1057 (S.D. Iowa 2009) ("[T]he determinative question is whether Artino breached his duty of loyalty to NCMIC when Artino obtained information from NCMIC's computers.").

[21] 18 U.S.C. Section 1030(e)(6).

information. The data may be located on government or private computers.

The crime involves two aspects:

1. Accessing a computer without authorization; and
2. Taking data

The crime is a felony if committed for:

1. a commercial purpose or private financial gain, or
2. if the value of the stolen data (or computer time) exceeds $5,000.00.

Civil Litigation

Although it is a criminal statute, in some circumstances the CFAA allows victims of specific kinds of loss or damage to file a civil lawsuit that seeks the imposition of injunctive or other equitable relief, as well as compensatory damages.

The major subsections of the CFAA are:

1. Obtaining National Security Information 18 U.S.C. Section 1030(a)(1): This section criminalizes the disclosure of information that is detrimental to national defense merging espionage with computer abuse.

   A violation may invoke the federal crimes of terrorism.
2. Accessing a Computer and Obtaining Information 18 U.S.C. Section 1030(a)(2): This section goes beyond the issue of hacking and is intended to address those who seek to acquire protected information by intentional and unauthorized computer access.

   A violation of this section may also raise issues of copyright infringement.
3. Trespassing in a Government Computer 18 U.S.C. Section 1030(a)(3): This section is intended to address unauthorized intrusion or hacking, it is not limited to computers that are strictly used by the government alone but includes computers with shared access and includes computers that are located outside the United States that are used in a manner that affects interstate or foreign commerce or communication of the United States.

4. Accessing to Defraud and Obtain Value 18 U.S.C. Section 1030(a)(4): This section criminalizes the unauthorized use of a computer used by the federal government, a bank, or a computer used in or affecting interstate or foreign commerce, to commit fraud.

   It may be utilized in conjunction with the CAN-SPAM Act that addresses "protected" computers, allowing the prosecution of hackers who use e-mail for a fraudulent purpose.

   A violation may also implicate other general federal criminal statutes, as well as laws addressing theft or fraud of federal property, theft or fraud related to financial institutions and those that prohibit theft or fraud involving property in or affecting interstate or foreign commerce.
5. Damaging a Computer or Information 18 U.S.C. Section 1030(a)(5): Added in 1996 and amended in the USA PATRIOT and Homeland Security Acts, this section establishes three offenses for damage to a computer based on the intent to intrude and cause damage. Anyone who intentionally obtains unauthorized access is punishable for any resulting damage regardless of whether he intended to cause it or was recklessly indifferent.

   As with paragraph (a)(1), a violation may also invoke the federal crimes of terrorism.
6. Trafficking in Passwords 18 U.S.C. Section 1030(a)(6): Although rarely used, this section addresses situations where hackers post passwords for a computer system on an electronic bulletin board and provides a civil remedy as well.
7. Threatening to Damage A Computer 18 U.S.C. Section 1030(a)(7): This section is intended to address situations where:
   1. A criminal has already stolen information and threatens to disclose it unless compensated, as well as situations where
   2. A criminal causes damage first, by accessing a computer without authority and encrypting critical data, followed by a threat that they will not reverse the problem unless paid.

In summary, the CFAA addresses situations where a computer is "victimized," while other laws address the use of computers to commit a crime. Other laws, which are discussed in the following sections, address identity theft, obscenity, pornography, and gambling, among other subjects.

Other Significant Federal Law

The Wiretap Act as Amended

In summary, this law, also known as Title III, regulates the use of wiretaps to investigate criminal conduct. It became a source for criminal prosecution in 1986 when Congress amended it to specifically cover "electronic communications" that is broad enough to cover network communication. It prohibits "any person," not just law enforcement, from making an illegal interception, disclosing, or using illegally intercepted information. The Wiretap Act is likely to be invoked whenever a criminal defendant has surreptitiously collected information from a computer.

Although complex, the Wiretap Act has three significant prohibitions, subject to a number of exceptions:

1. The interception of communications;
2. The disclosure of communications; and
3. The use of intercepted communications.

Intercepting a Communication 18 U.S.C. Section 2511(1)(a)

Arguably the most significant section of the Wiretap Act prohibits any person from intentionally intercepting, or attempting to intercept any wire, oral, or electronic communication. Generally, an act is not "intentional" if it is due to inadvertence or mistake. However, motive is irrelevant and a person who incorrectly believes that an interception was lawful is in violation of the law.

As part of the Electronic Communications Privacy Act, discussed later in this chapter, Congress changed the requisite intent from "willfully" to "intentionally" to address situations where a criminal defendant argued that they were ignorant of the law and therefore did not act "willfully."

"Intercept" is defined as

> '...the aural or other acquisition of the contents of any wire, electronic, or oral communication through the use of any electronic, mechanical, or other device.'[22] The terms 'contents,' 'wire communication,' 'electronic communication,' 'oral communication,' and 'electronic, mechanical, or other device,' are specifically defined in the statute.

---

[22] 18 U.S.C. Section 2510(4).

Although unstated in the law, courts have required that the acquisition be contemporaneous with the transmission, although "contemporaneous" may not be the same as "simultaneous." Interception of a transmission does not require that the defendant also listened to or read the communication, and a recording, alone, is sufficient to constitute a violation of the statute. Accessing a stored copy of a communication is not the equivalent of interception.

"Contents"

One court defined "contents" as any information concerning the substance, purport, or meaning of that communication. Congress amended the statute to exclude, from its coverage, the identity of the parties or the existence of the communication. Therefore, someone who learns that a communication is occurring, or who is able to tell who is communicating, has not violated the Wiretap Act.

"Wire, oral, or electronic communication"

"Wire communication" generally corresponds to traditional telephone conversations involving the human voice. "Oral communication" is vocal, spoken by a person in private. "Electronic communication" is intended to be a broad catchall phrase that covers any other kind of communication that occurs electronically, including communication involving a computer, rather than the human voice.

"An electronic, mechanical, or other device"

This requirement eliminates situations where unaided human senses are used to obtain the contents of a communication. To require otherwise would criminalize a situation where someone simply overhears a private conversation. Critically important to this issue is an expectation of privacy, as discussed in the chapter on privacy.

Disclosing an Intercepted Communication 18 U.S.C. Section 2511(1)(c)

Disclosure of the contents of a communication, as well as the nature of the communication is prohibited. Therefore, disclosure that an illegal interception occurred is not a violation. Nor is it a violation if the contents of the communication have already become public information or common knowledge. In addition, the disclosure must be to "any other person" meaning someone other than the person who intercepted the communication, or the parties whose communication was intercepted.

"Use of Content"

Although seemingly broad, this requires "...active employment of the contents of the illegally intercepted communication for some purpose."[23] Use of an intercepted password to gain access to a computer or intercepted confidential business information satisfies the requirement. Threatened disclosure to influence another constitutes a "use." Simply listening to an intercepted conversation is not a violation.

Exclusions

Arguably the most significant exclusion is the extension telephone. This exception allows employers to monitor employees' communications on extensions provided in the ordinary course of business.

The Significant Exceptions

Consent

An interception is lawful if the interceptor is a party to the communication or if a party consents to the interception, although a communication that is intercepted to commit a criminal or tortious act, such as blackmail, or an invasion of privacy may violate the act. Thus, an interception committed for a lawful, as well as an unlawful purpose is a violation of the law.

Consent may be express or implied

Consent may be implied where the surrounding circumstances indicate that the party knowingly agreed to the surveillance. This generally requires that the consenting party had actual notice of the monitoring

[23] *Peavy v. Harman*, 37 F.Supp.2d 495, 513 (1999).

and voluntarily chose to use the monitored system. Prison inmates that voluntarily use telephones that they know are monitored have impliedly consented and employees who knew that the employer monitored e-mail communication and was reminded on a daily basis about the monitoring, are deemed to have consented by implication.

Good faith

The “good faith” exception is commonly used to prevent prosecution of law enforcement officers relying on a warrant, court order or grand jury subpoena or an emergency request, as well as a service provider complying with a legal process, such as a government subpoena, where the legal process is later determined to be deficient. A good faith mistake of law may also fall under this exception.

“Accessible to the public”

Any communication that is readily accessible to the public, such as a public bulletin board, public chat room, or the like is exempt. This exception applies only to electronic communication and a significant issue is the lack of an expectation of privacy.

The First Amendment

The First Amendment may prevent prosecution when the disclosure of information of public concern was made by:

1. a third party not involved in the interception, as long as
2. the third party was under no duty to keep the information confidential.

Using an Intercepted Communication 18 U.S.C. Section 2511(1)(d)

As previously noted, although seemingly broad, “use” requires that the contents of the illegally intercepted communication be used for some purpose. “Use” does not include simply listening to an intercepted conversation. Because this section regulates conduct, not speech, it may address situations that would otherwise be protected by the First Amendment.

Unlawful Access to Stored Communications 18 U.S.C. Section 2701

This law is intended to address the confidentiality of communications that are stored by providers of electronic communication services prior to their final delivery to the intended recipients and applies where a third party was able to obtain, alter, or delete e-mail or voicemail.

A violation requires that the defendant accessed an electronic communication service (ECS) that is defined as any service that provides to users thereof the ability to send or receive wire or electronic communications. This applies to the computers of telephone companies, providers of e-mail services over the Internet, and hosts of an electronic bulletin board. This means that a home computer, anyone who maintains a website, such as Amazon, or simply uses the Internet does not qualify.

Under this law, voicemail is a wire communication, while e-mail and other forms of Internet communication that lacks a human voice are electronic communications.

Electronic Storage

This does not refer simply to the storage of information by electronic means and is specifically defined and refers to:

1. Temporary storage;
2. Made in the course of transmission;
3. By a provider of electronic communication services; and
4. To backups of intermediate communications.

Therefore, a communication that was received by a recipient's service provider but that has not yet been accessed by the recipient is in electronic storage. The communication reaches its final destination when a recipient retrieves the e-mail or voice mail. Although the Ninth Circuit disagrees, most court seem to hold that should a recipient choose to retain a copy of the communication on the service provider's system that communication is no longer in electronic storage since it is no longer in temporary intermediate storage incidental to electronic transmission nor is it a backup of such communication.

Purpose

In order to violate this law a party must have acted for purposes of commercial advantage, malicious destruction or damage, or private commercial gain, or in furtherance of any criminal or tortious act.

The Major Exceptions

Needless to say, the law exempts any person or entity providing a wire or ECS. The law also exempts conduct authorized by a user with respect to a communication of, or intended, for that user.

The Stored Wire and Electronic Communications and Transactional Records Access Act (18 U.S.C. Section 121)

The SCA restricts the government's ability to get information from social media sites, although social media sites are not technically an ISP. However, this is limited to non-criminal matters. In addition, messages older than 180 days, or that have already been opened by the user may be obtained by the government pursuant to a subpoena, which, unlike a warrant, may be issued by the government without judicial approval and without probable cause.

Identity Theft

The need for such laws is obvious. The FTC estimates that up to nine million Americans have their identity stolen each year. There are a number of federal laws that apply to this area.

Identify theft is defined as use of another's:

1. personally identifying information, such as name, date of birth, Social Security number or credit card number
2. without authorization
3. to commit fraud, or other crimes.

Federal law may also prohibit the:

1. production, transfer, or possession
2. of false or
3. illegally issued identification documents.

Federal law also prohibits the:

1. production, transfer, or possession of
2. a "document-making implement," specifically including computers.

"Transfer" includes:

1. making either false identification documents or the software or data used to make them available online.

A Number of Federal Laws apply to the subject of identity theft.

Identity Theft 18 U.S.C. Section 1028(a)(7)

Prior to 1998, identity theft was prosecuted under "false personation" (or "false impersonation") statutes that date back to the late 19th century.[24] False personation was generally defined as falsely assuming the identity of another to gain a benefit or avoid an expense. Unauthorized or illegal network intrusions are also likely to implicate laws on identity theft.

---

[24] See, for example, California Penal Code Section 529. (a) Every person who falsely personates another in either his or her private or official capacity, and in that assumed character does any of the following is punishable pursuant to subdivision (b): (1) Becomes bail or surety for any party in any proceeding whatever, before any court or officer authorized to take that bail or surety. (2) Verifies, publishes, acknowledges or proves, in the name of another person, any written instrument, with intent that the same may be recorded, delivered, or used as true. (3) Does any other act whereby, if done by the person falsely personated, he might, in any event, become liable to any suit or prosecution, or to pay any sum of money, or to incur any charge, forfeiture, or penalty, or whereby any benefit might accrue to the party personating, or to any other person. (b) By a fine not exceeding ten thousand dollars ($10,000), or by imprisonment in a county jail not exceeding one year, or imprisonment pursuant to subdivision (h) of Section 1170, or by both that fine and imprisonment.

The Identity Theft and Assumption Deterrence Act of 1998

This law made identity theft a federal crime and generally makes it a federal crime to:

1. Knowingly transfer or use;
2. Without lawful authority;
3. A means of identification of another person;
4. With the intent to commit; or
5. To aid or abet any unlawful activity;
6. That constitutes a violation of federal law; or
7. That constitutes a felony under any applicable state or local law.

While prior law emphasized financial institutions, this law made identity theft a crime against the individual whose identity was stolen and credit affected. The law closed certain loopholes that previously made it a crime to produce or possess false identity documents, but not to steal another's personal identifying information.

Aggravated Identity Theft 18 U.S.C. Section 1028A

Aggravated identity theft occurs when a defendant knowingly transfers, possesses, or uses, without lawful authority, a means of identification of another person during and in relation to any felony violation of certain enumerated federal offenses. The following are examples of individuals that may be guilty of aggravated identity theft:

"Carders"

Individuals who sell or trade stolen credit or debit card account information on online forums.

"Phishers"

Individuals who obtain the same kind of information as carders by way of fraudulent e-mails.

"Hackers"

Individual who may violate this section if they obtain identity or account information.

Access Device Fraud 18 U.S.C. Section 1029

The term "access device" is defined to mean any card, plate, code, account number, electronic serial number, mobile identification number, personal identification number, or other telecommunications service, equipment, or instrument identifier, or other means of account access that can be used, alone or in conjunction with another access device, to obtain money, goods, services, or any other thing of value, or that can be used to initiate a transfer of funds (other than a transfer originated solely by paper instrument).

This law prohibits the production, use, possession, or trafficking of unauthorized or counterfeit access devices, including new access devices that result from technological innovation. The definition of an "access device" also applies to offenses noted in the Identity Theft Penalty Enhancement Act of 2004 aforementioned and includes new access devices that result from technological innovation. Unauthorized access devices include lost, stolen, or revoked devices and a counterfeit device includes fictitious, altered, or forged devices.

Identity Theft Penalty Enhancement Act of 2004 18 U.S.C. Section 1028A

Created a new statutory crime of aggravated identity theft that requires a mandatory two-year sentence for any identity fraud crime where the identity in question belonged to another person. Established penalties for aggravated identity theft, when a defendant knowingly transfers, possesses, or uses, without lawful authority, a means of identification of another person during and in relation to any felony violation of certain enumerated federal offenses.

This law generally applies to those who:

1. Sell or trade stolen credit or debit card account information on online forums; or

2. Obtain the same kind of information by way of fraudulent e-mails (phishing).

Identity Theft Enforcement and Restitution Act of 2008

This law specifies that restitution orders for identity theft may include an amount equal to the value of the victim's time spent addressing the actual or intended harm of the identity theft or aggravated identity theft and provides for federal court jurisdiction where the offender and the victim live in the same state.

CAN-SPAM Act 18 U.S.C. Section 1037

The law applies to "electronic mail messaging" and generally provides a method to prosecute those who send substantial amounts of unsolicited commercial e-mail and addresses situations where the sender has:

1. Taken steps to conceal his identity or the source of the spam from recipients, ISPs, or law enforcement;
2. Sent sexually explicit e-mail that does not contain a marking or label that identifies as such.

This law authorizes the prosecution of those who personally perform the prohibited acts or who procures another to do so.

A commercial electronic mail message is any electronic mail message, the primary purpose of which, is the commercial advertisement or promotion of a commercial product or service, including content on an Internet website operated for a commercial purpose. Thus, while "electronic mail message" includes e-mail, it is not strictly limited to e-mail and may include other kinds of communication, including messages sent between users of social networking sites.

Multiple commercial e-mail messages are more than 100 electronic mail messages during a 24-hour period, more than 1,000 electronic mail messages during a 30-day period, or more than 10,000 electronic mail messages during a one-year period.

Mail and Wire Fraud

Mail Fraud Act of 1990 (18 U.S.C. Section 1341)

It is a federal crime to use the mail to defraud the public and includes commercial carriers such as Federal Express and the United Parcel Service. There are two basic elements to mail fraud:

1. Having devised or intending to devise a scheme to defraud, or to perform specified fraudulent acts; and
2. Use of the mail for the purpose of executing, or attempting to execute, the scheme (or specified fraudulent acts).

Fraud generally consists of a:

1. Material misrepresentation of a fact,
2. knowingly made,
3. with the intent to deceive another, and
4. on which a reasonable person could and would rely to his detriment.

Wire Fraud 18 (U.S.C. Section 1343)

"Whoever, having devised or intended to devise any scheme or artifice to defraud, or for obtaining money or property by means of false or fraudulent pretenses, representations, or promises, transmits, or causes to be transmitted by means of wire, radio, or television communication in interstate or foreign commerce, any writings, signs, signals, pictures, or sounds for the purpose of executing such scheme or artifice, shall be fined under this title or imprisoned not more than 20 years, or both. If the violation affects a financial institution, such person shall be fined not more than $1,000,000 or imprisoned not more than 30 years or both."

Federal law prohibits the use of interstate wire communications to further a fraudulent scheme to obtain money or property and applies to computer crimes. The penalties are severe and include fines, imprisonment up to 20 years or both and, in the case of a financial institution, 30 years in prison, a fine of not more than $1,000,000 or both.

Federal Wiretap Act (Title III or the Federal Wiretap Statute)

Enacted as part of the Omnibus Crime Control and Safe Streets Act of 1968 it prohibits the interception or attempt to intercept any "wire, oral, or electronic communication." The ECPA extended the prohibitions in the Omnibus Crime Control and Safe Streets Act of 1968 to include electronic communications intercepted during transmission.

The federal Wiretap Act requires that federal wiretap applications include:

1. a full and complete statement that
2. explains if alternative investigative techniques have been tried and failed;
3. why they "reasonably appear" unlikely to succeed if tried; or
4. that they are too dangerous.

In summary, an application for a federal wiretap must demonstrate that a less intrusive investigative procedure is not feasible. If federal law enforcement violated the Wiretap Act, a criminal defendant will try to exclude the damaging evidence as fruit of the poisonous tree, as discussed below.

This law is particularly significant in the prosecution of cybercrime. It has been applied to a variety of situations, including facsimile, telex, modem, and Internet transmissions, all of which fall under "wire, radio, or television communication(s)."

In summary, it is a crime to use wire, telegraph, telephone, television, the Internet, or e-mail with the intent to defraud.

Communication Interference (18 U.S.C. Section 1362)

"Whoever willfully or maliciously injures or destroys any of the works, property, or material of any radio, telegraph, telephone or cable, line, station, or system, or other means of communication operated or controlled by the United States, or used or intended to be used for military or civil defense functions of the United States, whether constructed or in the process of construction, or willfully or maliciously interferes in any way with the working or use of any such line, or system, or willfully or maliciously obstructs, hinders, or delays the transmission of any communication over any such line, or system, or attempts or conspires to do such an act, shall be fined under this title or imprisoned not more than ten years, or both."

The statute is broad and even covers privately owned lines and systems, even those that are not exclusively devoted to military or civil defense functions. The law is broad enough that it may apply to communication systems owned or operated by internet service providers (ISPs), if such systems are used, even if only occasionally, for communication by the government.

Freedom of Expression

While the foregoing represents some of the more significant issues that are related to business and the Internet, no discussion of criminal law would be complete without a discussion of expression that may involve a violation of criminal statutes. These issues are separate and apart from those that are discussed in Chapter 3. Although rare, there are certain categories of speech or expression that are not protected by the First Amendment and may result in criminal prosecution.

Examples of speech or expression that may result in criminal prosecution include:

1. Fighting words (more broadly, threatening speech)
   Generally, this includes speech or communication that is intended to incite violence. Generally, however, the speaker must pose a true threat, a serious intent to commit an unlawful, violent act against a specific person or group.

   Speech involving fighting words or "true threats" may include:
   a. sending threatening e-mail messages to a victim, or
   b. a public announcement on the Internet of an intention to commit an act that is racially motivated; and
2. Obscenity, including child pornography

What is the difference between "obscenity" and "pornography"?

The Definition of "Obscenity"

The Court established the test that determines whether material is obscene in three significant cases.[25] The three-part test as established by the Miller case is:

1. Whether the average person, applying contemporary adult community standards, finds that the matter, taken as a whole, appeals to prurient interests (i.e., an erotic, lascivious, abnormal, unhealthy, degrading, shameful, or morbid interest in nudity, sex, or excretion;
2. Whether the average person, applying contemporary adult community standards, finds that the matter depicts or describes sexual conduct in a patently offensive way (i.e., ultimate sexual acts, normal or perverted, actual or simulated, masturbation, excretory functions, lewd exhibition of the genitals, or sado-masochistic sexual abuse; and
3. Whether a reasonable person finds that the matter, taken as a whole, lacks serious literary, artistic, political, or scientific value.

In the Miller case the Supreme Court noted, "We acknowledge, however, the inherent dangers of undertaking to regulate any form of expression. State statutes designed to regulate obscene materials must be carefully limited. (Citation omitted). As a result, we now confine the permissible scope of such regulation to works which depict or describe sexual conduct. That conduct must be specifically defined by the applicable state law, as written, or authoritatively construed. (Footnote omitted). A state offense must also be limited to works which, taken as a whole, appeal to the prurient interest in sex, which portray sexual conduct in a patently offensive way, and which, taken as a whole, do not have serious literary, artistic, political, or scientific value."[26]

The Court went on to note, "The basic guidelines for the trier of fact must be: (a) whether 'the average person, applying contemporary community standards would find that the work, taken as a whole, appeals to the prurient interest, (citation omitted) whether the work depicts or

[25] *Miller v. California*, 413 U.S. 15, 24–25 (1973); *Smith v. United States*, 431 U.S. 291, 300–302, 309 (1977); *Pope v. Illinois*, 481 U.S. 497, 500–501 (1987).
[26] *Miller v. California*, 413 U.S. 15, 23–24 (1973).

describes, in a patently offensive way, sexual conduct specifically defined by the applicable state law; and (c) whether the work, taken as a whole, lacks serious literary, artistic, political, or scientific value....If a state law that regulates obscene material is thus limited, as written or construed, the First Amendment values applicable to the States through the Fourteenth Amendment are adequately protected by the ultimate power of appellate courts to conduct an independent review of constitutional claims when necessary."[27]

Thus, obscenity is not protected by the First Amendment and may result in criminal prosecution. Broadly, anything that fits the definition of the test that was enunciated in the Miller case, including, for example, visual depictions, spoken words or written text, may violate the law. Federal law makes it illegal to distribute, transport, sell, ship, mail, produce with intent to distribute or sell, or engage in the business of selling or transferring obscene material. So, although the law generally does not criminalize the private possession of obscene material, simply receiving such material may violate federal law that prohibits the use of the mails.[28]

Federal law strictly prohibits the distribution of obscene material to minors.

Pornography

Pornography is not "obscene" unless it meets the definition established by the Court in the Miller case aforementioned. Although pornography that is not obscene may not be banned, it may be regulated, thus allowing the government to enact reasonable restrictions, such as zoning laws.

However, in *New York v. Ferber*[29] the Court unanimously banned child pornography, even if it did not meet the test of obscenity as defined by the case in Miller. In doing so the Court upheld a law that prohibited the production, exhibition, or sale of any material that included actual or simulated sexual intercourse, deviate sexual intercourse, sexual bestiality, masturbation, sado-masochistic abuse, or lewd exhibition of the genitals by a child under the age of 16, because of its direct link to child abuse.

[27] *Ibid.*, at 24–25.

[28] https://www.justice.gov/criminal-ceos/obscenity.

[29] 458 U.S. 747 (1982).

In addition, the Court held that transmitting obscenity and child pornography, whether by the Internet or other means, is illegal for both adults and juveniles.[30]

Federal Law and Obscenity

Legislative attempts to address online pornography face constitutional challenges, chief among the barriers to prosecution is the First Amendment. Congressional attempts to address pornography include a variety of federal laws.

1. The Communications Decency Act (CDA) 1996: The CDA made it a crime to engage in online speech that was "indecent" or "patently offensive" if a minor could view the speech. However, in *Reno v. ACLU*,[31] the first major ruling by the Court on the regulation of material distributed via the Internet, the Supreme Court struck down portions of the law on the basis of the First Amendment holding that the terms "indecent" and "patently offensive" were unconstitutionally vague and overbroad. The Court noted, "In order to deny minors access to potentially harmful speech, the CDA effectively suppresses a large amount of speech that adults have a constitutional right to receive and to address to one another..." Other parts of the CDA, specifically the safe harbor provision of Section 230, discussed in the chapter on freedom of expression, remains in force.

The Children's Internet Protection Act

The Court upheld the Children's Internet Protection Act (CIPA) that required schools and libraries that accept federal funds to purchase computers or Internet access to block or filter obscenity, child pornography, and, with respect to minors, material that is "harmful to minors." A challenge to the law failed since filters may be disabled for *bona fide* research or other lawful purpose.

The Child Pornography Prevention Act of 1996 (CPPA) attempted to regulate virtual child pornography and made it a federal crime not only to

---

[30] *Reno v. ACLU*, 521 U.S. 844 (1998).

[31] 521 U.S. 844 (1997).

send images of children engaged in sexual activity, but also to use, for example, virtual children, or adults who appeared to be minors. In *Ashcroft v. Free Speech Coalition*,[32] the Court invalidated that section of the law that criminalized depictions that "appear to be" and "convey the impression" of a minor engaged in sexual conduct, even if the depiction does not involve an actual minor since it is not obscene as defined by the Miller test, nor actual child pornography as defined by the Ferber case. "The Government may not suppress lawful speech as the means to suppress unlawful speech. Protected speech does not become unprotected merely because it resembles the latter."[33]

Congress responded with the Prosecutorial Remedies and Other Tools to End the Exploitation of Children Today Act (PROTECT Act). Unsurprisingly, the constitutionality of the law was soon challenged. In *United States v. Williams*,[34] the Court reversed a decision by the Eleventh Circuit that held one component of the PROTECT Act, the "pandering provision" violated the First Amendment. The specific provision imposed criminal liability on anyone who knowingly advertises, promotes, presents, distributes, or solicits through the mails, or in interstate or foreign commerce by any means, including by computer, any material or purported material in a manner that reflects the belief, or that is intended to cause another to believe, that the material or purported material is, or contains (i) an obscene visual depiction of a minor engaging in sexually explicit conduct; or (ii) a visual depiction of an actual minor engaging in sexually explicit conduct. The Eleventh Circuit ruled that although the content described in subsections (i) and (ii) is not constitutionally protected, speech that advertises or promotes such content is protected by the First Amendment and held that the specific provision was unconstitutionally overbroad as well as unconstitutionally vague, in that it did not adequately and specifically describe the kind of speech that would result in criminal liability.

In overturning the Eleventh Circuit's decision, the Court upheld the PROTECT Act that banned the distribution of certain child pornography involving the use of actual children as constitutional and stated that the provision did not punish the solicitation or offering of virtual child pornography in compliance with the holding in Ashcroft, supra.

---

[32] 535 U.S. 234 (2002).

[33] *Ibid.*, at 255.

[34] 553 U.S. 285 (2008).

Other Federal Laws

Numerous other federal laws on the subject exist, some of which are discussed in the chapters on intellectual property.

The U.S. Safe Web Act

After passage of the CAN-SPAM Act, spam from servers in other nations increased.

The Federal Trade Commission lacked the authority to address this issue. The Safe Web Act allows the FTC to cooperate and share information with foreign agencies investigating and prosecuting Internet-based fraud and deception.

Safe Harbor for ISPs

ISPs have immunity for providing information to the FTC about possible unfair or deceptive actions in foreign jurisdictions.

Copyrights in Digital Information

As noted in Chapter 10, copyright is arguably the most important form of intellectual property protection on the Internet because:

1. so much of the material on the Internet consists of works of authorship, and
2. the nature of the Internet requires that data be copied to be transferred online.

Under prior law, criminal penalties for copyright violations could be imposed only if unauthorized copies were exchanged for financial gain. Now, criminal liability extends even to those who do not profit.

The Digital Millennium Copyright Act of 1998

This Act has established both civil and criminal penalties for anyone who:

1. circumvents encryption software or other technological antipiracy protection, as well as those who

2. manufacture or sell devices or services primarily designed or produced to circumvent encryption.

The law retains an exception for fair use in the case of educational and other non-commercial uses, i.e., to evaluate computer security, to protect personal privacy and to enable parents to monitor their children's use of the Internet.

The law also recognizes limited liability for ISPs. Thus, an ISP is not liable for any copyright infringement by a customer unless the ISP is aware of the subscriber's violation. An ISP may be held liable only if it fails to shut the subscriber down after learning of the violation. However, the copyright holder must sue promptly or the subscriber may have their online access restored.

Criminal Copyright Infringement and the Digital Millenium Copyright Act

While the usual remedy for copyright infringement is a civil lawsuit, the FBI is now involved in fighting piracy and prosecuting criminal copyright infringement. Conviction requires proof that the defendant intentionally violated a known legal duty in order to satisfy the *mens rea* or criminal intent element. Thus, "innocent" infringers may escape criminal but not civil, liability.

The Electronic Communications Privacy Act of 1986 (ECPA)

In summary, this law made it illegal to intentionally intercept certain electronic transmissions. While it originally applied to cell phone communication it was amended in 1994 to apply to cordless phone communication and e-mail. Unlike the Computer Fraud and Abuse Act (noted earlier), ECPA updates existing federal law on intercepting wire and electronic communications and addresses hacking by:

1. Establishing privacy rights for computer users; and
2. Allowing law enforcement to employ electronic surveillance to investigate computer crimes.

Federal Cyberstalking Law 18 U.S.C. Section 875

This law criminalizes the intentional use of electronic communications systems to place another in reasonable fear of death or serious bodily injury. In a fairly unusual case, John Rayne Rivello, a resident of Maryland, was arrested by the FBI for violating the law because he created a flashing strobe light image within an electronic communication that he sent to the recipient in Texas. The recipient suffered from epilepsy, which was known to the sender, and the flashing light triggered a seizure in the recipient. While federal charges in Texas[35] were dismissed without prejudice, the sender faced state criminal prosecution in Texas, as well as a civil lawsuit by the recipient in Maryland.[36]

Constitutional Protection for those Accused of a Crime

In addition, the discussion of criminal law would not be complete without a discussion of the constitutional protections that exist for those that are accused of a crime.

The Fourth Amendment

> "The right of the people to be secure in their persons, houses, papers, and effects, against unreasonable searches and seizures, shall not be violated, and no Warrants shall issue, but upon probable cause, supported by Oath or affirmation, and particularly describing the place to be searched, and the persons or things to be seized."

The Fourth Amendment thus has two requirements. First, it prohibits "unreasonable searches and seizures" by the government in the absence of a search warrant. Second, it requires that the search warrant be supported by probable cause. Thus, a "reasonable" search may not require a search warrant but must still be justified by probable cause.

---

[35] *United States of America v. John Rayne Rivello*, 3-17MJ192-BK (N.D. Texas).

[36] *Eichenwald v. Rivello*, 318 F.Supp.3d 766 (2018).

What constitutes a "search"?

As noted previously, in *Katz v. United States*,[37] the Court was asked to define what constitutes a "search." In summary, the Court held that the inquiry involves two issues. First, does the individual have a "reasonable" expectation of privacy? Second, is that reasonable expectation of privacy one that society is prepared to recognize as 'reasonable? A search may violate the Fourth Amendment, if the government conduct violates both:

1. the individual's subjective expectation of privacy, as well as
2. a privacy interest that society recognizes as reasonable.

As long as both prongs of the test are met, any evidence that is obtained may not be used at trial unless the government first obtained a search warrant. As an example of the two-step analysis, a person may have a reasonable expectation of privacy in a computer they own at home, but not a computer in the workplace or one provided by an employer.

Is there a reasonable expectation of privacy in trash?

Also noted previously, in *Greenwood v. California*,[38] the issue for the Court was whether a warrantless search of an individual's trash, which had been left at the curb, violated the Fourth Amendment. Law enforcement suspected Greenwood of dealing drugs. Because law enforcement lacked probable cause for a search of his residence, law enforcement searched trash bags left out for collection. The evidence obtained from the trash provided the probable cause for a search warrant to search Greenwood's residence. Greenwood challenged the validity of the search and the trial court held that the warrantless search violated the Fourth Amendment. An appellate court affirmed that decision. The California Supreme Court declined to hear the case. The prosecution then filed a writ of *certiorari* with the Supreme Court that was granted.

The Court ruled that Greenwood did not have a reasonable expectation of privacy, noting that it was common knowledge that trash in that location was "...readily accessible to animals, children, scavengers, snoops and other members of the public." And, the trash was left in that

[37] 389 U.S. 347 (1967).
[38] 486 U.S. 35 (1988).

location specifically so that the trash collector, a stranger, could and would take it. Quoting from Katz, supra., the Court noted that "[w]hat a person knowingly exposes to the public, even in his own home or office, is not a subject of Fourth Amendment protection."

Is there a reasonable expectation of privacy in e-mail?

The answer can be difficult and involves an analysis of the facts.

Smyth v. The Pillsbury Company[39]

Again as noted previously, although a civil case, the Smyth case provides a framework for the analysis that court's follow in determining a party's expectation of privacy in the context of a private employer. The defendant repeatedly assured its employees, including plaintiff, that all e-mail communications would remain confidential and privileged. Defendant further assured its employees, including plaintiff, that e-mail communications could not be intercepted and used by the defendant against its employees as grounds for termination or reprimand. Nonetheless, the plaintiff was terminated due to unprofessional comments that were contained in an e-mail. The court noted that it "...did not find a reasonable expectation of privacy in e-mail communications voluntarily made by an employee to his supervisor over the company e-mail system notwithstanding any assurances that such communications would not be intercepted by management. Once plaintiff communicated the alleged unprofessional comments to a second person (his supervisor) over an e-mail system which was apparently utilized by the entire company, any reasonable expectation of privacy was lost. Significantly, the defendant did not require plaintiff, as in the case of a urinalysis or personal property search to disclose any personal information about himself. Rather, plaintiff voluntarily communicated the alleged unprofessional comments over the company e-mail system. We find no privacy interests in such communications."[40]

---

[39] 914 F.Supp. 97 (E.D.Pa. 1996).

[40] *Ibid.*, at 101. Likely of significance for the court were threats in the e-mails to "kill the backstabbing bastards" as well as a reference to the planned holiday party as the "Jim Jones Koolaid affair."

City of Ontario, California v. Quon[41]

Although another civil case as previously mentioned, Quon provides an example of the Court's approach in deciding the issue of privacy when the government is involved, thus implicating the approach that is likely in a criminal prosecution. Quon was employed by the Ontario, California, Police Department (OPD). He was a police sergeant and member of OPD's Special Weapons and Tactics (SWAT) Team. The City issued pagers to Quon and other SWAT Team members in order to help the SWAT Team mobilize and respond to emergency situations.

> Before acquiring the pagers, the City announced a 'Computer Usage, Internet and E–Mail Policy' (Computer Policy) that applied to all employees. Among other provisions, it specified that the City 'reserves the right to monitor and log all network activity including e-mail and Internet use, with or without notice. Users should have no expectation of privacy or confidentiality when using these resources.' In March 2000, Quon signed a statement acknowledging that he had read and understood the Computer Policy.
>
> The Computer Policy did not apply, on its face, to text messaging. Text messages share similarities with e-mails, but the two differ in an important way. In this case, for instance, an e-mail sent on a City computer was transmitted through the City's own data servers, but a text message sent on one of the City's pagers was transmitted using wireless radio frequencies from an individual pager to a receiving station owned by Arch Wireless. It was routed through Arch Wireless' computer network, where it remained until the recipient's pager or cellular telephone was ready to receive the message, at which point Arch Wireless transmitted the message from the transmitting station nearest to the recipient. After delivery, Arch Wireless retained a copy on its computer servers. The message did not pass through computers owned by the City.
>
> Although the Computer Policy did not cover text messages by its explicit terms, the City made clear to employees, including Quon, that the City would treat text messages the same way as it treated e-mails. At an April 18, 2002 staff meeting at which Quon was present, the OPD officer responsible for the City's contract with Arch Wireless, told officers that messages sent on the pagers 'are considered e-mail messages. This means

[41] 580 U.S. 746 (2010).

that [text] messages would fall under the City's policy as public information and [would be] eligible for auditing.' The … comments were put in writing in a memorandum sent … to Quon and other City personnel.

Over the next few months, Quon exceeded his character limit three or four times. Each time he reimbursed the City. A decision was made … to determine whether the existing character limit was too low … or if the overages were for personal messages. Transcripts of certain text messages sent by Quon and the other employee who exceeded the character allowance were requested.

Before conducting a review, the City used Quon's work schedule … in order to eliminate any messages Quon sent while off duty … and reviewed the content of the messages Quon sent during work hours. The report noted that Quon sent or received 456 messages during work hours in the month of August 2002, of which no more than 57 were work related; he sent as many as 80 messages during a single day at work; and on an average workday, Quon sent or received 28 messages, of which only 3 were related to police business. The report concluded that Quon violated OPD rules … and he was allegedly disciplined.

Did Quon have a reasonable expectation of privacy? The parties disagreed. The record established that OPD, at the outset, made it clear that pager messages were not considered private. The City's Computer Policy stated that '[u]sers should have no expectation of privacy or confidentiality when using' City computers … and this policy extended to text messaging.

The disagreement, at least as respondents see the case, is over whether later statements by a member of the OPD overrode the official policy. Respondents contend that because an official with OPD told Quon that an audit would be unnecessary if Quon paid for the overage, Quon reasonably expected that the contents of his messages would remain private.

Even if Quon had a reasonable expectation of privacy in his text messages, petitioners did not necessarily violate the Fourth Amendment by obtaining and reviewing the transcripts. Although as a general matter, warrantless searches 'are *per se* unreasonable under the Fourth Amendment,' there are 'a few specifically established and well-delineated exceptions' to that general rule, citing the Katz case. In the Katz case, the Court held that the 'special needs' of the workplace justify one such exception. (Citations omitted).

Because the search was motivated by a legitimate work-related purpose, and because it was not excessive in scope, the search was reasonable

> ... For these same reasons — that the employer had a legitimate reason for the search, and that the search was not excessively intrusive in light of that justification — the Court also concludes that the search would be 'regarded as reasonable and normal in the private-employer context.'... The search was reasonable, and the Court of Appeals erred by holding to the contrary. Petitioners did not violate Quon's Fourth Amendment rights.

The Fifth and Sixth Amendments

Confessions

Among other requirements, a confession must be knowing and voluntary.[42] In *Miranda v. Arizona*,[43] the Court applied the exclusionary rule to confessions by requiring individuals in custody, prior to interrogation, to be informed of certain rights[44]:

1. The right to remain silent;
2. The right to have an attorney present during questioning;
3. The right to have an attorney appointed if the suspect cannot afford one.[45]

---

[42] *Davis v. United States*, 512 U.S. 452, 461(1994). After a suspect has knowingly and voluntarily waived his *Miranda* rights police may continue questioning "until and unless the suspect clearly requests an attorney."

[43] 384 U.S. 436 (1966).

[44] In *Berghuis v. Thompkins*, 560 U.S. 370 (2010) the Court held that both the Fifth and Sixth Amendments "... protect against compulsory self-incrimination by requiring an interrogation to cease when either right is invoked." In this case, after being advised of his Miranda rights, the accused remained silent during interrogation. However, at one point during the interrogation the accused was asked, "Do you pray to God to forgive you for shooting that boy down?" The suspect answered "Yes." The voluntary reply, after prolonged silence, acted as an implied waiver of his Miranda rights. "In sum, a suspect who has received and understood the Miranda warnings, and has not invoked his Miranda rights, waives the right to remain silent by making an uncoerced statement to the police."

[45] In Berghuis, supra., the suspect was provided with a form that contained the following admonishments: (1) You have the right to remain silent. (2) Anything you say can and will be used against you in a court of law. (3) You have a right to talk to a lawyer before answering any questions and you have the right to have a lawyer present with you while

The "public safety" exception to Miranda

In *New York v. Quarles*,[46] the Supreme Court held that an officer's concern for public safety can justify a failure to give *Miranda* warnings. In that case, a woman told police a man with a gun raped her. She also said the man entered a nearby store. An officer spotted a man in the store matching the description the victim gave and ran after him. The officer caught him, noticed he was wearing an empty gun holster, and handcuffed him. Moments later, other officers arrived. The officer then asked the man where the gun was. The man nodded in a certain direction and said, "The gun is over there." The officer then retrieved it. Clearly, the requirements established by *Miranda* applied to this situation — the officer interrogated the suspect while he was in handcuffs and surrounded by four officers but did not read the man his rights until after his incriminating statement.

When the defendant faced prosecution for illegal weapon possession, lower courts decided that the gun, and the man's statements about it, were inadmissible. The U.S. Supreme Court disagreed, deciding that *Miranda* does not apply to a situation where officers ask questions legitimately designed to protect their safety or that of the public.

Waiver

Suspects may waive their right to remain silent or their right to an attorney either expressly or impliedly. To expressly waive Miranda rights, a suspect must state (or sign something stating) that they waive the right to remain silent or the right to have an attorney present. Implied waiver means that the suspect acts in a way that indicates a knowing and voluntary waiver of Miranda rights, such as by making a voluntary, uncoerced statement as noted in *Berghuis v. Thompkins*, supra. A waiver may be withdrawn by a suspect at any time.

---

you are answering any questions. (4) If you cannot afford to hire a lawyer, one will be appointed to represent you before any questioning if you wish one. (5) You have the right to decide at any time before or during questioning to use your right to remain silent and your right to talk with a lawyer while you are being questioned."

[46] 467 U.S. 469 (1984).

Defenses to Criminal Liability

The Exclusionary Rule and the Fruit of the Poisonous Tree Doctrine

If the government conducts, for example, a warrantless search and the individual has a legitimate expectation of privacy that society accepts as reasonable, the defendant may seek to have the evidence of the illegal search excluded at the time of trial. The Exclusionary Rule is broad and applies to a variety of situations. Thus, evidence derived from an illegal search, arrest, or interrogation is inadmissible because the evidence (the fruit) was tainted by the illegality (the poisonous tree).

Did the Accused Lack the Necessary Mental State (mens rea)?

Insanity

A discussion of insanity, as with many other subjects in American law is complicated and depends, at least in part on state law. In *Clark v. Arizona*,[47] the Court cataloged state insanity defenses, counting four "strains variously combined to yield a diversity of American standards" for when to absolve mentally ill defendants of criminal culpability. The first strain asks about a defendant's "cognitive capacity" — whether a mental illness left him "unable to understand what he [was] doing" when he committed a crime. (Citation omitted). The second examines his "moral capacity" — whether his illness rendered him "unable to understand that his action [was] wrong." (Citation omitted). Those two inquiries, Clark explained, appeared as alternative pathways to acquittal in the landmark English ruling M'Naghten's Case,[48] 10 Cl. & Fin. 200, 8 Eng. Rep. 718 (H. L. 1843), as well as in many follow-on American decisions and statutes: If the defendant lacks either cognitive or moral capacity, he is not criminally responsible for his behavior. Yet a third "building block[ ]" of state insanity tests, gaining popularity from the mid-19th century on,

---

[47] 548 U.S. 735, 749 (2010).

[48] The M'Naghten rule in its original formulation required that, "at the time of the committing of the act, the party accused was laboring under such a defect of reason, from disease of the mind, as not to know the nature and quality of the act he was doing; or, if he did know it, that he did not know he was doing what was wrong."

focuses on "volitional incapacity" — whether a defendant's mental illness made him subject to "irresistible[ ] impulse[s]" or otherwise unable to "control[ ] his actions." (Citations omitted). And bringing up the rear, in Clark's narration, the "product-of-mental-illness test" broadly considers whether the defendant's criminal act stemmed from a mental disease. (Citation omitted).

The Court in Clark went on to note, "... even that taxonomy fails to capture the field's complexity. (Citation omitted). Most notable here, *M'Naghten*'s "moral capacity" prong later produced a spinoff, adopted in many States, that does not refer to morality at all. Instead of examining whether a mentally ill defendant could grasp that his act was *immoral*, some jurisdictions took to asking whether the defendant could understand that his act was *illegal*. (Citations omitted). That change in legal standard matters when a mentally ill defendant knew that his act violated the law yet believed it morally justified." (Citations omitted). A discussion of the intricacies of the insanity defense is beyond the scope of this text.

French Law Also Addresses the Issue of Insanity

Section 122-1 of the Penal Code notes that:

> A person who was suffering, at the time of the facts, from a psychic or neuropsychic disorder having abolished his discernment or the control of his actions, is not criminally liable.
>
> The person who was suffering, at the time of the facts, from a psychic or neuropsychic disorder having altered his discernment or hindered the control of his actions remains punishable. However, the court takes this circumstance into account when determining the penalty and setting the rules. If a custodial sentence is incurred, it is reduced by one third or, in the case of a crime punishable by criminal imprisonment or life imprisonment, is reduced to thirty years. The court may, however, by a specially reasoned decision in correctional matters, decide not to apply this reduction in sentence. When, after medical advice, the court considers that the nature of the disorder justifies it, it ensures that the sentence imposed allows the convicted person to receive treatment appropriate to his condition.

However, Section 122-1-1 goes on to note:

> The first paragraph of article 122-1 is not applicable if the temporary abolition of the discernment of the person or the control of his acts at the time of the commission of a crime or an offense results from the fact that, very close to the time of the action, the person voluntarily consumed psychoactive substances with the intention of committing the offense or an offense of the same nature or of facilitating its commission.

And Section 122-1-2 goes on to note:

> The reduction in sentence provided for in the second paragraph of Article 122-1 is not applicable in the event of a temporary alteration in the judgment of the person or in the control of his acts at the time of the commission of a crime or offense when this alteration results from the voluntary consumption, illicitly or manifestly excessive, of psychoactive substances.

Mistake of Fact

As previously noted, while ignorance of the law is not a defense either in the United States, or France, a mistake of fact may serve as a defense if it eliminates the required mental state (*mens rea*) that is necessary for the specific offense. The Model Penal Code, Section 2.04 notes:

1. Ignorance or mistake as to a matter of fact or law is a defense if:
   a. The ignorance or mistake negatives the purpose, knowledge, belief, recklessness or negligence required to establish a material element of the offense; or
   b. The law provides that the state of mind established by such ignorance or mistake constitutes a defense.
2. Although ignorance or mistake would otherwise afford a defense to the offense charged, the defense is not available if the defendant would be guilty of another offense had the situation been as he supposed. In such case, however, the ignorance or mistake of the defendant shall reduce the grade and degree of the offense of which he may be convicted to those of the offense of which he would be guilty had the situation been as he supposed.
3. A belief that conduct does not legally constitute an offense is a defense to a prosecution for that offense based upon such conduct when:

a. the statute or other enactment defining the offense is not known to the actor and has not been published or otherwise reasonably made available prior to the conduct alleged; or
b. he acts in reasonable reliance upon an official statement of the law, afterward determined to be invalid or erroneous, contained in (i) a statute or other enactment; (ii) a judicial decision, opinion or judgment; (iii) an administrative order or grant of permission; or (iv) an official interpretation of the public officer or body charged by law with responsibility for the interpretation, administration or enforcement of the law defining the offense.

French law is similar. Section 122-3 notes:
A person is not criminally liable if he justifies having believed, through an error in the law that he was unable to avoid, to be able to legitimately perform the act. And Section 122-4 goes on to note:

A person who performs an act prescribed or authorized by legislative or regulatory provisions is not criminally liable.

A person who performs an act ordered by the legitimate authority is not criminally liable, unless this act is manifestly illegal.

Necessity

This defense may be available where particular justification defenses, such as, but not limited to self-defense,[49] is not. The MPC notes that this defense applies to conduct the actor believes to be "necessary to avoid a harm or evil to himself or another," provided that "the harm or evil sought to be avoided by such conduct is greater than that sought to be prevented by the law defining the offense charged." This defense does not affect an accused's potential civil liability.

---

[49]As with American law, French law also recognizes self-defense. Section 122-5 notes that there is no criminal liability for a person "...who, in the face of an unjustified attack on himself or others, performs, at the same time, an act ordered by the necessity of the self-defense of himself or others, except if there is a disproportion between the means of defense employed and the seriousness of the attack. Is not criminally liable the person who, to interrupt the execution of a crime or misdemeanor against property, performs an act of defence, other than intentional homicide, when this act is strictly necessary for the purpose pursued. provided that the means employed are proportionate to the seriousness of the offence."

French Law, Section 122-7 also provides a defense for "necessity" and notes:

A person is not criminally liable who, faced with a present or imminent danger which threatens himself, others or property, performs an act necessary to safeguard the person or property, unless there is a disproportion between the means employed and the seriousness of the threat.

Other Constitutional Issues

As previously noted, both the Fourth Amendment requirement of, for example, probable cause, as well as the Fifth Amendment protection against self-incrimination may provide protection to those accused of a crime, although such protection applies only to "natural" persons and not, for instance, to a corporation or limited liability company.

Statute of Limitations

There is a statute of limitations for every crime except murder. However, the statute of limitations may be tolled, stops running, if, for instance, the accused flees the jurisdiction.

Jurisdictional Issues

Prosecution may be difficult for a variety of reasons. First, there are jurisdictional issues, as noted previously in this chapter, as well as Chapter 2. Generally, in the United States the federal government, or a state has jurisdiction over crimes that are committed within its boundaries. The Internet has challenged the issue of geographic boundaries. In addition, the anonymity offered by the Internet may make it difficult, if not impossible, to identify the perpetrator of a crime or the accused may reside in a foreign country that is beyond the reach of American courts.

Chapter 7

Contract Creation

Abstract

Our society cannot function without contracts. A contract involves the creation of both rights and responsibilities or obligations. The law of contracts, unlike most of our other subjects is part of the common law or judge-made law. While our common law traces its roots back to A.D. 1066 when William the Conqueror won the Battle of Hastings, French law traces its roots back to the Napoleonic Code. Entering into a contract, whether in-person or online, and whether in France, or the United States, involves similar requirements. The common law requirements for the creation of a contract can be strict and demanding and a failure to comply with even one of those requirements may affect the validity, and therefore the enforceability, of a contract. French requirements may be no less demanding.

Introduction

In the United States, contract law, unlike some of the other laws that have been discussed, is based on judge-made law or precedent, rather than statute. However, the issue of contract creation, particularly when dealing with consumers, is a matter that is subject to numerous court decisions as well as federal and state regulations. At the federal level, and as discussed in Chapter 4, the Federal Trade Commission (FTC) has strict regulations that apply, particularly to the subject of advertising, which may be of significance on the subject of contract creation.

One of the key differences between a civil and common law system is in the area of contracts. A common law system offers parties far greater freedom of contract. In a common law system, unlike a civil law system, generally, few clauses are required by law, although there are exceptions for contracts involving consumers.[1]

In this chapter, American requirements for contracts as established by the Restatement (Second) of Contracts (hereinafter referred to as "The Restatement") will be compared with the requirements established in the French Civil Code.[2] While the French Civil Code is binding, the Restatement is not, although it is persuasive.

Contract Creation in the United States

Whether created online in a written document, or verbally, all contracts must have certain required elements in order to be legally binding and enforceable. The same is not necessarily true in countries with a system that is based on civil law.

While the law of contracts is generally considered to be common law, statutory law also plays a significant issue, particularly with regard to advertising and the increasing use of contracts in the online environment. The one exception is in the area of commercial law in the U.S., which is based on statutory law.

The Uniform Commercial Code

Although referred to as "uniform" there are differences among the commercial codes that have been adopted by the states.

---

[1] https://ppp.worldbank.org/public-private-partnership/legislation-regulation/framework-assessment/legal-systems/common-vs-civil-law.

[2] References to French law in chapters seven and eight were obtained from both an unofficial English translation that is available at https://www.legifrance.gouv.fr/codes/texte_lc/LEGITEXT000006070721/ version in force November 18, 2023, as well as https://www.trans-lex.org/601101/_/french-civil-code-2016/. It should be noted that the Restatement (Second) of Torts also has relevance to certain aspects of the law of contracts, particularly with regard to the issue of misrepresentation. See, e.g. Restatement (Second), Torts Sections 532–536.

Creation of a Valid Contract

The common law generally requires that valid contracts in the United States must have four distinct elements:

1. Agreement (an offer and acceptance, mutual assent, a meeting of the minds);
2. Consideration — Something of value;
3. Contractual Capacity;
4. Legality.

The Restatement

Section 17, Requirement of a Bargain notes:

1. Except as stated in Subsection (2), the formation of a contract requires a bargain in which there is a manifestation of mutual assent to the exchange and a consideration.
2. Whether or not there is a bargain a contract may be formed under special rules applicable to formal contracts or under the rules stated in Sections 82–94.

Section 18, Manifestation of Mutual Assent notes:

Manifestation of mutual assent to an exchange requires that each party either make a promise or begin or render a performance.

Section 20, Effect of Misunderstanding notes:

1. There is no manifestation of mutual assent to an exchange if the parties attach materially different meanings to their manifestations and
   a. neither party knows or has reason to know the meaning attached by the other; or
   b. each party knows or each party has reason to know the meaning attached by the other.
2. The manifestations of the parties are operative in accordance with the meaning attached to them by one of the parties if:
   a. that party does not know of any different meaning attached by the other, and the other knows the meaning attached by the first party; or

b. that party has no reason to know of any different meaning attached by the other, and the other has reason to know the meaning attached by the first party.

When the Issue of Mutual Assent is Questioned

The Restatement Section 201 addresses both the interpretation of offers, as well as contracts and states,

1. Where the parties have attached the same meaning to a promise or agreement or a term thereof, it is interpreted in accordance with that meaning.
2. Where the parties have attached different meanings to a promise or agreement or a term thereof, it is interpreted in accordance with the meaning attached by one of them if at the time the agreement was made
   a. that party did not know of any different meaning attached by the other, and the other knew the meaning attached by the first party, or
   b. that party had no reason to know of any different meaning attached by the other, and the other had reason to know the meaning attached by the first party.
3. Except as stated in this Section, neither party is bound by the meaning attached by the other, even though the result may be a failure of mutual assent.

French law on the subject is similar to American law.

Article 1128 of the French Civil Code (hereinafter referred to generally as "Article" with the relevant number). "The following are necessary for the validity of a contract:

1. The consent of the parties;
2. Their capacity to contract;
3. Content which is lawful and certain."

Agreement in France is defined as an agreement (assent) by all parties to the terms as evidence by an offer and acceptance.

> Article 1101: A contract is a concordance of wills of two or more persons intended to create, modify, transfer, or extinguish obligations.

> Article 1113: A contract is formed by the meeting of an offer and an acceptance by which the parties demonstrate their will to be bound.

However, whether in France or the United States, not all agreements are legally enforceable. A contractual agreement only arises when the terms of the agreement impose legally enforceable obligations on the parties. An example would be an advertisement. In both the United States and France, an advertisement is generally considered to be an invitation to negotiate.

> Article 1114: An offer, whether made to a particular person or to persons generally, contains the essential elements of the envisaged contract, and expresses the will of the offeror to be bound in case of acceptance. Failing this, there is only an invitation to enter into negotiations.

Requirements of the Offer

The Restatement, Section 24 defines an offer and notes:

> An offer is the manifestation of willingness to enter into a bargain, so made as to justify another person in understanding that his assent to that bargain is invited and will conclude it.

An agreement, or, as the Restatement notes, a "bargain," is a promise or commitment to do or refrain from doing a specific act, now or in the future.

Therefore, the general requirements for a valid offer are:

1. An intent to create a binding obligation;
2. Terms that are reasonably certain;
3. Communication of the offer.

Intention

Whether the parties to a contract intend to enter into a binding agreement depends, in part, on their intent, as determined by a reasonable, objective person. French law on the subject is contained in Article 1127-1:

> An offer must set out in addition:
>
> 1. The different steps that must be followed to conclude the contract by electronic means;
> 2. The technical means by which the person to whom the offer is addressed, before the conclusion of the contract, may identify any errors in the data entry, and correct them;
> 3. The languages offered for the conclusion of the contract, which must include the French language;
> 4. Where appropriate, the ways in which the party issuing the offer is to file it, and the conditions for access to the filed contract;
> 5. The means of consulting electronically any business, professional or commercial rules to which the party issuing the offer intends (as the case may be) to be bound.

Interpretation

As noted previously, a contract should be interpreted as determined by a reasonable, objective person.

The Restatement, Section 33 notes:

1. Even though a manifestation of intention is intended to be understood as an offer, it cannot be accepted so as to form a contract unless the terms of the contract are reasonably certain.
2. The terms of a contract are reasonably certain if they provide a basis for determining the existence of a breach and for giving an appropriate remedy.
3. The fact that one or more terms of a proposed bargain are left open or uncertain may show that a manifestation of intention is not intended to be understood as an offer or as an acceptance.

French law is virtually identical and Item 1188 notes:

> The contract is interpreted according to the common intention of the parties rather than stopping at the literal meaning of the terms.
>
> When this intention cannot be detected, the contract is interpreted according to the meaning given to it by a reasonable person placed in the same situation.

Item 1189 goes on to clarify that:

> All the clauses of a contract are interpreted in relation to each other, giving each of them the meaning that respects the coherence of the act as a whole.
>
> When, in the common intention of the parties, several contracts contribute to the same operation, they are interpreted according to this operation.

Item 1190 also notes:

> In case of doubt, the contract by mutual agreement is interpreted against the creditor and in favor of the debtor, and the adhesion contract against the person who proposed it.

And Item 1191 states that:

> When a clause is capable of two meanings, the one which gives it an effect takes precedence over the one which does not cause it to produce any.

There are some situations where a serious intention to become bound (an "offer") may not exist. For example, offers made in anger, jest, or undue excitement, as determined by the reasonable objective person standard may not meet the requirements of a serious intention to become bound.

Situations that may not rise to the level of an offer include:

1. Advertisements
2. Price lists
3. Expressions of Opinion
4. Auctions

The Restatement Section 26 on Preliminary Negotiations notes:

> A manifestation of willingness to enter into a bargain is not an offer if the person to whom it is addressed knows or has reason to know that the person making it does not intend to conclude a bargain until he has made a further manifestation of assent.

Generally, an advertisement is considered an invitation to negotiate since, to hold otherwise, would potentially expose everyone who advertises to the possibility of a lawsuit for breach of contract, although there are exceptions.

Section 5 of the Federal Trade Commission Act states that unfair or deceptive acts or practices are unlawful. Section 12 specifically prohibits false ads that are likely to induce the purchase of food, drugs, devices, or cosmetics. Section 15 defines a false advertisement for purposes of Section 12 as one which is "misleading in a material respect."

Misleading Advertisements

While an advertisement may not be sufficient to create a binding agreement, there still may be an issue regarding deception that may give rise to legal liability. The United States Supreme Court has noted, "The determination whether an advertisement is misleading requires consideration of the legal sophistication of its audience."[3]

The issue of torts, as noted in Chapter 5 may also come into play on this subject. The Restatement (Second) of Torts Section 402B notes:

One engaged in the business of selling chattels who, by advertising, labels, or otherwise, makes to the public a misrepresentation of a material fact concerning the character or quality of a chattel sold by him is subject to liability for physical harm to a consumer of the chattel caused by justifiable reliance upon the misrepresentation, even though

a. it is not made fraudulently or negligently, and
b. the consumer has not bought the chattel from or entered into any contractual relation with the seller.

Carlill v. Carbolic Smoke Ball Company (1893) 1 QB 256

The Carbolic Smoke Ball Company advertised that 100 £. reward will be paid by the Carbolic Smoke Ball Company to any person who after having used the ball three times daily for two weeks according to the printed directions supplied with such ball contracts the increasing epidemic influenza, colds, or any diseases caused by taking cold. The ball will last a family several months, and can be refilled at a cost of 5 s. The advertisement went on to state, 1000 £ is deposited with the

[3] *Bates v. Arizona*, 433 U.S. 350, 383 n. 37 (1977).

Alliance Bank, shewing our sincerity in the matter. Carlill purchased a Carbolic Smoke Ball and used it as directed between November 20, 1891, to January 17, 1892, at which time she came down with the flu. The plaintiff sued to recover the 100 £ and a court found in her favor. The defendant appealed.

The court noted, We must first consider whether this was intended to be a promise at all, or whether it was a mere puff which meant nothing. Was it a mere puff? My answer to that question is NO, and I based my answer upon this passage: '1000 £. is deposited with the Alliance Bank, shewing our sincerity in the matter.' Now, for what was that money deposited or that statement made except to negative the suggestion that this was a mere puff and meant nothing at all? The deposit is called in aid by the advertiser as proof of his sincerity in the matter — that is, the sincerity of his promise to pay this 100 £. in the event which he has specified …

Then it is contended that it is not binding. In the first place, it is said that it is not made with anybody in particular. Now that point is common to the words of this advertisement and to the words of all other advertisements offering rewards … In point of law this advertisement is an offer to pay 100ℓ to anybody who will perform these conditions, and the performance of the conditions is the acceptance of the offer …

But then it is said, 'Supposing that the performance of the conditions is an acceptance of the offer, that acceptance ought to have been notified.' Unquestionably, as a general proposition, when an offer is made, it is necessary in order to make a binding contract, not only that it should be accepted, but that the acceptance should be notified. But is that so in cases of this kind? I apprehend that they are an exception to that rule, or, if not an exception, they are open to the observation that the notification of the acceptance need not precede the performance. This offer is a continuing offer. It was never revoked …

We, therefore, find here all the elements which are necessary to form a binding contract enforceable in point of law, subject to two observations. First of all it is said that this advertisement is so vague that you cannot really construe it as a promise …

… it strikes me that there are two, and possibly three, reasonable constructions to be put on this advertisement … Another meaning, and the one which I rather prefer, is that the reward is offered to any person who contracts the epidemic or other disease within a reasonable time after having used the smoke ball. Then it is asked, What is a reasonable time?… It strikes me that a reasonable time may be ascertained in a

> business sense and in a sense satisfactory to a lawyer, in this way; find out from a chemist what the ingredients are; find out from a skilled physician how long the effects of such ingredients on the system could be reasonably expected to endure so as to protect a person from an epidemic or cold, and in that way you will get a standard to be laid before a jury, or a judge without a jury, by which they might exercise their judgment as to what a reasonable time would be ...
>
> I come now to the last point which I think requires attention — that is, the consideration. It has been argued that this is a nudum pactum — that there is no consideration. We must apply to that argument the usual legal tests ... It is quite obvious that in the view of the advertisers a use by the public of their remedy, if they can only get the public to have confidence enough to use it, will react and produce a sales which is directly beneficial to them. Therefore, the advertisers get out of the use an advantage which is enough to constitute consideration.
>
> But there is another view. Does not the person who acts upon this advertisement and accepts the offer put himself to some inconvenience at the request of the defendants? It appears to me that there is a distinct inconvenience, not to say a detriment, to any person who so uses the smoke ball. I am of opinion, therefore, that there is ample consideration for the promise ...

Auctions

Offers to sell at auctions, whether online or live, are generally considered an invitation to submit a bid. In the auction setting, a bidder is the offeror. The auctioneer is the offeree who may accept or reject a bid.

Are Statements of Opinion Sufficient to Constitute an Offer That May Be Accepted?

The Restatement of Torts, Second, specifies that an opinion is a representation that expresses only the belief of the maker, without certainty, as to the existence of a fact, or his judgment as to quality, value, authenticity, or other matters of judgment.

Expert or Non-Expert?

While generally, an opinion is just that, an exception does exist. At common law, a consumer can generally rely on an expert opinion, such as that from an attorney, engineer, or someone with additional education or training. For this reason, representations of expert opinion will generally be regarded as representations of fact. Thus, statements by an expert or someone with expertise on a subject may rise to the level of fraud.

Puffing

The Carbolic Smoke Ball case refers to "puff." The term "puff" or "puffing" refers generally to an expression of opinion that is not made as a representation of fact. Thus, a seller has some latitude in puffing its goods, but it is not authorized to misrepresent them or to assign to them benefits that they do not possess. Statements made for the purpose of deceiving prospective purchasers cannot properly be characterized as mere puffing and may result in legal liability.

In addition, while puffing is generally legal, under certain circumstances, such statements may be considered deceptive by the FTC. As an example, the FTC noted, "False, misleading and deceptive advertising claims beamed at children tend to exploit unfairly a consumer group unqualified by age or experience to anticipate or appreciate the possibility that representations may be exaggerated or untrue."[4]

Is It Puffing or a Material Misrepresentation?

The FTC specifies that the answer requires a three-step process[5]:

1. Was there a representation, omission, or practice that is likely to mislead the consumer under the circumstances?
   Actions that are considered misleading or deceptive include:
   false or written representations,
   misleading price claims,
   sales of hazardous or defective products or services without adequate warnings,
   failure to disclose information regarding pyramid sales,
   use of bait-and-switch techniques,

[4]FTC Policy Statement on Deception October 14, 1983. https://www.ftc.gov/system/files/documents/public_statements/410531/831014deceptionstmt.pdf.

[5]https://www.ftc.gov/system/files/documents/public_statements/410531/831014deception stmt.pdf.

failure to perform promised services, and
failure to meet warranty obligations.

2. If so, the specific action or representation must be analyzed from the standpoint of a reasonable consumer. If the action or representation affects or is directed primarily at a particular group, "reasonableness" is determined by the perspective of that specific group.
3. Was the representation, omission, or practice material? Materiality is determined by asking whether the action or representation is likely to affect the consumer's conduct or decision with regard to a good or service.

If so, the action or representation is material and a consumer is likely to have made a different choice but for the deception.

Most deceptive trade practices or acts involve written or oral misrepresentations or omissions of material information.[6] Marketing and point-of-sales practices that are likely to mislead consumers will generally be considered deceptive.[7] In certain circumstances it is likely that materiality will be presumed[8]:

1. Express claims are generally considered to be material. In this regard the Supreme Court noted, "[i]n the absence of factors that would distort the decision to advertise, we may assume that the willingness of a business to promote its products reflects a belief that consumers are interested in the advertising."[9]
2. When a seller knew, or should have known, that a reasonable consumer would need omitted information in order to properly evaluate the product or service, or that claim was false, because the manufacturer intended the information or omission to have an effect;
3. When a seller knew, or should have known, that a reasonable consumer would need omitted information in order to properly evaluate the product or service, or that claim was false, because the manufacturer intended the information or omission to have an effect;
4. When evidence exists that a seller intended to make an implied claim;

[6] *Ibid.*

[7] *Ibid.*

[8] *Ibid.*

[9] *Central Hudson Gas & Electric Co. v. PSC*, 447 U.S. 557, 567 (1980).

5. Claims or omissions that significantly involve health, safety, or other areas that would be of concern to a reasonable consumer;
6. Information that concerns the purpose, safety, efficacy, or cost of the product or service;
7. Information that is related to the durability, performance, warranties, or quality of a product or service;
8. Information pertaining to a finding by another agency regarding the product may also be material.

A determination of materiality will generally result in a finding that a consumer is likely to be injured or damaged because of the representation, omission, sales practice, or marketing technique. And injury or damage is likely to exist if a reasonable consumer would have chosen differently, but for the deception. If different choices are likely, the claim is material and the likelihood of injury or damage is as well. Injury and/or damage are likely to be considered synonyms for "materiality."

A necessary part of the analysis also includes the consideration of whether the consumer's interpretation or reaction was reasonable under the circumstances? As the FTC noted,[10] "An advertiser cannot be charged with liability with respect to every conceivable misconception, however outlandish, to which his representations might be subject among the foolish or feeble-minded. Some people, because of ignorance or incomprehension, may be misled by even a scrupulously honest claim. Perhaps a few misguided souls believe, for example, that all 'Danish pastry' is made in Denmark. Is it therefore an action deception to advertise 'Danish pastry' when it is made in this country? Of course not. A representation does not become 'false and deceptive' merely because it will be unreasonably misunderstood by an insignificant and unrepresentative segment of the class of persons to whom the representation is addressed."

To be considered reasonable, the interpretation or reaction does not have to be the only one. An interpretation will be presumed reasonable if it is the one the seller intended to convey.[11] Accurate information in the text of an advertisement may not remedy a false headline since a reasonable consumer may review only the headline. Likewise, if the first contact between a seller and a consumer occurs through a deceptive practice, the

---

[10] https://www.ftc.gov/system/files/documents/public_statements/410531/831014deceptionstmt.pdf.

[11] *Ibid.*

law may be violated even if accurate information is provided later. And the reverse is also true. A secondary message that is understood by a reasonable consumer is likely to be deceptive even when the primary message is accurate.[12]

An interpretation may be considered reasonable even though it is not shared by a majority of consumers in the relevant class, or by particularly sophisticated consumers. A material statement or practice that misleads a significant minority of reasonable consumers is likely to be considered deceptive.[13]

Related to the issue of misrepresentation is the issue of good faith. In this regard, American and French law on the subject of contracts is in general agreement. In the United States, the Restatement (Second) of Contracts, Section 205 notes that the common law "imposes a duty of good faith and fair dealing upon the parties in performing and enforcing the contract."[14] The Restatement is notable for failing to require good faith as part of negotiation.

French law, Article 1112, however, specifies that,

> The initiative, progress and termination of pre-contractual negotiations are free. They must imperatively meet the requirements of good faith....[15]

Article 1112-1 addresses the subject of fraud, particularly in the area of a failure to disclose information and notes that,

> One of the parties who is aware of information whose importance is decisive for the consent of the other party must inform it when, legitimately, the latter is unaware of this information or trusts its co-contracting party.

---

[12] *Ibid.*

[13] *Ibid.*

[14] As noted in the chapter on Commercial Law, UCC Section 1-203 states that "Every contract or duty within this Act imposes an obligation of good faith in its performance or enforcement." And UCC 2-103(j) defines good faith as "honesty in fact and the observance of reasonable commercial standards of fair dealing."

[15] Although limited to the sale or lease of goods, the Uniform Commercial Code also requires good faith which Section 1-201(20) addresses and notes that "good faith," except as otherwise provided in Article 5, means honesty in fact and the observance of reasonable commercial standards of fair dealing.

However, this duty of information does not relate to the estimation of the value of the service.

Of decisive importance is information that has a direct and necessary connection with the content of the contract or the quality of the parties.

It is incumbent upon the person claiming that information was owed to him to prove that the other party owed it to him, and it is up to that other party to prove that he provided it.

The parties can neither limit nor exclude this duty.

In addition to the liability of the person who was bound by it, failure to comply with this duty to inform may lead to the cancellation of the contract under the conditions provided for in articles 1130 *et seq*.

Other Requirements for a Valid Contract

Terms that are reasonably certain are the second requirement for an effective offer.

The Restatement Section 33 on "Certainty" notes:

1. Even though a manifestation of intention is intended to be understood as an offer, it cannot be accepted so as to form a contract unless the terms of the contract are reasonably certain.
2. The terms of a contract are reasonably certain if they provide a basis for determining the existence of a breach and for giving an appropriate remedy.
3. The fact that one or more terms of a proposed bargain are left open or uncertain may show that a manifestation of intention is not intended to be understood as an offer or as an acceptance.

Reasonably necessary terms are required in order for a court to determine:

1. Whether an agreement was breached; and
2. The remedy.

The offeror, generally the seller, controls the offer and, in the absence of negotiation, the resulting contract. However, there are numerous variations and while there are standardized contracts with common terms (often referred to as "boilerplate"), the use of such a contract may present a problem. The clauses that are noted below may be a part of contracts that are offered business-to-business and business-to-consumer. However, particularly with business-to-business contracts, negotiation is common and may affect the terms of the offer or the acceptance and the following are unlikely to represent all of the necessary clauses.

1. Age verification
   a. When dealing with minors,
      i. as noted in Chapter 4, the Children's Online Privacy Protection Act protects children under the age of 13 and requires, among other things, "verifiable parental consent."
2. Acceptance
   a. The specific actions that an offeree must do to accept the offer;
      i. Clicking on "I accept".
3. Payment;
4. Warranties, if any:
   a. A representation by the seller regarding the quality, features or condition of the goods sold or leased;
   b. In the case of goods, the Uniform Commercial Code Section 2-312 and 2A-211 specify three kinds of warranties of title;
      i. 2-312(1)(a) Good and valid title
      ii. 2-312(1)(b), 2A-211(1) No Encumbrances
      iii. 2-312(3), 2A-211(2) No Infringements
   c. A seller or lessor may disclaim title warranties only by way of specific language;
   d. Express Warranties;
      i. A seller or lessor creates an express warranty by way of representations, in writing or verbally, about the quality, condition, or capabilities of the goods.
      ii. 2-313 and 2A-210 specify situations where an express warranty is created.
   e. Implied Warranties;
      i. 2-314, 2A-212 Implied Warranty of Merchantability.
      ii. 2-315, 2A-213 Implied Warranty of fitness for a particular purpose.
      iii. 2-314(3), 2A-212(3) Implied Warranties from prior course of dealing or trade usage or custom.

5. Warranty Disclaimers;
   a. 2-316(1), 2a-214(1) allow a seller or lessor to disclaim oral express warranties by including a written disclaimer that is clear and conspicuous and called to a buyer's or lessee's attention.
   b. The implied warranties of merchantability and fitness for a particular purpose are generally disclaimed by statements such as "sold as is, where is, with no warranties express or implied" "with all faults" unless excluded by state law.
   c. 2-316(2), 2A-214(4) a seller or lessor must specifically specify "merchantability" in order to exclude the warranty of merchantability. 2-316(2), 2A-214(4) specify that if contained within a writing, the exclusion must be conspicuous or presented in such a way as to call attention to a reasonable person.
   d. 2-316(3)(c) allows an implied warranty to be excluded or modified by course of dealing, course of performance, or usage of trade.
6. Refunds (if any);
7. Restocking fee (if any);
8. Returns (if any);
9. Exculpatory clauses;
   a. Non-liability for certain uses of the goods (i.e., commercial).
   b. The need for advice from an attorney or other professional.
10. Limitation-of-Liability clauses;
    a. A liquidated damages clause.
    b. A clause that specifies a limited remedy such as repair or replacement within a specified period of time.
    c. A refund limited to a specified amount, such as the total price paid or an amount paid during a specified time frame.
    d. Exclusion of special, incidental, or consequential damages.
    i. UCC 2-719 allows a party to exclude consequential damages unless the exclusion is unconscionable or causes the remedy to fail of its essential purpose.
11. Available Remedies;
    a. Generally, the warranty (if any), including limitations based on:
       Time;
       Use;
       Misuse or Abuse;
12. The Offeror's Privacy Policy;
    a. What will the offeror do with the personally identifiable information gathered?

13. Alternatives to Litigation;
    a. Mediation.
    b. Binding Arbitration.
    c. The prevailing party shall recover attorneys' fees and costs.
14. Choice-of-law;
    a. The specific state law or other regulation that applies in the event of a dispute.
15. Choice-of-forum;
    a. The specific location, court or forum where the dispute will be heard.
16. Merger Clause;
    a. This written contract contains the full and complete expression of the terms between the parties, intended to prevent the introduction of parol evidence.

Arguably the most important clause is that specified by the Restatement (Third) of Torts Section 18. A party whose conduct creates a risk of physical or emotional harm can fail to exercise reasonable care by failing to warn of the danger if

1. The defendant knows or has reason to know
    a. of that risk; and
    b. that those encountering the risk will be unaware of it; and
2. A warning might be effective in reducing the risk of harm.

Even if the party adequately warns of the risk that the defendant's conduct creates, the defendant can fail to exercise reasonable care by failing to adopt further precautions to protect against the risk if it is foreseeable that despite the warning some risk of harm remains.

And it is arguable that this duty to warn extends to advertising. In many, may be most situations, consumers are unlikely to read the entirety of an advertisement, or may be directed away from the importance of the qualifying clause by acts or statements of the seller. In addition, the longer the contract, the less likely it is that it will be read either in its entirety, or at all.

French Law, Civil Code Section 1245-14 is far more restrictive and notes,

> Clauses that aim to exclude or limit liability for defective products are prohibited and deemed unwritten.

However, for damage caused to goods which are not used by the victim mainly for his private use or consumption, the clauses stipulated between professionals are valid.

Item 1170 of the French Civil Code is similar to American law on the subject of unconscionable contracts and provides another restriction, noting 'Any clause which deprives the essential obligation of the debtor of its substance is deemed to be unwritten.'

Communication

Communication is the third requirement for an effective offer since, ordinarily, one cannot agree to a bargain without knowing that it exists.

Express and Implied Contracts

Express

The terms are fully and explicitly stated.
The terms may be

1. verbal, or
2. written

Implied contracts (Implied-in-fact contracts)

These contracts are implied from the conduct of the parties.

Requirements for Implied Contracts[16]

1. A party provided a good or service at the request of another;
2. The party providing the good or service reasonably expected to be compensated and the other party knew or should have known that compensation was customary;

[16] See, for instance UCC Section 1–201 "Agreement, as distinguished from 'contract,' means the bargain of the parties in fact, as found in their language or inferred from other circumstances, including course of performance, course of dealing or usage of trade as provided in Section 1–303."

3. The party requesting the goods or services had an opportunity to inquire about compensation but failed to do so.

Termination of an Offer

An offer may be terminated either by:

1. Action of the parties; or
2. Operation of law

The Restatement

Section 36 of the Methods of Termination of the Power of Acceptance notes:

1. An offeree's power of acceptance may be terminated by
   a. rejection or counter-offer by the offeree, or
   b. lapse of time, or
   c. revocation by the offeror, or
   d. death or incapacity of the offeror or offeree.
2. In addition, an offeree's power of acceptance is terminated by the non-occurrence of any condition of acceptance under the terms of the offer.

Action of the Parties

An offer may be terminated by the offerror by way of revocation.

The Restatement

Section 42, Revocation by Communication from Offeror Received by Offeree states:

> An offeree's power of acceptance is terminated when the offeree receives from the offeror a manifestation of an intention not to enter into the proposed contract.
>
> May be express or implied
>
> A specific statement; or
>
> An act inconsistent with an offer.

Action by the Offeree

An offer may be terminated by the offeree's rejection of the offer.

The Restatement Section 38 on Rejection notes:

1. An offeree's power of acceptance is terminated by his rejection of the offer, unless the offeror has manifested a contrary intention.
2. A manifestation of intention not to accept an offer is a rejection unless the offeree manifests an intention to take it under further advisement.

May be express or implied.

Counteroffer

The Restatement

Section 38 of the Rejection of Offer by Counter-Offer states:

> A counter-offer by the offeree, relating to the same matter as the original offer, is a rejection of the original offer, unless the offeror in his offer, or the offeree in his counter-offer states that in spite of the counter-offer the original offer shall not be terminated.

The Restatement Section 39 on Counter-offers goes on to note:

1. A counter-offer is an offer made by an offeree to his offeror relating to the same matter as the original offer and proposing a substituted bargain differing from that proposed by the original offer.
2. An offeree's power of acceptance is terminated by his making of a counteroffer, unless the offeror has manifested a contrary intention or unless the counteroffer manifests a contrary intention of the offeree.

Generally, a response that does not exactly reflect the offer may be considered a counteroffer because of the common law "mirror image" rule.

Article 1118 provides, in part, "An acceptance which does not conform to the offer has no effect, apart from constituting a new offer. Article 1119 of the French Civil Code goes on to note:

> The general conditions invoked by one party only have effect with regard to the other if they have been brought to the attention of the latter and if it has accepted them.
>
> In case of discrepancy between the general conditions invoked by either party, the incompatible clauses are without effect.
>
> In case of discrepancy between general conditions and special conditions, the latter takes precedence over the former.

Termination by Operation of Law

Under certain circumstances an offer may be terminated by operation of law. As the Restatement Section 261 (1981) notes, a party's duty to perform a contract will only be discharged if extraordinary circumstances, "the non-occurrence of which was a basic assumption on which the contract was made," make performance "so vitally different from what was reasonably to be expected as to alter the essential nature of that performance."

Termination by Lapse of Time

The Restatement Section 41 on Lapse of Time notes:

1. An offeree's power of acceptance is terminated at the time specified in the offer, or, if no time is specified, at the end of a reasonable time.
2. What is a reasonable time is a question of fact, depending on all the circumstances existing when the offer and attempted acceptance are made.
3. Unless otherwise indicated by the language or the circumstances, and subject to the rule stated in Section 49, an offer sent by mail is seasonably accepted if an acceptance is mailed at any time before midnight on the day on which the offer is received.

   If an offer specifies a particular time frame, the offer terminates automatically at that time.

   If an offer does not specify a particular time frame it terminates upon passage of a reasonable time.

What is reasonable depends on a variety of factors. For instance, an offer to sell fresh fruits and vegetables may terminate in a shorter period of time than an offer to sell nuts, bolts, and nails.

French law, contained in Article 1117 is similar, if not identical, and notes:

> The offer lapses on the expiry of the period set by its author or, failing that, on the expiry of a reasonable period.
>
> It is also in case of incapacity or death of its author, or death of its addressee.

Termination by Destruction of the Subject Matter

Destruction of the subject matter of the contract generally falls under the category of impossibility of performance. Generally, impossibility is a defense to a breach of contract action only when performance is rendered objectively impossible by an unanticipated event that could not have been foreseen or guarded against in the contract.[17] Thus, impossibility excuses a party's performance only when the destruction of the subject matter of the contract or the means of performance makes performance objectively impossible.[18]

Termination by Death or Incompetence of Either Party

The Restatement Section 48 on Death or Incapacity of Offeror or Offeree specifies that an offeree's power of acceptance is terminated when the offeree or offeror dies or is deprived of legal capacity to enter into the proposed contract. French law is identical. Article 1117 as noted above goes on to note that an offer lapses "...in the case of the incapacity or death of the offeror."

Termination by Supervening Illegality

One of the requirements for a binding contract is "legality." Therefore, a contract that was legal at the time of making, but became illegal, possibly by a change in the law, may discharge the parties. French law, article 1162 notes that a contract may not derogate from public policy either by its stipulations or by its purpose, whether or not this was known by all the parties.

[17] *Gap Inc. v. Ponte Gadea New York LLC.*, 524 F.Supp.3d 224, 237 (S.D.N.Y. 2021).
[18] *Kel Kim Corp. v. Cent. Markets, Inc.*, 70 N.Y.2d 900, 902 (1987).

Acceptance of an Offer

The Restatement Section 30 notes:

Form of Acceptance Invited

1. An offer may invite or require acceptance to be made by an affirmative answer in words, or by performing or refraining from performing a specified act, or may empower the offeree to make a selection of terms in his acceptance.
2. Unless otherwise indicated by the language or the circumstances, an offer invites acceptance in any manner and by any medium reasonable in the circumstances.

The Restatement Section 32 goes on to note:

Invitation of Promise or Performance

In case of doubt an offer is interpreted as inviting the offeree to accept either by promising to perform what the offer requests or by rendering the performance, as the offeree chooses.

The Restatement Section 50 defines acceptance and notes:

Acceptance of Offer Defined; Acceptance by Performance; Acceptance by Promise

1. Acceptance of an offer is a manifestation of assent to the terms thereof made by the offeree in a manner invited or required by the offer.
2. Acceptance by performance requires that at least part of what the offer requests be performed or tendered and includes acceptance by a performance which operates as a return promise.
3. Acceptance by a promise requires that the offeree complete every act essential to the making of the promise.

Section 53 goes on to note:

1. An offer can be accepted by the rendering of a performance only if the offer invites such an acceptance.

2. Except as stated in Section 69, the rendering of a performance does not constitute an acceptance if within a reasonable time the offeree exercises reasonable diligence to notify the offeror of non-acceptance.
3. Where an offer of a promise invites acceptance by performance and does not invite a promissory acceptance, the rendering of the invited performance does not constitute an acceptance if before the offeror performs his promise the offeree manifests an intention not to accept.

Words or Conduct that Signify Assent (Agreement) to the Terms of the Offer

Unequivocal Acceptance

Pursuant to the common law mirror-image rule, an acceptance must be:

1. Unequivocal,
2. and communicated to the offeror.

Materially different terms in an acceptance are generally considered a rejection and counteroffer.

Additional terms that are not material may not constitute a rejection and counteroffer.

French law on the subject of acceptance is contained in Article 1118:

> An acceptance is the manifestation of the will of the offeree to be bound on the terms of the offer.
>
> As long as the acceptance has not reached the offeror, it may be withdrawn freely provided that the withdrawal reaches the offeror before the acceptance.
>
> An acceptance which does not conform to the offer has no effect, apart from constituting a new offer.

Article 1127-2 goes on to note that:

> A contract is validly concluded only if the party to whom the offer is addressed had the possibility of verifying the detail of his order and its total price and of correcting any possible errors before confirming his order in order to express his definitive acceptance.

> The party issuing the offer must without undue delay acknowledge by electronic means the receipt of such an order which has been addressed to him.
>
> The order, the confirmation of acceptance of the offer, and the acknowledgement of receipt are deemed to have been received when the parties to whom they are addressed are able to have access to them.

Silence as an Acceptance

The Restatement

Ordinarily, silence does not constitute an acceptance, although the law recognizes exceptions.

The Restatement, Section 69, acceptance by silence or exercise of dominion notes that:

1. Where an offeree fails to reply to an offer, his silence and inaction operate as an acceptance in the following cases only:
   a. Where an offeree takes the benefit of offered services with reasonable opportunity to reject them and reason to know that they were offered with the expectation of compensation.
   b. Where the offeror has stated or given the offeree reason to understand that assent may be manifested by silence or inaction, and the offeree in remaining silent and inactive intends to accept the offer.
   c. Where because of previous dealings or otherwise, it is reasonable that the offeree should notify the offeror if he does not intend to accept.
2. An offeree who does any act inconsistent with the offeror's ownership of offered property is bound in accordance with the offered terms unless they are manifestly unreasonable. But if the act is wrongful as against the offeror it is an acceptance only if ratified by him.

French law on the subject of silence is virtually identical. Article 1120 notes:

> Silence does not count as acceptance except where so provided by legislation, usage, business dealings or other particular circumstances.

Contracts and the Internet

The United States

Federal law on electronic transactions

In the late 1990s it became clear that the development of online transactions required the need for electronic signatures. In 1995, Utah's Digital Signature Act became the first state law to accept the enforceability of electronic signatures. California and Illinois soon followed suit. The variations in state laws prompted the National Conference of Commissioners on Uniform State Laws to join the fray and bring uniformity to the process.

The Uniform Electronic Transactions Act (UETA)

The UETA gives electronic signatures the same legal effect as traditional handwritten signatures under the Statute of Frauds, although the UETA only applies to certain kinds of transactions and only if the parties have agreed to conduct the transaction electronically.

Electronic signature

An electronic signature is broadly defined as any electronic sound, symbol, or process that is both:

1. Attached to or associated with a record or contract; and
2. Executed with the intent to sign the record.

The UETA has been adopted by every state except New York as well as the District of Columbia, Puerto Rico, and the Virgin Islands. New York adopted similar laws that make electronic signatures legally enforceable. Therefore, electronic records and signatures are as legally binding as those on paper.

Limitation

However, the UETA applies only to electronic records and electronic signatures related to a "transaction." A transaction is defined as,

"An interaction between two or more people relating to business, commercial, or governmental activities." Therefore, this law does not apply to:

> Wills, trusts, or codicils;
>
> Transactions governed by the Uniform Commercial Code other than sections 1-107 and 1-206 and Articles 2 and 2A;
>
> Transactions related to the Uniform Computer Information Transactions Act;
>
> Other laws, if any, identified by a state.

In addition, the parties must have previously agreed to make electronic documents and signatures valid and binding. The parties' agreement may be written, verbal or even implied by the conduct of the parties.

Electronic Signatures in Global and National Commerce Act (E-SIGN)[19]

In summary, this act gives electronic signatures the same legal effect as handwritten signatures in all states or territories where federal law applies.[20] While individual states may decide to adopt the UETA or, as in the case of New York, a similar law, E-SIGN applies, as noted, in all states. The E-SIGN act grants legal recognition to electronic signatures and records as long as all parties to a contract choose to use electronic documents and to sign them electronically. This law allows the use of electronic records to satisfy any statute, regulation, or rule of law that requires that such information be provided in writing, if the consumer has affirmatively consented, in writing, to such use and has not withdrawn the consent.

This means that in order for an electronic signature to be valid and binding, the parties must have entered into an enforceable contract where the parties agree to be bound by such signatures. Therefore, the E-SIGN Act requires:

1. The consent of all the parties;
2. An intent to sign, which means that a party must have the option to opt out;

---

[19]Public Law 106-229, June 30, 2000. 15 U.S.C. Section 7001 *et seq.*

[20]https://www.govinfo.gov/content/pkg/PLAW-106publ229/pdf/PLAW-106publ229.pdf.

3. A visible mark, sound, symbol, or process that is;
4. Attributable and associated only with that signer; as well as
5. Retention so that the document is saved and may be viewed or printed by a party.

Signatures on Electronic Records

E-Signature Defined

An e-signature is "an electronic sound, symbol, or process attached to or logically associated with a record and executed or adopted by a person with the intent to sign the record." Typing a name or entering a "symbol" or even a "sound" may serve as a signature.

An electronic record is deemed sent when properly directed to the recipient in a form readable by the recipient's computer. This replaces the common law "mailbox rule." Although at least one court held that a typed name does not constitute a signature, software now creates an e-signature that is similar to a handwritten signature

Exclusions

As with the UETA, the E-SIGN Act has certain limitations and excludes from its coverage the following:

1. Court papers;
2. Divorce decrees;
3. Evictions;
4. Foreclosures;
5. Health insurance terminations;
6. Prenuptial *(antenuptial)* agreements;
7. Wills.

Both E-SIGN and UETA share a common purpose to assist commercial transactions.

French law on the subject of electronic signatures is similar. Section 1367 notes that:

> The signature necessary for the perfection of a legal act identifies its author. It expresses its consent to the obligations arising from this act.

When it is affixed by a public official, it confers authenticity on the act.

When it is electronic, it consists of the use of a reliable identification process guaranteeing its link with the act to which it is attached. The reliability of this process is presumed, until proven otherwise, when the electronic signature is created, the identity of the signatory assured, and the integrity of the act guaranteed, under conditions fixed by decree in Council of State.

French Law on Electronic Transactions specifies additional details that are similar to American law:

Article 1125:

Electronic means may be used to make available contractual stipulations.

Article 1126:

The information which is requested with a view to concluding a contract or that which is sent during its execution may be transmitted by e-mail if the recipient has accepted the use of this means.

Article 1127-1:

A person who, in a business or professional capacity, makes a proposal by electronic means for the supply of property or services, must make available the applicable contractual stipulations in a way which permits their storage and reproduction.

A person issuing an offer remains bound by it as long as it is made accessible by him by electronic means.

The offer further states:

1. The different steps to follow to conclude the contract electronically;
2. The technical means allowing the recipient of the offer, before the conclusion of the contract, to identify any errors made in the entry of data and to correct them;
3. The languages offered for the conclusion of the contract, including the French language;

4. If applicable, the methods of archiving the contract by the author of the offer and the conditions of access to the archived contract;

5. The means of consulting electronically the professional and commercial rules to which the author of the offer intends, where applicable, to comply.

Article 1127-2:

The contract is only validly concluded if the recipient of the offer has had the opportunity to check the details of his order and its total price and to correct any errors before confirming it to express his final acceptance.

The author of the offer must acknowledge receipt without undue delay, by electronic means, of the order sent to him.

The order, the confirmation of acceptance of the offer and the acknowledgment of receipt are considered received when the parties to whom they are addressed can have access to them.

Article 1127-3:

An exception is made to the obligations referred to in (subparagraphs) 1–5 of Article 1127-1 and the first two paragraphs of Article 1127-2 for contracts for the supply of goods or the provision of services which are concluded exclusively by exchange of e-mails.

The provisions of (subparagraphs) 1–5 of Article 1127-1 and Article 1127-2 may also be waived in contracts concluded between professionals.

Article 1127-4:

Apart from the cases provided for in Articles 1125 and 1126, the delivery of an electronic document is effective when the recipient, after having been able to read it, has acknowledged receipt.

If a provision provides that the writing must be read to the addressee, the delivery of an electronic writing to the person concerned under the conditions provided for in the first paragraph constitutes reading.

Item 1174:

When a written document is required for the validity of a contract, it may be drawn up and kept in electronic form under the conditions provided for in Articles 1366 and 1367 and, when an authentic document is required, by the second paragraph of Article 1369 which, as previously stated, may be drawn up in an electronic medium if it is created and stored on the conditions fixed by decree of the Council of State.

When a written mention by the hand of the person who undertakes is required, the latter may affix it in electronic form if the conditions of this affixing are such as to guarantee that it can only be carried out by himself.

Consideration

The Restatement Section 71 notes the requirements for consideration and states:

1. To constitute consideration, a performance or a return promise must be bargained for.
2. A performance or return promise is bargained for if it is sought by the promisor in exchange for his promise and is given by the promisee in exchange for that promise.
3. The performance may consist of:
   a. an act other than a promise, or
   b. a forbearance, or
   c. the creation, modification, or destruction of a legal relation.
4. The performance or return promise may be given to the promisor or to some other person. It may be given by the promisee or by some other person.

The purpose of this requirement is to distinguish a contract from a gift. In this regard, French law also notes the difference between a contract and a gift:

Article 1107: A contract is onerous where each of the parties receives a benefit from the other in return for what he provides.

It is gratuitous where one of the parties provides a benefit to the other without expecting or receiving anything in return.

Consideration generally is one of the requirements that is necessary for the creation of a contract. Consideration is generally defined as a detriment incurred or a benefit received.

The Restatement Section 79 addresses the "adequacy" of consideration, as well as the mutuality of obligation and notes:

If the requirement of consideration is met, there is no additional requirement of

a. a gain, advantage, or benefit to the promisor or a loss, disadvantage, or detriment to the promisee, or
b. equivalence in the values exchanged, or
c. "mutuality of obligation."

In summary, consideration consists of:

1. A promise to do something that a promisor has no prior legal duty to do;
2. Performing an action a promisor is not obligated to do; or
3. Refraining from performing a legal right.

Hamer v. Sidway, 79 Sickels 538 (N.Y., 1894)

William E. Story, Sr., was the uncle of William E. Story, 2d; that at the celebration of the golden wedding of Samuel Story and wife, father and mother of William E. Story, Sr., on March 20, 1869, in the presence of the family and invited guests, he promised his nephew that if he would refrain from drinking, using tobacco, swearing, and playing cards or billiards for money until he became 21 years of age, he would pay him the sum of $5,000. The nephew assented thereto, and fully performed the conditions inducing the promise. When the nephew arrived at the age of 21 years, and on January 31, 1875, he wrote to his uncle, informing him that he had performed his part of the agreement, and had thereby become entitled to the sum of $5,000. The uncle received the letter, and a few days later, and on the 6th day of February, he wrote and mailed to his nephew the following letter: "Buffalo, Feb. 6, 1875. W. E. Story, Jr. — Dear Nephew: Your letter of the 31st ult. came to hand all right, saying that you had lived up to the promise made to me several years ago. I have no doubt but you have, for which you shall have five thousand dollars, as I promised you. I had the money in the bank the day you was twenty-one years old that I intend for you, and you shall have the money certain …"

"The nephew received the letter, and thereafter consented that the money should remain with his uncle in accordance with the terms and conditions of the letter. The uncle died on the 29th day of January, 1887, without having paid over to his nephew any portion of the said $5,000 and interest …

"The defendant contends that the contract was without consideration to support it, and therefore invalid. He asserts that the promisee, by refraining from the use of liquor and tobacco, was not harmed, but benefited; that that which he did was best for him to do, independently of his uncle's promise, — and insists that it follows that, unless the promisor was benefited, the contract was without consideration, — a contention which, if well founded, would seem to leave open for controversy in many cases whether that which the promisee did or omitted to do was in fact of such benefit to him as to leave no consideration to support the enforcement of the promisor's agreement. Such a rule could not be tolerated, and is without foundation in the law. The exchequer chamber in 1875 defined "consideration" as follows: "A valuable consideration, in the sense of the law, may consist either in some right, interest, profit, or benefit accruing to the one party, or some forbearance, detriment, loss, or responsibility given, suffered, or undertaken by the other." Courts "will not ask whether the thing which forms the consideration does in fact benefit the promisee or a third party, or is of any substantial value to anyone. It is enough that something is promised, done, forborne, or suffered by the party to whom the promise is made as consideration for the promise made to him." …"In general a waiver of any legal right at the request of another party is a sufficient consideration for a promise." "Any damage, or suspension, or forbearance of a right will be sufficient to sustain a promise."…Pollock in his work on Contracts, (page 166,) after citing the definition given by the exchequer chamber, already quoted, says: "The second branch of this judicial description is really the most important one. 'Consideration' means not so much that one party is profiting as that the other abandons some legal right in the present, or limits his legal freedom of action in the future, as an inducement for the promise of the first.' Now, applying this rule to the facts before us, the promisee used tobacco, occasionally drank liquor, and he had a legal right to do so. That right he abandoned for a period of years upon the strength of the promise of the testator that for such forbearance he would give him $5,000. We need not speculate on the effort which may have been required to give up the use of those stimulants. It is sufficient that he restricted his lawful freedom of action within certain prescribed limits upon the faith of his uncle's agreement, and now, having fully performed the conditions imposed, it is of no moment whether such performance actually proved a benefit to the promisor, and the court will not inquire into it; but, were it a proper subject of inquiry, we see nothing in this record that would permit a determination that the uncle was not benefited in a legal sense."

Capacity

Another requirement for a valid contract. An individual's ability, oftentimes referred to as "capacity," to enter into a binding agreement may, under some circumstances be affected, by a variety of factors.

The Restatement Section 12 addresses the subject and notes:

1. No one can be bound by contract who has not legal capacity to incur at least voidable contractual duties. Capacity to contract may be partial and its existence in respect of a particular transaction may depend upon the nature of the transaction or upon other circumstances.
2. A natural person who manifests assent to a transaction has full legal capacity to incur contractual duties thereby unless he is
   a. under guardianship, or
   b. an infant, or
   c. mentally ill or defective, or
   d. intoxicated

Section 13, Persons Affected by Guardianship:

> A person has no capacity to incur contractual duties if his property is under guardianship by reason of an adjudication of mental illness or defect.

Section 14, Infants:

> Unless a statute provides otherwise, a natural person has the capacity to incur only voidable contractual duties until the beginning of the day before the person's eighteenth birthday.

Section 15, Mental Illness or Defect:

1. A person incurs only voidable contractual duties by entering into a transaction if by reason of mental illness or defect
   a. he is unable to understand in a reasonable manner the nature and consequences of the transaction, or
   b. he is unable to act in a reasonable manner in relation to the transaction and the other party has reason to know of his condition.
2. Where the contract is made on fair terms and the other party is without knowledge of the mental illness or defect, the power of avoidance under Subsection (1) terminates to the extent that the contract has been so performed in whole or in part or the circumstances have so changed that avoidance would be unjust. In such a case a court may grant relief as justice requires.

Section 16, Intoxicated Persons:

A person incurs only voidable contractual duties by entering into a transaction if the other party has reason to know that by reason of intoxication

a. he is unable to understand in a reasonable manner the nature and consequences of the transaction, or
b. he is unable to act in a reasonable manner in relation to the transaction.

French Law Article 1129 and the succeeding sections address the subject of capacity and note:

> In accordance with article 414-1, one must be of sound mind to give valid consent to a contract.

Article 1145:

> Every natural person is able to conclude a contract, except in the case of lack of capacity provided for by legislation.
>
> The capacity of legal persons is limited to acts useful for realizing their purpose as defined by their statutes and acts which are incidental to

them, in accordance with the rules applicable to each of those persons.

Article 1146:

The following lack the capacity to conclude a contract, to the extent to which legislation provides:

1. Minors who have not been emancipated;
2. Protected adults within the meaning of article 425.

Article 1147:

A lack of capacity to conclude a contract is a ground of relative nullity.

Article 1148:

Every person who lacks the capacity to contract may nonetheless effect independently day-to-day acts authorized by legislation or by usage, provided that they are concluded on normal terms.

Article 1149:

Day-to-day acts effected by a minor may be annulled on the ground of mere substantive inequality of bargain. However, nullity is not incurred where the substantive inequality results from an unforeseeable event.

The mere fact that a minor has made a declaration of majority does not constitute an obstacle to annulment.

A minor cannot escape from undertakings which he has entered into in the exercise of his business or profession.

Article 1151:

A contracting party who has capacity may defend an action for annulment brought against him by establishing that the act was useful to the protected person and was free from substantive inequality, or that he profited from it.

> Such a contracting party may also set up against an action for annulment the fact that the other party to the contract affirmed the act after gaining or regaining his capacity.

Legality

The creation of a binding agreement also requires that the purpose of the contract be legal. An offer to do something that is prohibited by federal or state statutory law is illegal. Thus, generally, an offer that involves fraud, a tort, or an illegal act is void and unenforceable.

The Restatement Section 178 addresses the subject of illegality on the basis of public policy and notes:

1. A promise or other term of an agreement is unenforceable on grounds of public policy if legislation provides that it is unenforceable or the interest in its enforcement is clearly outweighed in the circumstances by a public policy against the enforcement of such terms.
2. In weighing the interest in the enforcement of a term, account is taken of
   a. the parties' justified expectations,
   b. any forfeiture that would result if enforcement were denied, and
   c. any special public interest in the enforcement of the particular term.
3. In weighing a public policy against enforcement of a term, account is taken of
   a. the strength of that policy is manifested by legislation or judicial decisions,
   b. the likelihood that a refusal to enforce the term will further that policy,
   c. the seriousness of any misconduct involved and the extent to which it was deliberate, and
   d. the directness of the connection between that misconduct and the term.

French law also refers to the subject of public policy, and its effect on a contract. As previously noted, Article 1162 specifies that:

> A contract cannot derogate from public policy either by its stipulations or by its purpose, whether or not this was known by all the parties.

The Statute of Frauds

In certain situations, a contract must be in writing in order to be enforceable. The Restatement Section 131 notes the requirements for a writing or "memorandum" and notes:

Unless additional requirements are prescribed by the particular statute, a contract within the Statute of Frauds is enforceable if it is evidenced by any writing, signed by or on behalf of the party to be charged, which

a. reasonably identifies the subject matter of the contract,
b. is sufficient to indicate that a contract with respect thereto has been made between the parties or offered by the signer to the other party, and
c. states with reasonable certainty the essential terms of the unperformed promises in the contract.

Such contracts include:

1. Contracts involving the sale of an interest in land;
2. Contracts that cannot by their terms be performed within one year from the date of formation;
3. Collateral or secondary contracts, such as promises to answer for the debt of another;
4. Promises made in consideration of marriage;
5. UCC Sections 2-201(1) and UCC 2A-210(1) require that contracts for the sale of goods priced at $500 or more and lease contracts requiring payments of $1,000 or more.

Contract Creation in the European Union

Just as there are differences among the laws of the 50 states, as well as the District of Columbia, the same is true for the European Union. The common law system in England and Ireland are different from those in the United States, and different from the civil law systems of the continental European countries. And the differences in the legal systems of the various countries of the European Union, including those that utilize a civil law system, are likely to be far more significant than those in the United States.

Among the notable differences between the common law and civil law systems is freedom of contract. In the United States, except for commercial contracts and contracts involving consumers, parties are free to negotiate the terms of a contract. Even with regard to commercial law, the parties are free to specify the terms of a contract. Only in those situations where the parties failed or neglected to include a provision, will the commercial law come into play. Unless expressly prohibited by law, the parties are generally free to negotiate whatever terms they like.

In a civil law system, there may be less emphasis on specifying the terms of a contract since the contract will be controlled by the relevant code. The parties are not free to add to, vary, or delete terms that are required by the applicable code. However, there are differences even among the civil law systems.

In a civil law system disputes over a contract are generally decided on the basis of statutory law that is applied to the facts of a case, rather than the application of precedent, as in the United States.

The French Civil Code

A significant part of the French Civil Code is dedicated to the requirement of good faith, something that is required both by the American Uniform Commercial Code as well as the common law.

The French Civil Code on Contracts, Articles 1100–1386-1, specify, in detail, everything from the definition of a contract, as noted above, "A contract is a concordance of wills of two or more persons intended to create, modify, transfer or extinguish obligations") to the issue of proof ("A court may require an oath of its own initiative only in support of a claim, or of any defence which is set up against it, if the claim or defence is neither conclusively justified nor completely lacking in means of proof") and specifically leaves its "... probative value to the assessment of the court."

In addition, unlike the United States, in a civil law system, parties may not be required to swear an oath since self-interest is unlikely to be addressed by an oath.

Article 1102 notes that "Everyone is free to contract or not to contract, to choose the person with whom to contract, and to determine the content and form of the contract, within the limits imposed by legislation." However, Article 1102 goes on to note, "Contractual freedom does not allow derogation from rules which are an expression of public policy." And Article 1104 notes, "Contracts must be negotiated, formed and performed in good faith. This provision is a matter of public policy." This provision is arguably broader than the common law requirement. The Restatement (Second) of Contracts, Section 205 only "imposes a duty of good faith and fair dealing upon the parties in performing and enforcing the contract."[21] As previously noted, there is arguably no requirement about good faith in the negotiation of a contract.

Unlike the United States, Article 5 of the French Civil Code specifically removes a judge's discretion to create rules of general applicability when deciding a case, thus making it clear that only the legislature may create law.

In conclusion, a written code appears to reflect both a distrust of the judgment of individual judges as well as trust in the judgment of the legislature, as well as arguably creating a more transparent, impartial, and uniform basis for decisions. However, the approach may limit the flexibility that arises, at least in part, from, for instance, technological advances.

---

[21] The Uniform Commercial Code, on the other hand and as noted elsewhere, may allow a court to modify the terms of a commercial contract, particularly when a consumer is a party. Section 2-302(1) notes, "If the court as a matter of law finds the contract or any clause of the contract to have been unconscionable at the time it was made the court may refuse to enforce the contract, or it may enforce the remainder of the contract without the unconscionable clause as to avoid any unconscionable result."

Chapter 8

Contract Interpretation and Performance

Abstract

Ideally, all contracts are performed exactly as specified, to the satisfaction of all the parties. There are, however, exceptions where performance may be either more difficult, or impossible. The common law recognizes situations where a contract may not be enforced, or enforceable, for a variety of reasons. The common law also allows parties to insert clauses in their contract that may affect performance, whether there is a breach or not, and the available remedies.

The prior chapter discussed the requirements that are necessary to create a binding agreement, both in the United States as well as France. In the United States, prior to the creation of an agreement, the parties are called the "offeror," the one making the offer, and the "offeree," the one receiving the offer. Once there has been an unequivocal acceptance to an offer the parties then become the "promisor" and the "promisee."

Codes in countries with a civil law system specify the details of a contract from its creation to its performance or breach while a common law system may provide for more flexibility to the parties, although there are exceptions.

While most contracts are fulfilled exactly as promised, there are situations where that may not be possible and both the common and civil law systems provide for exceptions.

The Restatement (Second) of Contracts Section 1 defines a contract and notes that a contract is a promise or a set of promises for the breach of which the law gives a remedy, or the performance of which the law in some way recognizes as a duty.

Section 2

Promise; Promisor; Promisee; Beneficiary

1. A promise is a manifestation of intention to act or refrain from acting in a specified way, so made as to justify a promisee in understanding that a commitment has been made.
2. The person manifesting the intention is the promisor.
3. The person to whom the manifestation is addressed is the promisee.
4. Where performance will benefit a person other than the promisee, that person is a beneficiary.

Section 4

How a Promise May Be Made

A promise may be stated in words either oral or written, or may be inferred wholly or partly from conduct.

Performance

Contracts are normally discharged by full and complete performance. However, as with an offer, as noted in the prior chapter, a contract may also be discharged by:

1. agreement of the parties, or
2. operation of law.

Discharge by Performance

The Restatement Section 235 notes:

1. Full performance of a duty under a contract discharges the duty.
2. When performance of a duty under a contract is due any non-performance is a breach.

Substantial Performance

When a contract is not fully performed it may either be considered "substantial" performance, or a breach. The Restatement provides guidance on whether performance is substantial or not. If performance is not considered substantial it will generally be labeled a material breach of contract.

The Restatement Section 241 specifies the factors to consider when determining whether a performance is either substantial or a breach:

In determining whether a failure to perform is material, the following circumstances are significant:

a. The extent to which the injured party will be deprived of the benefit which he reasonably expected;
b. The extent to which the injured party can be adequately compensated for the part of that benefit of which he will be deprived;
c. The extent to which the party failing to perform or to offer to perform will suffer forfeiture;
d. The likelihood that the party failing to perform or to offer to perform will cure his failure, taking account of all the circumstances including any reasonable assurances;
e. The extent to which the behavior of the party failing to perform or to offer to perform comports with standards of good faith and fair dealing.

As with French law, the existence of good faith, as well as fair dealing is a significant element and a court may allow a party who, in good faith, performed substantially all of the terms of a contract to enforce the contract, usually payment. If, on the other hand, there is an absence of good faith, or an intentional failure to comply, there is likely a breach, unless the law provides for an excuse.

In summary, substantial performance will generally involve the following issues:

1. Was there a good faith effort to perform as promised in the contract, or an intentional failure?
2. Was there a minor deviation from the terms of the agreement that does not significantly affect the outcome of the performance?

In any event, in the United States, whether a performance was substantial or not may be determined by courts as a result of a lawsuit.

French Law on the subject of a breach of contract also includes a requirement of substantiality, although it is described in somewhat different terms:

Item 1184[1]:

> When the cause of nullity affects only one or more clauses of the contract, it only invalidates the entire act if this or these clauses constitute a determining element of the commitment of the parties or one of them.
>
> The contract is maintained when the law deems the clause unwritten, or when the purposes of the unrecognized rule require its maintenance.
>
> Item 1185:
>
> The exception of nullity is not prescribed if it relates to a contract, which has not received any execution.
>
> Item 1186:
>
> A validly formed contract lapses if one of its essential elements disappears....
>
> Item 1187:
>
> Lapse terminates the contract.
>
> It may give rise to restitution under the conditions provided for in Articles 1352–1352-9.

Effect of a Breach on the Duty to Perform

A critical issue is the effect that a breach will have on the other party's duty to perform, likely to be the duty to pay. A breach may result in either a termination of the other party's duty to perform or a temporary suspension of the duty to perform.

---

[1]Unless otherwise noted, all references to French law in this chapter were obtained from an unofficial English translation of the French Civil Code that is available at https://www.legifrance.gouv.fr/codes/texte_lc/LEGITEXT000006070721/ Version in force November 18, 2023.

The Restatement Section 243 addresses the subject of a breach of contract by non-performance and whether it constitutes a total breach, noting:

1. With respect to performances to be exchanged under an exchange of promises, a breach by non-performance gives rise to a claim for damages for total breach only if it discharges the injured party's remaining duties to render such performance, other than a duty to render an agreed equivalent under Section 240.
2. Except as stated in Subsection (3), a breach by non-performance accompanied or followed by a repudiation gives rise to a claim for damages for total breach.
3. Where at the time of the breach the only remaining duties of performance are those of the party in breach and are for the payment of money in installments not related to one another, his breach by non-performance as to less than the whole, whether or not accompanied or followed by a repudiation, does not give rise to a claim for damages for total breach.
4. In any case other than those stated in the preceding subsections, a breach by non-performance gives rise to a claim for total breach only if it so substantially impairs the value of the contract to the injured party at the time of the breach that it is just in the circumstances to allow him to recover damages based on all his remaining rights to performance.

Thus, if performance is substantial the other party's duty to perform may be temporarily suspended but is unlikely to be discharged. If the breach is material, the other party's duty to perform is discharged and the non-breaching party may sue for damages, if any.

French law provides several options in the event of substantial performance or a complete breach, all of which are similar to the options available in the United States.

Item 1217:

> The party toward whom the commitment has not been performed, or has been performed imperfectly, may:
>
> — Refuse to perform or suspend the performance of his own obligation;
> — Pursue the forced execution in kind of the obligation;
> — Obtain a price reduction;

— Cause the termination of the contract;
— Seek compensation for the consequences of non-performance.

Sanctions that are not incompatible may be cumulative; damages can always be added.

Item 1219:

A party may refuse to perform its obligation, even when it is due, if the other does not perform its own and if this non-performance is sufficiently serious.

Item 1220:

A party may suspend performance of its obligation when it is clear that its co-contracting party will not perform on the due date and that the consequences of this non-performance are sufficiently serious for it. This suspension must be notified as soon as possible.

As previously noted, a contract may be terminated either by action of the parties or by operation of law. The contract itself may provide for situations that result in the termination of the contract. French law recognizes this distinction as well.

Item 1224:

Termination results either from the application of a termination clause or, in the event of sufficiently serious non-performance, from notification by the creditor to the debtor or from a court decision.

French law wisely requires notification in the event of a perceived breach of contract, thus giving a party an opportunity to correct the breach.

Item 1226:

The creditor may, at his own risk, terminate the contract by notification. Except in an emergency, he must first give formal notice to the defaulting debtor to fulfill his commitment within a reasonable time. The formal notice expressly mentions that if the debtor fails to meet his obligation, the creditor will be entitled to terminate the contract.

When non-performance persists, the creditor notifies the debtor of the termination of the contract and the reasons for it.

> The debtor may at any time seise the judge to contest the resolution. The creditor must then prove the seriousness of the non-performance.

Is it a Material or a Minor Breach?

The difference may not always be clear. Generally, as previously noted, in the event of a minor breach, the other party's duty to perform may be suspended temporarily, but not entirely excused. And, once the minor breach is cured the non-breaching party's duty to perform (usually pay), is reinstated. In certain situations, a minor breach may justify a reduction in payment both in the United States and France. As French law notes in Item 1223:

> In the event of imperfect performance of the service, the creditor may, after formal notice and if he has not yet paid all or part of the service, notify the debtor as soon as possible of his decision to reduce it in such a way proportional to the price. The debtor's acceptance of the creditor's price reduction decision must be in writing.
>
> If the creditor has already paid, failing agreement between the parties, he may ask the judge to reduce the price.

Discharge of a Contract by Agreement of the Parties May Occur in Several Ways

Rescission or Rescission and Restitution

First, a contract may be discharged by rescission. That is, the parties agree to rescind a contract, returning the parties to their original positions prior to creation of the contract. An agreement to rescind a contract generally requires all of the elements that are necessary for the creation of the original agreement.

If the contract is executory on both sides, and neither party has performed, the agreement to rescind the contract is generally sufficient. In the event that the contract is partially executed or performed either partially, or in whole by one or both parties, rescission will generally require restitution by one or both parties, of the benefit that has been received.

Discharge by Novation

The Restatement of Contracts Section 424 defines novation as (a) a contract that discharges immediately a previous contractual duty or a duty to make compensation, (b) creates a new contractual duty, and (c) includes as a party one who neither owed the previous duty nor was entitled to its performance. And Section 280 of the Restatement of Contracts states that a novation means the substitution of a new party for a party in a previous contract.

Thus, in certain situations, a party to a contract may be unable to perform, either due to an injury or illness or some other legally valid excuse. In that situation, the parties to an agreement may rescind the original agreement and substitute a third party for one of the original parties.

French law also recognizes the necessity of a novation in certain situations, although the definition is not limited to a new party and may include a different obligation between existing parties.

Section 1329:

> Novation is a contract whose purpose is to substitute for an obligation, which it extinguishes, a new obligation which it creates.
>
> It can take place by substitution of obligation between the same parties, by change of debtor or by change of creditor.

Item 1330:

> Novation is not presumed; the will to operate it must clearly result from the act.

Item 1331:

> Novation takes place only if the old obligation and the new obligation are both valid, unless it has the declared purpose of substituting a valid commitment for a commitment tainted with a vice.

Discharge by Settlement Agreement

In the event of a dispute over the interpretation of a valid agreement the parties may agree to substitute a revised agreement to replace the original. In order to do so, all of the noted requirements for a valid contract must be met.

Discharge by Accord and Satisfaction

The Restatement of Contracts Section 281 addresses the subject of "Accord and Satisfaction" and notes that:

1. An accord is a contract under which an obligee promises to accept a stated performance in satisfaction of the obligor's existing duty. Performance of the accord discharges the original duty.
2. Until performance of the accord, the original duty is suspended unless there is such a breach of the accord by the obligor as discharges the new duty of the obligee to accept the performance in satisfaction. If there is such a breach, the obligee may enforce either the original duty or any duty under the accord.
3. Breach of the accord by the obligee does not discharge the original duty, but the obligor may maintain a suit for specific performance of the accord, in addition to any claim for damages for partial breach.

An accord and satisfaction typically arises when an original agreement cannot be performed as required by the terms of the agreement. This may be due to a variety of reasons, such as the unavailability of certain materials or services required by the existing agreement, and thus the subsequent performance is different from the performance that was originally promised. The accord is an agreement that is different from what was originally agreed to. The satisfaction is the performance of a different requirement, in accordance with the subsequent agreement.[2]

Discharge by Operation of Law

The law specifies that in certain situations a contract may be terminated.

Material Alteration

The Restatement Section 286 addresses the alteration of a writing and notes:

1. If one to whom a duty is owed under a contract alters a writing that is an integrated agreement or that satisfies the Statute of Frauds with

---

[2] *Valcon II, Inc. v. United States*, 26 Cl. Ct. 393, 397 (1992).

respect to that contract, the duty is discharged if the alteration is fraudulent and material.

2. An alteration is material if it would, if effective, vary any party's legal relations with the maker of the alteration or adversely affect that party's legal relations with a third person. The unauthorized insertion in a blank space in a writing is an alteration.

In order to be fraudulent, such an alteration must be done without assent or agreement.

Statutes of Limitations

In the event of a dispute over a requirement, litigation must be commenced within a specific period of time. Failing to sue within that specific time may eliminate the possibility of judicial assistance in resolving a dispute.

For verbal contracts, the statute of limitations is generally two to three years. For written contracts, the statute of limitations is generally four to five years. A statute of limitations recognizes that memories fade and documents may be lost or destroyed and is thus intended to bar stale claims.

Bankruptcy

Although bankruptcy generally terminates a contract, a party may still file a claim in bankruptcy court although any recovery is likely to be minimal.

Impossibility of Performance

The Restatement (Second) of Contracts Section 261 (1981) notes that a party's duty to perform a contract will only be discharged if extraordinary circumstances, "the non-occurrence of which was a basic assumption on which the contract was made," make performance "so vitally different from what was reasonably to be expected as to alter the essential nature of that performance." In addition, performance must be objectively, as opposed to subjectively, impossible. As Comment e to Restatement of Contracts Section 261 notes, the difference between objective and subjective impossibility "has been described as that between 'the thing cannot be done' and 'I cannot do it.'"

Thus, the intervening event must not only be unforeseen, but unforeseeable as well. Examples of objective impossibility of performance are the same as those noted in termination of the offer and include death or incapacity of a party prior to performance, destruction of the subject matter and illegality.

The Restatement Section 262 addresses the death or incapacity of a party whose performance was necessary for the contract and notes:

> If the existence of a particular person is necessary for the performance of a duty, his death or such incapacity as makes performance impracticable is an event the non-occurrence of which was a basic assumption on which the contract was made.

French law also addresses the issue of impossibility. Item 1351 notes:

> The impossibility of performing the service releases the debtor to the extent when it results from a case of *force majeure*[3] and it is final, unless he has agreed to take charge of it or he has been given notice beforehand.

Section 1351-1:

> When the impossibility of performance results from the loss of the thing due, the debtor put in default is nevertheless released if he proves that the loss would have similarly occurred if the obligation had been performed.
>
> However, he is required to transfer to his creditor the rights and actions attached to the thing.

The Restatement Section 263 addresses the subject of destruction, deterioration, or a failure to come into existence of something that was necessary for contract performance and notes:

> If the existence of a specific thing is necessary for the performance of a duty, its failure to come into existence, destruction, or such deterioration

---

[3] Black's Law Dictionary 657 (6th ed. 1990) notes that "force majeure" is French for superior or irresistible force.

as makes performance impracticable is an event the non-occurrence of which was a basic assumption on which the contract was made.

Commercial Impracticability

Related to the issue of impossibility of performance is commercial impracticability. The Restatement Section 261 addresses the subject of discharge by supervening impracticability[4] and notes:

> Where, after a contract is made, a party's performance is made impracticable without his fault by the occurrence of an event the non-occurrence of which was a basic assumption on which the contract was made, his duty to render that performance is discharged, unless the language or the circumstances indicate the contrary.

Thus, a court may excuse performance when it is significantly more difficult or expensive than originally contemplated. However, this defense is limited and requires that the party asserting it demonstrate that the performance is exceptionally difficult or costly and that the additional difficulty or expense was not foreseeable when the contract was made.

French law is virtually identical and Item 1218 notes:

> There is *force majeure* in contractual matters when an event beyond the control of the debtor, which could not reasonably have been foreseen at the time of the conclusion of the contract and the effects of which cannot be avoided by appropriate measures, prevents the performance of its obligation, by the debtor.
>
> If the impediment is temporary, the performance of the obligation is suspended unless the resulting delay justifies termination of the contract.

---

[4]The Uniform Commercial Code Section 2-615, discussed in the chapter on Commercial Law is similar and provides in relevant part, "Excuse by Failure of Presupposed Conditions. Except so far as a seller may have assumed a greater obligation and subject to the preceding section on substituted performance:

(a) Delay in delivery or non-delivery in whole or in part by a seller who complies with paragraphs (b) and (c) is not a breach of his duty under a contract for sale if performance as agreed has been made impracticable by the occurrence of a contingency the non-occurrence of which was a basic assumption on which the contract was made ...

If the impediment is final, the contract is automatically terminated and the parties are released from their obligations under the conditions provided for in Articles 1351 and 1351-1.

Item 1221:

The creditor of an obligation may, after formal notice, pursue its performance in kind unless such performance is impossible or if there is a manifest disproportion between its cost for the debtor in good faith and its interest for the creditor.

Item 1223:

In the event of imperfect performance of the service, the creditor may, after formal notice and if he has not yet paid all or part of the service, notify the debtor as soon as possible of his decision to reduce it in such a way proportional to the price. The debtor's acceptance of the creditor's price reduction decision must be in writing.

If the creditor has already paid, failing agreement between the parties, he may ask the judge to reduce the price.

Section 1231-1:

The debtor is condemned, if necessary, to the payment of damages either because of the non-execution of the obligation, or because of the delay in the execution, if he does not justify that the execution was prevented by *force majeure.*

Adhesion Contracts and Unconscionability

Generally, a court will not examine the 'fairness" of a contract, although exceptions do exist, particularly when a consumer is involved. A contract is unconscionable "when a party lacks a meaningful opportunity to agree to the clause terms either because of unequal bargaining power, as in an adhesion contract, or because the clause and its effects are not readily ascertainable upon a review of the contract."[5] Generally, in order for a

[5] *D.R. Horton, Inc. v. Green*, 120 Nev. 549, 553 (2004).

contract or contract provision to be unconscionable, it must be both procedurally and substantively unconscionable.[6]

Procedural unconscionability often involves the use of fine print or complicated, incomplete, or misleading language that fails to inform a reasonable person of the contractual language's consequences.[7] Substantive unconscionability focuses on the one-sidedness of the contract terms.[8]

French law is virtually identical and Item 1171 notes:

> In a contract of adhesion, any non-negotiable clause, determined in advance by one of the parties, which creates a significant imbalance between the rights and obligations of the parties to the contract is deemed unwritten.
>
> The assessment of the significant imbalance relates neither to the main purpose of the contract nor to the adequacy of the price to the service.

Unconscionability

The Restatement Section 208, addresses the subject of an unconscionable contract or an unconscionable term in a contract and recognizes the reality of litigation in America by giving a judge flexibility as to the remedy:

If a contract or term thereof is unconscionable at the time the contract is made a court may:

> refuse to enforce the contract, or
>
> may enforce the remainder of the contract without the unconscionable term, or
>
> may so limit the application of any unconscionable term as to avoid any unconscionable result.

[6] *United States Home Corp. v. Ballesteros Trust*, 134 Nev. 180 (2018).

[7] *Ibid.*, at 554.

[8] *Ibid.*, at 554.

Contract Interpretation

The Restatement Section 202 specifies rules in aid of interpretation of a contract and is similar to French law discussed in the prior chapter, noting:

1. Words and other conduct are interpreted in the light of all the circumstances, and if the principal purpose of the parties is ascertainable it is given great weight.
2. A writing is interpreted as a whole, and all writings that are part of the same transaction are interpreted together.
3. Unless a different intention is manifested,
   a. where language has a generally prevailing meaning, it is interpreted in accordance with that meaning;
   b. technical terms and words of art are given their technical meaning when used in a transaction within their technical field.
4. Where an agreement involves repeated occasions for performance by either party with knowledge of the nature of the performance and opportunity for objection to it by the other, any course of performance accepted or acquiesced in without objection is given great weight in the interpretation of the agreement.
5. Wherever reasonable, the manifestations of intention of the parties to a promise or agreement are interpreted as consistent with each other and with any relevant course of performance, course of dealing, or usage of trade.

The Restatement Section 203 also provides standards of preference in interpretation and notes:

> In the interpretation of a promise or agreement or a term thereof, the following standards of preference are generally applicable:
>
> a. An interpretation which gives a reasonable, lawful, and effective meaning to all the terms is preferred to an interpretation which leaves a part unreasonable, unlawful, or of no effect;
> b. Express terms are given greater weight than course of performance, course of dealing, and usage of trade, course of performance is given greater weight than course of dealing or usage of trade, and course of dealing is given greater weight than usage of trade;

c. Specific terms and exact terms are given greater weight than general language;
d. Separately negotiated or added terms are given greater weight than standardized terms or other terms not separately negotiated.

The Restatement Section 204 also provides guidance on supplying an omitted essential term:

> When the parties to a bargain sufficiently defined to be a contract have not agreed with respect to a term which is essential to a determination of their rights and duties, a term which is reasonable in the circumstances is supplied by the court.

French Law also provides guidance for interpretation of a contract and is virtually identical to American law.

Item 1188:

> The contract is interpreted according to the common intention of the parties rather than stopping at the literal meaning of its terms.
>
> When this intention cannot be detected, the contract is interpreted according to the meaning given to it by a reasonable person placed in the same situation.

Item 1189:

> All the clauses of a contract are interpreted in relation to each other, giving each of them the meaning that respects the coherence of the act as a whole.
>
> When, in the common intention of the parties, several contracts contribute to the same operation, they are interpreted according to this operation.

Item 1190:

> In case of doubt, the contract by mutual agreement is interpreted against the creditor and in favor of the debtor, and the adhesion contract against the person who proposed it.

Item 1191:

> When a clause is capable of two meanings, the one which gives it an effect takes precedence over the one which does not cause it to produce any.

Item 1192:

> Clear and precise clauses cannot be interpreted on pain of distortion.

Item 1194:

> Contracts bind not only to what is expressed therein, but also to all the consequences given to them by equity, usage or the law.

Contract Modification

Needless to say, the parties may modify contracts. In the United States, contract modification requires all the elements of contract creation that have been previously noted.[9] However, the matter is further complicated by the issue of "pre-existing duty."[10] The Restatement of the Law of Contracts, Section 89 addresses the modification of an executory contract and notes.

A promise modifying a duty under a contract not fully performed on either side is binding

a. if the modification is fair and equitable in view of circumstances not anticipated by the parties when the contract was made, or
b. to the extent provided by statute, or
c. to the extent that justice requires enforcement in view of material change of position in reliance on the promise.

---

[9]However, UCC 2-209 (1) changes that rule and notes, "(1) An agreement modifying a contract within this Article needs no consideration to be binding." However, the UCC tempers this statement by retaining the requirement of good faith. UCC 1-304 provides that every contract or duty within the Uniform Commercial Code imposes an obligation of good faith in its performance and enforcement.

[10]The Restatement Section 73 addresses the issue of pre-existing duty and notes that modifications without additional consideration by the promisee are likely to be the product of "an express or implied threat to withhold performance of a legal duty."

Thus, among other issues, contract modification requires mutual assent of the parties and French law is virtually identical.

Item 1193:

> Contracts may only be modified or revoked by mutual consent of the parties, or for causes permitted by law.

Item 1195:

> If a change in circumstances unforeseeable at the time of the conclusion of the contract makes performance excessively onerous for a party who had not agreed to assume the risk, the latter may request a renegotiation of the contract from its co-contracting party. It continues to perform its obligations during the renegotiation.
>
> In the event of refusal or failure of the renegotiation, the parties may agree to the termination of the contract, on the date and under the conditions that they determine, or request by mutual agreement the judge to proceed with its adaptation. Failing agreement within a reasonable time, the judge may, at the request of a party, revise the contract or terminate it, on the date and under the conditions that he sets.

Contract Provisions Limiting Remedies

As noted in the prior chapter, and this is particularly true in contracts with consumers, limitations must be clear and understandable. Contract provisions that limit remedies tend to fall into several categories:

1. No damages may be recovered for certain kinds of breaches or that damages are limited to a certain amount;
2. The only remedy for breach is replacement or repair of the item or a refund of the purchase price.

Exculpatory clauses are another form of limitation. This limitation is common in certain areas, such as skydiving and releases a party from liability in the event of a monetary loss, physical injury, or death, regardless of fault.

Enforceability of Limitation-of-Liability Clauses

While limitation-of-liability clauses are common in certain areas, and generally enforceable in the event of negligence, there are exceptions. It is unlikely that a court will enforce a limitation-of-liability clause that involve fraud, intentional torts, illegal acts, or a violation of public policy.

Defenses to the Enforceability of a Contract

There are several issues that may affect voluntary assent and thus the enforceability of a contract.

Fraudulent Misrepresentation

Although fraud is a tort it may also affect the mutual assent requirement of a contract since the innocent party has not voluntarily consented to the terms and therefore there is no mutual assent.

The Restatement of Contracts, Section 162 addresses the situation when a misrepresentation is fraudulent or material and notes:

1. A misrepresentation is fraudulent if the maker intends his assertion to induce a party to manifest his assent and the maker
   a. knows or believes that the assertion is not in accord with the facts, or
   b. does not have the confidence that he states or implies in the truth of the assertion, or
   c. knows that he does not have the basis that he states or implies for the assertion.
2. A misrepresentation is material if it would be likely to induce a reasonable person to manifest his assent, or if the maker knows that it would be likely to induce the recipient to do so.

Related to that is the issue of negligent misrepresentation. Negligent misrepresentation is similar to fraudulent misrepresentation but lacks the element of intent as noted in Section 162(1) aforementioned.

And, while fraudulent or negligent misrepresentation may generally involve an assertion, as noted earlier, that is not always the case.

The Restatement Section 161 addresses the situation when non-disclosure is equivalent to an assertion:

> A person's non-disclosure of a fact known to him is equivalent to an assertion that the fact does not exist in the following cases only:
>
> a. Where he knows that disclosure of the fact is necessary to prevent some previous assertion from being a misrepresentation or from being fraudulent or material.
> b. Where he knows that disclosure of the fact would correct a mistake of the other party as to a basic assumption on which that party is making the contract and if non-disclosure of the fact amounts to a failure to act in good faith and in accordance with reasonable standards of fair dealing.
> c. Where he knows that disclosure of the fact would correct a mistake of the other party as to the contents or effect of a writing, evidencing or embodying an agreement in whole or in part.
> d. Where the other person is entitled to know the fact because of a relation of trust and confidence between them.

However, the issue of misrepresentation, whether negligent or intentional, requires another key factor.

The Restatement Section 167 notes:

> A misrepresentation induces a party's manifestation of assent if it substantially contributes to his decision to manifest his assent.

Thus, the issue is one of whether the misrepresentation was a substantial factor that induced a party to enter into a contract.

An additional issue in this area is one of "opinion." Did the statement constitute a representation, or only an opinion? The Restatement Section 168 addresses reliance on assertions of opinion and notes:

1. An assertion is one of opinion if it expresses only a belief, without certainty, as to the existence of a fact or expresses only a judgment as to quality, value, authenticity, or similar matters.
2. If it is reasonable to do so, the recipient of an assertion of a person's opinion as to facts not disclosed and not otherwise known to the recipient may properly interpret it as an assertion

a. that the facts known to that person are not incompatible with his opinion, or
b. that he knows facts sufficient to justify him in forming it.

The Restatement Section 169 addresses those situations when reliance on an assertion of opinion is not justified and therefore may not give rise to liability in the event of litigation:

> To the extent that an assertion is one of opinion only, the recipient is not justified in relying on it unless the recipient
>
> (a) stands in such a relation of trust and confidence to the person whose opinion is asserted that the recipient is reasonable in relying on it; or
> (b) reasonably believes that, as compared with himself, the person whose opinion is asserted has special skill, judgment or objectivity with respect to the subject matter; or
> (c) is for some other special reason particularly susceptible to a misrepresentation of the type involved.

Unsurprisingly, French law also addresses the issue of fraudulent, or intentional, misrepresentation. Article 1137 notes:

> The fraud is the fact for a contracting party to obtain the consent of the other by maneuvers or lies.
>
> Also constitutes fraud the intentional concealment by one of the contracting parties of information which he knows is decisive for the other party.
>
> However, the fact that a party does not reveal to its co-contracting party its estimate of the value of the service does not constitute fraud.

Item 1138:

> Fraud is also constituted if it emanates from the representative, business manager, agent, or standing surety of the contracting party. It is still so when it emanates from a conniving third party.

Item 1139:

> The error resulting from fraud is always excusable; it is a cause of nullity even if it concerns the value of the service or a simple reason for the contract.

Undue Influence

The Restatement Section 177 addresses the situation when undue influence makes a contract voidable:

1. Undue influence is unfair persuasion of a party who is under the domination of the person exercising the persuasion or who by virtue of the relation between them is justified in assuming that that person will not act in a manner inconsistent with his welfare.
2. If a party's manifestation of assent is induced by undue influence by the other party, the contract is voidable by the victim.
3. If a party's manifestation of assent is induced by one who is not a party to the transaction, the contract is voidable by the victim unless the other party to the transaction in good faith and without reason to know of the undue influence either gives value or relies materially on the transaction.

In the case of undue influence, a dominant party, for instance a parent with a child, is able to take advantage of the other, negating the victim's voluntary assent to the terms of the agreement.

Mistake

In certain situations, a mistake may, but not necessarily will, affect the validity of a contract. Mistake can take many forms, including a bilateral mistake, or a mistake on the part of both parties to a contract. A unilateral mistake is a mistake by one party to a contract. The other issue is whether it is a mistake of fact, or a mistake of value.

The Restatement Section 151. Defines "mistake" and notes:

> A mistake is a belief that is not in accord with the facts.

The Restatement Section 152 goes on to note those situations when a mistake of both parties makes a contract voidable:

1. Where a mistake of both parties at the time a contract was made as to a basic assumption on which the contract was made has a material

effect on the agreed exchange of performances, the contract is voidable by the adversely affected party unless he bears the risk of the mistake under the rule stated in Section 154.
2. In determining whether the mistake has a material effect on the agreed exchange of performances, account is taken of any relief by way of reformation, restitution, or otherwise.

Restatement Section 153 addresses those situations when a mistake of one party makes a contract voidable:

> Where a mistake of one party at the time a contract was made as to a basic assumption on which he made the contract has a material effect on the agreed exchange of performances that is adverse to him, the contract is voidable by him if he does not bear the risk of the mistake under the rule stated in Section 154, and
>
> a. the effect of the mistake is such that enforcement of the contract would be unconscionable, or
> b. the other party had reason to know of the mistake or his fault caused the mistake.

Restatement Section 154 addresses those situations when a party bears the risk of a mistake:

A party bears the risk of a mistake when

> a. the risk is allocated to him by agreement of the parties; or
> b. he is aware, at the time the contract is made, that he has only limited knowledge with respect to the facts to which the mistake relates but treats his limited knowledge as sufficient; or
> c. the risk is allocated to him by the court on the ground that it is reasonable in the circumstances to do so.

French law on the subject is virtually identical.

Article 1130 provides that:

> Mistake, fraud, and duress vitiate consent where they are of such a nature that, without them, one of the parties would not have contracted or would have contracted on substantially different terms.

> Their decisive character is assessed in the light of the person and the circumstances in which consent was given.

Article 1132 also addresses the subject of mistake and goes on to note:

> Mistake of law or of fact, as long as it is not inexcusable, is a ground of nullity of the contract where it bears on the essential qualities of the act of performance owed or of the other contracting party.
>
> Mistake is a ground of nullity whether it bears on the act of performance of one party or of the other.
>
> Acceptance of a risk about a quality of the act of performance rules out mistake in relation to this quality.

Article 1134:

> Mistake about the essential qualities of the other contracting party is a ground of nullity only as regards contracts entered into on the basis of considerations personal to the party.

Article 1135:

> Mistake about mere motive, extraneous to the essential qualities of the act of performance owed or of the other contracting party is not a ground of nullity unless the parties have expressly made it a decisive element of their consent.
>
> However, mistake about the motive for an act of generosity is a ground of nullity where, but for the mistake, the donor would not have made it.

Article 1136:

> A mistake as to value is not a ground of nullity where, in the absence of a mistake about the essential qualities of the act of performance, a contracting party makes only an inaccurate valuation of it.

Duress

Improper threats, for example of violence, may also affect the mutual assent of one party to a contract. The Restatement Section 176 notes those situations when a threat is improper:

1. A threat is improper if
   a. what is threatened is a crime or a tort, or the threat itself would be a crime or a tort if it resulted in obtaining property;
   b. what is threatened is a criminal prosecution;
   c. what is threatened is the use of civil process and the threat is made in bad faith; or
   d. the threat is a breach of the duty of good faith and fair dealing under a contract with the recipient.
2. A threat is improper if the resulting exchange is not on fair terms, and
   a. the threatened act would harm the recipient and would not significantly benefit the party making the threat;
   b. the effectiveness of the threat in inducing the manifestation of assent is significantly increased by prior unfair dealing by the party making the threat; or
   c. what is threatened is otherwise a use of power for illegitimate ends.

In summary, a threat that the threatening party has no right to make, that is wrongful (tortious) or illegal (criminal) affects the voluntariness of the consent. Note that a threat of civil litigation may be considered improper only if it is made in bad faith.

French law is virtually identical. Item 1140 notes:

> There is violence when a party engages under the pressure of a constraint which inspires him with the fear of exposing his person, his fortune, or those of his relatives to considerable harm.

Item 1142 goes into additional details and, similar to American law, addresses the issue of litigation.

> The threat of legal action does not constitute violence. The situation is different when the remedy is diverted from its purpose or when it is invoked or exercised to obtain a manifestly excessive advantage.

Item 1143:

> There is also violence when a party, abusing the state of dependence in which its co-contractor finds itself with regard to it, obtains from it a commitment which it would not have subscribed to in the absence of such constraint and derives a manifestly excessive advantage.

Other Defenses

The Statute of Frauds

As noted in the prior chapter, in certain situations a contract must be in writing to be enforceable.

French law also requires that certain contracts be in writing in order to be enforceable.

Article L131-2 notes that:

> The performance, publishing and audiovisual production contracts defined in this title must be recorded in writing. The same applies to free execution authorizations.
>
> Contracts by which copyright is transferred must be evidenced in writing.
>
> In all other cases, the provisions of Articles 1359–1362 of the Civil Code are applicable.

As noted, the French Civil Code also addresses the subject of a written contract and notes:

Item 1359:

> The legal act relating to a sum or a value exceeding an amount fixed by decree must be proven in writing under a private or authentic signature.
>
> It cannot be proved in addition to or against a writing establishing a legal act, even if the sum or the value does not exceed this amount, except by another writing under private or authentic signature.
>
> Anyone whose claim exceeds the threshold mentioned in the first paragraph cannot be exempted from proof in writing by restricting his request.
>
> The same applies to anyone whose claim, even less than this amount, relates to the balance or part of a claim greater than this amount.

Item 1365:

> Writing consists of a series of letters, characters, numbers or any other signs or symbols with an intelligible meaning, whatever their medium.

Item 1366:

> Electronic writing has the same probative force as writing on paper, provided that the person from whom it emanates can be duly identified and that it is drawn up and stored in conditions such as to guarantee its integrity.

Item 1360:

> The rules provided for in the preceding article receive exceptions in the event of material or moral impossibility of obtaining a writing, if it is customary not to establish a writing, or when the writing has been lost by *force majeure.*

Merger Clause

A "merger" clause consists of a statement in a written document that the document is the full and complete agreement of the parties, excluding all other representations, usually, but not necessarily verbal. A merger clause may be rendered invalid by fraud.

Illegality

As noted in the prior chapter, the Restatement Section 178 addresses those situations when a term of a contract is rendered unenforceable because it violates public policy:

1. A promise or other term of an agreement is unenforceable on grounds of public policy if legislation provides that it is unenforceable or the interest in its enforcement is clearly outweighed in the circumstances by a public policy against the enforcement of such terms.
2. In weighing the interest in the enforcement of a term, account is taken of

   a. the parties' justified expectations;
   b. any forfeiture that would result if enforcement were denied; and
   c. any special public interest in the enforcement of the particular term.
3. In weighing a public policy against enforcement of a term, account is taken of
   a. the strength of that policy is manifested by legislation or judicial decisions;
   b. the likelihood that a refusal to enforce the term will further that policy;
   c. the seriousness of any misconduct involved and the extent to which it was deliberate; and
   d. the directness of the connection between that misconduct and the term.

However, in most, if not all legal systems, there are exceptions. The Restatement Section 198 addresses those situations where a party to a contract is "excusably ignorant" or not equally in the wrong:

> A party has a claim in restitution for performance that he has rendered under or in return for a promise that is unenforceable on grounds of public policy if
>
> a. he was excusably ignorant of the facts or of legislation of a minor character, in the absence of which the promise would be enforceable; or
> b. he was not equally in the wrong with the promisor.

Is a Contract for the Sale or Distribution of Marijuana Illegal and Therefore Unenforceable?

Mann v. Gullickson, Northern District of California, 2016 WL 6473215

> Around March 2014, Mann sold two businesses to Gullickson … (1) Illinois DP, LLC a/k/a Dispensary Permits.com ("DP") a consulting business for state-regulated marijuana dispensary or cultivation licenses; and (2) weGrow Enterprises, Inc. ("weGrow") a franchise hydroponic

retail operation (collectively, the "Companies"). Gullickson, as consideration, forgave a $10,000 loan to Mann and executed a Promissory Note ("Note") agreeing to pay Mann an additional $400,000 in three installments. Mann alleges Gullickson has failed to make payments as required under the Note and sued. The defendant filed a motion for summary judgment.

At its core, this case consists of a simple breach of contract claim. But to decide whether the parties' business agreement is enforceable, the Court must navigate the conflict created by the prohibition of medical marijuana under federal law and the legalization of medical marijuana under California law. Specifically, this Order addresses whether Defendant and Cross-Claimant Sara Gullickson is excused from performing her obligations under a contract formed in California because the contract relates to the medical marijuana industry. Pending before the Court is Gullickson's Motion for Summary Judgment, in which she asks the Court to invalidate the parties' agreement under the federal Controlled Substances Act. By way of a contract, the defendant agreed to pay $400,000 as part of a purchase related to the medical marijuana industry. Is the contract void for illegality? Gullickson ... contends the parties' agreement is void *ab initio* because it relates to medical marijuana, which is still a prohibited substance under the federal Controlled Substances Act ("CSA"), even if legal in the states where the Companies operate and the parties' contracts were formed. At the hearing on this matter, Gullickson conceded that her counterclaims would be subject to dismissal if the Court granted her summary judgment on the basis asserted in her motion.

That said, where a party challenges enforcement of a contract based on the defense of illegality under federal law, there is some question about whether to apply state or federal law. The parties did not directly address this dispute in their papers. For purposes of ruling on this Motion, the Court is bound by the Ninth Circuit's recognition that "[b]oth federal law and California law begin from the core proposition that whatever flexibility may otherwise exist with regard to the enforcement of 'illegal' contracts, courts will not order a party to a contract to perform an act that is in direct violation of a positive law directive, even if that party has agreed, for consideration, to perform that act." "California law includes federal law" and thus, "a violation of federal law is a violation of law for purposes of determining whether or not a contract is unenforceable as contrary to the public policy of California." Gullickson urges the Court to use this rule to void the parties' contracts entirely — but both California courts and the Ninth Circuit have applied a more nuanced approach. Having reviewed the materials in the record, the Court finds it could grant relief in this case that does not require Gullickson to violate the CSA. Mann's suit seeks Gullickson's full payment for the businesses he sold to her. Mandating that payment does not require Gullickson to possess, cultivate, or distribute marijuana, or to in any other way require her to violate the CSA. Gullickson attempts to argue otherwise by suggesting 'she has no other means' to pay Mann other than to operate the Companies. But this argument fails for at least two reasons. First, semantically Gullickson's declaration only says that she '*had* no other means to the pay for the businesses' — there is no evidence in the record that she currently *has* no other means to pay for the Companies. Second, even if these businesses are Gullickson's only livelihood, she has not shown the only way to operate them is in a way that violates the CSA. In other words, if the Court ordered payment, and Gullickson's only way to pay was by making these businesses operational, that situation would not necessarily require Gullickson to be involved in the medical marijuana industry; Gullickson has not shown otherwise. Thus, … ordering payment on the parties' contract would not mandate illegal conduct.

Remedies

In General

The Restatement Section 344 notes that:

> Judicial remedies under the rules stated in this Restatement serve to protect one or more of the following interests of a promisee:
>
> (a) his 'expectation interest,' which is his interest in having the benefit of his bargain by being put in as good a position as he would have been in had the contract been performed;
> (b) his 'reliance interest,' which is his interest in being reimbursed for loss caused by reliance on the contract by being put in as good a position as he would have been in had the contract not been made; or
> (c) his 'restitution interest,' which is his interest in having restored to him any benefit that he has conferred on the other party.

Monetary Damages

Duty to Mitigate Damages

All parties to a contract have a duty to mitigate their damages in the event of a breach. The Restatement Section 350 notes that:

1. Except as stated in Subsection (2), damages are not recoverable for loss that the injured party could have avoided without undue risk, burden or humiliation.
2. The injured party is not precluded from recovery by the rule stated in Subsection (1) to the extent that he has made reasonable but unsuccessful efforts to avoid loss. There does not appear to be a corresponding duty to mitigate damages in France.

The Measure of Damages for a Breach of Contract

The Restatement Section 347 notes that:

> Subject to the limitations stated in Sections 350–353, the injured party has a right to damages based on his expectation interest as measured by
>
> a. the loss in the value to him of the other party's performance caused by its failure or deficiency; plus
> b. any other loss, including incidental or consequential loss, caused by the breach; less
> c. any cost or other loss that he has avoided by not having to perform.

As discussed in Chapter 5, a lawsuit for a tort is intended to put the plaintiff in the same position they would have occupied but for the tort. The same is true for a breach of contract. Generally, in a breach of contract lawsuit the plaintiff is entitled to recover compensatory damages, for losses that directly result from the breach, as well as consequential damages that cover related, foreseeable damages.

The rule regarding recovery of consequential damages was established by a case from England that was decided in the 18th century.

Hadley v. Baxendale, 9 Exch. 341, 156 Eng. Rep. 145 (1854)

> … the plaintiffs carried on the business of millers and mealmen in copartnership, and were proprietors and occupiers of the City

Steam-Mills, in the city of Gloucester, and were possessed of a steam-engine, by means of which they worked the said mills, and therein cleaned corn, and ground the same into meal … and a certain portion of the said steam-engine, to wit, the crank shaft of the said steam-engine, was broken …, whereby the said steam-engine was prevented from working, and the plaintiffs were desirous of having a new crank shaft made … and had ordered the same … (from a company) who had contracted to make the said new shaft for the plaintiffs; but before they could complete the said new shaft it was necessary that the said broken shaft should be forwarded to their works at Greenwich, in order that the said new shaft might be made so as to fit the other parts of the said engine which were not injured, and so that it might be substituted for the said broken shaft; … and the defendants, before and at the time of the making of the said promises, were common carriers of business of common carriers … and the plaintiffs, at the request of the defendants, delivered to them as such carriers the said broken shaft, to be conveyed by the defendants as such carriers from Gloucester to the said W. Joyce & Co., at Greenwich, and there to be delivered for the plaintiffs on the second day after the day of such delivery … and in consideration thereof the defendants then promised the plaintiffs to convey the said broken shaft from Gloucester to Greenwich, and there on the said second day to deliver the same to the said W. Joyce & Co. for the plaintiffs. And although such second day elapsed before the commencement of this suit, yet the defendants did not nor would deliver the said broken shaft at Greenwich on the said second day, but wholly neglected and refused so to do for the space of seven days after the said shaft was so delivered to them …

The second count stated, that, the defendants … did not nor would use due or proper care or diligence in or about the carrying or conveying or delivering the said broken shaft as aforesaid, within such reasonable time as aforesaid, but wholly neglected and refused so to do; and by reason of the carelessness, negligence, and improper conduct of the defendants, the said broken shaft was not delivered for the plaintiffs to the said W. Joyce & Co., or at Greenwich, until the expiration of a long and unreasonable time after the defendants received the same as aforesaid, and after the time when the same should have been delivered for the plaintiffs; and by reason of the several premises, the completing of the said new shaft was delayed for five days, and the plaintiffs were prevented from working their said steam-mills … for the space of five days beyond the time that they otherwise would have been prevented from so doing, and they thereby were unable to supply many of their customers with flour, sharps, and bran during that period, and were obliged to buy flour to supply some of their other customers ... and were deprived of gains and profits which otherwise would have accrued to them, and were unable to employ their workmen, to whom they were compelled to pay wages during that period, and were otherwise injured, and the plaintiffs claim.

The delivery of the shaft at Greenwich was delayed by some neglect; and the consequence was, that the plaintiffs did not receive the new shaft for several days after they would otherwise have done, and the working of their mill was thereby delayed, and they thereby lost the profits they would otherwise have received.

The principle upon which damages are assessed is founded upon that of rendering compensation to the injured party. The important subject is ably treated in Sedgwick on the Measure of Damages. And this particular branch of it is discussed in the third chapter, where, after pointing out the distinction between the civil and the French law, he says ... It is sometimes said, in regard to contracts, that the defendant shall be held liable for those damages only which both parties may fairly be supposed to have at the time contemplated as likely to result from the nature of the agreement, and this appears to be the rule adopted by the writers upon the civil law...

Now we think the proper rule in such a case as the present is this:– Where two parties have made a contract which one of them has broken, the damages which the other party ought to receive in respect of such breach of contract should be such as may fairly and reasonably be considered either arising naturally, i.e., according to the usual course of things, from such breach of contract itself, or such as may reasonably be supposed to have been in the contemplation of both parties, at the time they made the contract, as the probable result of the breach of it. Now, if the special circumstances under which the contract was actually made were communicated by the plaintiffs to the defendants, and thus known to both parties, the damages resulting from the breach of such a contract, which they would reasonably contemplate, would be the amount of injury which would ordinarily follow from a breach of contract under these special circumstances so known and communicated. But, on the other hand, if these special circumstances were wholly unknown to the party breaking the contract, he, at the most, could only be supposed to

> have had in his contemplation the amount of injury which would arise generally, and in the great multitude of cases not affected by any special circumstances, from such a breach of contract. For, had the special circumstances been known, the parties might have specially provided for the breach of contract by special terms as to the damages in that case; and of this advantage it would be very unjust to deprive them. Now the above principles are those by which we think the jury ought to be guided in estimating the damages arising out of any breach of contract.
>
> Suppose the plaintiffs had another shaft in their possession put up or putting up at the time, and that they only wished to send back the broken shaft to the engineer who made it; it is clear that this would be quite consistent with the above circumstances, and yet the unreasonable delay in the delivery would have no effect upon the intermediate profits of the mill. Or, again, suppose that, at the time of the delivery to the carrier, the machinery of the mill had been in other respects defective, then, also, the same results would follow. Here it is true that the shaft was actually sent back to serve as a model for the new one, and that the want of a new one was the only cause of the stoppage of the mill, and that the loss of profits really arose from not sending down the new shaft in proper time, and that this arose from the delay in delivering the broken one to serve as a model. But it is obvious that, in the great multitude of cases of millers sending off broken shafts to third persons by a carrier under ordinary circumstances, such consequences would not, in all probability, have occurred; and these special circumstances were here never communicated by the plaintiffs to the defendants. It follows therefore, that the loss of profits here cannot reasonably be considered such a consequence of the breach of contract as could have been fairly and reasonably contemplated by both the parties when they made this contract. For such loss would neither have flowed naturally from the breach of this contract in the great multitude of such cases occurring under ordinary circumstances, nor were the special circumstances, which, perhaps, would have made it a reasonable and natural consequence of such breach of contract, communicated to or known by the defendants. The Judge ought, therefore, to have told the jury that upon the facts then before them they ought not to take the loss of profits into consideration at all in estimating the damages. There must therefore be a new trial in this case.

The critical issue for the recovery of consequential damages is foreseeability.

The Restatement Section 351 addresses this subject and affirms the limitations in the case from England:

1. Damages are not recoverable for loss that the party in breach did not have reason to foresee as a probable result of the breach when the contract was made.
2. Loss may be foreseeable as a probable result of a breach because it follows from the breach
   a. in the ordinary course of events, or
   b. as a result of special circumstances, beyond the ordinary course of events, that the party in breach had reason to know.
3. A court may limit damages for foreseeable loss by excluding recovery for loss of profits, by allowing recovery only for loss incurred in reliance, or otherwise if it concludes that in the circumstances justice so requires in order to avoid disproportionate compensation.

French Law is virtually identical to American, as well as English law and notes in Section 1231-3:

> The debtor is only liable for the damages and interest which were foreseen or which could have been foreseen at the time of the conclusion of the contract, except when the non-performance is due to gross negligence or willful misconduct.

Section 1231-4:

> Even in the event that the non-performance of the contract results from a gross or fraudulent fault, the damages only include what is an immediate and direct consequence of the non-performance.

Section 1231-2:

> The damages due to the creditor are, in general, for the loss he has incurred and the gain of which he has been deprived, except for the exceptions and modifications below.

Liquidated Damages

A liquidated damages clause specifies a payment to be made in the event that a party to a contract fails to perform as agreed. A critical issue for a court in awarding liquidated damages is whether the term is a liquidated damages clause, which is enforceable, or a penalty clause, which is not. The subject is addressed in the Restatement Section 356:

1. Damages for breach by either party may be liquidated in the agreement but only at an amount that is reasonable in the light of the anticipated or actual loss caused by the breach and the difficulties of proof of loss. A term fixing unreasonably large liquidated damages is unenforceable on grounds of public policy as a penalty.
2. A term in a bond providing for an amount of money as a penalty for non-occurrence of the condition of the bond is unenforceable on grounds of public policy to the extent that the amount exceeds the loss caused by such non-occurrence.

Courts have noted that when a party challenges a liquidated damages provision, the court must step back and examine it in light of what the parties knew at the time the contract was formed and in light of an estimate of the actual damages caused by the breach.[11] Courts have gone on to note that, in addition, liquidated damages must have some relation to actual damages.[12]

As one court in Ohio[13] noted,

> Where the parties have agreed on the amount of damages, ascertained by estimation and adjustment, and have expressed this agreement in clear and unambiguous terms, the amount so fixed should be treated as liquidated damages and not as a penalty, if the damages would be (1) uncertain as to amount and difficult of proof, and if (2) the contract as a whole is not so manifestly unconscionable, unreasonable, and disproportionate in amount as to justify the conclusion that it does not express the true intention of the parties, and if (3) the contract is consistent with the conclusion that it was the intention of the parties that damages in the amount stated should follow the breach thereof.

French law also addresses the issue of liquidated damages, although by a different name.

Section 1231-5 notes:

> When the contract stipulates that the party who fails to perform it will pay a certain sum as damages, a greater or lesser sum cannot be awarded

[11] *Lake Ridge Academy v. Carney*, 66 Ohio St. 376, 382 (1993).

[12] 3 Restatement of the Law 2d, Contracts (1981) 157, Section 356(1).

[13] *Kent State University v. Ford*, 25 N.E. 3d 868 (2015).

to the other party. Nevertheless, the judge may, even *ex officio*, moderate or increase the penalty thus agreed upon if it is manifestly excessive or derisory.

When the commitment has been partially executed, the agreed penalty may be reduced by the judge, even *ex officio*, in proportion to the interest that the partial execution has procured for the creditor, without prejudice to the application of the previous paragraph.

Any stipulation contrary to the two preceding paragraphs is deemed unwritten.

Except for definitive non-performance, the penalty is incurred only when the debtor is put in default.

Equitable Remedies

Although rare, there are situations where monetary damages are inadequate to compensate a party. In that situation, a party may seek an equitable remedy. The Restatement Section 359 addresses this situation and notes:

1. Specific performance or an injunction will not be ordered if damages would be adequate to protect the expectation interest of the injured party.
2. The adequacy of the damage remedy for failure to render one part of the performance due does not preclude specific performance or injunction as to the contract as a whole.
3. Specific performance or an injunction will not be refused merely because there is a remedy for breach other than damages, but such a remedy may be considered in exercising discretion under the rule stated in Section 357.

Specific Performance

Rescission (May Also Require Restitution)

Rescission terminates a contract and may either be unilateral, on the part of one party, or bilateral if it involves both parties to a contract. Unilateral rescission is available in the event that a contract is not performed, or there is a material breach of contract. As with the French law, the rescinding party must give prompt notice of the rescission. In certain situations, such as partial performance, restitution may be required and the parties must promptly return money or items or their value if they cannot be returned.

French law, Item 1229 addresses this subject although by a different term:

> The resolution terminates the contract.
>
> The resolution takes effect, depending on the case, either under the conditions provided for by the termination clause, or on the date of receipt by the debtor of the notification made by the creditor, or on the date fixed by the judge or, failing that, on the day of the court summons.
>
> When the services exchanged could only be used by the complete execution of the terminated contract, the parties must return all of what they have procured from each other. When the services exchanged have found their usefulness as the reciprocal performance of the contract progresses, there is no need for restitution for the period prior to the last service not having received its consideration; in this case, the resolution is qualified as termination.
>
> Refunds take place under the conditions set out in Articles 1352–1352-9.

Item 1231:

> Unless the non-performance is final, damages are only due if the debtor has previously been given formal notice to perform within a reasonable time.

Restitution

As noted previously, in certain situations the parties must promptly return money or items or their value if they cannot be returned.

The Restatement Section 158 addresses this subject and notes:

1. In any case governed by the rules stated in this Chapter, either party may have a claim for relief including restitution under the rules stated in Section 240 and 376.
2. In any case governed by the rules stated in this Chapter, if those rules together with the rules stated in Chapter 16 will not avoid injustice, the court may grant relief on such terms as justice requires including protection of the parties' reliance interests.

French law is identical and Item 1352 notes:

> The restitution of a thing other than a sum of money takes place in kind or, when this is impossible, in value, estimated on the day of restitution.

Section 1352-1:

> The person who returns the item is liable for damage and deterioration which has reduced its value, unless he is in good faith and these are not due to his fault.

Section 1352-2:

> The person who, having received it in good faith, has sold the thing shall only refund the price of the sale.
>
> If he received it in bad faith, he owes the value on the day of restitution when it is higher than the price.

Section 1352-3:

> Restitution includes the fruits and the value of the enjoyment that the thing has procured.
>
> The value of the enjoyment is assessed by the judge on the day he rules.
>
> Unless otherwise stipulated, the restitution of the fruits, if they are not found in kind, takes place according to an estimated value on the date of reimbursement, according to the state of things on the day of payment of the obligation.

Section 1352-5:

> To set the amount of refunds, account is taken of the expenses necessary for the preservation of the thing and of those which have increased its value, within the limit of the estimated capital gain on the day of the refund.

Section 1352-6:

> The return of a sum of money includes interest at the legal rate and taxes paid in the hands of the person who received it.

Section 1352-7:

> Anyone who received in bad faith owes the interest, the fruits he has received or the value of the enjoyment from the date of payment.
>
> Anyone who has received it in good faith only owes them from the day of the request.

Section 1352-8:

> The restitution of a provision of service takes place in value. This is assessed on the date it was provided.

Reformation

Occasionally mistakes are made when reducing a verbal agreement to a written agreement. In that situation, the assistance of a court may be necessary to reform the written document to conform to the terms of the verbal agreement.

The Restatement Section 155 addresses the situation where there is a bilateral mistake, a mistake on the part of both parties that satisfies the requirements for reformation:

> Where a writing that evidences or embodies an agreement in whole or in part fails to express the agreement because of a mistake of both parties as to the contents or effect of the writing, the court may at the request of a party reform the writing to express the agreement, except to the extent that rights of third parties such as good faith purchasers for value will be unfairly affected.

The Restatement Section 157 goes on to explain the effect of a fault on the party that is seeking relief and notes:

> A mistaken party's fault in failing to know or discover the facts before making the contract does not bar him from avoidance or reformation under the rules stated in this Chapter, unless his fault amounts to a failure to act in good faith and in accordance with reasonable standards of fair dealing.

Stambovsky v. Ackley, 169 A.D.2d 254 (1991)

In the following case, although the plaintiff sought rescission and not reformation, for obvious reasons, the case is instructive on a variety of issues, including a merger clause.

> Plaintiff, to his horror, discovered that the house he had recently contracted to purchase was widely reputed to be possessed by poltergeists, reportedly seen by defendant seller and members of her family on numerous occasions over the last nine years. Plaintiff promptly commenced this action seeking rescission of the contract of sale. The trial court reluctantly dismissed the complaint, holding that plaintiff has no remedy at law in this jurisdiction. The plaintiff appealed.
>
> From the perspective of a person in the position of plaintiff herein, a very practical problem arises with respect to the discovery of a paranormal phenomenon: 'Who you gonna' call?' as the title song to the movie 'Ghostbusters' asks. Applying the strict rule of caveat emptor to a contract involving a house possessed by poltergeists conjures up visions of a psychic or medium routinely accompanying the structural engineer and Terminix man on an inspection of every home subject to a contract of sale. It portends that the prudent attorney will establish an escrow account lest the subject of the transaction come back to haunt him and his client — or pray that his malpractice insurance coverage extends to supernatural disasters. In the interest of avoiding such untenable consequences, the notion that a haunting is a condition which can and should be ascertained upon reasonable inspection of the premises is a hobgoblin which should be exorcised from the body of legal precedent and laid quietly to rest.
>
> It has been suggested by a leading authority that the ancient rule which holds that mere non-disclosure does not constitute actionable misrepresentation 'finds proper application in cases where the fact undisclosed is patent, or the plaintiff has equal opportunities for obtaining information which he may be expected to utilize, or the defendant has no reason to think that he is acting under any misapprehension'. (Citation omitted). However, with respect to transactions in real estate, New York adheres to the doctrine of caveat emptor and imposes no duty upon the vendor to disclose any information concerning the premises … unless there is a confidential or fiduciary relationship between the parties … or some conduct on the part of the seller which constitutes 'active concealment'

...[dummy ventilation system constructed by seller]; [foundation cracks covered by seller]). Normally, some affirmative misrepresentation ... [industrial waste on land allegedly used only as farm]; (citation omitted) [land containing valuable minerals allegedly acquired for use as campsite]) or partial disclosure ... [existence of third unopened street concealed]; [escrow agreements securing lien concealed]) is required to impose upon the seller a duty to communicate undisclosed conditions affecting the premises ...

Caveat emptor is not so all-encompassing a doctrine of common law as to render every act of non-disclosure immune from redress, whether legal or equitable. 'In regard to the necessity of giving information which has not been asked, the rule differs somewhat at law and in equity, and while the law courts would permit no recovery of *damages* against a vendor, because of mere concealment of facts *under certain circumstances,* yet if the vendee refused to complete the contract because of the concealment of a material fact on the part of the other, equity would refuse to compel him so to do, because equity only compels the specific performance of a contract which is fair and open, and in regard to which all material matters known to each have been communicated to the other' ...Even as a principle of law, long before exceptions were embodied in statute law ... the doctrine was held inapplicable to contagion among animals, adulteration of food, and insolvency of a maker of a promissory note and of a tenant substituted for another under a lease ... Common law is not moribund ... Where fairness and common sense dictate that an exception should be created, the evolution of the law should not be stifled by rigid application of a legal maxim.

Where a condition which has been created by the seller materially impairs the value of the contract and is peculiarly within the knowledge of the seller or unlikely to be discovered by a prudent purchaser exercising due care with respect to the subject transaction, nondisclosure constitutes a basis for rescission as a matter of equity. Any other outcome places upon the buyer not merely the obligation to exercise care in his purchase but rather to be omniscient with respect to any fact which may affect the bargain. No practical purpose is served by imposing such a burden upon a purchaser. To the contrary, it encourages predatory business practice and offends the principle that equity will suffer no wrong to be without a remedy.

Defendant's contention that the contract of sale, particularly the merger or 'as is' clause, bars recovery of the buyer's deposit is unavailing. Even an express disclaimer will not be given effect where the facts are peculiarly within the knowledge of the party invoking it ... Moreover, a fair reading of the merger clause reveals that it expressly disclaims only representations made with respect to the physical condition of the premises and merely makes general reference to representations concerning 'any other matter or things affecting or relating to the aforesaid premises.' As broad as this language may be, a reasonable interpretation is that its effect is limited to tangible or physical matters and does not extend to paranormal phenomena. Finally, if the language of the contract is to be construed as broadly as defendant urges to encompass the presence of poltergeists in the house, it cannot be said that she has delivered the premises 'vacant' in accordance with her obligation under the provisions of the contract rider.

In the case at bar, defendant seller deliberately fostered the public belief that her home was possessed. Having undertaken to inform the public at large, to whom she has no legal relationship, about the supernatural occurrences on her property, she may be said to owe no less a duty to her contract vendee. It has been remarked that the occasional modern cases which permit a seller to take unfair advantage of a buyer's ignorance so long as he is not actively misled are 'singularly unappetizing.' (Citation omitted). Where, as here, the seller not only takes unfair advantage of the buyer's ignorance but has created and perpetuated a condition about which he is unlikely to even inquire, enforcement of the contract (in whole or in part) is offensive to the court's sense of equity. Application of the remedy of rescission, within the bounds of the narrow exception to the doctrine of caveat emptor set forth herein, is entirely appropriate to relieve the unwitting purchaser from the consequences of a most unnatural bargain.

Accordingly, the judgment of the Supreme Court, New York... entered April 9, 1990, which dismissed the complaint ... should be modified, on the law and the facts and in the exercise of discretion, and the first cause of action seeking rescission of the contract reinstated, without costs.

Contract Performance in France

Generally, in countries with a system of civil law, contracts tend to be organized into various categories, including sales, employment, leases, as well as contracts for work or contracts for services. And there may be differences in the requirements or terms that are required by law. Because of requirements established by the codes, contracts in countries with a civil law system are likely to be far shorter than the equivalent contract in the United States.

Therefore, interpretation of a contract is likely to focus on consent, that is, what the parties intended. As noted in the prior chapter, Article 1128 of the French Civil Code notes, "The following are necessary for the validity of a contract:

1. The consent of the parties;
2. Their capacity to contract;
3. Content which is lawful and certain."

And, as with the common law, French Civil Code Article 1130 notes, "Mistake, fraud and duress vitiate consent where they are of such a nature that, without them, one of the parties would not have contracted or would have contracted on substantially different terms." Article 1132 goes on to note, "Mistake of law or of fact, as long as it is not inexcusable, is a ground of nullity of the contract where it bears on the essential qualities of the act or performance owed or of the other contracting party." And Article 1139 notes, "A mistake induced by fraud is always excusable. It is a ground of nullity even if it bears on the value of the act of performance or on a party's mere motive."

Rights of a Third Party Under Contract Law

The Restatement Section 302 on Intended and Incidental Beneficiaries notes that,

1. Unless otherwise agreed between promisor and promisee, a beneficiary of a promise is an intended beneficiary if recognition of a right to performance in the beneficiary is appropriate to effectuate the intention of the parties and either
   a. the performance of the promise will satisfy an obligation of the promisee to pay money to the beneficiary; or
   b. the circumstances indicate that the promisee intends to give the beneficiary the benefit of the promised performance.
2. An incidental beneficiary is a beneficiary who is not an intended beneficiary.

Thus, the law distinguishes between intended beneficiaries and incidental beneficiaries.

Third-Party Beneficiaries

Intended Beneficiaries

The original parties to a contract may agree that a third party shall benefit from the contract. Life insurance contracts are an example. Thus, intended beneficiaries have legal rights related to a contract and may sue to enforce the contract.[14]

French law is similar. Item 1205 notes that one can stipulate for others:

> One of the contracting parties, stipulating it, can make the other, promising it, promise to perform a service for the benefit of a third party, the beneficiary. The latter may be a future person but must be precisely designated or be able to be determined during the execution of the promise

And Section 1205 notes that:

> The beneficiary is vested with a direct right to the performance against the promisor from the stipulation.
>
> However, the stipulator may freely revoke the stipulation as long as the beneficiary has not accepted it.
>
> The stipulation becomes irrevocable when the acceptance reaches the stipulator or the promisor.

Incidental Beneficiaries

Incidental beneficiaries, unlike intended beneficiaries, have no rights under a contract.

[14] *Lawrence v. Fox*, 20 N.Y. 268 (1859).

French law, Item 1199 similarly restricts the rights of incidental beneficiaries and notes,

> The contract only creates obligations between the parties.
>
> Third parties may neither request performance of the contract nor be forced to perform it, subject to the provisions of this section and those of Chapter III of Title IV.

The Transfer of Rights and Obligations under a Contract

Assignment

The Restatement Section 317 addresses the power of a party to assign their rights to a contract and notes,

1. An assignment of a right is a manifestation of the assignor's intention to transfer it by virtue of which the assignor's right to performance by the obligor is extinguished in whole or in part and the assignee acquires a right to such performance.
2. A contractual right can be assigned unless
   a. the substitution of a right of the assignee for the right of the assignor would materially change the duty of the obligor, or materially increase the burden or risk imposed on him by his contract, or materially impair his chance of obtaining return performance, or materially reduce its value to him; or
   b. the assignment is forbidden by statute or is otherwise inoperative on grounds of public policy; or
   c. assignment is validly precluded by contract.

Unless prohibited by law, the terms of the contract, or other limited considerations, duties under a contract are generally assignable. However, there is a concern. Generally, the assignor remains liable for performance of the contract by the assignee.

French law also authorizes assignment and Item 1216 notes:

> A contractor, the assignor, may assign its status as a party to the contract to a third party, the assignee, with the agreement of its co-contractor, the assignee.

> This agreement may be given in advance, in particular in the contract concluded between the future transferor and the transferee, in which case the transfer takes effect with regard to the transferee when the contract concluded between the transferor and the transferee is notified to him or when takes not.
>
> The transfer must be recorded in writing, on pain of nullity.

Item 1216-1 is similar to American law on the subject of assignment and notes that:

> If the assignee has expressly consented to it, the assignment of the contract releases the assignor for the future.
>
> Failing this, and unless there is a clause to the contrary, the transferor is jointly and severally liable for the performance of the contract.

Delegation

Related to the subject of assignment is delegation. A party to a contract may be able to delegate their duties under the contract.

The Restatement Section 318 addresses this subject and notes,

1. An obligor can properly delegate the performance of his duty to another unless the delegation is contrary to public policy or the terms of his promise.
2. Unless otherwise agreed, a promise requires performance by a particular person only to the extent that the obligee has a substantial interest in having that person perform or control the acts promised.
3. Unless the obligee agrees otherwise, neither delegation of performance nor a contract to assume the duty made with the obligor by the person delegated discharges any duty or liability of the delegating obligor.

A party may generally assign their rights under a contract, although there are limitations, for instance, when a contract expressly forbids assignment. Likewise, a party may delegate their duties under a contract, although the delegator retains liability for non-performance, as well as personal liability in the event of a negligent act by the delegate. That problem may be avoided by way of a novation as discussed earlier.

French law is similar and Section 1336 of the French Civil Code notes that,

> Delegation is an operation by which one person, the delegator, obtains from another, the delegate, that he finds himself to a third person, the delegate, who accepts him as a debtor.
>
> The delegate may not, unless otherwise stipulated, set up against the delegate any exception drawn from his relations with the delegator or from the relations between the latter and the delegate.

And Item 1338 goes on to note that,

> When the delegator is a debtor of the delegate but the latter has not discharged him of his debt, the delegation gives the delegate a second debtor. The payment made by one of the two debtors releases the other, proportionally.

Chapter 9

Sales and Leases

Abstract

Contracts for the sale of goods, unlike the last two chapters, involve state statutory law rather than the common law. The Uniform Commercial Code (UCC), Article 2 establishes the requirements for such contracts and covers both the sale and lease of "goods." Although not entirely "uniform," Article 2 and 2A of the Uniform Commercial Code have been adopted by all states except Louisiana. The Uniform Commercial Code, as the name implies, applies to commercial transactions, and was intended to, and does benefit business, whether the contract is entered into in-person or online. The UCC eases the formality of the common law when it comes to entering into certain contracts. Those who are unfamiliar with its requirements risk entering into a contract unknowingly. While coverage of the entirety of Article 2 is far beyond the scope of this chapter, there are certain key issues that are critical for business.

While the two preceding chapters on contracts are based on the common law, this chapter is based on state statutory law. As has been previously noted, the United States is considered a common law country, although a substantial amount of law is statutory, including the law of commercial transactions, the Uniform Commercial Code. German law, and remember that Germany is a civil law country, had a major influence on the development of the Uniform Commercial Code.[1]

Section 1-102 of the Uniform Commercial Code (UCC) specifies that its purpose is "... to simplify, clarify and modernize the law governing commercial transactions." Section 1-304 goes on to note that "every contract or duty within the Uniform Commercial Code imposes an obligation of good faith in its performance and enforcement" although it does not, by its terms, apply to negotiation. In this regard, the UCC is similar to French law which has a similar requirement. Article 1104 of the French Civil Code notes that "contracts must be negotiated, formed and performed in good faith." In addition, the German Civil Code, Section 242[2] states that "an obligor has a duty to perform according to the requirements of good faith, taking customary practice into consideration."

The UCC does not apply to all contracts. Section 2-102 notes that the UCC applies as long as "... the item involved is movable and is not money or an investment security." Movable items include personal property. Needless to say, houses and the land upon which they are built are not movable. The UCC does not apply to services and items such as the following:

1. stocks,
2. bank accounts,
3. intellectual property, such as patents, copyrights and trademarks.

Although intellectual property is considered personal property, it is intangible and therefore excluded from coverage under the UCC.

Nor does the UCC apply if the parties wish to establish different requirements. UCC 1-302 notes the following:

(a) Except as otherwise provided in subsection (b) or elsewhere in [the Uniform Commercial Code], the effect of provisions of [the Uniform Commercial Code] may be varied by agreement.
(b) The obligations of good faith, diligence, reasonableness, and care prescribed by [the Uniform Commercial Code] may not be

[1] James Whitman, *Commercial Law and the American Volk: A note on Llewellyn's German Sources for the Uniform Commercial Code*, 97 Yale L.J. 158 (1987).

[2] https://www.gesetze-im-internet.de/englisch_bgb/englisch_bgb.html. Accessed November 18, 2023.

disclaimed by agreement. The parties, by agreement, may determine the standards by which the performance of those obligations is to be measured if those standards are not manifestly unreasonable. Whenever [the Uniform Commercial Code] requires an action to be taken within a reasonable time, a time that is not manifestly unreasonable may be fixed by agreement.

(c) The presence in certain provisions of [the Uniform Commercial Code] of the phrase 'unless otherwise agreed', or words of similar import, does not imply that the effect of other provisions may not be varied by agreement under this section."

All of the common law requirements that are noted in the prior chapters, such as offer and acceptance, consideration, capacity, and legality, are required to create a binding contract under the UCC, UNLESS modified by the UCC, but the UCC requires far less formality than the common law.

Contract Creation Under the UCC

The Restatement (Second) of Contracts, Section 19, notes generally that parties may enter into a contract by written or spoken words or by other actions or by failure to act. UCC 2-204 is similar and notes that any contract for the sale of goods may be made in any manner sufficient to show agreement, including conduct by both parties which recognizes the existence of such a contract. The UCC will control the interpretation of a contract for the sale or lease of goods when there is a conflict between the common law rules and the UCC.

Definitions

Sale: Article 2-106(1) states that a sale occurs when there is a "passing of title from seller to buyer for a price." The title consists of the legal right of ownership to an item. Therefore, if legal title does not pass, there has not been a sale as defined by the UCC.

Lease: Article 2A[3] deals with the lease of certain personal property and specifies that it applies to a transaction that creates a lease, or sublease, of goods. The lessor sells the right to the following:

---

[3] 2A-102, 2A-103(1)(k).

1. possession and use of goods,
2. pursuant to a lease.

The lessee acquires possession and use of goods, but not title.

Title: UCC Section 2-401 specifies that a party may hold legal title to a good if

1. the good exists and
2. has been "identified" to the contract.

Section 2-401 allows the parties to determine when title passes and notes:

If the parties do not specify when the title passes, then

1. the title passes to the buyer when the seller completes all obligations regarding the delivery of the goods or
2. the title passes to the buyer when the seller delivers the title documents if the goods do not need to be moved.

The passage of the title is related to the risk of loss that is normally addressed by way of insurance.

Goods: As previously noted, the UCC applies to "goods" and Section 2-105(1) defines goods as follows:

1. all things (including specially manufactured things),
2. which are movable,
3. at the time of identification to the contract for sale.

In addition to being movable, the UCC requires that goods must be tangible, which, as noted above, does not apply to certain items of personal property. In addition, the UCC does not apply to real estate or intangibles such as the following:

1. stocks,
2. bonds,
3. services.

However, the UCC may apply to certain goods that are associated with real estate, such as the following:

1. oil,
2. gas,
3. minerals,
4. if severance or separation is performed by the seller,
5. growing crops or timber to be cut, regardless of who severs.

Since most contracts cover both goods and services, it presents a dilemma. Does the UCC or the common law control the interpretation of the contract? The courts use the predominant-factor test that asks whether the primary value of the contract is goods or services. Whichever is more valuable will determine whether the UCC or common law controls the interpretation of the contract.

Other Requirements of the UCC

Merchants and Nonmerchants

Is one or more of the parties a merchant or nonmerchant? The UCC's rules may vary significantly, depending on whether the buyer or seller is a merchant.

As noted previously, UCC Section 1-203 requires that all parties to a contract controlled by Article 2 be held to a standard of "good faith." Section 1-201 of the UCC goes on to define "good faith" as "honesty in fact in the conduct or transaction concerned." Merchants are held to an even higher standard than consumers because of their business expertise.

UCC Section 2-104 defines a merchant as one of the following:

1. a person, who regularly deals in goods involved in the transaction,
2. a person, who by occupation presents himself as having knowledge or skill specialized to the transaction,
3. a person, who employs an agent who holds himself out as having particular knowledge or skill about the goods involved.

Given the breadth of the definition, it is likely that a company doing business over the Internet will be considered a merchant and, therefore, held to a higher standard in all transactions.

The Creation of Sales and Lease Contracts

The UCC controls when a contract does not address a particular issue or the parties want to alter or modify the UCC's requirements.

Offer

The common law specifies that an offer can be revoked at any time before acceptance, although as noted, an option contract is an exception to that rule. Once an offer is met with an unqualified acceptance, a contract is formed.

The UCC is somewhat different and notes that a contract may exist even if the moment of its making is unclear.[4] The UCC is similar to the common law in that an offer may be revoked at any time prior to acceptance but also provides an exception.

Section 2-205 covers the issue of a merchant's firm offer and notes the following: "A merchant's firm offer arises when a merchant-offeror gives assurances in a signed writing that the offer will remain open."

The offer remains open for

1. the stated time or
2. a reasonable time not to exceed three months.

French law is similar to the UCC with regard to an offer. Civil Code Article 1116 provides that an offer "... cannot be retracted before the expiry of the period set by its author or, failing that, the end of a reasonable period." In addition, this section also notes that withdrawal or retraction of the offer in violation of this prohibition prevents the conclusion of the contract. However, the retraction also creates "... the extra-contractual liability of its author under the conditions of common law without obliging him to compensate for the loss of the benefits expected from the contract."

Requirements for a Merchant's Firm Offer pursuant to UCC 2-205 or 2A-205 for leases arise when a merchant provides assurances in a signed writing that an offer will remain open.

---

[4] 2-204(2), 2A-204(2).

UCC Section 2-205 goes on to specify the details:

> An offer by a merchant to buy or sell goods in a signed writing which by its terms gives assurance that it will be held open is not revocable, for lack of consideration, during the time stated or if no time is stated for a reasonable time, but in no event may such period of irrevocability exceed three months; but any such term of assurance on a form supplied by the offeree must be separately signed by the offeror.

UCC Section 1-201(37) specifies "general definitions" and notes that "Signed" includes using any symbol executed or adopted with present intention to adopt or accept a writing.

Section 3-401 of the UCC goes into greater detail and states the following:

a. A person is not liable on an instrument unless
   i. the person signed the instrument or
   ii. the person is represented by an agent or representative who signed the instrument and the signature is binding on the represented person under Section 3-402.
b. A signature may be made
   i. manually or by means of a device or machine and
   ii. by the use of any name, including a trade or assumed name, or by a word, mark, or symbol executed or adopted by a person with present intention to authenticate a writing."

UCC 1-201(37) notes that "writing" includes printing, typewriting, or any other intentional reduction to tangible form. "Written" has a corresponding meaning. In some sections, the UCC refers to a "record." UCC 1-201(31) notes that a "Record" means information that is inscribed on a tangible medium or that is stored in an electronic or other medium and is retrievable in perceivable form. Thus, a "record" as well as a "writing" may include electronic communication, such as an e-mail.

UCC 1-201(12) also specifies that a "contract," as distinguished from an "agreement," means the total legal obligation that results from the parties' agreement as determined by the Uniform Commercial Code as supplemented by any other applicable laws.

Other Sections of the UCC on Acceptance

Section 2-204

A sales contract "may be made in any manner sufficient to show agreement" between the parties. Therefore, unlike the common law, which requires a definite acceptance in response to an officer, an agreement may exist even if the moment when an offer is met with an unqualified acceptance is unclear.

Acceptance Under the UCC

The UCC provides a variety of methods for an offer to be accepted. Section 2-206(1) notes that unless otherwise unambiguously indicated by the language or circumstances,

a. an offer to make a contract shall be construed as inviting acceptance in any manner and by any medium reasonable under the circumstances;
b. an order or other offer to buy goods for prompt or current shipment shall be construed as inviting acceptance either by a prompt promise to ship or by the prompt or current shipment of conforming or nonconforming goods, but such a shipment of nonconforming goods does not constitute an acceptance if the seller seasonably notifies the buyer that the shipment is offered only as an accommodation to the buyer;
   1. Where the beginning of a requested performance is a reasonable mode of acceptance, an offeror who is not notified of acceptance within a reasonable time may treat the offer as having lapsed before acceptance.

This section allows an acceptance to be made in any manner that is reasonable under the circumstances. Therefore, an acceptance by way of the Internet is likely to be legally sufficient.

Section 2-207(1) goes on to note the following:

> A contract is formed when the offeree communicates a definite acceptance, even if the acceptance includes terms that are additional to or different from those in the offer, unless acceptance is expressly made conditional on assent to the additional or different terms.

2. The additional terms are to be construed as proposals for addition to the contract. Between merchants, such terms become part of the contract unless

(a) the offer expressly limits acceptance to the terms of the offer,
(b) they materially alter it, or
(c) notification of objection to them has already been given or is given within a reasonable time after notice of them is received.

3. Conduct by both parties which recognizes the existence of a contract is sufficient to establish a contract for sale although the writings of the parties do not otherwise establish a contract. In such cases, the terms of the particular contract consist of those terms on which the writings of the parties agree, together with any supplementary terms, incorporated under any other provisions of this Act.

UCC 2-507 addresses the "perfect tender" rule.

As with the common law, a seller or lessor must provide goods that meet the requirement of the contract, referred to as "conforming" goods. "Conforming" goods conform exactly to the requirements of the contract. Nonconforming goods are goods that do not match the specific requirements of the contract, even if only in slight detail.

Under the UCC, the prompt shipment of nonconforming goods constitutes both an acceptance, creating a contract, as well as a breach of that contract *unless* the seller seasonably notifies the buyer that the nonconforming goods are offered as an accommodation. This is likely to be addressed by way of a contract that specifically gives a seller such an option.

Additional Terms

The common law "mirror image" rule requires the acceptance to exactly "mirror" the offer. Anything short of that may be considered a rejection and a counteroffer. However, the analysis is complicated by the common law's "last shot" rule. The party that sent the last form, usually the offeror, dictated the terms governing the transaction.[5] The UCC rejects the mirror image rule and modifies the last shot rule.

[5] Caroline N. Brown, *Restoring Peace in the Battle of the Forms: A Framework for Making the Uniform Commercial Code Section 2-207 Work*, 69 N.C. L. REV. 893, 902 (1991) (noting that under the common law rule, the offeree became the master of the commercial contract created pursuant to an exchange of forms).

UCC 2-207(1) specifies the following:

1. A definite and seasonable expression of acceptance or a written confirmation which is sent within a reasonable time operates as an acceptance even though it states terms additional to or different from those offered or agreed upon, unless acceptance is expressly made conditional on assent to the additional or different terms.
2. The additional terms are to be construed as proposals for addition to the contract. Between merchants, such terms become part of the contract unless
   a. the offer expressly limits acceptance to the terms of the offer;
   b. they materially alter it; or
   c. notification of objection to them has already been given or is given within a reasonable time after notice of them is received.

As previously noted, UCC 2-207(3) states that "conduct by both parties which recognizes the existence of a contract is sufficient to establish a contract for sale although the writings of the parties do not otherwise establish a contract. In such cases, the terms of the particular contract consist of those terms on which the writings of the parties agree, together with any supplementary terms incorporated under any other provisions of this Act."

Thus, under the UCC, an acceptance with additional terms may be a valid acceptance and not a rejection. The test that is used by the courts is a relatively simple one: Does it appear that the parties intended to form a contract? If the answer is in the affirmative, a contract has been formed.

However, the UCC adds an additional consideration to the issue. Whether the additional terms become a part of the contract depends, at least in part, on whether the parties are merchants or nonmerchants.

UCC 2-207(2) notes that if the acceptance includes terms additional to or different from those in the offer and one (or both) parties is (are) a nonmerchant, the contract is formed on the terms of the original offer. If both parties are merchants, UCC 2-207(2) notes that the additional terms become part of the contract unless

1. the original offer expressly limited acceptance to its terms;
2. the new or changed terms materially alter the contract; or
3. the offeror objects to the new or changed terms within a reasonable period of time.

What is a "Material" Alteration?

Comment four to UCC 2-207 defines material alteration as a term that would "result in surprise or hardship if incorporated without express awareness by the other party …" and goes on to summarize the foregoing by noting that the purpose of subsection (2)(b) is the "avoidance of oppression and unfair surprise." Comment four provides examples of additional terms that "would normally 'materially alter' the contract," such as disclaimers of implied warranties of merchantability and fitness for a particular purpose. Comment five notes the issue of "unreasonable surprise" and specifies additional terms that do NOT involve the element of unreasonable surprise, such as the payment of interest on overdue accounts and reasonable limits on remedies in the event of breach.

In an effort to put the foregoing into practical terms, one court resorted to tort law and noted the following: "To carry the burden of showing surprise, a party must establish that, under the circumstances, it cannot be presumed that a reasonable merchant would have consented to the additional term."[6] Another court noted that unreasonable surprise is measured by "both the subjective element of what a party actually knew and the objective element of what a party should have known."[7] At least some courts have clarified that in order to constitute "hardship," a term must rise to the level of substantial economic hardship.[8]

Open Terms

Under the common law, a contract must have sufficient terms for a court to be able to fashion a remedy in the event of a breach. The UCC is less demanding. UCC 2-204(3) provides that a contract will not fail for indefiniteness as long as

1. the parties intended to make a contract and
2. there is a reasonably certain basis for the court to grant an appropriate remedy.

[6] Carr v. Michael Weinig, AG 2006 WL 2355867 (N.D.N.Y. Aug. 14, 2006).
[7] Bayway Ref. Co. v. Oxygenated Mktg. & Trading A.G., 215 F.3d 219, 224 (2d Cir. 2000).
[8] ISRA Vision AG v. Burton Industries, Inc., 654 F.Supp.2d 638 (E.D. Mich. 2009).

While this usually requires a specified quantity, there are two exceptions.[9]

Open Price Term

UCC 2-305 provides the following:

1. The parties if they so intend can conclude a contract for sale even though the price is not settled. In such a case, the price is a reasonable price at the time for delivery if
   (a) nothing is said as to price; or
   (b) the price is left to be agreed by the parties and they fail to agree; or
   (c) the price is to be fixed in terms of some agreed market or other standard as set or recorded by a third person or agency and it is not so set or recorded.
2. A price to be fixed by the seller or by the buyer means a price for him to fix in good faith.
3. When a price left to be fixed otherwise than by agreement of the parties fails to be fixed through fault of one party, the other may at his option treat the contract as canceled or himself fix a reasonable price.
4. Where, however, the parties intend not to be bound unless the price be fixed or agreed and it is not fixed or agreed there is no contract. In such a case, the buyer must return any goods already received or if unable to do so must pay their reasonable value at the time of delivery and the seller must return any portion of the price paid on account.

Note, much like French law, the requirement of good faith. The price is to be fixed in "good faith." As previously noted, UCC Section 1-201(20) states that "good faith," except as otherwise provided in Article 5, means honesty in fact and the observance of reasonable commercial standards of fair dealing.

[9]A requirements contract that requires a seller to agree to provide all or a specified amount that will satisfy the buyer's requirements, and an output contract where the buyer agrees to buy all or a stated amount of what the seller manufactures or produces.

French Law

French Civil Code Article 1164 notes the following:

> In framework contracts it may be agreed that the price will be fixed unilaterally by one of the parties, subject to the requirement that the latter must provide the reason for the amount if it is challenged.

The requirement of "good faith" is critical to the Uniform Commercial. As noted in Chapter 7, the common law also requires good faith in "performance or enforcement." However, this creates a potential issue in situations where the terms of the contract are unreasonable or, as specified by the UCC, "unconscionable." The UCC makes no mention of a requirement of good faith in the creation of a contract, although UCC Section 2-103(b) seemingly closes that loophole by specifying that "Good Faith" in the case of a merchant means honesty in fact and the observance of reasonable commercial standards of fair dealing in the trade.

Although unreasonableness is likely to be the fault of one of the parties to the contract, in the absence of a mistake, the other party is not necessarily without a remedy, particularly if the aggrieved party is a consumer. UCC Section 2-302(1) may allow a court to modify the terms of a contract. The section notes the following: "If the court as a matter of law finds the contract or any clause of the contract to have been unconscionable at the time it was made the court may refuse to enforce the contract, or it may enforce the remainder of the contract without the unconscionable clause, or it may so limit the application of any unconscionable clause as to avoid any unconscionable result."

Since the UCC refers to "unconscionable," it also provides not a definition, but rather a "test". Under Section 2-302(1), the test of unconscionability is "whether, in the light of the general commercial background and the commercial needs of the particular trade or case, the clauses involved are so one-sided as to be unconscionable under the circumstances existing at the time of the making of the contract... The principle is one of the prevention of oppression and unfair surprise and not of disturbance of allocation of risks because of superior bargaining power."

The need for good faith in the area of commercial law is at least partly related to the need for commercial contracts to sometimes leave certain terms unspecified. Thus, for instance, the UCC may allow the parties to leave the price unspecified. In the absence of good faith, such an approach may be an invitation to litigation.

Acceptance

As noted previously, acceptance under the common law must meet the mirror image rule requirements. In addition, the issue of acceptance is further complicated by whether the contract is unilateral or bilateral. UCC 2-206 specifies the following:

1. Unless otherwise unambiguously indicated by the language or circumstances,
   a. an offer to make a contract shall be construed as inviting acceptance in any manner and by any medium reasonable in the circumstances;
   b. an order or other offer to buy goods for prompt or current shipment shall be construed as inviting acceptance either by a prompt promise to ship or by the prompt or current shipment of conforming or nonconforming goods, but such a shipment of nonconforming goods does not constitute an acceptance if the seller seasonably notifies the buyer that the shipment is offered only as an accommodation to the buyer.
2. Where the beginning of a requested performance is a reasonable mode of acceptance, an offeror who is not notified of acceptance within a reasonable time may treat the offer as having lapsed before acceptance.

"Nonconforming" goods are goods that do not meet the requirements established by the contract. The prompt shipment of nonconforming goods is both an acceptance and a breach unless the seller seasonably notified the buyer that it is offered as an accommodation. The notice of accommodation must clearly indicate that shipment is not an acceptance and no contract has been formed unless the parties' agreement specifies otherwise. An accommodation is a counteroffer which the recipient is free to accept or reject.

Consideration

Both the common law and UCC require consideration. However, there is a significant difference when it comes to the issue of contract modification. The common law requires a contract modification to be supported by consideration, whereas the UCC does not. UCC 2-209(1) states that the UCC does not require a contract modification to be supported by new consideration although it again requires good faith (UCC 1-304 noted above). In addition, a contract may require a modification to be in writing in which case only those changes agreed to in a signed writing may be enforceable.

Parol Evidence

Due to its flexibility compared to the common law, it is much more likely that litigation involving a contract that is controlled by the UCC will require verbal testimony to explain the terms of a contract. Therefore, UCC Section 2-202 notes the following:

> Terms with respect to which the confirmatory memoranda of the parties agree or which are otherwise set forth in a writing intended by the parties as a final expression of their agreement ... may not be contradicted by evidence of any prior agreement or of a contemporaneous oral agreement but may be explained or supplemented
>
> a. by course of dealing or usage of trade (Section 1-205) or by course of performance (Section 2-208); and
> b. by evidence of consistent additional term unless the court finds the writing to have been intended also as a complete and exclusive statement of the terms of the agreement.

Section 1-205 specifies that when parties have had regular dealings, their prior actions may be used to resolve a dispute. However, there is an exception to the UCC rules with regard to parol evidence. UCC 2-209(2) specifies that if a nonmerchant enters into a written contract with a merchant that forbids oral modification, the clause is not binding unless the nonmerchant signs a separate agreement accepting the requirement. If a contract modification brings a contract within the UCC requirements for a written contract, as noted above, this modification must generally be in writing, subject to certain exceptions, in order to be enforceable.

The Statute of Frauds

As noted in the chapters on contracts, the common law requires that certain contracts be in writing in order to be enforceable. The UCC also requires certain contracts to be in writing in order to be enforceable. UCC 2-201 specifies the following:

1. Except as otherwise provided in this section, a contract for the sale of goods for the price of $500 or more is not enforceable by way of action or defense unless there is some writing sufficient to indicate that a contract for sale has been made between the parties and signed by the party against whom enforcement is sought or by his authorized agent or broker. A writing is not insufficient because it omits or incorrectly states a term agreed upon, but the contract is not enforceable under this paragraph beyond the quantity of goods shown in such writing.
2. Between merchants if within a reasonable time a writing in confirmation of the contract and sufficient against the sender is received and the party receiving it has reason to know its contents, it satisfies the requirements of subsection (1) against such party unless written notice of objection to its contents is given within 10 days after it is received.
3. A contract which does not satisfy the requirements of subsection (1) but which is valid in other respects is enforceable
    a. if the goods are to be specially manufactured for the buyer and are not suitable for sale to others in the ordinary course of the seller's business and the seller, before notice of repudiation is received and under circumstances which reasonably indicate that the goods are for the buyer, has made either a substantial beginning of their manufacture or commitments for their procurement; or
    b. if the party against whom enforcement is sought admits in his pleading, testimony or otherwise in court that a contract for sale was made, but the contract is not enforceable under this provision beyond the quantity of goods admitted; or
    c. with respect to goods for which payment has been made and accepted or which have been received and accepted (Section 2-606). French Civil Code Article 1383 addresses admissions and distinguishes between judicial and extra-judicial. Article 1381-1 notes that a purely oral extra-judicial admission is not recognized, except in the situation where legislation permits proof by any means. Its probative value is left to the assessment of the court.

In the case of contracts between merchants, UCC Section 2-201(2) provides an additional exception and notes the following:

> Between merchants, if within a reasonable time a writing in confirmation of the contract and sufficient against the sender is received and the party receiving it has reason to know its contents, it satisfied the (writing) requirements … against such party unless written notice of objection to its contents is given within ten days after it is received.
>
> French Civil Code Article 1381-1 notes that a purely oral extra-judicial admission is not recognized except in the situation where legislation permits proof by any means. Its probative value is left to the assessment of the court. In addition, 1383 et seq. addresses the issue of an admission.

Warranties

A warranty is a representation by the seller or lessor about the quality, condition and/or features of the goods. These representations may be either verbal or in writing. There are express warranties, which are specifically stated by the merchant, as well as warranties of title and implied warranties that are implied by law, unless excluded.

Among the most significant warranties is the warranty of title that covers three different subjects. UCC Section 2-312 states that a seller warrants that good title is transferred to the buyer and that the goods are free of any claim of infringements or liens, unless those are disclosed to the buyer and are a part of most sales contracts.

UCC 2-312 specifies the following:

1. Subject to subsection (2), there is in a contract for sale a warranty by the seller that
   a. the title conveyed shall be good, and its transfer rightful and
   b. the goods shall be delivered free from any security interest or other lien or encumbrance of which the buyer at the time of contracting has no knowledge.
2. A warranty under subsection (1) will be excluded or modified only by specific language or by circumstances which give the buyer reason to know that the person selling does not claim the title in himself or that he is purporting to sell only such right or title as he or a third person may have.

3. Unless otherwise agreed, a seller who is a merchant regularly dealing in goods of the kind warrants that the goods shall be delivered free of the rightful claim of any third person by way of infringement or the like, but a buyer who furnishes specifications to the seller must hold the seller harmless against any such claim which arises out of compliance with the specifications.

However, also as noted, UCC 2-316(1) permits a party to disclaim or modify the warranty of title, at the time the contract is formed, as long as there is

1. language that is specific and conspicuous or
2. the circumstances of a sale, such as a sheriff's sale provide notice to the buyer.

UCC Section 2-313(1) specifies the method by which express warranties are created and notes that express warranties are created by the seller as follows:

a. Any affirmation of fact or promise made by the seller to the buyer which relates to the goods and becomes part of the basis of the bargain creates an express warranty that the goods shall conform to the affirmation or promise.
b. Any description of the goods which is made part of the basis of the bargain creates an express warranty that the goods shall conform to the description.
c. Any sample or model which is made part of the basis of the bargain creates an express warranty that the whole of the goods shall conform to the sample or model.

An express warranty may be found in a seller's or lessor's advertising or promotional material, statements, verbal or otherwise by a sales representative, or a sales or lease contract. A merger clause in a written document that disclaims any verbal representations may be effective.

Puffery

As discussed in the chapters on contracts, not all statements rise to the level of a warranty. UCC 2-313(2) notes the following: "It is not necessary to the creation of an express warranty that the seller use formal words such as 'warrant' or 'guarantee' or that he have a specific intention to make a warranty, but an affirmation merely of the value of the goods or a statement purporting to be merely the seller's opinion or commendation of the goods does not create a warranty." However, comment eight acknowledges that some opinion statements, where they are a part of the "basis of the bargain" or when the seller holds himself out as an expert, may rise to the level of a warranty.

However, the analysis is far more complicated. "Only a foolish lawyer will be quick to label a seller's statement as puffs or not puffs, and only a reckless one will label a seller's statement at all without carefully examining such factors as the nature of the defect (was it obvious or not) and the buyer's and seller's relative knowledge."[10]

Implied Warranties

A warranty that is "implied" is implied by the law in certain circumstances. The implied warranty of merchantability is created automatically in every sale or lease by a merchant who deals in the kind of goods sold or leased. UCC Section 2-314 notes that merchants impliedly warrant that the goods they sell or lease must meet two warranties:

1. Unless excluded or modified (Section 2-316), a warranty that the goods shall be merchantable is implied in a contract for their sale if the seller is a merchant with respect to goods of that kind. Under this section, the serving for value of food or drink to be consumed either on the premises or elsewhere is a sale.
2. Goods to be merchantable must be at least such as:
   a. pass without objection in the trade under the contract description;
   b. in the case of fungible goods are of fair average quality within the description;
   c. are fit for the ordinary purposes for which such goods are used;
   d. run, within the variations permitted by the agreement, of even kind; quality and quantity within each unit and among all units involved;
   e. are adequately contained, packaged, and labeled as the agreement may require;
   f. conform to the promise or affirmations of fact made on the container or label if any.

---

[10] James J. White & Robert S. Summers, *Uniform Commercial Code 336* (4th ed. 1995).

Subsection (3) goes on to note the following: "Unless excluded or modified (Section 2-316) other implied warranties may arise from course of dealing or usage of trade." This warranty does not require knowledge on the part of the merchant that the goods were not merchantable. Thus, under this section, when both parties have knowledge of a well-recognized trade custom, a court will infer that both parties intended for that custom to apply. A course of dealing or trade usage may also serve to modify or exclude an implied warranty.

UCC 2-315 creates the implied warranty of fitness for a particular purpose and states as follows: "Where the seller at the time of contracting has reason to know any particular purpose for which the goods are required and that the buyer is relying on the seller's skill or judgment to select or furnish suitable goods, there is unless excluded or modified under the next section an implied warranty that the goods shall be fit for such purpose."

What is unique about the implied warranty of fitness for a particular purpose is that it is not limited to "merchants." Thus, the warranty under UCC 2-315 may arise as long as the seller or lessor knows:

1. the particular purpose for which the goods will be used and
2. also that the buyer is relying on the skill and judgment of the seller.

Under the implied warranty of fitness for a particular purpose, while goods may be merchantable, they may be unfit for a particular purpose. A "particular" purpose differs from the "ordinary" purpose for which goods are used and relates to "merchantability." In addition, UCC 2-315 does not require actual knowledge of the particular purpose. It is sufficient if the merchant knew or had reason to know of the buyer's particular purpose. This may arise in situations where, for instance, the circumstances of the sale are sufficient to give the seller actual knowledge or a reason to know of the buyer's particular purpose. However, in what appears to be a similar requirement to the "basis of the bargain," requirement that is found in UCC 2-313(2), noted above, UCC 2-315 requires actual reliance by the buyer on the seller's "skill and judgment."

Webster v. Blue Ship Tea Room, 347 Mass. 421, (1964)

The plaintiff, who had been born and brought up in New England (a fact of some consequence), ordered clam chowder and crabmeat salad.

Within a few minutes, she received tidings to the effect that 'there was no more clam chowder,' whereupon she ordered a cup of fish chowder. Presently, there was set before her 'a small bowl of fish chowder.' She had previously enjoyed a breakfast about 9 A.M. which had given her no difficulty. The fish chowder contained haddock, potatoes, milk, water and seasoning. The chowder was milky in color and not clear. The haddock and potatoes were in chunks (also a fact of consequence). 'She agitated it a little with the spoon and observed that it was a fairly full bowl ... It was hot when she got it, but she did not tip it with her spoon because it was hot ... but stirred it in an up and under motion. She denied that she did this because she was looking for something, but it was rather because she wanted an even distribution of fish and potatoes.' 'She started to eat it, alternating between the chowder and crackers which were on the table with ... [some] rolls. She ate about 3 or 4 spoonfuls then stopped. She looked at the spoonfuls as she was eating. She saw equal parts of liquid, potato and fish as she spooned it into her mouth. She did not see anything unusual about it. After 3 or 4 spoonfuls she was aware that something had lodged in her throat because she couldn't swallow and couldn't clear her throat by gulping and she could feel it. This misadventure led to two esophagoscopies at the Massachusetts General Hospital, in the second of which ... a fish bone was found and removed. The sequence of events produced injury to the plaintiff which was not insubstantial.'

The court noted as follows: 'We must decide whether a fish bone lurking in a fish chowder, about the ingredients of which there is no other complaint, constitutes a breach of implied warranty under applicable provisions of the Uniform Commercial Code, the annotations to which are not helpful on this point.' As the judge put it in his charge, 'Was the fish chowder fit to be eaten and wholesome? ... [N]obody is claiming that the fish itself wasn't wholesome... But the bone of contention here — I don't mean that for a pun — but was this fish bone a foreign substance that made the fish chowder unwholesome or not fit to be eaten?'

A namesake of the plaintiff, Daniel Webster, had a recipe for fish chowder which has survived into a number of modern cookbooks and in which the removal of fish bones is not mentioned at all. One old time recipe recited in the New English Dictionary study defines chowder as 'A dish made of fresh fish (esp. cod) or clams, stewed with slices of pork or bacon, onions, and biscuit. "Cider and champagne are sometimes added."' Hawthorne, in *The House of the Seven Gables* ... speaks of '[a] codfish of sixty pounds, caught in the bay, [which] had been dissolved into the rich liquid of a chowder.' A chowder variant, cod 'Muddle,' was made in Plymouth in the 1890s by taking 'a three or four pound codfish, head added. Season with salt and pepper and boil in just enough water to keep from burning. When cooked, add milk and piece of butter.' The recitation of these ancient formulae suffices to indicate that in the construction of chowders in these parts in other years, worries about fish bones played no role whatsoever.

Thus, we consider a dish which for many long years, if well made, has been made generally as outlined above. It is not too much to say that a person sitting down in New England to consume a good New England fish chowder embarks on a gustatory adventure which may entail the removal of some fish bones from his bowl as he proceeds. We are not inclined to tamper with age old recipes by any amendment reflecting the plaintiff's view of the effect of the Uniform Commercial Code upon them. We are aware of the heavy body of case law involving foreign substances in food, but we sense a strong distinction between them and those relative to unwholesomeness of the food itself … and a fish bone in a fish chowder … In any event, we consider that the joys of life in New England include the ready availability of fresh fish chowder. We should be prepared to cope with the hazards of fish bones, the occasional presence of which in chowders is, it seems to us, to be anticipated, and which, in the light of a hallowed tradition, do not impair their fitness or merchantability. We are most impressed, however, by Allen v. Grafton, (citation omitted) …, where in Ohio, the Midwest, in a case where the plaintiff was injured by a piece of oyster shell in an order of fried oysters, Mr. Justice Taft (now Chief Justice) in a majority opinion held that 'the possible presence of a piece of oyster shell in or attached to an oyster is so well known to anyone who eats oysters that we can say as a matter of law that one who eats oysters can reasonably anticipate and guard against eating such a piece of shell …

Thus, while we sympathize with the plaintiff who has suffered a peculiarly New England injury … Judgment for the defendant.

Warranty Disclaimers

Warranty disclaimers require specific and unambiguous language in a way that avoids surprise.

UCC 2-316 notes the following:

1. Words or conduct relevant to the creation of an express warranty and words or conduct tending to negate or limit warranty shall be construed wherever reasonable as consistent with each other; but subject to the provisions of this Article on parol or extrinsic evidence (Section 2-202), negation or limitation is inoperative to the extent that such construction is unreasonable.
2. Subject to subsection (3), to exclude or modify the implied warranty of merchantability or any part of it, the language must mention merchantability and in case of a writing must be conspicuous, and to exclude or modify any implied warranty of fitness, the exclusion must be by a writing and conspicuous. Language to exclude all implied warranties of fitness is sufficient if it states, for example, that "There are no warranties which extend beyond the description on the face hereof."
3. Notwithstanding subsection (2)
   a. unless the circumstances indicate otherwise, all implied warranties are excluded by expressions like "as is", "with all faults," or other language which in common understanding calls the buyer's attention to the exclusion of warranties and makes plain that there is no implied warranty;
   b. when the buyer before entering into the contract has examined the goods or the sample or model as fully as he desired or has refused to examine the goods there is no implied warranty with regard to defects which an examination ought in the circumstances to have revealed to him;
   c. an implied warranty can also be excluded or modified by course of dealing or course of performance or usage of trade.

Conspicuous

UCC 1-201(10) defines "Conspicuous" with reference to a term, means so written, displayed, or presented that a reasonable person against which it is to operate ought to have noticed it. Whether a term is "conspicuous" or not is a decision for the court. Conspicuous terms include the following:

1. a heading in capitals equal to or greater in size than the surrounding text, or in contrasting type, font, or color to the surrounding text of the same or lesser size; and

2. language in the body of a record or display in larger type than the surrounding text or in contrasting type, font, or color to the surrounding text of the same size, or set off from surrounding text of the same size by symbols or other marks that call attention to the language.

International Issues

Contracts for the International Sale of Goods

The United Nations Convention on Contracts for the International Sale of Goods (CISG) was intended to provide a modern, uniform, and fair regime for contracts for the international sale of goods.[11] The CISG applies to the international sale of goods whenever contracts for the sale of goods are concluded between parties with a place of business in Contracting States.[12]

While the CISG, as with the UCC, does not apply to a contract for services, among the notable differences between the CISG and the UCC is the fact that the CISG does not apply to consumer sales. The text of the CISG together with an explanatory note is available on the UNCITRAL website in all official United Nations languages.[13]

---

[11] https://uncitral.un.org/en/texts/salegoods/conventions/sale_of_goods/cisg.

[12] *Ibid.*

[13] https://uncitral.un.org/sites/uncitral.un.org/files/media-documents/uncitral/en/19-09951_e_ebook.pdf.

Chapter 10

Copyright

Abstract

Copyrights are likely the most significant form of intellectual property protection when it comes to the Internet since so much of the material on the Internet is copyrighted. In order for the material to be transferred online, it must be copied. The law has changed to reflect the changes in technology. Originally, copyright infringement could be prosecuted only when a copy of something, such as music, was exchanged for financial gain. That is why most, if not all tape decks in years gone by, came with two slots, allowing the purchaser to make copies of cassettes. The copy was not as good as the original. With the development of computers and "ripping and burning" technology, the copies are identical to the original, thus requiring a change in the law. What makes this area of the law difficult is that a reproduction need not be identical to the original, nor copy the original in its entirety. If the form or expression of an idea is copied, there may be infringement. As with all subjects, there are a variety of defenses that are available, the most obvious one being fair use. Once the copyright expires, the material enters the public domain and may be used by others.

Introduction

This area of the law is complex. As the United States Patent and Trademark Office (USPTO) notes, "There is an area of overlap between copyright and design patent statutes where the author/inventor can secure both a copyright and a design patent. Thus, an ornamental design may be copyrighted as a work of art and may also be a subject matter of a design patent."[1]

Copyright has been a part of the American legal landscape since colonial times when many of the colonies adopted copyright laws.[2] Upon ratification, the Constitution empowered Congress to enact laws on the subject of copyright. Article 1, Section 8, Clause 8 states that "Congress shall have Power … To promote the Progress of Science and useful Arts, by securing for limited Times to Authors and Inventors the exclusive Right to their respective Writings and Discoveries."

In May 1790, when Congress enacted the first federal copyright law, the U.S. Copyright Office did not exist. Authors and publishers recorded their claims with federal district courts and submitted copies of their works, at that time consisting of books, maps, and charts, in support of their applications. Called "deposits," these materials were stored in a variety of places, including in the U.S. Department of State and the U.S. Department of the Interior.[3]

In 1897, Congress established and funded the U.S. Copyright Office as a separate department within the Library of Congress and created the position of Register of Copyrights. Since then, the Register has been appointed by, and works under the general direction of, the Librarian of Congress. This appointment authority, however, required that the Librarian thereafter be appointed with the advice and consent of the Senate.[4]

The functions of the U.S. Copyright Office are mentioned in Title 17 of the U.S. Code, which includes the provisions of the Copyright Act as well as chapters on the Digital Millenium Copyright Act (DMCA), vessel designs, and other *sui generis* protection and exemptions.[5]

---

[1] U.S. Copyright Office Bulletin 3, Copyright Enactments 1783–1900, at 9-29 (listing copyright laws enacted by Connecticut, Massachusetts, Maryland, New Jersey, New Hampshire, Rhode Island, Pennsylvania, South Carolina, Virginia, North Carolina, Georgia, and New York between 1783 and 1786), available at www.copyright.gov/history/Copyright_Enactments_1783-1973.pdf.

[2] *Ibid.*

[3] https://copyright.gov/comp3/chap100/ch100-general-background.pdf.

[4] *Ibid.*

[5] *Ibid.*

Federal Law

The Copyright Act of 1976 as Amended[6]

The primary source of law in the United States is the Copyright Act of 1976 as amended, covering literary or artistic productions of a specified type, in addition to a number of international agreements. Works created after January 1, 1978, are automatically given statutory copyright protection for:

1. The life of the author plus 70 years after the author's death;
2. Works made for hire[7] and anonymous or pseudonymous works, 95 years from publication or 120 years from creation, whichever is shorter; or
3. For works by more than one author (joint works), the copyright expires 70 years after the death of the last surviving author.

These time periods reflect extensions contained in the Copyright Term Extension Act. Works created before 1978 are subject to a different time frame.

Section 102(a) of the Copyright Act addresses the subject matter of copyright, and subsection (b) specifies what is not eligible for copyright protection:

---

[6] 17 U.S.C. Sections 101 *et seq.*

[7] Section 101 of the Copyright Act notes that A "work made for hire" is — (1) a work prepared by an employee within the scope of his or her employment; or (2) a work specially ordered or commissioned for use as a contribution to a collective work, as a part of a motion picture or other audiovisual work, as a translation, as a supplementary work, as a compilation, as an instructional text, as a test, as answer material for a test, or as an atlas, if the parties expressly agree in a written instrument signed by them that the work shall be considered a work made for hire. For the purpose of the foregoing sentence, a "supplementary work" is a work prepared for publication as a secondary adjunct to a work by another author for the purpose of introducing, concluding, illustrating, explaining, revising, commenting upon, or assisting in the use of the other work, such as forewords, afterwords, pictorial illustrations, maps, charts, tables, editorial notes, musical arrangements, answer material for tests, bibliographies, appendixes, and indexes, and an "instructional text" is a literary, pictorial, or graphic work prepared for publication and with the purpose of use in systematic instructional activities.

a. Copyright protection subsists, in accordance with this title, in original works of authorship fixed in any tangible medium of expression, now known or later developed, from which they can be perceived, reproduced, or otherwise communicated, either directly or with the aid of a machine or device. Works of authorship include the following categories:
   i. Literary works;
   ii. Musical works, including any accompanying words;
   iii. Dramatic works, including any accompanying music;
   iv. Pantomimes and choreographic works;
   v. Pictorial, graphic, and sculptural works;
   vi. Motion pictures and other audiovisual works;
   vii. Sound recordings; and
   viii. Architectural works.
b. In no case does copyright protection for an original work of authorship extend to any idea, procedure, process, system, method of operation, concept, principle, or discovery, regardless of the form in which it is described, explained, illustrated, or embodied in such work.

Copyright protection gives the copyright holder the right to reproduce, distribute, and perform or display the work and prevents others from copying or exploiting the creation without permission.

Section 106 of the Copyright Act lists the author's exclusive rights in a copyrighted work:

"Subject to sections 107 through 122, the owner of copyright under this title has the exclusive rights to do and to authorize any of the following:

1. to reproduce the copyrighted work in copies or phonorecords;
2. to prepare derivative works based upon the copyrighted work;
3. to distribute copies or phonorecords of the copyrighted work to the public by sale or other transfer of ownership, or by rental, lease, or lending;
4. in the case of literary, musical, dramatic, and choreographic works, pantomimes, and motion pictures and other audiovisual works, to perform the copyrighted work publicly;
5. in the case of literary, musical, dramatic, and choreographic works, pantomimes, and pictorial, graphic, or sculptural works, including the

individual images of a motion picture or other audiovisual work, to display the copyrighted work publicly; and
6. in the case of sound recordings, to perform the copyrighted work publicly by means of a digital audio transmission."

In summary, copyright laws have been interpreted to promote both the creation and dissemination of creative works.[8] The Copyright Act protects "original works of authorship" that are "fixed in any tangible medium of expression ..."[9] Section 106 of the Act provides copyright holders with specified exclusive rights including the right to reproduce works, prepare derivative works, distribute works, and in certain cases, to publicly perform and display works. It also specifies certain exceptions and limitations to these exclusive rights.[10]

Under prior law, works were protected for a specific initial term and could be renewed for an additional renewal term. The 1976 Act does not require renewal. Generally, the Act protects works based on the time frame of the author's life plus 70 years.[11] In the case of an anonymous work, a pseudonymous work, or a work made for hire, the copyright lasts for a term of 95 years from the year of its first publication, or a term of 120 years from the year of its creation, whichever expires first.[12]

Congress added numerous exceptions and limitations to the statute,[13] including Section 107 that codified the judicially created fair use doctrine and Section 108 that specified certain exceptions for libraries and archives.

---

[8] See, e.g., Golan, 132 S. Ct. at 888–889. "[t]he Framers intended copyright itself to be the engine of free expression." *Harper & Row Publishers, Inc. v. Nation Enterprises et al.*, 471 U.S. 539, 558 (1985); see also Golan, 132 S. Ct. at 890 ("By establishing a marketable right to the use of one's expression, copyright supplies the economic incentive to create and disseminate ideas.").

[9] 17 U.S.C. Section 102(a).

[10] See 17 U.S.C. Sections 107–122.

[11] 17 U.S.C. Section 302(a)

[12] 17 U.S.C. Section 302(c).

[13] Sections 107–122.

Requirements for Copyright

An Original Work of Authorship

Federal courts have been called upon to decide issues that are not specifically addressed by the 1976 Act and therefore certain copyright law doctrines derive from court decisions. Among the issues decided by the court is the extent of creativity that is necessary for a work to qualify as a "work of authorship" under the Act. Section 102(a) of the Act states that "[c]opyright protection subsists ... in original works of authorship fixed in any tangible medium of expression, now known or later developed, from which they can be perceived, reproduced, or otherwise communicated, either directly or with the aid of a machine or device."

As the courts have noted, originality is "the bedrock principle of copyright" and "the very premise of copyright law".[14] "To qualify for copyright protection, a work must be original to the author," which means that the work must be "independently created by the author" and it must possess "at least some minimal degree of creativity."[15]

Independent Creation

The term "independent creation" means that the author created the work without copying from other works.[16] Court decisions have emphasized that "originality" is not a synonym for "novelty."[17] Therefore, a work may be an "independent creation" "even though it closely resembles other works so long as the similarity is fortuitous and not the result of copying."[18] Therefore, if two authors created works that are similar or even identical, each work may be registered as long as the authors did not copy from each other.

---

[14] *Feist Publications, Inc. v. Rural Telephone Service Co., Inc.*, 499 U.S. 340, 347 (1991).
[15] *Ibid.* at 345.
[16] *Ibid.*
[17] *Ibid.*
[18] *Ibid.*

Creativity

A work of authorship must possess "some minimal degree of creativity" to sustain a copyright claim.[19] "[T]he requisite level of creativity is extremely low." Even a "slight amount" of creative expression will suffice. "The vast majority of works meet the requirement as they possess some creative spark, 'no matter how crude, humble or obvious it might be.'"[20] Thus, while an author's creation need not "be presented in an innovative or surprising way," it "cannot be so mechanical or routine as to require no creativity whatsoever." A work that it is "entirely typical," "garden-variety," or "devoid of even the slightest traces of creativity" does not satisfy the originality requirement.[21] "[T]here is nothing remotely creative" about a work that merely reflects "an age-old practice, firmly rooted in tradition and so commonplace that it has come to be expected as a matter of course."[22] And, a work that "does not possess the minimal creative spark required by the Copyright Act" because the author's expression is "obvious" or "practically inevitable" is not protected by copyright.[23]

Although the creativity standard is low, it is not bottomless.[24] "There remains a narrow category of works in which the creative spark is utterly lacking or so trivial as to be virtually nonexistent. Such works are incapable of sustaining a valid copyright."[25]

The author's expression need not be novel, and it does not need to "be presented in an innovative or surprising way."[26] Note also that "Originality is … distinguished from novelty; there must be independent creation, but it need not be invention in the sense of striking uniqueness, ingeniousness, or novelty."[27] Thus, a work may be original, although it is neither new nor inventive or even if "it closely resembles other works."[28] As a result, the fact that a work is new, innovative, or even unique does

---

[19] *Ibid.* at 348, 362.

[20] *Ibid.* at 346.

[21] *Ibid.* at 362.

[22] *Ibid.* at 363.

[23] *Ibid.*

[24] *Ibid.* at 362.

[25] *Ibid.* at 359.

[26] *Ibid.* at 362.

[27] *L. Batlin & Son v. Snyder*, 536 F.2d 486, 490 (1976).

[28] *Feist*, 499 U.S. at 345.

not necessarily mean that it contains a sufficient amount of creative expression to satisfy the originality requirement.

In addition, the Copyright Office will not consider the truth or falsity of the facts outlined in a work of authorship nor the soundness or the unsoundness of the views that are expressed. As one court explained, "The gravity and immensity of the problems, theological, philosophical, economic and scientific, that would confront a court if this view were adopted are staggering to contemplate. It is surely not a task lightly to be assumed, and we decline the invitation to assume it."[29]

Requirements for Works That May Be Copyrighted

Provided that a work falls within one or more of the categories of authorship that is defined in Section 102(a) of the Copyright Act, it may be registered with the U.S. Copyright Office. Works that fall outside one or more of these categories are not copyrightable subject matter and cannot be registered. Section 102(a) of the Copyright Act states that works of authorship include the following categories:

Literary works
Musical works, including any accompanying words
Dramatic works, including any accompanying music
Pantomimes and choreographic works
Pictorial, graphic, and sculptural works
Motion pictures and other audiovisual works
Sound recordings
Architectural works.

Literary Works

The Copyright Act defines a literary work as "works, other than audiovisual works, expressed in words, numbers, or other verbal or numerical symbols or indicia, regardless of the nature of the material objects, such as books, periodicals, manuscripts, phonorecords, film, tapes, disks, or cards, in which they are embodied."[30] A literary work is a non-dramatic work that

---

[29] *Belcher v. Tarbox*, 486 F. 2d 1087, 1088 (1973).
[30] 17 U.S.C. Section 101.

explains, describes, or narrates a particular subject, theme, or idea through the use of narrative, descriptive, or explanatory text, rather than dialog or dramatic action. Generally, non-dramatic literary works are intended to be read; they are not intended to be performed before an audience.

Examples of non-dramatic literary works include:

Fiction;
Non-fiction;
Poetry;
Directories;
Catalogs;
Textbooks;
Reference works;
Advertising copy;
Compilations of information;
Computer programs;
Databases.

Fixed in a Tangible Medium

As previously noted, a literary work may be registered with the U.S. Copyright Office if it has been "fixed in any tangible medium of expression, now known or later developed, from which [it] can be perceived, reproduced, or otherwise communicated."[31] A literary work is considered "fixed in a tangible medium of expression" when it has been embodied "in a copy or phonorecord, by or under the authority of the author" that "is sufficiently permanent or stable to permit [the work] to be perceived, reproduced, or otherwise communicated for a period of more than a transitory duration."[32] There are a vast number of methods by which a literary work may be fixed in a tangible medium of expression. Examples include:

A poem written on paper;
A short story saved in a computer file;
An article printed in a periodical; or
A novel embodied in an audio recording.

---

[31] 17 U.S.C. Section 102(a).

[32] 17 U.S.C. Section 101 defining "fixed".

What May Not Be Copyrighted

Section 102(a) of the Copyright Act specifies that, among other requirements, copyright protection extends only to "original works of authorship." This has been interpreted to mean that works that have not been fixed in a tangible medium of expression, works that have not been created by a human being, and works that are not eligible for copyright protection in the United States do not satisfy this requirement. Likewise, the copyright law does not protect works that do not constitute copyrightable subject matter or works that do not contain a sufficient amount of original authorship, such as:

An idea, procedure, process, system, method of operation, concept, principle, or discovery;
Facts;
Research;
Typeface or mere variations of typographic ornamentations;
Format and layout;
Book designs;
Names, titles, slogans, or other short phrases;
Numbers;
Works consisting entirely of information that is common property, such as standard calendars, height and weight charts, schedules of sporting events, and lists or tables taken from public documents or other common sources;
A mere listing of ingredients or contents;
Blank forms;
Scènes à faire;
Familiar symbols and designs;
U.S. government works;
Government edicts.

Websites

For purposes of copyright registration, the U.S. Copyright Office defines the registrable content of a "website" as a webpage or set of interconnected webpages, including a homepage, located on the same computer or server that is, fixed together on that computer or server, and prepared and maintained as a collection of information by a person, group, or organization.

A key element of a website is that the user can browse through the content on the site by scrolling through each webpage, by using internal hypertext links, or by using a search feature. A database, on the other hand, does not disclose the underlying content to the user but instead requires a search query to find and access particular information contained within the database that matches the parameters of each query.

As with any medium for copyrightable expression, such as a book, DVD, or CD-ROM, it is the content of the website — not the medium of expression — that comprises the copyrightable authorship that may be registered with the U.S. Copyright Office. Therefore, a website may, or may not be copyrightable in and of itself since it is only a vehicle for the dissemination of content, a medium of fixation, for works of original authorship. Therefore, although a website may contain copyrightable subject matter that falls within one or more of the categories of authorship that are set forth in Section 102(a), and/or it may qualify as a compilation, a collective work, or a derivative work, a website in and of itself is not explicitly recognized as copyrightable subject matter.

The potentially copyrightable authorship elements of a website are:

> Content that is made perceptible on the website's pages in the form of text or digital files;
>
> Compilation authorship in the way in which the copyrightable text and/or digital files are selected, coordinated, and/or arranged on a particular webpage, or the way in which the pages of the overall website are selected, coordinated, and/or arranged, such as the manner or hierarchy in which the pages are connected or linked to each other;
>
> Underlying markup language or style sheets that structure, arrange, and coordinate the manner in which the user views or otherwise perceives the content on the site through the user's browser.

However, unlike physical objects such as books and magazines, websites are dynamic and face a significant issue. Copyright protection in the United States extends only to fixed works of authorship that fall under the categories provided in Section 102(a) of the Copyright Act. Therefore, the Copyright Office will register a claim in website content only as it exists at the time that the application is received. The Office will not register a claim in website content as it may exist in the future if that content has not yet been fixed.

In addition, other material related to a website may not be copyrightable. Examples of uncopyrightable material include, but are not limited to:

Ideas, such as plans for future websites;
Functional design elements;
Domain names and hypertext links;
The layout, format, or "look and feel" of a website;
Common, unoriginal material, such as names, icons, or familiar symbols.

User-Generated Content (UGC)

Websites that allow users to post content that they created, such as comments, reviews, photographs, or videos must address the issue of user-generated content. Generally, the user is the author of any original expression that he or she creates and posts to a website, and the user owns the copyright in that material unless he or she transfers ownership of all the exclusive rights to the website owner pursuant to a valid, signed, written transfer of ownership.

An individual author may be asked to accept the terms of service for a website before the author uploads UGC to that site. If the terms of service state that the website becomes the owner of all the exclusive rights in any works that are lawfully uploaded to that site, the author may be deemed to have transferred ownership of the copyright in that UGC through a written, digitally signed transfer agreement.[33]

The Publication Requirement

The publication requirement applies to work published after January 1, 1978. For works created after or published after January 1, 1978, Section

---

[33] See *Metropolitan Regional Information Systems v. American Home Realty Network, Inc.*, 722 F. 3d 591 (2013).

101 of the Copyright Act defines publication as "the distribution of copies or phonorecords of a work to the public by sale or other transfer of ownership, or by rental, lease, or lending..."[34] and goes on to state that "offering to distribute copies or phonorecords to a group of persons for purposes of further distribution, public performance, or public display, constitutes publication." However, "...(a) public performance or display of a work does not, in and of itself, constitute publication" and public performance is not necessarily a "publication."

Does Posting on the Internet Qualify as "Publication"?

At this time there does not appear to be a consensus on the issue.

Notice of Copyright

A variety of international agreements, including the Berne Convention, The Berne Convention Implementation Act of 1988, and the Uruguay Round Agreements Act amended the Copyright Act of 1976 and its notice requirement.

Although notice is optional for unpublished works, foreign works, or works published on or after March 1, 1989, the U.S. Copyright Office encourages notice for the following reasons:

> It puts potential users on notice that copyright is claimed in the work;
>
> In the case of a published work, a notice may prevent a defendant in a copyright infringement action from attempting to limit its liability for damages or injunctive relief based on an innocent infringement defense;
>
> It identifies the copyright owner at the time the work was first published for parties seeking permission to use the work;
>
> It identifies the year of first publication, which may be used to determine the term of copyright protection in the case of an anonymous work, a pseudonymous work, or a work made for hire;

[34] 17 U.S.C. Section 101.

It may prevent the work from becoming an orphan work by identifying the copyright owner and/or specifying the term of the copyright.[35]

French law on the subject of copyrights is primarily found within the French Intellectual Property Code, Articles L 111-1 to L 343-7. However, as in America, French law is also shaped by international agreements to which France is a party, such as:

The Berne Convention for the Protection of Literary and Artistic Works of 1886;
The Rome Convention for the Protection of Performers, Producers of Phonograms and Broadcasting Organizations of 1961;
The World Intellectual Property Organization (WIPO) Performances and Phonograms Treaty of 20 December 1996 (WPPT);
The 1995 Agreement on Trade-Related Aspects of Intellectual Property Rights (TRIPS), notably on copyright and related rights; and
The WIPO Copyright Treaty of 1996.

In addition, in certain respects, the law of the European Union is also part of the French copyright law.

The French Intellectual Property Code[36] specifies the requirements for copyright and is similar to American law in its requirements:

Article L111-1 is similar to Section 106 and specifies the rights of the creator:

The author of a work of the mind enjoys over this work, by the mere fact of its creation, an exclusive intangible property right and enforceable against all.

This right includes intellectual and moral attributes as well as patrimonial attributes, which are determined by books I and III of this code.

The existence or conclusion of a work or service contract by the author of an intellectual work does not derogate from the enjoyment of the right recognized by the first paragraph, subject to the exceptions provided for

[35] See 17 U.S.C. Sections 401(d), 402(d), 405(b), 406(a), 504(c)(2).

[36] The information was taken from the French Code *de la propriete intellectuelle*, translated into English and the version in force on June 13, 2022.

in this code. Subject to the same reservations, there is also no derogation from the enjoyment of this same right when the author of the intellectual work is an agent of the State, of a local authority, of an establishment of an administrative nature, an independent administrative authority endowed with legal personality, the Banque de France, the Institut de France, the Académie française, the Académie des inscriptions et belles-lettres, the Academy of Sciences, Academy of Fine Arts or

The provisions of Articles L121-7-1 and L131-3-1 to L131-3-3 do not apply to agents who are authors of works whose disclosure is not subject, by virtue of their statute or the rules which govern their functions, with no prior control of the hierarchical authority.

Article L111-2:

The work is deemed to be created, independently of any public disclosure, by the mere fact of the realization, even unfinished, of the author's design.

Article L123-1 and the following articles address the length of copyright protection.

The author enjoys, throughout his life, the exclusive right to exploit his work in any form whatsoever and to derive a pecuniary profit from it.

On the death of the author, this right persists for the benefit of his successors in title during the current calendar year and the seventy years that follow.

Article L123-2:

For collaborative works, the calendar year taken into consideration is that of the death of the last living collaborator.

For audiovisual works, the calendar year taken into consideration is that of the death of the last living person of the following collaborators: the author of the script, the author of the spoken text, the author of the musical compositions with or without words specially produced for the work, the main director.

Article L123-3:

For pseudonymous, anonymous or collective works, the duration of the exclusive right is seventy years from January 1 of the calendar year following that in which the work was published. The date of publication is determined by any mode of proof of common law, and in particular by legal deposit.

In the event that a pseudonymous, anonymous or collective work is published in installments, the period runs from January 1 of the calendar year following the date on which each element was published.

When the author(s) of anonymous or pseudonymous works have made themselves known, the duration of the exclusive right is that provided for in Articles L. 123-1 or L. 123-2.

The provisions of the first and second paragraphs are only applicable to pseudonymous, anonymous or collective works published during the seventy years following the year of their creation.

However, when a pseudonymous, anonymous or collective work is disclosed at the end of the period mentioned in the preceding paragraph, its owner, by succession or by other title, who publishes it or has it published enjoys an exclusive right of twenty-five years from January 1 of the calendar year following that of publication.

Article L123-4:

For posthumous works, the duration of the exclusive right is that provided for in article L. 123-1. For posthumous works disclosed after the expiry of this period, the duration of the exclusive right is twenty-five years from January 1 of the calendar year following that of publication.

The right to exploit posthumous works belongs to the author's heirs if the work is disclosed during the period provided for in Article L. 123-1.

If the disclosure is made after the expiration of this period, it belongs to the owners, by succession or otherwise, of the work, who make or cause to be made the publication.

> Posthumous works must be the subject of a separate publication, except in the case where they constitute only a fragment of a previously published work. They may only be attached to previously published works by the same author if the author's heirs still enjoy the right of exploitation over them.

Article L112-2 is similar to Section 102(a) and notes the works that may be covered by copyright:

> [The following are] considered in particular as works of the mind within the meaning of this code:
>
> 1. Books, brochures and other literary, artistic and scientific writings;
> 2. Lectures, speeches, sermons, pleadings and other works of the same nature;
> 3. Dramatic or dramatico-musical works;
> 4. Choreographic works, circus acts and tricks, pantomimes, the implementation of which is fixed in writing or otherwise;
> 5. Musical compositions with or without words;
> 6. Cinematographic works and other works consisting of animated sequences of images, with or without sound, together referred to as audiovisual works;
> 7. Works of drawing, painting, architecture, sculpture, engraving, lithography;
> 8. Graphic and typographical works;
> 9. Photographic works and those produced using techniques analogous to photography;
> 10. Works of applied art;
> 11. Illustrations, geographical maps;
> 12. Plans, sketches and plastic works relating to geography, topography, architecture and science;
> 13. Software, including preparatory design material;
> 14. The creations of the seasonal clothing and adornment industries. Seasonal clothing and adornment industries are deemed to be those industries which, due to the requirements of fashion, frequently renew the form of their products, and in particular sewing, fur, lingerie, embroidery, fashion, shoes, gloves, leather goods, the manufacture of high-end or special haute couture fabrics, the production of adornments and bootmakers and the factories of upholstery fabrics.

Article R122-3 goes into additional detail about the kind of works that are subject to copyright protection and notes:

> The works mentioned in article R. 122-1 are original graphic or plastic works created by the author himself, such as paintings, collages, paintings, drawings, engravings, prints, lithographs, sculptures, tapestries, ceramics, glassware, photographs and plastic creations on audiovisual or digital media.
>
> Works produced in a limited number of copies and under the responsibility of the author are considered as original works of art within the meaning of the preceding paragraph if they are numbered or signed or duly authorized in another way by the author. These are in particular:
>
> a. The original etchings, prints and lithographs drawn in limited numbers from one or more plates;
> b. Editions of sculpture, within the limit of twelve copies, numbered copies and artist's proofs combined;
> c. Handmade tapestries and works of textile art, based on original models provided by the artist, within the limit of eight copies;
> d. Enamels executed entirely by hand and bearing the artist's signature, within the limit of eight numbered copies and four artist's proofs;
> e. Signed photographic works, within the limit of thirty copies, regardless of format and medium;
> f. Plastic creations on audiovisual or digital support within the limit of twelve copies.

Copyright Protection

In summary, copyright holders possess a variety of rights, including:

1. The right to make copies of their work and control others who wish to make copies;
2. Create derivative (transformative) works such as adaptations, translations, and sequels to a movie;
3. Distribute copies of the work, including sales, leasing, and rentals of the work;
4. Perform the work publicly.

"Public" generally refers to a performance that occurs in a place open to the public. In addition, it would also apply to a performance in a place where a substantial number of individuals outside of a normal circle of a family and social acquaintances are gathered. It may also apply to a work that is performed publicly by digital transmission, although this only applies to sound recordings, but also includes streaming.

French law on the subject is similar to American law and, in particular Section 106. Article L122-1 addresses the author's rights and notes:

> The right of exploitation belonging to the author includes the right of representation and the right of reproduction.

Article L122-2 defines what constitutes the "public" and notes:

> The representation consists in the communication of the work to the public by any process whatsoever, and in particular:
>
> 1. By public recitation, lyrical performance, dramatic performance, public presentation, public projection and transmission in a public place of the televised work;
> 2. By television broadcasting.
>
> Television broadcasting means the broadcasting by any telecommunications process of sounds, images, documents, data and messages of any kind.
>
> The transmission of a work to a satellite is assimilated to a performance.

Article L122-2-1 goes on to note additional requirements for satellite transmission and notes:

> The right of representation of a work broadcast by satellite is governed by the provisions of this code as soon as the work is transmitted to the satellite from the national territory.

Article L122-3 addresses the issue of "reproduction" and notes:

> Reproduction consists in the material fixing of the work by any process which allows it to be communicated to the public in an indirect way.

> It can be carried out in particular by printing, drawing, engraving, photography, molding and any process of the graphic and plastic arts, mechanical, cinematographic or magnetic recording.
>
> For works of architecture, reproduction also consists in the repeated execution of a standard plan or project.

State Law

Copyright protection in the United States is governed by federal law and Section 301(a) of the 1976 Act preempts all similar protections provided by state law, other than with respect to sound recordings fixed before February 15, 1972, as provided under Section 301(c) of the Act. However, preemption only applies when a state law provides protection that is equivalent to the protection specified in the Copyright Act, for example, the rights that are equivalent to any of the exclusive rights under Section 106 of the Act in fixed works of authorship that fall within the subject matter of copyright.

Some of the kinds of protection that states may offer is specified in Section 301(b) and (c) of the 1976 Act. For example, state protection may apply to:

i. Works not fixed in a tangible medium of expression;
ii. Non-subscription broadcast transmission of pre-1972 sound recordings;
iii. State and local landmarks, historic preservation, zoning, or building codes relating to architectural works protected under Section 102(a)(8) of the Act; and
iv. Causes of actions for acts that took place before January 1, 1978.

Territoriality

U.S. copyright law generally applies only to acts that take place in the United States, including the Commonwealth of Puerto Rico and U.S. territories.[37] However, the Berne Convention specifies that national law applies to foreign works, and the law of the country in which infringement

---

[37] *Subafilms, Ltd. v. MGM-Pathe Communications Co.*, 24 F.3d 1088, 1094–1095 (1994).

takes place generally applies to infringement disputes.[38] And, while copyright infringement occurring in the United States is governed by U.S. law, courts in the U.S. may look to the law of the foreign country where ownership of the work was established or transferred when questions are raised concerning foreign ownership and copyright origin.[39]

Infringement

17 U.S.C. Section 501(a) states that "anyone who violates any of the exclusive rights of the copyright owner…is an infringer of the copyright." Infringement occurs when someone other than the copyright owner exercises the exclusive right of the copyright owner unlawfully, although there are exceptions specified in Sections 107–122 of the Copyright Act.

Among the exceptions to a claim of infringement is "fair use."

Fair Use

Section 107 notes, "… the fair use of a copyrighted work, including such use by reproduction in copies or phonorecords or by any other means specified by that section, for purposes such as criticism, comment, news reporting, teaching (including multiple copies for classroom use), scholarship, or research, is not an infringement of copyright. In determining whether the use made of a work in any particular case is a fair use the factors to be considered shall include —

1. the purpose and character of the use, including whether such use is of a commercial nature or is for nonprofit educational purposes;
2. the nature of the copyrighted work;
3. the amount and substantiality of the portion used in relation to the copyrighted work as a whole; and
4. the effect of the use upon the potential market for or value of the copyrighted work."

---

[38] Berne Convention for the Protection of Literary and Artistic Works, Art. 5(1)(c)(3), September 9, 1886, as revised in Paris on July 24, 1971, and amended on September 28, 1979, S. Treaty Doc. No. 99-27 (1986).

[39] See, e.g., *Itar-Tass Russian News Agency v. Russian Kurier, Inc.*, 153 F.3d 82, 88-92 (2d Cir. 1998).

The fourth factor is likely to be the most significant.

Unsurprisingly, French law also addresses, and allows the “fair use” of portions of a copyrighted work, although not so specified.

Article L122-5-4:

I. “Pursuant to 12 of Article L. 122-5, and subject to the provisions of II and III of this article, the representation or reproduction of extracts from works may be carried out without authorization from the authors, for the exclusive purposes of illustration in the context of education and professional training, including apprenticeship, and for the development and distribution of subjects for examinations or competitions organized as an extension of the teaching, exclusion of any activity for recreational purposes and to the extent justified by the non-commercial purpose pursued.

II. “This representation or reproduction takes place under the responsibility of an educational establishment:

in its premises or in other places, for an audience composed mainly of pupils, students or teachers directly concerned by the act of teaching or training requiring this representation or reproduction;

or by means of a secure digital environment accessible only to pupils, students and teaching staff of this establishment.

“In the event that the acts of representation and reproduction are carried out by means of a digital environment in a cross-border context within the European Union, they are deemed to take place only on the territory of the State where the establishment is established.

“Acts of performance or reproduction of extracts from works mentioned in this I are compensated by compensation negotiated on a flat-rate basis.

“II. The provisions of I do not apply to acts of reproduction and representation in digital form when adequate licenses authorize these acts for illustration purposes in the context of education and professional training and meet to the needs and specificities of the establishments are offered in a visible manner to the educational establishments. A Conseil d’Etat decree defines the conditions of visibility of the proposals and fixes the list of establishments for which the proposal is addressed to the competent ministers.

The conditions for granting the licenses mentioned in the preceding paragraph are based on objective and transparent criteria. The amount of remuneration requested in return for these licenses is reasonable.

Under the conditions provided for in Articles L. 324-8-1 to L. 324-8-6, the appropriate licenses issued by an approved collective management organization may be extended to holders of rights who are not members of this organization by order of the minister responsible for the culture.

"III. The provisions of I do not apply to acts of reproduction and representation in a form other than digital of works designed for educational purposes and musical scores.

"IV. The provisions of this article do not apply to the transfer of the right of reproduction by reprography mentioned in Article L. 122-10."

See also French Law L122-5, noted below, on the subject of "fair use."

Does "Embedding" Constitute Infringement?

"Embedding" refers to including or "embedding" a photograph or video on a webpage, blog, or social media by way of linking. Whether this constitutes infringement or not involves two schools of thought.

The "Server" Rule[40]

A website that includes a copyrighted work must have a copy of the item in the computer's memory in order for it to be considered infringement. Therefore, when an image is "embedded' it is linked to the server where the copyrighted work is stored and the work remains on that third-party's server. Therefore, it is not fixed in the alleged infringer's server memory and does not constitute infringement.

However, another court specifically rejected the "server rule" and observed, "When the Copyright Act was amended in 1976, the words 'tweet,' 'viral,' and 'embed' invoked thoughts of a bird, a disease, and a reporter."[41] The court went on to note, "Having carefully considered the embedding issue, this Court concludes, for the reasons discussed below, that when defendants caused the embedded Tweets to appear on their websites, their actions violated plaintiff's exclusive display right; the fact that the image was hosted on a server owned and operated by an unrelated

---

[40] *Perfect 10, Inc. v.* Amazon.com, 487 F.3d 701 (2007).

[41] *Goldman v. Breitbart News Network*, LLC, 302 F.Supp.3d 585 (2018).

third party (Twitter) does not shield them from this result."[42] Another court pointedly observed that "… the server rule is contrary to the text and legislative history of the Copyright Act."[43]

Platform License

In *Sinclair v. Ziff Davis, LLC*,[44] the plaintiff Sinclair, a professional photographer, publicly shared a copyrighted photo on her public Instagram page that was viewable by the general public. A party, Mashable offered to license the photo from Sinclair, but Sinclair rejected the offer. Nonetheless, Mashable proceeded to embed Sinclair's original Instagram post in its article, relying on Instagram's "Platform Policy, Terms of Use, and Privacy Policy." That policy stated that, by posting content to Instagram the user "grant[s] to Instagram a non-exclusive, fully paid and royalty-free, transferable, sub-licensable, worldwide license to the Content that you post on or through [Instagram]…"

Instagram's Privacy Policy allowed users to revoke Instagram's sub-licensable right by designating the content at issue as "private." Because Sinclair posted the photograph publicly the judge initially opined that, "Plaintiff made her choice. This Court cannot release her from the agreement she made." In so doing the court dismissed the copyright claim. However, upon reconsideration the court refused to dismiss the plaintiff's copyright claim on the basis of the sub-license defense. That, however, is not the only issue.

Is "Embedding" a "Public Display"?

The issue of "embedding" presents an additional issue, although at present there does not seem to be a consensus among the courts. Thus, while the answer at this point is uncertain, the conservative approach is to assume that a party should obtain permission before embedding another's photo from, for instance, a social media site.

French law also addresses the issue of online content and "authorization" and specifically notes in Article L137-2:

---

[42] *Ibid.* at 586.

[43] *Nicklen v. Sinclair Broadcast*, 551 F.Supp.3d 188 (2021).

[44] 343 F.Supp.3d 342 (2020).

I. "By providing access to works protected by copyright uploaded by its users, the provider of an online content sharing service performs an act of representation of these works for which it must obtain the authorization of the holders of rights, without prejudice to the authorizations that he must obtain under the right of reproduction for the reproductions of the said works that he makes.

II. 2 and 3 of I of article 6 of law n 2004-575 of June 21, 2004 on confidence in the digital economy are not applicable to the provider of the online content sharing service for acts of exploitation carried out by him.

III. 1. In the absence of authorization from the rights holders, the provider of an online content sharing service is liable for acts of unauthorized exploitation of works protected by copyright, unless he demonstrates that he has met all of the following conditions:
   a. He has made his best efforts to obtain authorization from the rights holders who wish to grant this authorization;
   b. It has made its best efforts, consistent with high industry standards of professional care, to ensure the unavailability of specific works for which rightsholders have provided it, directly or indirectly through a third party that they appointed,
   c. It has in any case acted promptly, upon receipt of a sufficiently reasoned notification from the rightholders, to block access to the works covered by the notification or to withdraw them from its service, and has made its best efforts to prevent these works from being uploaded in the future, pursuant to b;
2. To determine whether the provider of the online content sharing service has complied with its obligations under 1, the following elements are taken into account in particular:
   a. The type, audience and size of the service, as well as the type of works uploaded by users of the service;
   b. The availability of suitable and efficient means as well as their cost for the service provider;
3. By way of derogation from the conditions set out in 1, for a period of three years from the date on which the service is made available to the public within the European Union and on the condition that it has an annual turnover of less than ten million euros calculated in accordance with Recommendation 2003/361/EC of the European Commission of 6 May 2003 concerning the

definition of micro, small and medium-sized enterprises, in the event of the absence of authorization from the holders of rights, the supplier of an online content sharing service is liable for acts of unauthorized exploitation of copyrighted works unless it demonstrates that it has met the following conditions:

a. He has made his best efforts to obtain authorization from the rights holders and has acted promptly, when he has received a notification in accordance with the procedures provided for in c of 1, to block access to the works subject to notice or to remove them from its service;
b. In the event that the average monthly number of its unique visitors in the European Union has exceeded five million during the previous calendar year, it has also made its best efforts to avoid new uploads of works making the object of the notification for which the rightholders have provided it, directly or indirectly via a third party they have designated, with the relevant and necessary information.

   "The provider of the online content sharing service that invokes the application of this 3 to its service provides supporting evidence attesting to the required audience and turnover thresholds;

4. The provider of an online content sharing service acts solely on the basis of relevant and necessary information or notifications provided, directly or indirectly via a third party designated by them, by the rights holders.

IV. The contracts under which the authorizations mentioned in I are granted are, within the limits of their purpose, deemed to also authorize the acts of representation performed by the user of this service on the condition that the latter does not act for commercial purposes or that the revenue generated by the content uploaded by this user is not significant.

V. The measures taken within the framework of this article do not give rise either to the identification of individual users, or to the processing of personal data except when this is in accordance with the law n 78-17 of January 6, 1978 relating to information technology, files and freedoms and Regulation (EU) 2016/679 of April 27, 2016 on the protection of individuals with regard to the processing of personal data and on the free movement of such data, and repealing Directive 95/46/EC."

Defenses to Infringement

Separate and apart from the exceptions that are noted previously, the Copyright Act provides a number of defenses to a claim of infringement. Among them are:

Independent Development

Works that are created independently, with no knowledge of a copyrighted work, whether only similar, but even if it is identical, do not constitute infringement.

1. The First Sale Doctrine 17 U.S.C. Section 109: An individual who knowingly purchases a copy of a copyrighted work from the holder of the copyright obtains the right to sell, display, or otherwise dispose of that specific copy of the copyrighted item. However, the protection of the first sale doctrine does not extend to any person who has acquired possession of the copy or phonorecord from the copyright owner by rental, lease, loan, or otherwise, without acquiring ownership of it.[45] Items that are distributed pursuant to a licensing agreement, rather than a sale, such as software, are not covered by the first sale doctrine.

   French Law also addresses the "first sale" doctrine and notes in Article L122-3-1:

   > "As soon as the first sale of one or more material copies of a work has been authorized by the author or his successors in title on the territory of a Member State of the European Community or of another State party to the agreement on the European Economic Area, the sale of these copies of this work can no longer be prohibited in the Member States of the European Community and the States party to the Agreement on the European Economic Area."

2. *Scènes à Faire*: A "scene to be made" or "scene that must be done" refers to a scene or element that is commonly found in a work of that genre, and are also exempt from a claim of copyright infringement. For example, a court held that a motion picture about "…any account based on experiences in poverty-stricken, crime-ridden environments,

---

[45] 17 U.S.C. Section 109(d).

depictions of bribery, prostitution, purse-snatching and neighborhood hostility to law enforcers are inevitable."[46]

French law on the subject is similar but covers a wide variety of issues, including the issue of infringement. As part of that French law also addresses the issue of "public" performance as well as the French equivalent of "fair use." Article L122-5 notes:

> When the work has been disclosed, the author cannot prohibit:
>
> 1. Private and free performances performed exclusively within a family circle;
> 2. Copies or reproductions made from a lawful source and strictly reserved for the private use of the copyist and not intended for collective use, with the exception of copies of works of art intended to be used for identical to those for which the original work was created and copies of software other than the backup copy established under the conditions provided for in II of Article L. 122-6-1 as well as copies or reproductions an electronic database;
> 3. Provided that the name of the author and the source are clearly indicated:
>   a. Analyzes and short quotations justified by the critical, polemical, educational, scientific or informative nature of the work in which they are incorporated;
>   b. Press reviews;
>   c. The dissemination, even in full, by means of the press or television, as current information, of speeches intended for the public delivered in political, administrative, judicial or academic assemblies, as well as in public meetings of political order and official ceremonies;
>   d. Reproductions, in whole or in part, of graphic or plastic works of art intended to appear in the catalog of a judicial sale carried out in France for the copies made available to the public before the sale for the sole purpose of describing the works of art offered for sale;

[46] *Walker v. Time Life Films, Inc.*, 615 F.Supp. 430 (1985), cited in *Williams v. Crichton*, 84 F.3d 581 (1996). The court in Walker specifically noted, "...copyright protection does not extend to historical or contemporary facts, material traceable to common sources or in the public domain, and *scènes à faire.*"

e. The representation or reproduction of extracts from works, except for works designed for educational purposes and musical scores, for the exclusive purposes of illustration in the context of research, provided that this representation or reproduction is intended, in particular by means of a digital work space, for a public composed mainly of researchers directly concerned by the research activity requiring this representation or this reproduction, that it is not the subject of any publication or dissemination to a third party to the public thus constituted, that the use of this representation or this reproduction does not give rise to any commercial exploitation and that it is compensated by a remuneration negotiated on a fixed basis without prejudice to the transfer of the right of reproduction by reprography mentioned in article L. 122-10;

4. Parody, pastiche and caricature, taking into account the laws of the genre;
5. The acts necessary for access to the content of an electronic database for the needs and within the limits of the use provided for by contract;
6. Temporary reproduction of a transitory or incidental nature, when it is an integral and essential part of a technical process and when its sole purpose is to allow the lawful use of the work or its transmission between third parties by the route of a network using an intermediary; however, this provisional reproduction, which can only relate to works other than software and databases, must not have any specific economic value;
7. Under the conditions provided for in Articles L. 122-5-1 and L. 122-5-2, the reproduction and representation by legal persons and by establishments open to the public, such as libraries, archives, documentation centers and multimedia cultural spaces, with a view to strictly personal consultation of the work by persons suffering from one or more impairments of motor, physical, sensory, mental, cognitive or psychic functions and impeded by the fact of these deficiencies, to access the work in the form in which the author makes it available to the public;

   These prevented persons may also, with a view to a strictly personal consultation of the work, carry out, by themselves or through the intermediary of a natural person acting on their behalf, acts of reproduction and representation;

8. The reproduction of a work and its representation carried out for conservation purposes or intended to preserve the conditions of its consultation for the purposes of research or private study by individuals, in the premises of the establishment and on terminals dedicated by libraries accessible to the public, by museums or by archives services, provided that they do not seek any economic or commercial advantage;
9. The reproduction or representation, in whole or in part, of a graphic, plastic or architectural work of art, by means of the written, audiovisual or online press, for the exclusive purpose of immediate information and in direct relation with this last, subject to clearly indicating the name of the author.

   The first paragraph of this 9 does not apply to works, in particular photographic or illustrative works, which themselves aim to report information;
10. Copies or digital reproductions of a work for the purpose of text and data mining carried out under the conditions provided for in Article L. 122-5-3;
11. Reproductions and representations of architectural works and sculptures, permanently placed on the public highway, made by natural persons, excluding any use of a commercial nature;
12. The representation or reproduction of extracts from works for the exclusive purposes of illustration in the context of education and professional training, under the conditions provided for in Article L. 122-5-4;
13. The representation and reproduction of an unavailable work within the meaning of Article L. 138-1, under the conditions provided for in Article L. 122-5-5.

   Reproductions or representations which, in particular by their number or their format, would not be in strict proportion with the exclusive aim of immediate information pursued or which would not be directly related to the latter give rise to remuneration of the authors on the basis of the agreements or tariffs in force in the professional sectors concerned.

   The exceptions listed in this article may not interfere with the normal exploitation of the work or cause undue prejudice to the legitimate interests of the author.

The terms of application of this article, in particular the characteristics and conditions of distribution of the documents mentioned in d of 3, are specified by decree in Council of State.

Remedies For Copyright Infringement

17 U.S.C. Section 504

a. Except as otherwise provided by this title, an infringer of copyright is liable for either
   1. The copyright owner's actual damages and any additional profits of the infringer, as provided by Subsection (b); or
   2. Statutory damages, as provided by Subsection (c).
b. **Actual Damages and Profits:** The copyright owner is entitled to recover the actual damages suffered by him or her as a result of the infringement, and any profits of the infringer that are attributable to the infringement and are not taken into account in computing the actual damages. In establishing the infringer's profits, the copyright owner is required to present proof only of the infringer's gross revenue, and the infringer is required to prove his or her deductible expenses and the elements of profit attributable to factors other than the copyright work.
c. **Statutory damages:** (1) Except as provided in clause (2) of this subsection, the copyright owner may elect, at any time before final judgment is rendered, to recover, instead of actual damages and profits, an award of statutory damages for all infringements involved in the action, with respect to any one work, for which any one infringer is liable individually, or for which any two or more infringers are liable jointly and severally, in a sum of not less than $750 or more than $30,000 as the court considers just. For the purposes of this subsection, all the parts of a compilation or derivative work constitute one work.

   (2) In a case where the copyright owner sustains the burden of proving, and the court finds, that infringement was committed willfully, the court in its discretion may increase the award of statutory damages to a sum of not more than $150,000. In a case where the infringer sustains the burden of proving, and the court finds, that such infringer was not aware and had no reason to

believe that his or her acts constituted an infringement of copyright, the court in its discretion may reduce the award of statutory damages to a sum of not less than $200. The court shall remit statutory damages in any case where an infringer believed and had reasonable grounds for believing that his or her use of the copyrighted work was a fair use under Section 107, if the infringer was: (i) an employee or agent of a non-profit educational institution, library, or archives acting within the scope of his or her employment who, or such institution, library, or archives itself, which infringed by reproducing the work in copies or phonorecords; or (ii) a public broadcasting entity which or a person who, as a regular part of the non-profit activities of a public broadcasting entity (as defined in Section 118(f)) infringed by performing a published non-dramatic literary work or by reproducing a transmission program embodying a performance of such work.

(3) A. In a case of infringement, it shall be a rebuttable presumption that the infringement was committed willfully for purposes of determining relief if the violator, or a person acting in concert with the violator, knowingly provided or knowingly caused to be provided materially false contact information to a domain name registrar, domain name registry, or other domain name registration authority in registering, maintaining, or renewing a domain name used in connection with the infringement.

B. Nothing in this paragraph limits what may be considered willful infringement under this section.

C. For purposes of this paragraph, the term "domain name" has the meaning given that term in Section 45 of the Act entitled "An Act to provide for the registration and protection of trademarks used in commerce, to carry out the provisions of certain international conventions, and for other purposes" approved July 5, 1946 (commonly referred to as the "Trademark Act of 1946"; 15 U.S.C. 1127).

D. Additional damages in certain cases. In any case in which the court finds that a defendant proprietor of an establishment who claims as a defense that its activities were exempt under Section 110(5) did not have reasonable grounds to believe that its use of a copyright work was exempt under

> such section, the plaintiff shall be entitled to, in addition to any award of damages under this section, an additional award of two times the amount of the license fee that the proprietor of the establishment concerned should have paid the plaintiff for such use during the preceding period of up to 3 years.

In summary, civil remedies are monetary damages, including actual damages and lost profits, court costs and attorneys' fees, as well as the equitable remedy of an injunction. A federal court may also require that the infringing goods be impounded and destroyed.

Penalties to be applied in cases of criminal copyright infringement (violations of 17 U.S.C. Section 506(a)), are specified in 18 U.S.C. Section 2319. Criminal penalties may be imposed if the infringement was

1. Willful and "for purposes of commercial advantage or private financial gain," or
2. The infringement involves the willing reproduction or distribution of multiple copies with a value that exceeds $1,000 within 180 days.

In such a case the infringer may be fined and imprisoned.

French law on the subject of infringement is similar and also provides for both civil and criminal remedies.

Article L332-1:

> Any author of a work protected by Book I of this Part, his successors in title or his assigns may sue for infringement. To this end, these persons are entitled to have any bailiffs proceed, assisted if necessary by experts appointed by the plaintiff, on an order issued on request by the competent civil court, either to the detailed description, with or without deduction of samples, or the actual seizure of the allegedly infringing works as well as any related document. The order may authorize the actual seizure of any document relating to the allegedly infringing works in the absence of the latter.
>
> The court can order the detailed description or the actual seizure of the materials and instruments used to produce or distribute the works illicitly.

To this end, the court may order:

1. Seizure of copies constituting an illicit reproduction of an intellectual work protected by Book I of this Part or of any copy, product, device, device, component or means infringing the technical measures and information mentioned, respectively, in Articles L. 331-5 and L. 331-11;
2. The seizure, whatever the day and time, of copies constituting an illicit reproduction of the work, already manufactured or in the process of being manufactured, or of the copies, products, apparatus, devices, components or means, manufactured or during manufacture, affecting the technical measures and the information mentioned, respectively, in Articles L. 331-5 and L. 331-11, of the recipes made, as well as of the illicitly used copies;
3. Seizure of receipts from any reproduction, representation or distribution, by any means whatsoever, of an intellectual work, carried out in violation of the rights of the author or resulting from an infringement of technical measures and the information mentioned, respectively, in Articles L. 331-5 and L. 331-11;
4. The actual seizure of illicit works or products suspected of infringing copyright or their delivery into the hands of a third party in order to prevent their introduction or circulation in commercial circuits.

The competent civil court may also order:

a. The suspension or extension of performances or public performances in progress or already announced;
b. The suspension of any production in progress aimed at the illicit reproduction of a work or the carrying out of an attack on the technical measures and the information mentioned, respectively, in Articles L. 331-5 and L. 331-11.

It may make the execution of the measures it orders subject to the provision by the plaintiff of guarantees intended to ensure the possible compensation of the defendant if the action for infringement is subsequently deemed unfounded or the seizure annulled.

It may, in the same manner, order the measures provided for in this article at the request of the holders of neighboring rights defined in Book II of this part.

Article 335-1 provides additional information and notes:

> The competent judicial police officers may proceed, as soon as the offenses provided for in Articles L. 335-4 to L. 335-4-2 are observed, to the seizure of phonograms and videograms illicitly reproduced, copies and objects manufactured or imported illicitly, of any copy, product, device, device, component or means infringing the technical measures and information mentioned respectively in Articles L. 331-5 and L. 331-11 as well as the seizure of equipment specially installed for such purposes actions.

And Article 335-2 addresses the subject of counterfeiting and specifies that:

> Any edition of writings, musical composition, drawing, painting or any other production, printed or engraved in whole or in part, in defiance of the laws and regulations relating to the property of the authors, is an infringement and any infringement is an offense.
>
> Counterfeiting in France of works published in France or abroad is punishable by three years' imprisonment and a fine of 300,000 euros.
>
> The same penalties will apply to the debit, export, import, transshipment or detention for the aforementioned purposes of infringing works.
>
> When the offenses provided for in this article have been committed by an organized gang, the penalties are increased to seven years' imprisonment and a fine of 750,000 euros.

Article 335-3-1 addresses the subject of fines and imprisonment:

> I.- A fine of 3,750 euros is imposed for knowingly infringing, for purposes other than research, an effective technical measure as defined in Article L.331-5, in order to alter the protection of a work by decoding, decryption or any other personal intervention intended to circumvent, neutralize or eliminate a protection or control mechanism, when this infringement is carried out by means other than the use of a technological application , an existing device or component mentioned in II.
>
> II.-Is punished by six months' imprisonment and a fine of 30,000 euros the fact of knowingly procuring or offering to others, directly or

indirectly, means designed or specially adapted to undermine an effective technical measure as defined in Article L. 331-5, by one of the following methods:

1. By manufacturing or importing a technological application, device or component, for purposes other than research;
2. By holding with a view to sale, loan or rental, by offering for these same purposes or by making available to the public in any form whatsoever a technological application, a device or a component;
3. By providing a service for this purpose;
4. By encouraging the use or by ordering, designing, organizing, reproducing, distributing or disseminating advertising in favor of one of the processes referred to in 1 to 3.

III.-These provisions are not applicable to acts carried out for computer security purposes, within the limits of the rights provided for by this code.

Article 335-5

In the event of a conviction based on one of the offenses defined in Articles L. 335-2 to L 335-4-2, the court may order the total or partial, permanent or temporary closure, for a maximum period of five years of the establishment used to commit the offence.

The temporary closure cannot lead to either termination or suspension of the employment contract, or any pecuniary damage to the employees concerned. When the permanent closure leads to the dismissal of the staff, it gives rise, apart from the notice indemnity and the dismissal indemnity, to the damages provided for in Articles L. 122-14-4 and L. 122-14-5 of the labor code in the event of termination of the employment contract. Non-payment of these indemnities is punishable by six months' imprisonment and a fine of 3,750 euros.

Article 335-6:

Individuals guilty of one of the offenses provided for in Articles L. 335-2 to L. 335-4-2 may also be ordered, at their own expense, to withdraw from commercial channels objects deemed infringing and anything that has served or was intended to commit the offence.

The court may pronounce the confiscation of all or part of the revenue obtained by the offense as well as that of all phonograms, videograms, objects and copies that are infringing or illicitly reproduced, as well as equipment specially installed with a view to carrying out the offence.

It may order the destruction, at the expense of the convicted person, or the return to the injured party of objects and things withdrawn from commercial channels or confiscated, without prejudice to any damages.

It may also order, at the expense of the convicted person, the posting of the judgment or the dissemination of the judgment pronouncing the sentence, under the conditions provided for in Article 131-35 of the Criminal Code.

Article 335-7-2:

To pronounce the penalty of suspension provided for in Articles L. 335-7 and L. 335-7-1 and determine its duration, the court takes into account the circumstances and the seriousness of the offense as well as the personality of its author, and in particular his professional or social activity, as well as his socio-economic situation. The length of the sentence pronounced must reconcile the protection of intellectual property rights and respect for the right to express oneself and communicate freely, in particular from one's home.

Article 335-9:

If the perpetrator of one of the offenses provided for and punishable by this chapter is or has been bound by agreement with the injured party, the penalties incurred are doubled.

Other Federal Laws

The Digital Millennium Copyright Act

Also noted in Chapter 5, Congress passed this law in 1998 and amended the U.S. copyright law to address important parts of the relationship between copyright and the Internet. The three main updates were (1) establishing protections for online service providers in certain situations if their users engage in copyright infringement, including by creating the notice-and-takedown system, which allows copyright owners to inform online service providers about infringing material so it can be taken down; (2) encouraging copyright owners to give greater access to their works in digital formats by providing them with legal protections against unauthorized access to their works (for example, hacking passwords or circumventing encryption); and (3) making it unlawful to provide false copyright management information (for example, names of authors and copyright owners, titles of works) or to remove or alter that type of information in certain circumstances.

In addition, The Digital Millennium Copyright Act of 1998 also served to implement United States treaty obligations and to move the nation's copyright law into the digital age.[47] In particular, obligations established by the World Intellectual Property Organization (WIPO) and the legal prohibitions against circumvention of technological protection measures employed by copyright owners to protect their works, and against the removal or alteration of copyright management information, were required in order to meet U.S. treaty obligations.[48]

As with the Communication Decency Act, discussed in Chapter 5, the DMCA established limited liability for ISPs, addressing issues such as:

1. Fair use, and
2. Public domain.

Since copyright protection exists only for a specified amount of time, once that time period has elapsed the work enters the public domain and is freely usable.

3. Creative commons
4. Direct licensing

[47] https://www.copyright.gov/reports/studies/dmca/dmca_executive.html.
[48] *Ibid.*

The Benefits of Copyright Registration

Registration is a requirement in order to sue for infringement. 17 U.S.C. Section 410(c) states that if a valid claim to copyright is registered prior to publication or within five years after, the registration is *prima facie* evidence of a valid copyright. 7 U.S.C. Section 412 goes on to note that the copyright owner may recover statutory damages and attorneys' fees for infringement but only if the work is registered before infringement or within three months of first publication.[49] 17 U.S.C. Section 504(c)(2) provides for an increase in statutory damages to not more than $150,000 in the event of willful infringement and Section 401(d) precludes the defense of innocent infringement when the work that was infringed contains a notice of copyright. This is particularly important since 17 U.S.C. Section 504(c)(2) provides that if a defendant successfully asserts the defense of innocent infringement the judge may reduce the statutory damages, if any, to as low as $200 per infringement.

Other International Laws

Trade-Related Aspects of Intellectual Property Rights (TRIPS)

The TRIPS Agreement protects seven forms of intellectual property, including copyrights, patents trademarks, and trade secrets. It allows for certain limitations and exceptions in an effort to balance intellectual property with interests in public health as well as economic development. The TRIPS Agreement became effective in 1995 as part of the agreement that established the World Trade Organization. Developed countries were to implement the agreement by January 1, 1996. Developing-country members and members in transition to a market economy were to implement the requirements by January 1, 2000. Least-developed members were given until January 1, 2006, to implement the requirements with the possibility of a delay upon request. All members of the World Trade Organization must provide broad intellectual property rights and remedies, both civil and criminal, and prohibit discrimination.

[49] 17 U.S.C. Section 504 addresses the subject of statutory damages and Section 505 addresses the issue of costs and attorneys' fees.

Limitations

The TRIPS Agreement does not address newer technologies such as the Internet and digital copyright issues, advanced biotechnology, as well as international harmonization and the effort to create uniform global standards.

The World Intellectual Property Organization (WIPO)

WIPO addressed digital copyright issues by way of the WIPO Copyright Treaty (WCT) and the WIPO Performances and Phonograms Treaty (WPPT), referred to as the Internet Treaties.

The Berne Convention for the Protection of Literary and Artistic Works

WIPO notes that the Berne Convention, adopted in 1886, deals with the protection of works and the rights of their authors. It provides creators such as authors, musicians, poets, painters, and others with a way to control how their works are used, by whom, and on what terms. All countries that are signatories to the convention must recognize an author's copyright, regardless of the author's nationality.

Notice Requirements

Copyright notice is not needed under the Berne Convention for works published after March 1, 1989.

The European Union

Revised its copyright law under the Berne Convention and extended the protection for music from 50 to 70 years, a reflection of the rise of illegal downloads.

French Law implemented international obligations, in part through L111-5 which notes:

Subject to international conventions, the rights recognized in France for authors of software by this code are recognized for foreigners on the condition that the law of the State of which they are nationals or in the territory of which they have their domicile, their registered office social security or an effective establishment grants protection to software created by French nationals and by persons residing in France or having an effective establishment.

Chapter 11

Trademarks and Service Marks

Abstract

A trademark is a distinctive marking that a manufacturer applies to a product to indicate its source. However, not all trademarks are subject to protection. In order to be protected a trademark must be "strong," fanciful, arbitrary, or suggestive. An infringing mark need not be identical to the original in order to infringe. The test is a "likelihood of confusion in the minds of the public." Some words or phrases are not inherently distinctive and do not acquire protection until the public associates the word or phrase with a particular company. Microsoft "Windows" is an example of a word that achieved a secondary meaning in the minds of the public. Not all companies produce a product or a good, such as an Apple Ipad™. Some companies provide a service. The law of service marks is similar to the law of trademarks. Another area is trade dress, a concept that applies to the image or impression created by a product or its packaging. The law with regard to trade dress, as with service marks, is the same as trademarks and the test, again, is a likelihood of confusion in the minds of the public.

The United States

Generally, a trademark is a word, phrase, symbol, letters, numbers, design, color or colors, sounds including music or other distinctive sounds, images, logos, scents, or a combination of those that is used to identify the goods from a particular entity.[1] A service mark[2] identifies the source of a service from a particular entity. It is how customers recognize the source of a product or service in the marketplace and distinguish that particular source from its competitors.

The Purpose of Trademark Law

"The purpose underlying any trade-mark statute is two-fold. One is to protect the public so it may be confident that, in purchasing a product bearing a particular trade-mark which it favorably knows, it will get the product which it asks for and wants to get. Secondly, where the owner of a trade-mark has spent energy, time, and money in presenting to the public the product, he is protected in his investment from its misappropriation by pirates and cheats. This is the well-established rule of law protecting both the public and the trade-mark owner."[3]

By protecting trademarks, Congress hoped "to protect the public from deceit, to foster fair competition, and to secure to the business community the advantages of reputation and good will by preventing their diversion from those who have created them to those who have not. This is the end to which this bill is directed."[4]

---

[1] 15 U.S.C. Section 1127 notes, "The term 'trademark' includes any word, name, symbol, or device, or any combination thereof—

(1) used by a person, or

(2) which a person has a *bona fide* intention to use in commerce and applies to register on the principal register established by this chapter, to identify and distinguish his or her goods, including a unique product, from those manufactured or sold by others and to indicate the source of the goods, even if that source is unknown."

[2] 15 U.S.C. Section 1127, "The term 'service mark' means any word, name, symbol, or device, or any combination thereof—

(1) used by a person, or

(2) which a person has a *bona fide* intention to use in commerce and applies to register on the principal register established by this chapter, to identify and distinguish the services of one person, including a unique service, from the services of others and to indicate the source of the services, even if that source is unknown. Titles, character names, and other distinctive features of radio or television programs may be registered as service marks notwithstanding that they, or the programs, may advertise the goods of the sponsor."

[3] S. Rep. No. 1333, 79th Cong., 2d Sess., 3 (1946).

[4] *Ibid.* at 4.

Therefore, a trademark or service mark (a "mark") serves three general purposes:

It serves to identify the source of a particular product or service;

It provides legal protection for a good or service;

It helps to prevent counterfeiting and fraud.

However, the purpose of trademark law has expanded to benefit and protect the value of a brand. A brand is likely to sell a variety of goods or services in many different markets and marks serve to protect the brand across the different markets.

As part of that the law also allows the owner to control how that word or phrase is used with the owner's specific goods or services. Although a party may become an owner as soon as a mark is used with specific goods or services, the rights associated with that mark are limited to the geographic area associated with the goods or services.

Although United States trademark law is controlled primarily by the Lanham Act, the common law also plays a part. Common law trademark rights are acquired automatically when a business uses a name or logo in commerce, and are enforceable in state courts. Marks registered with the U.S. Patent and Trademark Office are given a higher degree of protection in federal courts than unregistered marks, although both registered and unregistered trademarks are granted some degree of federal protection under the Lanham Act 43(a).

The Lanham Act[5] as Amended

The Lanham Act was intended to make "actionable the deceptive and misleading use of marks" and "to protect persons engaged in…commerce against unfair competition." (Citation omitted). Section 43(a) "prohibits a broader range of practices than does Section 32," which applies to registered marks, (citation omitted), but it is common ground that Section 43(a) protects qualifying unregistered trademarks and that the general principles qualifying a mark for registration under Section 2 of the Lanham Act are

[5] 15 U.S.C. Sections 1051 *et seq.*

for the most part applicable in determining whether an unregistered mark is entitled to protection under Section 43(a). (Citations omitted)."[6]

As previously noted, a trademark is defined in 15 U.S.C. Section 1127 as including "any word, name, symbol, or device or any combination thereof" used by any person "to identify and distinguish his or her goods, including a unique product, from those manufactured or sold by others and to indicate the source of the goods, even if that source is unknown." In order to be registered, a mark must be capable of distinguishing the applicant's goods from those of others.[7] Marks are often classified in categories of generally increasing distinctiveness: (1) generic; (2) descriptive; (3) suggestive; (4) arbitrary; or (5) fanciful.[8]

The Lanham Act is the original federal law that established the requirements for trademark registration and protects the owner of a federally registered mark against the use of:

1. the same, or
2. confusingly similar marks, if
3. use is likely to result in consumer confusion, or
4. if dilution of a famous mark is likely to occur.

Trademark Eligibility

The law established two basic requirements that must be met for a mark to be eligible for trademark protection:

1. It must be in use in commerce[9]; and
2. It must be distinctive.[10]

---

[6] *Two Pesos, Inc. v. Taco Cabana, Inc.*, 505 U.S. 763, 766 (1992).

[7] 15 U.S.C. Section 1052.

[8] *Abercrombie & Fitch Co. v. Hunting World, Inc.*, a537 F.2d 4, 9 (1976).

[9] 15 U.S.C. Section 1051(b)(3)(B).

[10] 15 U.S.C. Section 1051(b)(3)(D) "...that, to the best of the verifier's knowledge and belief, no other person has the right to use such mark in commerce either in the identical form thereof or in such near resemblance thereto as to be likely, when used on or in connection with the goods of such other person, to cause confusion, or to cause mistake, or to deceive."

The "Use in Commerce"[11] Requirement

The law defines a trademark as a mark used in commerce or registered with a *bona fide* intent to use it in commerce.[12] If a mark does not meet that requirement at the time the application is filed, registration may still be allowed if the applicant establishes a good faith intent to use the mark in commerce at a later date.[13] The exclusive right to a trademark is awarded to the first to use it in commerce.

The "Distinctive" Requirement

The general rule regarding distinctiveness is clear: An identifying mark is distinctive and capable of being protected if it either (1) is inherently distinctive or (2) has acquired distinctiveness through secondary meaning.[14] In addition, eligibility for protection under Section 43(a) requires non-functionality and a likelihood of confusion.[15]

The second requirement, that a mark be distinctive, addresses a trademark's capacity to identify and distinguish the source of particular goods from one producer and not another. Trademarks are traditionally divided into four categories of distinctiveness: arbitrary/fanciful, suggestive,

---

[11] 15 U.S.C. Section 1127 notes, "The term 'use in commerce' means the *bona fide* use of a mark in the ordinary course of trade, and not made merely to reserve a right in a mark. For purposes of this chapter, a mark shall be deemed to be in use in commerce —

(1) on goods when —

(A) it is placed in any manner on the goods or their containers or the displays associated therewith or on the tags or labels affixed thereto, or if the nature of the goods makes such placement impracticable, then on documents associated with the goods or their sale; and

(B) the goods are sold or transported in commerce, and

(2) on services when it is used or displayed in the sale or advertising of services and the services are rendered in commerce, or the services are rendered in more than one State or in the United States and a foreign country and the person rendering the services is engaged in commerce in connection with the services."

[12] 15 U.S.C.Section 1127 states, "The word 'commerce' means all commerce which may lawfully be regulated by Congress."

[13] 15 U.S.C. Section 1051.

[14] Restatement (Third) of Unfair Competition Section 13 and Comment a.

[15] *Two Pesos, Inc. v. Taco Cabana, Inc.*, 505 U.S. 763, 768 (1992).

descriptive, and generic.[16] If a mark is categorized as either arbitrary/fanciful or suggestive, it is considered to be inherently distinctive, and exclusive rights to the mark are determined solely by priority of use. Strong marks are creative or unique.

A trademark that is categorized as descriptive is only protectable as a trademark if it has acquired a secondary meaning in the minds of the consuming public. Secondary meaning is also necessary to establish trademark protection for a personal name or a geographic term. Generic terms are not eligible for trademark protection because they refer to a general class of products rather than indicating a unique source. Generic terms are the common, everyday name for a good or service, such as "bicycle," or "bagel shop." A mark may be generic *ab initio* and refused registration, or it may become generic over time through use such as "aspirin."

Secondary Meaning

Secondary meaning is used generally to indicate that a mark or dress has come through use to be uniquely associated with a specific source.[17] To establish secondary meaning, a manufacturer must show that, in the minds of the public, the primary significance of a product feature or term is to identify the source of the product rather than the product itself.[18]

Registration with the USPTO

In the United States a party can establish common law rights to a mark, even in the absence of registration, strictly by use of the mark in commerce. Therefore, while a party is not required to register a mark, registration provides greater protection. Registration with the USPTO may create nationwide rights in the mark.

Using the trademark symbols TM, SM, and ®

The symbol is intended to inform both consumers and competitors that a particular entity has laid claim to the mark. A party is allowed to use "TM"

---

[16] *Zatarain's, Inc. v. Oak Grove Smoke House, Inc.*, 698 F.2d 786 (1983).

[17] Restatement (Third) of Unfair Competition Section 13 Comment e.

[18] *Inwood Laboratories, Inc. v. Ives Laboratories, Inc.*, 456 U.S. 844, 851, n. 11 (1982).

for goods and "SM" for services even if the party has not yet filed an application with the USPTO. Once a mark is registered the owner may use ® with the mark.

French Law

French law also notes that a mark is used to distinguish the products or services of a company. "Distinctiveness" is a necessary part of that, but, as in the United States, only one of several requirements.

Article L711-1[19]:
A product or service mark is a sign used to distinguish the products or services of a natural or legal person from those of other natural or legal persons. This sign must be able to be represented in the national register of marks in such a way as to allow any person to determine precisely and clearly the object of the protection conferred on its holder.

Article L711-2 states that a mark:
Cannot be validly registered and, if registered, may be declared void:

1. A sign which cannot constitute a trademark within the meaning of Article L. 711-1;
2. A mark devoid of any distinctive character;
3. A trademark composed exclusively of elements or indications that may be used to designate, in trade, a characteristic of the product or service, and in particular the species, quality, quantity, destination, value, origin geographical, the time of production of the good, or the provision of the service;
4. A brand composed exclusively of elements or indications that have become customary in everyday language or in the fair and constant habits of the trade;
5. A sign consisting exclusively of the shape or another characteristic of the product imposed by the very nature of this product, necessary to obtain a technical result or which gives this product substantial value;

[19]This, and all other references to French law, unless otherwise noted, are taken from the translation of the French Intellectual Property Code in force June 14, 2022 as translated by Google Translate, or from wipolex-res.wipo.int/edocs/lexdocs/laws/en/fr/fr467en.html

6. A trademark excluded from registration pursuant to Article 6 of the Paris Convention for the Protection of Industrial Property in the absence of authorization from the competent authorities;
7. A mark contrary to public order or the use of which is legally prohibited;
8. A mark likely to deceive the public, in particular as to the nature, quality, or geographical origin of the product or service;
9. A mark excluded from registration by virtue of national legislation, European Union law, or international agreements to which France or the Union are parties, which provide for the protection of designations of origin and geographical indications, traditional mentions for wines and traditional specialties guaranteed;
10. A trademark consisting of the denomination of an earlier plant variety, registered in accordance with Book VI of this Code, European Union law or international agreements to which France or the Union are parties, which provide for the protection of plant varieties, or reproducing it in its essential elements, and which relates to plant varieties of the same species or of a closely related species;
11. A trademark whose filing was made in bad faith by the applicant.

In the cases provided for in 2, 3, and 4, the distinctive character of a mark may be acquired following the use that has been made of it.

Article L711-3 establishes limitations on what may be protected:

I. Cannot be validly registered and, if registered, is likely to be declared void, a trademark infringing prior rights having an effect in France, in particular:

1. An earlier mark:
    a. When it is identical to the earlier mark and the goods or services it designates are identical to those for which the earlier mark is protected;
    b. When it is identical or similar to the earlier mark and the goods or services it designates are identical or similar to those for which the earlier mark is protected, if there is, in the mind of the public, a risk of confusion including the risk of association with the earlier mark;
2. An earlier registered trademark or an application for a trademark subject to its subsequent registration, enjoying a reputation in France or,

in the case of a European Union trademark, a reputation in the Union, when the later mark is identical or similar to the earlier mark, whether or not the goods or services it designates are identical or similar to those for which the earlier mark is registered or applied for and when the use of this later mark without just reason would take unfair advantage of the distinctive character or reputation of the earlier mark, or that it would harm them;

3. A denomination or a company name, if there is a risk of confusion in the mind of the public;
4. A commercial name, a sign, or a domain name, the scope of which is not only local, if there is a risk of confusion in the mind of the public;
5. A registered geographical indication mentioned in Article L. 722-1 or an application for a geographical indication subject to the approval of its specifications and subsequent registration;
6. Copyright;
7. Rights resulting from a protected design or model;
8. A right to the personality of a third party, in particular to his family name, his pseudonym or his image;
9. The name, image, or reputation of a local authority or a public establishment for inter-municipal cooperation;
10. The name of a public entity, if there is a risk of confusion in the mind of the public.

II. A prior mark within the meaning of 1 of I means:

1. A registered French trademark, a European Union trademark, or a trademark that has been the subject of an international registration with effect in France;
2. An application for registration of a mark mentioned in 1, subject to its subsequent registration;
3. A well-known trademark within the meaning of Article 6 bis of the Paris Convention for the protection of industrial property.

The anteriority of a registered mark is assessed with regard to the date of the application for registration, taking into account, where applicable, the right of priority invoked or the seniority validly claimed by a European Union mark within the meaning of article L. 717-6.

III. Cannot be validly registered and, if registered, is liable to be declared void, a mark whose registration has been requested by the agent or representative of the holder of a mark protected in a State party to the Paris Convention for the Protection of Industrial Property, in its own name and without the authorization of the holder, unless this agent or this representative justifies his approach.
In summary, to obtain a trademark in France the mark must be:

Represented so as to allow any person to determine precisely and clearly the subject

matter of the protection granted to its owner;

Distinctive;

Not deceptive;

Lawful; and

Available.

The Coca-Cola Co. v. The Koke Co. of America

This is a bill in equity brought by the Coca-Cola Company to prevent the infringement of its trade-mark Coca-Cola and unfair competition with it in its business of making and selling the beverage for which the trade-mark is used. The District Court gave the plaintiff a decree. (Citation omitted). This was reversed by the Circuit Court of Appeals. Citation omitted). Subsequently a writ of *certiorari* was granted by this Court. (Citation omitted).

Both the Courts below agree that subject to the one question to be considered the plaintiff has a right to equitable relief. Whatever may have been its original weakness, the mark for years has acquired a secondary significance and has indicated the plaintiff's product alone. It is found that defendant's mixture is made and sold in imitation of the plaintiff's and that the word 'Koke' was chosen for the purpose of reaping the benefit of the advertising done by the plaintiff and of selling the imitation as and for the plaintiff's goods. The only obstacle found by the Circuit Court of Appeals in the way of continuing the injunction granted below was its opinion that the trade-mark in itself and the advertisements accompanying it made such fraudulent representations to the public that the plaintiff had lost its claim to any help from the Court. That is the question upon which the writ of *certiorari* was granted and the main one that we shall discuss.

Of course a man is not to be protected in the use of a device the very purpose and effect of which is to swindle the public. But the defects of a plaintiff do not offer a very broad ground for allowing another to swindle him. The defence relied on here should be scrutinized with a critical eye. The main point is this: Before 1900 the beginning of the good will was more or less helped by the presence of cocaine, a drug that, like alcohol of caffeine or opium, may be described as a deadly poison or as a valuable item of the pharmacopoeia according to the rhetorical purposes in view. The amount seems to have been very small, but it may have been enough to begin a bad habit and after the Food and Drug Act of June 30, 1906, … if not earlier, long before this suit was brought, it was eliminated from the plaintiff's compound. Coca leaves still are used, to be sure, but after they have been subjected to a drastic process that removes from them every characteristic substance except a little tannin and still less chlorophyl. The cola nut, at best, on its side furnishes but a small portion of the caffeine, which now is the only element that has appreciable effect. That comes mainly from other sources. It is argued that the continued use of the name imports a representation that has ceased to be true and that the representation is reinforced by a picture of coca leaves and cola nuts upon the label and by advertisements, which however were many years before this suit was brought, that the drink is an 'ideal nerve tonic and stimulant,' etc., and that thus the very thing sought to be protected is used as a fraud.

The argument (*sic*) does not satisfy us. We are dealing here with a popular drink not with a medicine, and although what has been said might suggest that its attraction lay in producing the expectation of a toxic effect the facts point to a different conclusion. Since 1900 the sales have increased at a very great rate corresponding to a like increase in advertising. The name now characterizes a beverage to be had at almost any soda fountain. It means a single thing coming from a single source, and well known to the community. It hardly would be too much to say that the drink characterizes the name as much as the name the drink. In other words 'Coca-Cola' probably means to most persons the plaintiff's familiar product to be had everywhere rather than a compound of particular substances … we see no reason to doubt that, as we have said, it has acquired a secondary meaning in which perhaps the product is more emphasized than the producer but to which the producer is entitled. The coca leaves and whatever of cola nut is employed may be used to justify the continuance of the name or they may affect the flavor as the plaintiff contends, but before this suit was brought the plaintiff had advertised to the public that it must not expect and would not find cocaine, and had eliminated everything tending to suggest cocaine effects except the name and the picture of the leaves and nuts, which probably conveyed little or nothing to most who saw it. It appears to us that it would be going too far to deny the plaintiff relief against a palpable fraud because possibly here and there an ignorant person might call for the drink with the hope for incipient cocaine intoxication. The plaintiff's position must be judged by the facts as they were when the suit was begun, not by the facts of a different condition and an earlier time.

The decree of the District Court restrains the defendant from using the word 'Dope'. The plaintiff illustrated in a very striking way the fact that the word is one of the most featureless known even to the language of those who are incapable of discriminating speech. In some places it would be used to call for Coca-Cola. It equally would have been used to call for anything else having about it a faint aureole of poison. It does not suggest Coca-Cola by similarity and whatever objections there may be to its use, objections which the plaintiff equally makes to its application to Coca-Cola, we see no ground on which the plaintiff can claim a personal right to exclude the defendant from using it.

The product including the coloring matter is free to all who can make it if no extrinsic deceiving element is present. The injunction should be modified also in this respect.

This case was the predecessor to the Lanham Act of 1946 which represented a codification of common law principles.

Trademark Registration in the United States

Generally, the registration process takes 12–18 months.[20] If opposed the process may take years.

[20] https://www.uspto.gov/trademarks/basics/how-long-does-it-take-register.

Benefits

The "TM" symbol may be used to demonstrate:

1. a claim to a common law right; or
2. that registration is pending.

In the United States only marks that are registered with the USPTO can use the ® symbol.

Federal registration gives the registrant:

1. Legal presumption of the validity and ownership of the mark;
2. The exclusive right to use the mark nationwide on or in connection with the goods or services listed on the registration, even in areas of the country where the trademark is not used;
3. A listing of the mark in the USPTO online databases;
4. Constructive notice of a claim of ownership[21] as well as the date of constructive use of the mark as of the filing date[22];
5. The authority to notify the U.S. Customs Service of the trademark to block imports of infringing goods[23];
6. The basis to obtain registration in foreign countries.

Pursuant to federal law, after 5 years of continuous and substantial exclusive use the registration achieves "incontestable" status.[24] Once a mark is incontestable:

1. The registration is conclusive evidence of the validity of the registered mark and its registration;
2. Of the registrant's ownership of the mark; and
3. The owner's exclusive right to use the registered mark in commerce.

Another benefit of federal registration is that:

The registration may not be challenged by third parties on the basis that:

---

[21] 15 U.S.C. Section 1072.

[22] 15 U.S.C. Section 1057(c).

[23] 15 U.S.C. Section 1124.

[24] 15 U.S.C. Section 1065.

1. The mark is merely descriptive of the goods or services;
2. The mark is a geographic place that will convey a goods-place or service-place association in the minds of consumers; or
3. The mark is merely a surname.

Trademark Registration in France

Pursuant to Article L. 712-1, registration is necessary. However, well-known trademarks may be granted protection without registration.[25]

Not all Marks are Entitled to Protection

Although a trademark is broadly defined, a requirement for registration is that a mark must be capable of distinguishing the applicant's goods from those of others.[26] Whether in the United States or France, as previously noted, the stronger and more distinctive the mark, the easier it is to register and enforce.[27] To be entitled to protection, a mark must be sufficiently distinct that a consumer may identify the manufacturer of the goods easily and be able to distinguish between those goods and competing products.

Strong Marks

Strong trademarks are suggestive, fanciful, or arbitrary and are protected as inherently distinctive without demonstrating secondary meaning and receive automatic protection since they identify a particular product's source as opposed to describing the product itself.

Fanciful

Invented words that only have meaning in relation to their goods or services such as Exxon® for petroleum or Pepsi® for soft drinks.[28]

---

[25] Article 6 bis of the WIPO Paris Convention for the Protection of Industrial Property 1883 (Paris Convention).

[26] 15 U.S.C. Section 1052.

[27] *Abercrombie & Fitch Co. v. Hunting World, Inc.*, 537 F.2d 4 (1976).

[28] https://www.uspto.gov/trademarks/basics/strong-trademarks.

Arbitrary

Actual words that have no association with the underlying goods or services. Apple® is registered as a trademark for computers as well as other products. Apple® is unique.

Suggestive

Words that suggest some quality about the product or service but do not specifically state that quality and require imagination, thought, or perception to understand the product or service. Coppertone® for sun-tanning products conveys the impression of a deep, dark tan but does not specifically state so.[29]

Descriptive

Describe some aspect of the good or service such as an ingredient, quality, characteristic, function, feature, purpose, or use[30] without identifying or distinguishing the source of those goods or services. Descriptive trademarks may only be registered in certain limited situations such as when the mark achieves a secondary meaning. Suggestive, arbitrary, and fanciful trademarks are inherently distinctive, whereas a descriptive mark may not be, at least initially.

Some examples of descriptive trademarks are:

"Creamy" for yogurt;

"Apple pie" for potpourri.[31]

However, a descriptive mark may not be registered or enforced unless and until the mark has achieved a secondary meaning, at which time the public associates the term with a particular source.

---

[29] *Ibid.*

[30] In re Chamber of Commerce of the U.S. 675 F.3d 1297 (2012).

[31] https://www.uspto.gov/trademarks/basics/strong-trademarks.

Acquired Distinctiveness or Secondary Meaning

15 U.S.C. Section 1052(f)

A proposed mark that is not inherently distinctive may still be registered with the USPTO on the basis of acquired distinctiveness, or "secondary meaning" if it has become distinctive to the applicant's goods or services in commerce.[32]

> A term which is descriptive ... may, through usage by one producer with reference to his product, acquire a special significance so that to the consuming public the word has come to mean that the product is produced by that particular manufacturer ... The crux of the secondary meaning doctrine is that the mark comes to identify not only the goods but the source of those goods. To establish secondary meaning, it must be shown that the *primary* significance of the term in the minds of the consuming public is not the product but the producer. This may be an anonymous producer, since consumers often buy goods without knowing the personal identity or actual name of the manufacturer.[33]

Once a secondary meaning has been achieved a mark is considered distinctive and is protected.

For example, a shade of color may qualify for protection when customers associate the color with the product. Examples include:

Tiffany™ blue

Home Depot™ orange

John Deere™ green

UPS™ brown

French law also addresses the issue of acquired distinctiveness or secondary meaning, if the mark has acquired a "distinctive character." Article L. 712-7 notes:

The Director General of the National Institute of Industrial Property rejects the application for registration:

---

[32] https://tmep.uspto.gov/RDMS/TMEP/current#/current/TMEP-1200d1e10316.html.

[33] *Ralston Purina Co. v. Thomas J. Lipton, Inc.*, 341 F.Supp. 129, 133 (1972).

1. If it does not meet the conditions provided for in Article L. 712-2;
2. If the mark does not meet the conditions set out in 1 and 5 to 10 of Article L. 711-2;
3. If the mark is devoid of any distinctive character pursuant to 2, 3 and 4 of Article L. 711-2, unless the applicant establishes that the mark has acquired a distinctive character following the use made of it before the filing date;
4. If the opposition to which it is the subject is upheld pursuant to Article L. 712-4.

When the grounds for rejection affect the application only in part, only partial rejection is made.

Generic Terms

Generic words are the common, everyday name for a good or service. Since they do not indicate a source, they do not function as trademarks and may not be registered or enforced as a trademark.[34] Examples include "Bicycle" and "Bagel shop" for a bagel shop.[35] "Aspirin" has become generic. Competitors may call their product "aspirin" but may not call it "genuine aspirin."

French law also addresses the issue of genericism. Article L714-6 restricts protection in certain situations and notes that an owner…

Incurs the forfeiture of his rights (as the) holder of a mark which has become by his doing:

a. The customary trade name of the product or service;
b. likely to mislead, in particular on the nature, quality, or geographical origin of the product or service.

The Scope of Protection

Because a mark is connected to specific goods or services the owner must specifically identify the particular goods or services that are associated with the mark. Doing so identifies the scope of use and generally allows

[34] *Bayer v. United Drug Co.*, 272 F. 505 (1921).

[35] https://www.uspto.gov/trademarks/basics/strong-trademarks.

the owner to prevent others from using the same, or confusingly similar trademark for related goods or services without permission.

Common Law Protection for Trademarks

Generally, use of a protectable mark on goods or services that are used in the ordinary course of trade automatically creates a common law right although protection is generally limited to a defined geographic area where the mark is known and used, such as a state. As with a registered mark the owner owns the rights for as long as the mark is used to identify and distinguish its goods or services.

Use in Commerce

Federal Law

"Use in commerce" means the *bona fide* use of a mark in the ordinary course of trade and not done simply to reserve a right in a mark.[36] Factors that the USPTO may consider when determining if there has been a "*bona fide* use of a mark in the ordinary course of trade" are:

1. The amount of use;
2. The nature or quality of the transaction; and
3. What is typical use within a particular industry.

French law also addresses the issue of "use in commerce" although in somewhat different terms. Article L714-5 notes that an owner,

> Incurs the forfeiture of his rights the holder of the mark who, without just cause, has not made serious use of it, for the products or services for which the mark is registered, for an uninterrupted period of five years. The starting point of this period is fixed at the earliest on the date of registration of the mark according to the methods specified by a decree in Council of State.

---

[36] 15 U.S.C. Section 1127.

The following is assimilated to use within the meaning of the first paragraph:

1. Use made with the consent of the owner of the mark;
2. The use made by a person authorized to use the collective mark or the guarantee mark;
3. The use of the mark, by the holder or with his consent, in a modified form that does not alter its distinctive character, whether or not the mark is registered in the name of the holder in the form used;
4. The affixing of the mark to products or their packaging, by the owner or with his consent, exclusively for export.

Other Federal Laws on Marks

The Federal Trademark Dilution Act[37] (1995)

This law amended the Lanham Act. Previously, federal law prohibited the unauthorized use of the same mark on competing — or non-competing but "related" — goods or services only when such use was likely to cause confusion. The amendment provided protection for "famous"[38] trademarks regardless of a showing of competition or likelihood of confusion.

Dilution involves issues with regard to both "blurring"[39] and "tarnishment".[40] Blurring occurs when the distinctiveness of a famous

---

[37] 15 U.S.C. Section 1125(c).

[38] 15 U.S.C. 1125(c)(2)(A) "For purposes of paragraph (1), a mark is famous if it is widely recognized by the general consuming public of the United States as a designation of source of the goods or services of the mark's owner. In determining whether a mark possesses the requisite degree of recognition, the court may consider all relevant factors, including the following:

(i) The duration, extent, and geographic reach of advertising and publicity of the mark, whether advertised or publicized by the owner or third parties.

(ii) The amount, volume, and geographic extent of sales of goods or services offered under the mark.

(iii) The extent of actual recognition of the mark.

(iv) Whether the mark was registered under the Act of March 3, 1881, or the Act of February 20, 1905, or on the principal register."

[39] 15 U.S.C. Section 1125(c)(2)(B).

[40] 15 U.S.C. Section 1125(c)(2)(C).

mark is impaired by association with another similar mark or trade name. Tarnishment occurs when the reputation of a famous mark is harmed by association with another similar mark or trade name.

Examples of "famous" trademarks include Apple™, Coca-Cola™, and McDonald's™.

The factors that are to be considered by a court include[41]:

1. The duration, extent, and geographic reach of advertising and publicity of the mark;
2. The amount of volume and geographic extent of sales of goods and services offered under the mark;
3. The extent of actual recognition of the mark.

Trademark Infringement

The Lanham Act prohibits the use of "any reproduction, counterfeit, copy, or colorable imitation of a registered mark" where "such use is likely to cause confusion, or to cause mistake, or to deceive."[42]

Whenever a mark is used in its entirety, or duplicated to such an extent that there is a likelihood of confusion, whether intentionally or not, the trademark has been infringed (used without authorization).

Infringement does not require that the competing mark be identical. The critical issue is whether there is a likelihood of confusion. Establishing infringement under the Lanham Act for either a registered mark[43] or an unregistered mark[44] requires the plaintiff to demonstrate that:

1. The plaintiff has a valid and legally protectable mark;
2. The plaintiff owns the mark; and
3. There is a likelihood of confusion.[45]

Although registration of a trademark is not necessary in order to sue for infringement, registration furnishes proof of the date of inception of the trademark's use which may go to the issue of damages.

---

[41] 15 U.S.C. Section 1125(c)(2)(A).

[42] 15 U.S.C. Section 1141(1)(a).

[43] 15 U.S.C. Section 1114.

[44] 15 U.S.C. Section 1125(a).

[45] See, e.g., *A&H Sportswear, Inc. v. Victoria's Secret Stores, Inc.*, 237 F.3d 198 (2000).

In summary, only those trademarks that are sufficiently distinctive from competing trademarks are entitled to protection.

Likelihood-of-Confusion

The most common reason for the USPTO to deny registration to an applicant is a likelihood-of-confusion either with a pre-existing mark or a pre-existing application.[46]

The key factors[47] that influence the USPTO's decision include the following:

1. The marks are similar in their sound, appearance, meaning, or commercial impression; and
2. The products and/or services are related to such an extent that it is likely that consumers would mistakenly believe that they come from the same source.

To prove a likelihood of confusion a plaintiff must demonstrate that "an appreciable number of ordinarily prudent purchasers are likely to be mislead, or … simply confused, as to the source of the goods in question."[48]

Among the non-exclusive list of factors that a court may consider are:

1. The strength of the plaintiff's mark;
2. The degree of similarity between the plaintiff and defendant's marks;
3. The proximity of the products and/or services;
4. Defendant's good faith in adopting the mark;
5. Evidence of actual confusion, usually by surveys;
6. The likelihood the plaintiff will bridge the gap and move into that market;
7. The quality of the defendant's product or services; and
8. The sophistication of the purchasers.[49]

---

[46] https://tmsearch.uspto.gov/webaka/html/Likelihood/Likelihood_of_Confusion.html.

[47] In re E.I. du Pont de Nemours & Co., 476 F.2d. 1357 (1973) specifies 13 factors that the U.S.P.T.O. may consider.

[48] *Mobil Oil Corp. v. Pegasus Petroleum Corp.*, 818 F.2d 254 (1987).

[49] See, e.g., *Mobil Oil Corp. v. Pegasus Petroleum Corp.*, 818 F.2d 254 (1987) citing the factors noted in *Polaroid Corp. v. Polarad Elecs. Corp.*, 287 F.2d 492 (1961).

French law on the subject is virtually identical. Article L721-8 notes:

I. Without prejudice to Articles L. 115-16 of the Consumer Code and L. 722-1 of this code, registered names are protected against:

1. Any direct or indirect commercial use of a registered name with regard to products not covered by the registration, when these products are comparable to those registered under this name or when this use makes it possible to take advantage of the reputation of the name protected;
2. Any usurpation, imitation or evocation, even if the true origin of the products or services is indicated or if the protected name is translated or accompanied by an expression such as "kind," "type," "method," "way," "imitation," or a similar expression;
3. Any other false or misleading indication as to the source, origin, nature, or essential qualities of the product which appears on the wrapping or packaging, on advertising or on documents relating to the product concerned, as well as against the use for packaging of a container likely to create an erroneous impression of the origin of the product;
4. Any other practice likely to mislead the consumer as to the true origin of the product.

When a geographical indication contains in itself the name of a product considered as generic, the use of this generic name is not considered contrary to 1 or 2 of this I.

II. The geographical indication, the specifications of which have been approved under the conditions provided for in this section, can never be considered as having a generic character and falling into the public domain.

Other Claims That a Plaintiff May Assert

The Lanham Act[50] allows for other claims, including:

1. Trade dress infringement;
2. False advertisement;

---

[50] 15 U.S.C. Section 1125.

3. Unfair competition;
4. Cybersquatting.

Defenses to a Claim of Infringement

Fair use[51]

The Lanham Act[52] specifies that: "The following shall not be actionable under this subsection:

A. Any fair use, including nominative or descriptive …, including use in connection with:
   i. Advertising or promotion that permits consumers to compare goods or services; or
   ii. Identifying or parodying, criticizing, or commenting upon the famous mark owner or the goods or services of the famous mark owner.
B. All forms of news reporting and news commentary.
C. Any noncommercial use of a mark."

The Lanham Act also exempts certain uses of registered trademarks from infringement claims when the use of the name, term, or device is "a use, otherwise than as a mark, of a term or device that is descriptive of and used fairly and in good faith only to describe goods or services of [a] party, or their geographic origin."[53]

One court described the two different kinds of fair use this way: "We distinguish two types of fair use: 'classic fair use,' in which 'the defendant has used the plaintiff's mark to describe the defendant's *own* product,' and 'nominative fair use,' in which the defendant has used the plaintiff's mark 'to describe the plaintiff's product' for the purpose of, for example, comparison to the defendant's product."[54] Other courts refer to the two kinds of fair use defense as nominative and descriptive fair use.

---

[51] The subject of fair use is also addressed in Chapter 10.

[52] 15 U.S.C. Section 1125(c)(3)(A)–(c)(3)(C).

[53] 15 U.S.C. Section 1115(b)(5)(A)–(C).

[54] *Cairns v. Franklin Mint Co.*, 292 F.3d 1139, 1150 (9th Cir. 2002).

Nominative fair use generally is permissible as long as:

1. The product or service in question is not readily identifiable without use of the trademark;
2. Only so much of the mark as is reasonably necessary to identify the product or service is used; and
3. Use of the mark does not suggest sponsorship or endorsement by the trademark owner.[55]

Nominative fair use generally applies to, among other areas, comparative advertising, parody, and non-commercial use of trademarks in academic articles and media reports.

To prove nominative fair use a defendant must show:

1. The product or service cannot be readily identified without using the trademark, since the trademark is descriptive;
2. The user only used so much of the mark as was necessary for the identification; and
3. The use did not suggest sponsorship or endorsement by the trademark owner.

Descriptive fair use[56]

In this case the trademark is merely descriptive, rather than identifying its source, and does not imply sponsorship or endorsement.[57] Descriptive fair use permits use of another's trademark to describe the user's products or services, rather than as a trademark to indicate the source of the goods or services. This usually is appropriate where the trademark

---

[55] *New Kids on the Block v. News Am. Publishing, Inc.*, 971 F.2d 302 (1992).

[56] 15 U.S.C. Section 1115(b)(4).

[57] See, e.g., *Playboy Enterprises, Inc. v. Welles*, 279 F.3d 796 (9th Cir. 2002) where the court noted that the defendant, who established a fan club and correctly described herself as a former Playboy Playmate of the Year, "…has not attempted to trick consumers into believing that they are viewing a Playboy-endorsed website… [S]he does not use the classic Playboy bunny logo, she inserted disclaimers which clearly state that the website is not endorsed by PEI, and the font of the Playmate of the Year 1981 title is not … [the] Playboy magazine font."

concerned has a descriptive meaning in addition to its secondary meaning as a trademark.

> Inhibitor Technology Corporation produces a line of rust-inhibiting products containing a substance called volatile corrosion inhibitor (VCI). This line of products is branded with the federally registered trademark THE INHIBITOR. More than a decade later the WD-40 Company introduced a new line of products. One of the WD-40 products — WD-40 Specialist Long-Term Corrosion Inhibitor, which contains VCI and a purpose similar to that of Inhibitor Technology Corporation's products — contains on its packaging the word 'inhibitor'. Inhibitor Technology Corporation sued WD-40 alleging trademark infringement and unfair competition under both federal and Illinois law.[58]

The district court granted summary judgment in favor of WD-40 finding that WD-40's use of the word "inhibitor" on the label of WD-40 Specialist Long-Term Corrosion Inhibitor was a non-trademark descriptive fair use of the word and the appellate court affirmed.

To prove descriptive fair use a defendant must prove:

1. Use other than as a mark;
2. In a descriptive manner; and
3. In good faith.[59]

Expressive Works

When a party uses another's mark in the title or content of an expressive work a court will consider the competing First Amendment and trademark interests and do not generally preclude the use unless the public interest in avoiding consumer confusion outweighs the public interest in free expression. Among the questions that a court may ask are:

1. Does the mark have artistic relevance to the underlying work?
2. Does use of the mark explicitly mislead consumers regarding the source or content of the work?

---

[58] *Sorenson v. WD-40 Company*, 792 F.3d 712 (2015).

[59] *Cairns v. Franklin Mint*, 292 F.3d at 1150–1151.

Laches as a Defense

Since the Lanham Act does not specify a statute of limitations courts rely on "laches" (Latin for "lax"). Laches is a defense developed by courts of equity to protect defendants against unreasonable, prejudicial delay in commencing suit thus serving to bar the plaintiff whose unreasonable delay in prosecuting a claim or protecting a right has worked a prejudice to the defendant.[60] The limit imposed by laches generally starts to run when the owner knew, or should have known, of the infringement.

To assert the defense of laches a defendant must demonstrate that:

1. The plaintiff had knowledge of the defendant's use of its mark;
2. Plaintiff delayed acting without justification; and
3. Defendant will be prejudiced by allowing plaintiff to assert its rights.

French law specifies a statute of limitations. Article L716-4-5 notes that, any action for infringement brought by the owner of an earlier mark against a later mark is inadmissible:

1. When the owner of the earlier mark has tolerated the use of the later mark for a period of five consecutive years with knowledge of this use and for the products or services for which the use was tolerated, unless its filing was made in bad faith;
2. When, at the request of the proprietor of the later mark, the plaintiff in the action for infringement on the basis of an earlier mark does not provide the evidence required, as the case may be, by Article L. 716-2- 3 or by article L. 716-2-4.

Article L716-4-3 provides an additional defense to infringement in the event that a mark has not been used for a minimum of 5 years.

Any action for infringement is inadmissible when, at the request of the defendant, the owner of the mark cannot provide proof:

1. That the mark has been the subject, for the products or services for which it is registered and which are invoked in support of the claim,

[60] *Petrella v. Metro-Goldwyn-Mayer, Inc.*, 572 U.S. 663 (2014).

genuine use during the 5 years preceding the date on which the claim for infringement was filed, under the conditions provided for in Article L. 714-5;

2. Or that there were just reasons for its non-use.

Certification Mark

While a certification mark is protected under the Lanham Act, it serves a different function. A certification mark is generally owned by a trade association or similar group but used by someone other than the owner to demonstrate that the goods or services conform to the requirements established by the owner.[61] The owner establishes standards for certification but is not, itself, allowed to use the mark.[62] The certification mark's owner is required to license the use of the mark to anyone whose goods or services meet the established standards.[63]

15 U.S.C. Section 1127 specifies three general categories for certification:

1. Regional or other origin,
2. Material, mode of manufacture, quality, accuracy, or
3. Other characteristics of such person's goods or services or that the work or labor on the goods or services was performed by members of a union or other organization.

French law provides for an equivalent mark. Article L715-1 notes that:

> A guarantee mark is a mark thus designated at the time of its filing and capable of distinguishing the products or services for which the material, the method of manufacture or service, the quality, the precision, or other characteristics are guaranteed.
>
> The provisions of this book are applicable to warranty marks subject to the specific provisions provided in this section.

[61] 15 U.S.C. Section 1127.
[62] 15 U.S.C. Section 1064.
[63] 15 U.S.C. Section 1064.

As with American law, Article L715-4 provides for certain limitations related to such marks:

> In addition to the grounds for rejection or nullity provided for in Articles L. 712-7 and L. 714-3, respectively, a guarantee mark is refused registration or, if registered, is liable to be declared null when it does not comply with the provisions of Articles L. 715-1 to L. 715-3 or that its rules of use are contrary to public order.
>
> A guarantee mark shall also be refused registration or, if registered, may be declared invalid where it risks misleading the public as to its character or meaning, in particular where it is likely to not appear as a warranty mark.

Article L721-1 refers to the French Consumer Code and provides a definition for issues with regard to "origin." The rules relating to the determination of designations of origin are set by Article L. 115-1 of the Consumer Code:

Article L. 115-1:

> An appellation of origin is the denomination of a country, region or locality used to designate a product originating therein and whose quality or characteristics are due to the geographical environment, including natural factors and human factors.

Article L721-2 and the following Articles go on to note:

> A geographical indication is the name of a geographical area or a specific place used to designate a product, other than agricultural, forestry, food, or sea, which originates there and which has a specific quality, reputation, or other characteristics that can be attributed essentially to this geographical origin. The conditions of production or processing of this product, such as cutting, extraction, or manufacture, comply with specifications approved by the decision taken pursuant to Article L. 411-4.

Article L721-7:

The specification of a geographical indication specifies:

1. Its name;
2. The product concerned;
3. The delimitation of the geographical area or the associated determined place;
4. The quality, reputation, traditional know-how, or other characteristics possessed by the product concerned and which can be attributed essentially to this geographical area or to this specific place, as well as the elements establishing the link between the product and the geographical area or associated determined location;
5. The description of the development, production, and transformation process, including the production or transformation operations which must take place in the geographical area or the determined place as well as those which guarantee the characteristics mentioned in 4°;
6. The identity of the defense and management body, its statutes, the list of initial operators it represents, and the financial terms of their participation;
7. The methods and frequency of inspections, the type of organization mentioned in Article L. 721-9 in charge of carrying them out, as well as the methods of financing these inspections. The terms include in particular the product control points and specific labeling elements;
8. The reporting or record-keeping obligations that operators must meet in order to allow verification of compliance with the specifications;
9. The procedures for formal notice and exclusion of operators in the event of non-compliance with the specifications;
10. Provisional financing of the defense and management body;
11. The specific labeling elements;
12. Where applicable, the social and environmental commitments made by the operators grouped together within the defense and management body.

Collective Mark

15 U.S.C. Section 1127 notes that the term "collective mark" means a trademark or service mark,

(1) used by the members of a cooperative, an association, or other collective group or organization, or
(2) which such cooperative, association, or other collective group or organization has a *bona fide* intention to use in commerce and applies to register on the principal register established by this chapter, and includes marks indicating membership in a union, an association, or other organization.

French law also recognizes a collective mark.[64] Article L715-6 notes that:

> A collective mark is a mark thus designated at the time of its filing and capable of distinguishing the products or services of the persons authorized to use it by virtue of its rules of use.
>
> The provisions of this book are applicable to collective marks subject to the specific provisions provided in this section.

Trade Dress

Trade dress consists not of words or symbols, but of a product's packaging or, broadly, its total "image" and overall appearance.[65] It may include features such as size, shape, color or color combinations, texture, graphics, or even particular sales techniques.[66] Over time courts have accepted that packages or images may be as arbitrary, fanciful, or suggestive as words or symbols.

Thus, although originally interpreted far more restrictively, federal courts are now in agreement that Section 43(a) creates a federal cause of

---

[64] The French National Institute of origin and quality (Institute National de l'origin et de la qualite (INAO)) is responsible for the recognition and protection of official signs identifying the quality and origin of agricultural food, and forestry.

[65] See, for instance, *Two Pesos, Inc. v. Taco Cabana, Inc.*, 505 U.S. 763 (1992) where the trial court described a restaurant's trade dress to "...include the shape and general appearance of the exterior of the restaurant, the identifying sign, the interior kitchen floor plan, the decor, the menu, the equipment used to serve food, the servers' uniforms and other features reflecting on the total image of the restaurant."

[66] *John H. Harland Co. v. Clarke Checks, Inc.*, 711 F.2d 966, 980 (1983); Restatement (Third) of Unfair Competition Section 16, comment a.

action for trademark and trade dress infringement claims.[67] The Court noted, "Whether we call the violation infringement, unfair competition or false designation of origin, the test is identical — is there a 'likelihood of confusion?'"[68] The expansion by the courts is unsupported by the text, although Congress has revisited this statute from time to time, and has accepted the "judicial legislation" that has created this federal cause of action.[69]

Examples include but are not limited to:

1. Distinctive elements of a restaurant such as McDonald's or International House Of Pancakes;
2. Product packaging such as the fluted design of a Coca-Cola bottle[70] or the polar bear and sunburst images of the package of the "Klondike" ice cream bar;
3. Color,[71] such as shoes with a distinct color of the sole;
4. The shape of a Hershey Kiss chocolate.

Trade Names

15 U.S.C. Section 1127 broadly notes, "The terms 'trade name' and 'commercial name' mean any name used by a person to identify his or her business or vocation." More specifically, a trade name is any word or words, a symbol, or combination of words and symbols, used by a person to identify that person's business, vocation, or occupation and to distinguish it from the business of others. A trade name or commercial name symbolizes the reputation of a person's business, vocation, or occupation as a whole. By comparison, a trademark identifies a person's goods, while a service mark identifies a person's service.[72]

If a person owns a trade name, then that person has the exclusive right to use the name or to control the use of confusingly similar variations of the name by others in the market.

[67] *Ibid.*, at 780.

[68] *Ibid.*

[69] *Ibid.*

[70] https://www.uspto.gov/trademarks/basics/trademark-examples.

[71] https://www.uspto.gov/trademarks/basics/trademark-examples.

[72] https://www.ce9.uscourts.gov/jury-instructions/node/230.

A trademark is always connected to the specific goods or services that are sold to customers with that trademark. Trade names may not be registered under the Lanham Act unless they function to identify the source of particular goods or services rather than merely identifying the company itself. A trade name may be protected as a trademark if the trade name is the same as the name of the company's trademarked product.

Trade names may generally be registered with a state and common law protection exists for unusual or fanciful trade names against the use of confusingly similar company names.

Remedies for Infringement

While the usual remedy is an injunction, the Lanham Act, 15 U.S.C. Section 1117(a), allows a plaintiff to recover:

Defendant's profits (the most common remedy);

Damages sustained by the plaintiff; and

The costs of the action, including

Attorneys' fees;

Actual damages including:

Lost sales or revenue;

Sales at lower prices;

Harm to market reputation; or

The cost of corrective advertising.

The plaintiff may also seek destruction of the infringing goods.

The Lanham Act also states that when "assessing damages the court may enter judgment, according to the circumstances of the case, for any sum above the amount found as actual damages, not exceeding three times such amount." Such recovery generally requires a showing of willfulness.

French law specifies similar damages that a plaintiff may recover. L716-4-10 notes that:

To fix the damages, the court takes into consideration separately:

1. The negative economic consequences of the infringement, including loss of profit and loss suffered by the injured party;

2. The moral prejudice caused to the latter;
3. And the profits made by the counterfeiter, including the savings in intellectual, material, and promotion investments that he has made from the counterfeit.

However, the court may, as an alternative and at the request of the injured party, award a lump sum as damages. The sum is greater than the amount of royalties or fees that would have been due if the infringer had requested authorization to use the right which he infringed. The sum is not exclusive of compensation for the moral damage caused to the injured party.

As with American law, French law also allows, in the case of counterfeiting or willfulness, additional remedies, including, but not limited to destruction of the goods as well as the machinery and materials that were used in their creation. Article L716-4-11 notes that:

> In the event of a civil conviction for counterfeiting, the court may order, at the request of the injured party, that the products recognized as infringing products and the materials and instruments having mainly been used in their creation or manufacture be recalled from the commercial circuits, definitively excluded from these circuits, destroyed or confiscated for the benefit of the injured party.
>
> The court may also order any appropriate measure of publicity for the judgment, in particular its display or publication in full or in extracts in the newspapers or on the online public communication services it designates, according to the methods it specifies.
>
> The measures mentioned in the first two paragraphs are ordered at the expense of the infringer.

And French law, as with American law, also provides for criminal penalties. Article L716-9 notes that:

> Any person, with a view to selling, supplying, offering for sale or renting goods presented under an infringing mark, is punished by 4 years of imprisonment and a fine of €400,000:
>
> a. To import, export, re-export, or transship goods presented under an infringing mark;
> b. To industrially produce goods presented under an infringing mark;
> c. To give instructions or orders for the commission of the acts referred to in a and b.

When the offenses provided for in this article have been committed in an organized gang or on an online public communication network or when the facts relate to goods dangerous to the health, safety of humans or animals, the penalties are increased to 7 years of imprisonment and a fine of €750,000.

Article L. 716-11-1:
In addition to the penalties provided for in Articles L. 716-9 and L. 716-10, the court may order the total or partial, permanent or temporary closure, for a maximum period of 5 years, of the establishment used to commit the crime.

The temporary closure cannot lead to either termination or suspension of the employment contract, or any pecuniary damage to the employees concerned. When the permanent closure leads to the dismissal of the staff, it gives rise, apart from the notice indemnity and the dismissal indemnity, to the damages provided for in Articles L. 1235-2 to L. 1235-5 and L. 1235-11 to L. 1235-13 of the Labor Code in the event of termination of the employment contract. Non-payment of these indemnities is punishable by six months of imprisonment and a fine of €3,750.

International Trademark Registration

The Protocol Relating to the Madrid Agreement Concerning the International Registration of Mark ("the Madrid Protocol")

This agreement is one of two treaties that comprise the Madrid System for international registration of trademarks. The protocol provides a cost-effective way for trademark owners to ensure protection for their marks in multiple countries by way of an application with a single office, in one language, with one set of fees, in one currency.

Although there is no "worldwide trademark" or a "worldwide trademark registration," an owner may register a trademark in multiple countries by way of the Madrid Protocol. This allows an owner to file a single application that may then be applied to any of the over 100 member countries, so long as the owner meets the legal requirements for registration in those countries.

Chapter 12

Patents

Abstract

Generally, it is said that a patent gives an inventor the exclusive right to an invention for a specified amount of time. In truth, a patent gives the owner the right to exclude others from making or selling the invention for a specified period of time. Originally, American law gave a patent to the first to invent. Because of issues with the original law, America's law on patents was changed in the fairly recent past in order to bring it more closely in line with the patent laws of other developed nations. While the definition of what is patentable is quite broad, requiring only that the invention, process, discovery, or design be novel, useful, and not obvious in light of current technology, there are limitations. In order for there to be patent infringement it is not necessary that all of the features of a product be copied. Once a patent expires it enters the public domain. So, for instance, medicine that was originally protected by a patent becomes "generic" when the patent expires. As with most intellectual property issues, proving infringement is a slow, expensive process that serves to discourage litigation.

Introduction

The Constitution

As noted in the chapters on copyright as well as trade and service marks, the Constitution of the United States gives Congress the authority to enact laws relating to intellectual property, including patents, in Article I, Section 8, Clause 8 that states "Congress shall have power…to promote the progress of science and useful arts, by securing for limited times to authors and inventors the exclusive right to their respective writings and discoveries."

Federal Law

The U.S. Patent Act[1]

Pursuant to the Constitution Congress has, from time to time, enacted various laws relating to patents. The first patent law was enacted in 1790. The patent laws underwent a general revision on July 19, 1952. On November 29, 1999, Congress enacted the American Inventors Protection Act of 1999 (AIPA), which further revised the patent laws.

The Leahy–Smith America Invents Act

Passed by Congress and signed into law in 2011 it went into effect in 2012 and 2013. The delay recognized the magnitude and complexity of the change. Arguably one of the most significant changes to the American patent system since the Patent Act of 1952. This law changed America from the first-to-invent (FTI) to the first inventor-to-file (FITF), similar to the European system. The law also expanded the definition of "prior art" that bars patentability involving situations such as:

Public use

Sales

Publications, and

Other public disclosures available to the public regardless of the location;

Other than publications by the inventor within one year of filing.

[1]35 U.S.C. Sections 1 *et seq.*

What is a Patent?

A patent is a grant of property rights by the U.S. government through the U.S. Patent and Trademark Office. This property right allows an inventor "to exclude others from making, using, offering for sale, or selling the invention throughout the United States or importing the invention into the United States" for a limited time in exchange for public disclosure of the invention when the patent is granted.

Generally, the term of a new patent is 20 years[2] from the date on which the patent application was filed in the United States, or, in special cases, from the date and earlier related application was filed, subject to the payment of maintenance fees.

U.S. patent grants are effective only within the United States, U.S. territories, and U.S. possession. Under certain circumstances, patent term extensions or adjustments may be available.[3]

The right conferred by the patent grant is, in the language of the statute and of the grant itself, "the right to exclude others from making, using, offering for sale, or selling" the invention in the United States or "importing" the invention into the United States. Patent protection does not start until the actual grant of a patent.

French law is similar. Article L. 611-2 notes that patents are granted for a period of 20 years from the day the application is filed and also notes, as is true in America, that patents cannot be renewed or extended, except for pharmaceutical and phytopharmaceutical patents, the protection of which can be extended for a specific additional period of time.

What a Patent is Not

What is granted is not the right to make, use, offer for sale, sell, or import, but the right to exclude others from making, using, offering for sale, selling, or importing the invention. The right conferred by the patent grant

[2] 35 U.S.C. Section 154.

[3] 35 U.S.C. Section 156 specifies extensions up to 5 years for medical devices, drugs, and food or color additives.

extends throughout the United States, but not beyond. The basic requirements for patentability in the United States include:

1. A patentable subject matter;
2. Utility;
3. Novelty;
4. Non-obviousness; and
5. Enablement.

35 U.S.C. Section 101 broadly defines the categories of patentability as any process, machine, manufacture, or composition of matter, or improvement thereof. Although within certain limits, the Supreme Court ruled that Congress intended what is patentable to "include anything under the sun that is made by man."[4] Therefore, the obvious limitations, according to the Court, are the laws of nature, physical phenomena, and abstract ideas. In summary, anything made by a human is potentially patentable, whereas that which results from nature, whether living or not, is not.

The French Intellectual Property Code is similar. Article L611-10 subparagraph 1 notes that the invention must be:

New;

Involve an inventive step; and

Be capable of industrial application.

Article 611-10 subparagraphs 2,3, and 4 provide additional clarification by specifying that which is excluded from patentability and are noted below. Article 611-11 provides additional clarification and notes in part:

> An invention is considered new if it is not included in the state of the art.
>
> The state of the art consists of everything that has been made available to the public before the date of filing of the patent application by a written or oral description, use or any other means....

---

[4] *Diamond v. Chakrabarty*, 447 U.S. 303 (1980).

Article L611-14 states that an invention involves an "inventive step" "… if, for a person skilled in the art, it does not result in an obvious way from the state of the art…"

Article 611-15 defines an "industrial application" "… if its object can be made or used in any kind of industry, including agriculture."

Requirements for a Patent in the United States

Utility

35 U.S.C. Section 101 defines the issue of "utility." The USPTO has developed guidelines for this subject. The guidelines state that the claimed utility must be credible, specific, and substantial.[5] Credible utility means that logic and facts support the claim of utility, or that a person of ordinary skill in the art would accept that the invention is currently capable of the claimed use. In addition, the utility must be specific to the subject matter that is claimed and not a general utility that may apply to a broad category of inventions. "Substantial" utility requires that the invention have a specific and current real-world application.

Novelty

35 U.S.C. Section 102 has two separate requirements. Novelty requires that, prior to invention by the applicant, the invention was not known nor used by others in this country, nor patented or described in a printed publication in this country or another country. In summary, the novelty requirement demands that the invention be new. However, 35 U.S.C. Section 102(b) establishes another requirement that must be met. There is a statutory bar requiring that the patent must not have been in public use or on sale in this country, or patented or described in a printed publication in this or another country more than one year prior to the date of the U.S. patent application. Thus, an inventor must apply for a patent within a specified period of time and an inventor who delays applying for a patent may lose the right to seek patent protection by way of that delay.

---

[5] https://www.uspto.gov/sites/default/files/web/menu/utility.pdf.

Non-obviousness

35 U.S.C. Section 103 asks whether the subject matter that is sought to be patented would be obvious to a person having ordinary skill in the art at the time of the invention. If so, the invention is not patentable.

Enablement

35 U.S.C. Section 112 has three requirements and states, "The specification shall contain a written description of the invention, and of the manner and process of making and using it, in such full, clear, concise, and exact terms as to enable any person skilled in the art to which it pertains … to make and use the same, and shall set forth the best mode contemplated by the inventor of carrying out his invention." As part of this, the specification must describe the invention with sufficient detail that a person with ordinary skill in the art would be able to make and use the claimed invention without "undue experimentation".[6] Last, 35 U.S.C. Section 112 also requires that the applicant disclose the best mode of utilizing the invention. Once it is established that the applicant did disclose the best mode it must be determined whether the applicant disclosed sufficient information to enable a person of ordinary skill in the art to practice the best mode of application.

The USPTO explains that the "enablement" requirement refers to the requirement of Section 112(a), first paragraph, that the specification describes how to make and use the invention. This is intended to ensure that the invention is communicated to the interested public in a meaningful way. The information provided by the inventor must be sufficient to inform those skilled in the relevant art how to both make and use the claimed invention.[7]

Requirements for a Patent in France

As previously noted, Article L611-10 subparagraph 1 *et seq*. define both what is patentable, as well as what is not:

---

[6]In re Wands, 858 F.2d 730 (1988). However, in *Amgen, et al. v. Sanofi, et al.*, 143 S.Ct. 399 (2022) (cert. granted) the Court has agreed to address the issue of the extent of information that must be disclosed.

[7]https://www.uspto.gov/web/offices/pac/mpep/s2164.html.

1. Are patentable, in all the technological fields, the new inventions implying an inventive step and susceptible of industrial application.
2. Are not considered as inventions within the meaning of the first paragraph of this article in particular:
   a. Discoveries as well as scientific theories and mathematical methods;
   b. Aesthetic creations;
   c. Plans, principles and methods in the exercise of intellectual activities, in matters of gambling or in the field of economic activities, as well as computer programs;
   d. Presentations of information.
3. The provisions of 2 of this article only exclude the patentability of the elements listed in the said provisions insofar as the patent application or the patent concerns only one of these elements considered as such.
4. Subject to the provisions of Articles L. 611-16 to L. 611-19, inventions relating to a product made up in whole or in part of biological material, or to a process for producing, process or use biological material.
   Biological material is considered to be material that contains genetic information and can reproduce itself or be reproduced in a biological system.

In summary, what is patentable in France must be new, involve an inventive step, be capable of industrial application, and not fall within certain excluded categories.

Article L611-2 defines the kinds of patents and the length of patent protection in France and notes:

The industrial property titles protecting inventions are:

1. Patents of invention, issued for a period of twenty years from the date of filing of the application;
2. Utility certificates, issued for a period of ten years from the date of filing of the application;
3. Supplementary protection certificates attached to a patent under the conditions provided for in Article L. 611-3, taking effect on the legal term of the patent to which they relate for a period not exceeding seven years from this term and seventeen years from the issuance of the marketing authorization mentioned in this same article…

> The provisions of this book concerning patents are applicable to utility certificates with … certain exceptions.
>
> Patent protection begins when the patent application is published.

Kinds of Patents

The United States

There are three basic kinds of patents, including utility, design, and plant patents.[8] Utility patents may be granted to anyone who invents or discovers any new and useful process, machine, article of manufacture, or composition of matter, or any new and useful improvement thereof. A design patent may be granted to anyone who invents a new, original, and ornamental design for an article of manufacture. A plant patent may be granted to anyone who invents or discovers and asexually reproduces any distinct and new variety of plant. This chapter focuses on utility patents.

35 U.S.C. Section 101 states that utility patents may be obtained for whoever invents or discovers a new, non-obvious, and useful:

Process

Machine

Article of manufacture

Composition of matter, or

Improvement of any of the above.

In addition to utility patents, patent protection is also available for:

1. Ornamental design of an article of manufacture; or
2. Asexually reproduced plant varieties by design and plant patents.

The term "process" is defined as a process, act, or method, and primarily includes industrial or technical processes. The word "machine" used in the statute is obvious. "Manufacture" refers to articles that are

[8] https://www.uspto.gov/patents/basics/general-information-patents.

made and includes all manufactured articles. The phrase "composition of matter" relates to chemical compositions and may include mixtures of ingredients; as well as new chemical compounds.

In summary, these classes of subject matter taken together include practically everything that may be made by a human as well as the processes for making the products.

Useful

The word "useful" requires that the subject matter have a useful purpose and includes "operativeness." A machine that will not perform the intended purpose is not considered "useful," and therefore would not be patentable.

What is Not Patentable in the United States

As previously noted, interpretations of the statute by the courts have defined the limits of the field of subject matter that can be patented, thus it has been held that the laws of nature, physical phenomena, and abstract ideas are not patentable subject matter. A patent may be granted for a new machine, manufacture, etc., as previously noted but not for the idea or suggestion. In addition, in order to be patentable, the invention must also be

1. Novel.[9] That is, the patent must be new and unique;
2. Non-obvious.[10] An "obvious" invention, which is not patentable, is one that may have been made by someone that is:

   skilled in the area, and
   familiar with the subject matter.

As previously noted, French law is virtually identical as specified in Article L611-10.

[9]35 U.S.C. Section 102.

[10]35 U.S.C. Section 103.

Article L611-11 also addresses the requirement that the subject of the invention be "new" and notes:

> An invention is considered new if it is not included in the state of the art.
>
> The state of the art consists of everything that has been made available to the public before the date of filing of the patent application by a written or oral description, use or any other means.
>
> The content of French patent applications and European or international patent applications designating France, as filed, which have a filing date prior to that mentioned in second paragraph of this article and which were only published on that date or a later date.
>
> The second and third paragraphs do not exclude the patentability of a substance or composition included in the state of the art for the implementation of the methods referred to in Article L. 611-16, provided that its use for the any of these methods are not included in the state of the art.
>
> The second and third paragraphs also do not exclude the patentability of a substance or composition referred to in the fourth paragraph for any specific use in any method referred to in Article L. 611-16, provided that this use is not included in the state of the art.

Article L611-14 goes into additional detail and notes the requirement that the invention must be new, involve an inventive step, and be non-obvious:

> An invention is considered to involve an inventive step if, for a person skilled in the art, it does not result in an obvious way from the state of the art....

Article L611-15 addresses the issue of "useful" noting:

> An invention is considered susceptible of industrial application if its object can be made or used in any kind of industry, including agriculture.

Similar to American law, Article L611-16 limits the coverage of patentability by excluding from patentability a specified "method."

> Are not patentable the methods of surgical or therapeutic treatment of the human or animal body and the diagnostic methods applied to the human or animal body. This provision does not apply to products, in particular substances or compositions, for the implementation of one of these methods.

Article L611-17 is also reflective of the American rule that denies patentability to something that is offensive to public morals and notes:

> Inventions whose commercial exploitation would be contrary to the dignity of the human person, to public order or to good morals are not patentable, this contravention not being able to result from the sole fact that this exploitation is prohibited by a legislative or regulatory provision.

French law, Article L611-10 and L611-19 *et seq.* expand on the definition that is provided in L611-16 to include other areas that are not patentable:

> Discoveries, scientific theories and mathematical methods.
>
> Aesthetic creations.
>
> Schemes, rules and methods for performing a mental act, playing a game or conducting business, and computer programs.
>
> Presentations of information.
>
> Methods for treatment of the human or animal body by surgery or therapy and diagnostic methods practiced on the human or animal body.
>
> Inventions whose commercial exploitation would be inconsistent to public policy or morality.
>
> Human body at the various stages of its formation and development, and the simple discovery of one of its elements, including the sequence or partial sequence of a gene, including:
>
> > processes for cloning of human beings;
> >
> > processes for modifying the germ line genetic identity of human beings;

use of human embryos for industrial or commercial purposes;

total or partial sequences of a gene as such.

Animal varieties.

Plant varieties.

Essentially biological processes for the production of plants and animals.

Processes for modifying the genetic identity of animals which are likely to cause them suffering without substantial medical benefit to man or animal, and also animals resulting from these processes.

Other Limitations on Patents

"New"

In order for an invention to be patentable in the United States it must be new as defined in the patent law, which provides that an invention cannot be patented if:

1. the claimed invention was patented, described in a printed publication, or in public use, on sale, or otherwise available to the public before the effective filing date of the claimed invention; or
2. the claimed invention was described in a patent issued (by the U.S.) or in an application for patent published or deemed published (by the U.S.), in which the patent or application, as the case may be, names another inventor and was effectively filed before the effective filing date of the claimed invention.[11]

However, there are certain limited exceptions to patent prohibitions to the two categories that are noted immediately above. An exception may apply to:

1. a "disclosure made one year or less before the effective filing date of the claimed invention;" but only if

[11] https://www.uspto.gov/patents/basics/general-information-patents.

2. "the disclosure was made by the inventor or joint inventor or by another who obtained the subject matter disclosed … from the inventor or joint inventor" for example:
   a. a lecture or speech at a scientific meeting;
   b. a statement made on a radio talk show;
   c. a YouTube™ video; or
   d. a website or other on-line material.

The "Publication" Requirement

> 'Publication' of patent applications is required by the American Inventors Protection Act of 1999 for most plant and utility patent applications filed on or after November 29, 2000. Upon the filing of a plant or utility application on or after November 29, 2000, an applicant may request that the application not be published, but only if the invention has not been and will not be the subject of an application filed in a foreign country that requires publication 18 months after filing (or earlier claimed priority date) or under the Patent Cooperation Treaty.

Publication occurs after the expiration of an 18-month period following the earliest effective filing date or priority date claimed by an application. Following publication, the application for patent is no longer held in confidence by the Office and any member of the public may request access to the entire file history of the application.

Publication allows an applicant to assert provisional rights:

> To recover a reasonable royalty from a third party that infringes a published application claim provided that actual notice is given to the third party by the applicant; and
>
> The patent issues from the application with a substantially identical claim.
>
> The foregoing allows an inventor to obtain damages for a pre-grant patent infringement.

Patent Rights

As previously noted, the grant confers:

1. "the right to exclude others from making, using, offering for sale, or selling the invention throughout the United States or importing the invention into the United States" and its territories and possessions for which the term of the patent shall be generally 20 years from the date on which the application for the patent was filed in the United States; or,
2. "if the application contains a specific reference to an earlier filed application under 35 U.S.C. 120, 121 or 365(c), from the date of the earliest such application was filed, and subject to the payment of maintenance fees as provided by law."

Since a patent does not grant the right to make, use, offer for sale, or sell or import the invention but only grants the exclusive nature of the right, any person is ordinarily free to make, use, offer for sale, or sell or import anything he or she pleases, regardless of a grant from the government. Since the patent does not grant the right to make, use, offer for sale, or sell, or import the invention, the patentee's own right to do so is dependent upon the rights of others and whatever general laws might be applicable.

A patentee, merely because he or she has received a patent for an invention, is not thereby authorized to make, use, offer for sale or sell, or import the invention if doing so would violate any law.

Examples

1. An inventor of a new automobile who has obtained a patent thereon would not be entitled to use the patented automobile in violation of the laws of a state requiring a license;
2. Nor may a patentee sell an article, the sale of which may be forbidden by law, merely because a patent has been obtained.
3. Neither may a patentee make, use, offer for sale or sell, or import his or her own invention if doing so would infringe the prior rights of others.

Therefore, a patentee may not violate the

1. federal antitrust laws, such as by resale price agreements or entering into a combination in restraint of trade, or
2. the pure food and drug laws, by virtue of having a patent.

Design and Utility Patents

The vast majority of patent applications are for a utility patent. Generally, a "utility patent" applies to the way an article is used and works,[12] while a "design patent" protects the way an article looks.[13] Although utility and design patents offer separate protection, the utility and design of an article may not be easily separated and an article may possess both functional and ornamental characteristics.

Design Patents[14]

As previously noted, a design patent may be granted to anyone who invents a new, original, and ornamental design for an article of manufacture; and applies to the invention of any new and non-obvious ornamental design for an article of manufacture.

The design patent protects only the appearance of an article, but not its structural or functional features. A design patent issued prior to May 13, 2015, has a term of 14 years from grant. Effective May 13, 2015, the patent term has been revised to 15 years from the date of patent grant for design patents issuing from both national design applications under chapter 16 and international design applications designating the United States.

However, there are limitations. 35 U.S.C. 171 specifies that "A design for an article of manufacture that is dictated primarily by the function of the article lacks ornamentality and is not proper statutory subject matter... In addition, Section 171 also requires that to be patentable a design must be 'original.'" Thus, a design that is reflective of a well-known or naturally occurring object or person may not meet the test of "originality" as required by the law. Last, a design that could be considered offensive to any race, religion, gender, ethnic group, or nationality is not a proper subject matter for a design patent.

French law also addresses the subject of design. Article L511-1 addresses the design of an item and notes:

---

[12]35 U.S.C. 101.

[13]35 U.S.C. 171.

[14]The principal statutes governing design patents are 35 U.S.C 171, 172, 173, 102, 103, 112, and 132.

> The appearance of a product, or part of a product, characterized in particular by its lines, contours, colors, shape, texture or materials, may be protected as a design or model. These characteristics may be those of the product itself or of its ornamentation.
>
> Is regarded as a product any industrial or artisanal object, in particular the parts designed to be assembled in a complex product, the packaging, the presentations, the graphic symbols and the typographical characters, with the exclusion however of the computer programs.

Article L511-2 addresses the issue of originality and notes one of the limitations of a design patent:

> Only the design or model that is new and has its own character can be protected.
>
> Article L511-3:
>
> A design or model is regarded as new if, on the date of filing of the application for registration or on the date of the claimed priority, no identical design or model has been disclosed. Designs or models are considered identical when their characteristics differ only in insignificant details.
>
> Article L511-4:
>
> A design or model has its own character when the overall visual impression it arouses in the informed observer differs from that produced by any design or model disclosed before the date of filing of the application for registration or before the date of claimed priority.
>
> For the appreciation of the specific character, it is taken into account the freedom left to the creator in the realization of the drawing or model.
>
> Article L511-6:
>
> A design or model is deemed to have been disclosed if it has been made available to the public by publication, use or any other means. There is

no disclosure where the design or model could not reasonably have been known, according to current business practice in the sector concerned, by professionals operating in the European Community, before the date of filing of the application for registration or before the claimed priority date.

However, the design or model is not deemed to have been disclosed to the public by the mere fact that it was disclosed to a third party under the express or implicit condition of secrecy.

When it took place within the twelve months preceding the date of filing of the application or the date of the claimed priority, the disclosure is not taken into account:

a. If the design or model has been disclosed by the creator or his successor in title, or by a third party on the basis of information provided or acts performed by the creator or his successor in title;
b. Or if the design or model has been disclosed as a result of abusive behavior against the creator or his successor in title.

The twelve-month period provided for in this article does not apply when the disclosure occurred before October 1, 2001.

Article L511-7 mirrors a requirement that applies in the United States:

Designs or models contrary to public order or morality are not protected.

Article L511-8 requires, as in America, that the design and function of the article be separable and, if they are not, the design may not be patentable:

Is not subject to protection:

1. The appearance, the characteristics of which are exclusively imposed by the technical function of the product;
2. The appearance of a product whose exact shape and size must necessarily be reproduced so that it can be mechanically associated with another product by contact, connection, placement inside or outside exterior under conditions allowing each of these products to fulfill its function.

However, a design which is intended to allow multiple assemblies or connections to products which are interchangeable within a modularly designed assembly may be protected.

Article L513-1 addresses the length of protection and notes:

The registration takes effect, from the date of filing of the application, for a period of five years, which can be extended by periods of five years up to a maximum of twenty-five years.

Designs or models filed before October 1, 2001, remain protected, without possible extension, for a period of twenty-five years from their date of filing. Designs or models whose protection was extended, before October 1, 2001, for a further period of twenty-five years remain protected until the expiry of this period.

Patent Infringement

35 U.S.C. 271 defines patent infringement and notes:

a. Except as otherwise provided ... whoever without authority makes, uses, offers to sell, or sells any patented invention, within the United States, or imports into the United States any patented invention during the term of the patent ..., infringes the patent;
b. Whoever actively induces infringement of a patent shall be liable as an infringer;
c. whoever offers to sell or sells within the United States or imports into the United States a component of a patented machine, manufacture, combination, or composition, or a material or apparatus for use in practicing a patented process, constituting a material part of the invention, knowing the same to be especially made or especially adapted for use in an infringement of such patent, and not a staple article or commodity of commerce suitable for substantial noninfringing use, shall be liable as a contributory infringer.

In summary, unless authorized by the patent owner, usually by way of a license, infringement occurs when anyone makes, uses, or offers to sell something that has all the elements of a patented claim, or its equivalent, while the patent is in effect. The prohibited act must occur in the United States, or a violating product must be imported into the United States after being created abroad.

French law uses similar language and Articles L. 613-3 and L. 613-4 note that the following actions, occurring on French territory, constitute infringement:

> Making, offering, putting on the market, using, importing, exporting or transferring a product which is the subject matter of the patent, or stocking a product for such purposes;
>
> Using a process which is the subject matter of the patent or, when the third party knows, or it is obvious in the circumstances that the use of the process is prohibited without the consent of the owner of the patent, offering the process for use;
>
> Offering, putting on the market, using, importing, exporting or transferring a product obtained directly by a process which is the subject matter of the patent, or stocking a product for such purposes;
>
> Supplying or offering to supply to a person other than a person entitled to work the patented invention, the means of implementing the invention with respect to an essential element thereof where the third party knows, or it is obvious from the circumstances, that such means are suited and intended for putting the invention into effect.

Defenses to Patent Infringement in the United States

Defenses, in both the United States and France include, but are not limited to:

1. A challenge to the validity of the patent;
2. That the actions of the defendant do not constitute infringement;
3. Prior commercial use.

The validity of a patent may be challenged in a variety of ways, even if the patent has already been granted. Any defense is likely to start with an analysis of the statutory requirements. Does the article meet the requirements as established by the law?

The Defense of "Prior Commercial Use"

This defense generally arises when an alleged infringer has effectively treated a method or process as a trade secret and its use would not qualify as a previous public use to invalidate the patent. The America Invents Act expanded this defense from its prior availability involving only a patent for a business method to "subject matter consisting of a process, or consisting of a machine, manufacture, or composition of matter use in a manufacturing or other commercial process." This defense includes pre-marketing regulatory review and non-profit laboratory use.

This defense requires that the alleged infringer demonstrate that their use occurred:

1. At least one year prior to the earlier of the effective filing date of the patent; or
2. The date on which the inventor publicly disclosed the invention.

However, this defense is limited. Infringement is determined primarily by the language of the claims of the patent and, if what the defendant is making does not fall within the language of any of the claims of the patent, there is no literal infringement.

Defenses to Patent Infringement in France

Articles L. 613-23 *et seq.* and Articles R. 613-44 *et seq.* specify the defenses that are available. As with the United States, defenses to patent infringement in France may be based, for instance, on the literal language of the statute. Thus, defenses include, but are not limited to:

Invalidity of the patent. That is, the patent does not meet the requirements for a patent, such as a:

Lack of novelty;

Lack of inventive step;

Lack of industrial application;

The invention is excluded subject matter; or,

That the acts do not constitute infringement.

Remedies for Patent Infringement

The United States

Generally, a lawsuit may not be filed until a patent is issued, although 35 U.S.C. Section 154(d) states that a patent owner may obtain reasonable royalty damages for specified infringing activities that occurred prior to a patent's issuance. In such a case the patent holder must demonstrate that:

1. The infringing activities occurred after the publication of the patent application;
2. The patented claims are substantially identical to the claims in the published applications; and
3. The infringer had actual notice of the published patent application.

The remedies that are available for patent infringement include royalties, lost profits, attorneys' fees and, if the infringement is willful, treble damages. In addition, if an infringer is found to have deliberately infringed a patent ("willful" infringement) "enhanced" damages may be awarded up to three times the damages found or assessed.

35 U.S.C. Section 284 specifies that the successful plaintiff is entitled to "… damages adequate to compensate for the infringement, but in no event less than a reasonable royalty." "Reasonableness" is determined by the standard practices of the specific industry most relevant to the invention, as well as any other relevant or similar royalty history of the patentee.

35 U.S.C. Section 285 notes that legal fees may also be assessed if the case is deemed "exceptional." An injunction may be available but only if the patent holder proves:

1. It has suffered irreparable injury; and
2. An injunction serves the public interest.

If damages will adequately compensate the plaintiff an injunction may not be available.

France

Article L615-7 provides guidance to a court and specifies that to fix the damages, the court should consider separately:

1. The negative economic consequences of the infringement, including loss of profit and loss suffered by the injured party;
2. The moral prejudice caused to the latter;
3. And the profits made by the counterfeiter, including the savings in intellectual, material, and promotional investments that he has made from the counterfeit.

However, the court may, as an alternative and at the request of the injured party, award a lump sum as damages. This sum is greater than the amount of royalties or fees that would have been due if the infringer had requested authorization to use the right which he infringed. This sum is not exclusive of compensation for the moral damage caused to the injured party.

Similar to American law, Article L615-7-1 permits additional remedies, including the possibility of destruction of the infringing goods, along with destruction of the materials and tools "mainly" used in their creation or manufacture:

> In the event of a civil conviction for counterfeiting, the court may order, at the request of the injured party, that the products recognized as infringing products and the materials and instruments having mainly been used in their creation or manufacture be recalled from the commercial circuits, definitively excluded from these circuits, destroyed or confiscated for the benefit of the injured party.
>
> The court may also order any appropriate measure of publicity for the judgment, in particular its display or publication in full or in extracts in the newspapers or on the online public communication services it designates, according to the methods it specifies.
>
> The measures mentioned in the first two paragraphs are ordered at the expense of the infringer.

And, as with American law, French law also allows for criminal proceedings. Article L615-14 addresses the issue of willful infringement and notes:

> Willful infringement of the rights of the owner of a patent, as defined in Articles L. 613-3 to L. 613-6, shall be punishable by three years' imprisonment and a fine of 300,000 euros. When the offense was committed in an organized gang or on an online public communication network or when the facts relate to goods dangerous to the health or safety of humans or animals, the penalties are increased to seven years imprisonment and a fine of 750,000 euros.

Notice Requirements

35 U.S.C. Section 287(a) notes that "patentees, and persons making, offering for sale, or selling within the United States any patented article for or under them, or importing any patented article into the United States, may give notice to the public that the same is patented, either by fixing thereon the word "patent" or the abbreviation "pat.", together with the number of the patent, or by fixing thereon the word "patent" or the abbreviation "pat." together with an address of a posting on the Internet, accessible to the public without charge for accessing the address, that associates the patented article with the number of the patent, or when, from the character of the article, this cannot be done, by fixing to it, or to the package wherein one or more of them is contained, a label containing a like notice."

The notice requirement is particularly important since the section goes on to note that "[i]n the event of failure so to mark, no damages shall be recovered by the patentee in any action for infringement, except on proof that the infringer was notified of the infringement and continued to infringe thereafter, in which event damages may be recovered only for infringement occurring after such notice. Filing of an action for infringement shall constitute such notice."

International Agreements

Since the rights granted by a U.S. patent extend only throughout the territory of the United States and have no effect in a foreign country, an inventor who wishes patent protection in other countries must apply for a patent in each of the other countries or in regional patent offices. Almost every country has its own patent law, and a person seeking a patent in a particular country must make an application for a patent in that country, in accordance with the requirements of that country.[15]

One way to obtain patent protection in a number of countries is to file a national patent application with the respective national patent office based on the Patent Cooperation Treaty noted below. For example, the European Patent Office (EPO) accepts regional patent applications or grants patents. In certain regions, a patentee may obtain a regional patent that is valid in some or all of its member states.[16]

The Paris Convention for the Protection of Industrial Property

More than 155 countries including the United States are signatories.[17]

Among the more significant requirements of the treaty is uniform treatment. Each signatory guarantees to the citizens of the other countries the same rights in patent and trademark matters that it gives to its own citizens.[18]

The treaty also provides for the right of priority in the case of patents, trademarks, and industrial designs (design patents). This right means that, on the basis of a regular first application filed in one of the member countries, the applicant may, within a certain period of time, apply for protection in all the other member countries. These later applications will then be regarded as if they had been filed on the same day as the first application. Thus, these later applicants will have priority over applications for the same invention that may have been filed during the same period of time by other persons.

Of considerable importance is that these later applications, being based on the first application, will not be invalidated by any acts accomplished in the interval, such as, for example, publication or exploitation of the invention, the sale of copies of the design, or use of the trademark. The time within which the subsequent applications may be filed in the other countries is 12 months in the case of first applications for patent and 6 months in the case of industrial designs and trademarks.

---

[15] https://www.uspto.gov/ip-policy/ipr-toolkits.

[16] https://www.wipo.int/patents/en/faq_patents.html.

[17] https://www.wipo.int/export/sites/www/pct/en/basic_facts/faqs_about_the_pct.pdf.

[18] https://www.uspto.gov/web/offices/pac/mpep/mpep-9035-appx-p.html.

The Patent Cooperation Treaty (PCT)

The PCT is an international treaty making it possible to seek patent protection for an invention simultaneously in a large number of countries by filing a single application instead of filing several separate national or regional patent applications. Any resident or national of a signatory (referred to as a "contracting state") may file a single international application that has the effect of national patent applications (and certain regional patent applications) in some or all PCT contracting states.[19]

More than 140 countries, including the United States, are signatories. The treaty facilitates the filing of applications for patents on the same invention in member countries by providing, among other things, centralized filing procedures and a standardized application format. The timely filing of an international application affords applicants an international filing date in each country which is designated in the international application and provides:

1. a search for the invention, and
2. a later time period within which the national applications for patent must be filed.

In the case of inventions made in the United States, U.S. law requires the patentee to obtain a license from the Director of the USPTO before applying for a patent in a foreign country. Such a license is required if the foreign application is to be filed before an application is filed in the United States or before the expiration of 6 months from the filing of an application in the United States unless a filing receipt with a license grant was issued earlier. The filing of an application for a U.S. patent constitutes the request for a license and the granting or denial of such request is indicated in the filing receipt mailed to each applicant.

After 6 months from the U.S. filing, a license is not required unless the invention has been ordered to be kept secret. If the invention has been ordered to be kept secret, the consent to the filing abroad must be obtained from the Director of the USPTO during the period the order of secrecy is in effect.

---

[19] https://www.uspto.gov/patents/basics/international-protection/patent-cooperation-treaty.

The Office of International Patent Cooperation

Established in 2014 to support and improve the international patent system. The office leads efforts to assist U.S. inventors and businesses in protecting their patent rights worldwide and supports the global innovation community.[20]

Artificial Intelligence (AI) and Patents

Some commentators have expressed concern about AI and the need to revise the laws on patents noting that the patent law assumes that inventors are human. Among the issues that have been identified is whether an invention is considered "non-obvious" to a person skilled in the art. In at least one case, researchers used an algorithm to identify elements that would treat bacterial infections. One researcher stated that the algorithm was capable of learning new patterns that were unknown to human experts, thus satisfying the requirement that the invention was not obvious.

Until courts have had an opportunity to address the issue, something that may occur in the reasonably near future, the issue will remain unresolved.

[20] https://www.uspto.gov/patents/basics/international-patent-cooperation.

Chapter 13

Trade Secrets

Abstract

Trade secrets protect matters that cannot, or should not, be patented, trademarked, or copyrighted. The most obvious trade secret is arguably the formula for Coca-Cola™. The formula for Gatorade™ was patented since it could easily be reverse-engineered, thus giving the formula protection from competition for a number of years. Once the patent expired, the formula entered the public domain and competitors were free to copy it. A trade secret is anything of value that a competitor would like to know about another company. While trade secrets have long been protected by the common law, federal and state laws have been enacted on the subject. The federal Economic Espionage Act makes theft of trade secrets a federal crime.

Introduction

The Commission on the Theft of American Intellectual Property estimates that the theft of trade secrets costs the U.S. economy $300 billion a year.[1] The threat is not limited to the United States. The European Centre for International Political Economy (ECIPE), a Brussels-based think tank, described in its report on cybercrime an economic impact caused by cyber

[1] https://eiexchange.com/content/30-how-much-are-your-trade-secrets-worth-heres-how.

theft of €60 billion loss in economic growth in the EU and a consequential potential loss of 289,000 jobs.[2] The same document goes on to note:

> There is a basic problematic issue: the general lack of awareness among European companies on the threat posed by cyber theft of trade secrets and the measures that should be put in place to prevent it. This is especially true for Small and Medium Enterprises (SMEs), because of their limited capacity to invest in advanced cybersecurity defence measures. At the same time, European SMEs, which constitute the vast majority of the entrepreneurial sector, are inadequate in establishing the nature and quantity of stolen data. This translates in a limited availability of data on cyber theft of trade secrets across the EU.

The Need for Trade Secret Protection

As the prefatory note to the Uniform Trade Secrets Act (UTSA) with 1985 Amendments observes,

> A valid patent provides a legal monopoly for seventeen years[3] in exchange for public disclosure of an invention. If, however, the courts ultimately decide that the Patent Office improperly issued a patent, an invention will have been disclosed to competitors with no corresponding benefit. In view of the substantial number of patents that are invalidated by the courts, many businesses now elect to protect commercially valuable information through reliance upon the state law of trade secret protection. *Kewanee Oil Co. v. Bicron Corp.*, 416 U.S. 470 (1974), which establishes that neither the Patent Clause of the United States Constitution nor the federal patent laws pre-empt state trade secret protection for patentable or unpatentable information, may well have increased the extent of this reliance...

Notwithstanding the commercial importance of state trade secret law to interstate business, this law has not developed satisfactorily. In the first place, its development is uneven. Although there typically are a

---

[2] The scale and impact of industrial espionage and theft of trade secrets through cyber – PwC Study.pdf.

[3] See Chapter 12 for current information on this issue.

substantial number of reported decisions in states that are commercial centers, this is not the case in less populous and more agricultural jurisdictions. Secondly, even in states with significant litigation, there is undue uncertainty concerning the parameters of trade secret protection and the appropriate remedies for the misappropriation of a trade secret. One commentator observed: "Under technological and economic pressures, industry continues to rely on trade secret protection despite the doubtful and confused status of both common law and statutory remedies. Clear, uniform trade secret protection is urgently needed…" Comment, "Theft of Trade Secrets: The Need for a Statutory Solution," 120 U. Pa. L. Rev., 378, 380–381 (1971). In spite of this need, the most widely accepted rules of trade secret law, Section 757 of the Restatement of Torts, were among the sections omitted from the Restatement of Torts, 2d (1978). The Uniform Act codifies the basic principles of common law trade secret protection, preserving its essential distinctions from patent law.

The Definition of a Trade Secret

International

The World Intellectual Property Organization (WIPO) arguably has the simplest definition of a trade secret[4]:

In general, to qualify as a trade secret, the information must be:

> Commercially valuable because it is secret;
>
> Be known only to a limited group of persons; and
>
> Be subject to reasonable steps taken by the rightful holder of the information to keep it secret, including the use of confidentiality agreements for business partners and employees.

The Definition of a Trade Secret in the United States

Originally, as noted previously, protection for trade secrets was a matter of state law and each state developed a definition. A variety of efforts have been undertaken to address the issues created by this situation.

---

[4] https://www.wipo.int/tradesecrets/en/.

The Restatement (Second) Torts Section 757[5] stated that a trade secret may consist of any formula, pattern, device, or compilation of information which is used in one's business, and which gives him an opportunity to obtain an advantage over competitors who do not know or use it. Comment b provides additional guidance and notes:

> A trade secret may consist of any formula, patterns, device or compilation of information which is used in one's business, and which gives him an opportunity to obtain an advantage over competitors who do not know or use it. It may be a formula for a chemical compound, a process of manufacturing, treating or preserving materials, a pattern for a machine or other device, or a list of customers. It differs from other secret information in a business (see Section 759) in that it is not simply information as to single or ephemeral events in the conduct of the business, as, for example, the amount or other terms of a secret bid for a contract or the salary of certain employees, or the security investments made or contemplated, or the date fixed for the announcement of a new policy, or for bringing out a new model or the like. A trade secret is a process or device for continuous use in the operation of the business. Generally, it relates to the production of goods, as, for example, a machine or formula for the production of an article. It may, however, relate to the sale of goods or to other operations in the business, such as a code for determining discounts, rebates or other concessions in a price list or catalogue, or a list of specialized customers, or a method of bookkeeping or other office manager.

The adoption of the UTSA by the vast majority of states and the District of Columbia represented an effort to correct the problems created by the lack of uniformity among state laws. The UTSA defines a "trade secret" as information, including a formula, pattern, compilation, program, device, method, technique, or process that:

> Derives independent economic value, actual or potential, from not being generally known to, and not being readily ascertainable by proper means by, other persons who can obtain economic value from its disclosure or use; and

[5] As noted, the Restatement of Torts dropped trade secrets in 1978. Trade secrets are now addressed by the Restatement of Unfair Competition.

Is the subject of efforts that are reasonable under the circumstances to maintain its secrecy.

To address concerns about the theft of trade secrets, in 1996 Congress passed and the president signed into law the Economic Espionage Act of 1996.[6] The act was intended to address the growing problem of theft of trade secrets and contains two separate provisions that criminalized the theft or misappropriation of trade secrets.[7] The first provision is directed at foreign economic espionage and requires that the theft of the trade secret be done to benefit a foreign government, instrumentality, or agent.[8] The second provision criminalizes the commercial theft of trade secrets, regardless of who benefits.[9]

While the Economic Espionage Act of 1996, criminalized the theft of trade secrets it did not provide for a civil remedy. That oversight was corrected in 2016 when the federal government passed the Defend Trade Secrets Act (DTSA).[10] The DTSA adopted the definition of "trade secret" from the Economic Espionage Act of 1996.[11] The definition states that trade secrets consist of all forms and types of financial, business, scientific, technical, economic, or engineering information, including patterns, plans, compilations, program devices, formulas, designs, prototypes, methods, techniques, processes, procedures, programs, or codes, whether tangible or intangible, and whether or how stored, compiled, or memorialized physically, electronically, graphically, photographically, or in writing if the owner thereof has taken reasonable measures to keep such information secret, and, the information derives independent economic value, actual or potential, from not being generally known to, and not being readily ascertainable through proper means by another person who can obtain economic value from the disclosure or use of the information.[12]

---

[6] 18 U.S.C. Sections 1831–1839.

[7] https://www.justice.gov/archives/jm/criminal-resource-manual-1122-introduction-economic-espionage-act.

[8] 18 U.S.C. Section 1831.

[9] 18 U.S.C. Section 1832.

[10] 18 U.S.C. Sections 1836–1839.

[11] 18 U.S.C Sections 1832(a), 1839 (3).

[12] 18 U.S.C. Section 1839.

Is It a Trade Secret or Something Else?

Although determining whether something is a trade secret or not may be difficult, as discussed later, among other issues, there are a few preliminary requirements. First, the subject matter of a trade secret must be a secret. Therefore, matters of public knowledge or of general knowledge in an industry cannot become a trade secret. Likewise, a trade secret is generally limited to the particular business in which it is used, although it need not be limited to one individual in a business. It may be shared with others in the business under certain limited conditions. Regardless, a substantial element of secrecy must exist, so that, except by the use of improper means, it would be difficult to acquire the information.

Another issue is whether something is a trade secret or an employee's general knowledge? An employee's general skills, knowledge, and experience may not rise to the level of a trade secret. The Restatement (Third) of Unfair Competition notes that:

> Information that forms the general skill, knowledge, training, and experience of an employee cannot be claimed as a trade secret by a former employer even when the information is directly attributable to an investment of resources by the employer in the employee...Whether particular information is properly regarded as a trade secret of the former employer or as a part of the general skill, knowledge, training, and experience of the former employee depends on the facts and circumstances of the particular case.[13]

The distinction between general knowledge and experience and a trade secret is likely to be every bit as vague as the definition of a trade secret itself. The general skills and knowledge acquired during the course of employment are "... things an employee is free to take and use in later pursuits, especially if they do not take the form of written records, compilations or analyses."[14] This is distinguishable from "know-how." "...'[k] now how' takes on a meaning far beyond simply assembling components. Rather, it is the ability, gained from trial and error, experimentation and the expenditure of many dollars in investment which collective gave (the

[13] Restatement (Third) of Unfair Competition Section 42 comment d (1995).

[14] *AMP, Inc. v. Fleischhacker*, 823 F.2d 1199, 1207 (1987).

employer) this type of know-how. This know-how is distinguishable from an individual's general knowledge and skill."[15]

However, aside from the requirement of secrecy, there are a number of key features to a trade secret. As noted earlier, the Restatement (Second) of Torts stated that "A trade secret may consist of any formula, patterns, device, or compilation of information which is used in one's business, and which gives him an opportunity to obtain an advantage over competitors who do not know or use it." This is similar to the definition in the Restatement (Third) of Unfair Competition, Section 39 (1995)[16] although the Restatement of Unfair Competition has a definition that is broader than that noted in the Restatement of Torts. As comment five notes, "The definition of 'trade secret' contains a reasonable departure from the Restatement of Torts (First) definition which required that a trade secret be 'continuously used in one's business.'" The broader definition in the proposed Act extends protection to a plaintiff who has not yet had an opportunity or acquired the means to put a trade secret to use. The definition includes information that has commercial value from a negative viewpoint, for example, the results of lengthy and expensive research which proves that a certain process will not work could be of immense value to a competitor.

The UTSA Section 1(4) of 1985[17] also provides guidance and notes:

4. "Trade secret" means information, including a formula, pattern, compilation, program, device, method, technique, or process, that:
   i. derives independent economic value, actual or potential, from not being generally known to, and not being readily ascertainable by proper means by, other persons who can obtain economic value from its disclosure or use, and

---

[15] *S.I. Handling Sys., Inc. v. Heisley*, 581 F. Supp. 1553 (1984).

[16] A trade secret is any information that can be used in the operation of a business or other enterprise and that is sufficiently valuable and secret to afford an actual or potential economic advantage over others.

[17] (4) "Trade secret" means information, including a formula, pattern, compilation, program, device, method, technique, or process, that: (i) derives independent economic value, actual or potential, from not being generally known to, and not being readily ascertainable by proper means by, other persons who can obtain economic value from its disclosure or use, and (ii) is the subject of efforts that are reasonable under the circumstances to maintain its secrecy.

ii. is the subject of efforts that are reasonable under the circumstances to maintain its secrecy.

The Restatement of Torts Section 757 notes the factors that are considered in determining trade secret status that still seem to be in widespread use. Those factors include:

> The extent to which the information is known outside of the business;
>
> The extent to which it is known by employees and others involved in the business;
>
> The extent of measures taken by the business to guard the secrecy of the information;
>
> The value of the information to the business and its competitors;
>
> The amount of effort or money expended by the business in developing the information;
>
> The ease or difficulty with which the information could be properly acquired or duplicated by others.

Examples of a Trade Secret

An exhaustive list of trade secrets is impossible. The WIPO again provides a good summary of potential trade secrets and notes:

> Trade secrets encompass both technical information, such as information concerning manufacturing processes, pharmaceutical test data, designs and drawings of computer programs, and commercial information, such as distribution methods, lists of suppliers and clients, and advertising strategies.
>
> A trade secret may be also made up of a combination of elements, each of which by itself is in the public domain, but where the combination, which is kept secret, provides a competitive advantage.
>
> Other examples of information that may be protected by trade secrets include financial information, formulas and recipes and source codes.
>
> Therefore, trade secrets may include, but are not limited to:

customer lists[18]

formulas, such as the formula for Coca Cola™; and

manufacturing processes.[19]

In summary, a trade secret is information that is valuable, secret, and the subject of reasonable efforts by the owner to keep it a secret. This is generally consistent with the law of France on the subject.

Obtaining a Trade Secret By Improper Means

The UTSA specifies the methods that a trade secret may be obtained in a way that are likely to give rise to litigation, either civil, contractual and/or tort, or criminal[20]:

1. "Improper means" includes theft, bribery, misrepresentation, breach or inducement of a breach of a duty to maintain secrecy, or espionage through electronic or other means;
2. "Misappropriation" means:
   i. acquisition of a trade secret of another by a person who knows or has reason to know that the trade secret was acquired by improper means; or
   ii. disclosure or use of a trade secret of another without express or implied consent by a person who
      A. used improper means to acquire knowledge of the trade secret; or
      B. at the time of disclosure or use, knew or had reason to know that his knowledge of the trade secret was

[18] See, e.g., *Morlife Inc. v. Perry*, 56 Cal. App. 4th 1514 (1997) where a court held that customer identities may be protected as trade secrets as long as the identities are not generally known to the industry. The court identified three factors to be considered in determining whether something is a trade secret: 1. How the information is stored; 2. Who has access to the information; and 3. Whether the information is subject to a confidentiality agreement.

[19] See, e.g., *Gates Rubber Co. v. Bando Chemical Industries Ltd.*, 9 F.3d 823 (1993) holding that manufacturing specifics that are not publicly available may qualify as a trade secret.

[20] UTSA Section 101, 14 U.L.A. 438 (amended 1985).

I. derived from or through a person who had utilized improper means to acquire it;

II. acquired under circumstances giving rise to a duty to maintain its secrecy or limit its use; or

III. derived from or through a person who owed a duty to the person seeking relief to maintain its secrecy or limit its use; or

C. before a material change of his [or her] position, knew or had reason to know that it was a trade secret and that knowledge of it had been acquired by accident or mistake.

Note that this list is not exhaustive. The Restatement of Torts, Section 757, Comment (f) specifically notes that a complete catalogue of improper means is not possible and that the foregoing is simply a partial listing.

Needless to say, there are methods to obtain a trade secret legally. The Restatement of Torts, Section 757, Comment (f), notes that:

Proper means include:

1. Discovery by independent invention;
2. Discovery by "reverse engineering", that is, by starting with the known product and working backward to find the method by which it was developed. The acquisition of the known product must, of course, also be by a fair and honest means, such as purchase of the item on the open market for reverse engineering to be lawful;
3. Discovery under a license from the owner of the trade secret;
4. Observation of the item in public use or on public display;
5. Obtaining the trade secret from published literature.

French Law

The Definition of Undisclosed Know-How and Business Information ("Trade Secrets") in France

European efforts to address the issue of trade secrets culminated in Directive (EU) 2016-943 of June 8, 2016, the "Trade Secrets Directive."[21]

[21] https://www.wipo.int/wipolex/en/legislation/details/16435.

In France, this directive was implemented by way of Law No. 2018-670 of July 30, 2018, and validated by the French Constitutional Council on July 26, 2018.[22]

Article L151-1 of the French Commercial ("Trade") code[23] defines a "trade secret" and notes:

> Any information meeting the following criteria is protected by trade secrecy:
>
> 1. It is not, in itself or in the exact configuration and assembly of its elements, generally known or easily accessible for people familiar with this type of information because of their sector of activity;
> 2. It has a commercial value, actual or potential, because of its secret nature;
> 3. It is the subject on the part of its legitimate holder of reasonable protection measures, taking into account the circumstances, to preserve its secrecy.

Article L151-2:

> The legitimate holder of a trade secret is anyone who has control of it in a lawful manner.

Article L151-3:

> The modes of lawfully obtaining a trade secret are:
>
> 1. An independent discovery or creation;
> 2. The observation, study, disassembly, or test of a product or an object which has been made available to the public or which is lawfully in the possession of the person who obtains the information, except contractual stipulation prohibiting or limiting the obtaining of secrecy.

---

[22] https://www.august-debouzy.com/en/blog/1258-trade-secrets-better-protected-by-french-law-and-by-the-courts.

[23] This is a Google Translate English translation of the French trade code effective June 14, 2022.

Article L151-4 notes that obtaining a trade secret is unlawful when it is carried out without the consent of its legitimate holder and results from:

1. Unauthorized access to any document, object, material, substance, or digital file which contains the secret or from which it can be deduced, or from an unauthorized appropriation or copying of these elements;
2. Any other behavior considered, given the circumstances, as unfair and contrary to commercial practice.

And Article L151-5 goes on to note that:

> The use or disclosure of a trade secret is unlawful when it is carried out without the consent of its legitimate holder by a person who has obtained the secret under the conditions mentioned in Article L. 151-4 or who acts in breach of an obligation not to disclose the secret or to limit its use.
>
> The production, offer, or placing on the market, as well as the import, export, or storage for these purposes of any product resulting significantly from a breach of trade secrecy are also considered to be illicit where the person carrying out these activities knew, or ought to have known in the circumstances.

Article L151-6 provides additional guidance and notes:

> Obtaining, using or disclosing a trade secret is also considered unlawful when, at the time of obtaining, using or disclosing the secret, a person knew, or should have known, given the circumstances, that this secret had been obtained, directly or indirectly, from another person who used or disclosed it unlawfully within the meaning of the first paragraph of Article L. 151-5.

However, French law goes on to note certain limitations to the protection that is afforded to trade secrets. Article L151-8 notes:

> On the occasion of a proceeding relating to an attack on business secrecy, the secret is not opposable when its obtaining, use, or disclosure has taken place:

1. To exercise the right to freedom of expression and communication, including respect for freedom of the press, and freedom of information as proclaimed in the Charter of Fundamental Rights of the European Union;
2. To reveal, with the aim of protecting the general interest and in good faith, an illegal activity, a fault or reprehensible behavior, including during the exercise of the right to alert defined in article 6 of the law n 2016-1691 of December 9, 2016 relating to transparency,

Thus, whether in America or France, among other requirements, in order to be a "trade secret" it must be valuable, secret, and the owner must take reasonable measures to maintain the confidentiality of the trade secret.

Protecting a Trade Secret

What are "Reasonable" Protection Measures?

As with the word "secret' there is no specific definition of what constitutes reasonable efforts. A court is likely to evaluate a variety of factors, including the efforts by the company to protect the trade secret. Courts require a variety of efforts, including, but not limited to, confidentiality agreements,[24] restricted access,[25] and passwords.[26] Such efforts necessarily involve a variety of considerations, including,

1. The security of the location where the secret is stored;
2. The security of the electronic location of the secret, including limitations on the use of electronic devices;
3. Limitations on the personnel that have access to the information as well as contracts with those that do have access; and,
4. Advising all employees, including newly hired employees, existing employees as well as employees that are retiring or otherwise leaving their employment on the existence of trade secret information.

The foregoing will also necessarily involve considerations of:

---

[24] See, e.g., *Tyson Metal Prods., Inc. v. McCann*, 546 A.2d 119, 122 (1988).

[25] See, e.g., *Capsonic Group, Inc. v. Plas-Met Corp.*, 361 N.E.2d 41, 44 (1977).

[26] See, e.g., *Schalk v. State*, 767 S.W.2d 441, 443 (1988).

1. The effort and expense that was incurred to develop the information;
2. The effort and expense to maintain the secrecy;
3. The value of the information, both as to the owner, as well as competitors.

The foregoing list should not be considered exhaustive.

Misappropriation[27] (Infringement)

The United States

The UTSA defines infringement as:

1. The acquisition of a trade secret by another who knows or has reason to know that the trade secret was acquired by improper means; or
2. Any disclosure or use of a trade secret of another without express or implied consent that was knowingly obtained by an improper means.

An "improper means" includes:

1. Theft;
2. Bribery;
3. Misrepresentation;
4. Breach or inducement of a breach of a duty to maintain secrecy; or
5. Espionage through electronic or other means.

Acquisition of a Trade Secret by Lawful Means

French Law

Similar to the law in America, the French Commercial Code, Section L 151-3 notes that acquisition is lawful when the trade secret is obtained as a result of independent discovery or creation, or of the observation, disassembly, or testing of a product that has been made available to the public (or, as previously noted, "reverse" engineering).

---

[27]The misappropriation of trade secrets is considered a form of unfair competition and is discussed in the Restatement (Third) of Unfair Competition.

Other situations where acquisition is unlawful are noted in the following sections. L 151-4 notes that acquisition is unlawful when the trade secret is acquired without the consent of the trade secret holder by

i. Unauthorized access to, appropriation of, or copying or, more generally;
ii. Any other conduct which, under the circumstances, is considered dishonest and contrary to commercial practices.

Other situations where acquisition of a trade secret is unlawful are specified in Article L151-5 which notes that:

> The use or disclosure of a trade secret is unlawful when it is carried out without the consent of its legitimate holder by a person who has obtained the secret under the conditions mentioned in Article L. 151-4 or who acts in breach of an obligation not to disclose the secret or to limit its use.
>
> The production, offer, or placing on the market, as well as the import, export, or storage for these purposes of any product resulting significantly from a breach of trade secrecy are also considered to be a use unlawful when the person carrying out these activities knew, or ought to have known in view of the circumstances, that this secret was being used unlawfully within the meaning of the first paragraph of this article.

And Article L 151-6 notes that:

> Obtaining, using, or disclosing a trade secret is also considered unlawful when, at the time of obtaining, using, or disclosing the secret, a person knew, or should have known at given the circumstances, that this secret had been obtained, directly or indirectly, from another person who used or disclosed it unlawfully within the meaning of the first paragraph of Article L 151-5.

However, French law, as is true with American law, also recognizes certain limitations. Article L. 151-7 notes that:

> Trade secrecy is not enforceable when the obtaining, use, or disclosure of the secret is required or authorized by European Union law,

> international treaties, or agreements in force or national law, in particular in the exercise of the powers of investigation, control, authorization, or sanction of the jurisdictional or administrative authorities.

And Article L. 151-8 goes on to note that:

> On the occasion of a proceeding relating to an attack on business secrecy, the secret is not opposable (recognized) when its obtaining, use, or disclosure has taken place:
>
> 1. To exercise the right to freedom of expression and communication, including respect for freedom of the press, and freedom of information as proclaimed in the Charter of Fundamental Rights of the European Union[28];
> 2. To reveal, with the aim of protecting the general interest and in good faith, an illegal activity, a fault, or reprehensible behavior, including during the exercise of the right to alert defined in Article 6 of the Law No. 2016-1691 of December 9, 2016 relating to transparency, the fight against corruption and the modernization of economic life under the conditions defined in Articles 6 and 8 of the same law;
> 3. For the protection of a legitimate interest recognized by European Union law or national law.

And last, Article 151-9 notes that:

> On the occasion of a proceeding relating to a breach of business secrecy, the secrecy is not opposable when:

[28] In this regard, French law is virtually identical to American law and specifically the issue of the First Amendment. As noted by David Greene, Trade Secrets, the First Amendment and the Challenges of the Internet Age, 23 Hastings Comm. & Ent. L.J. 537 (2001). Available at: https://repository.uclawsf.edu/hastings_comm_ent_law_journal/vol23/iss3/2/, "Trade secrets directly conflict with First Amendment rights of free speech and free press when trade secret holders seek to restrict the publication of their trade secrets by others. Indeed, the Uniform Trade Secrets Act provides for injunctions against the disclosure of trade secrets as a primary remedy. However, First Amendment principles, if applied fully, can make it extremely difficult to obtain such relief, especially when the publisher owes no duty of confidentiality to the owner of the secret."

> 1. Obtaining business secrecy occurred within the framework of the exercise of the right to information and consultation of employees or their representatives;
> 2. The disclosure of trade secrets by employees to their representatives occurred within the framework of the legitimate exercise by the latter of their functions, insofar as this disclosure was necessary for this exercise.
>
> The information thus obtained or disclosed remains protected by trade secrecy with regard to persons other than the employees or their representatives who have knowledge of it.

Article L 152-2 establishes a five-year statute of limitations "... from the day on which the legitimate holder of trade secrets knew or should have known of the last fact which is the cause."

Trade Secrets and Criminal Law

The United States

In certain situations, as noted earlier, theft of a trade secret may implicate criminal law. Under Section 1832(a) of the Economic Espionage Act of 1996, misappropriating a trade secret used in interstate commerce or foreign commerce may result in fines or imprisonment. Congress enacted the Defend Trade Secrets Act (DTSA)[29] as an amendment to the Economic Espionage Act,[30] a federal criminal statute. The DTSA added a private civil cause of action.

French law is similar and Article L621-1 notes:

> The penalties for the violation of trade secrets are provided for in Article L. 1227-1 of the Labor Code which states:
>
> The act of a director or an employee revealing or attempting to reveal a trade secret is punishable by imprisonment for two years and a fine of 30,000 euros.

---

[29] 18 U.S.C. Section 1836 *et seq.*

[30] 18 U.S.C. Sections 1831–1839. The Act generally defines "economic espionage" as the theft or misappropriation of trade secrets intending or knowing that the offense will benefit "any foreign government, foreign instrumentality, or foreign agent." See 18 U.S.C Section 1831.

> The court may also pronounce, as an additional penalty, for a maximum period of five years, the prohibition of civic, civil and family rights provided for by article 131-26 of the penal code.

Section 131-26 of the French penal code allows a judge to impose the following penalties as well and states that:

> The prohibition of civic, civil and family rights relates to:
>
> 1. The right to vote;
> 2. eligibility;
> 3. the right to exercise a judicial function or to be an expert before a court, to represent or assist a party before the courts;
> 4. the right to testify in court other than to make simple statements;
> 5. the right to be tutor or curator; this prohibition does not exclude the right, after assent of the guardianship judge, after hearing the family council, to be guardian or curator of one's own children.
>
> The prohibition of civic, civil, and family rights may not exceed a period of 10 years in the event of conviction for a crime and a period of 5 years in the event of a conviction for an offence.
>
> The court may order the prohibition of all or part of these rights.
>
> Prohibition of the right to vote or ineligibility pronounced pursuant to this article entails prohibition or incapacity to exercise a public function.

Remedies

The United States

The UTSA expressly displaced all other civil remedies for misappropriation aside from those based on the law of contracts.[31] The remedies that are available depend on whether the misappropriation is threatened or actual.[32] For actual misappropriation a court is likely to award damages. For threatened misappropriation an injunction is the appropriate remedy.

---

[31] Unif. Trade Secrets Act with 1985 Amendments Section 7.

[32] As will be discussed, there is also the issue of inevitable disclosure.

The DTSA notes that the available remedies[33] include:

> An injunction to preserve evidence and prevent trade secret disclosure, provided that it does not:
>
> Prevent a person from entering into an employment relationship; and
>
> That any conditions placed on the employment relationship are based on evidence of threatened misappropriation and not merely on the information the person knows; or
>
> Otherwise, conflict with an applicable state law prohibiting restraints on the practice of a lawful profession, trade, or business;
>
> Compensatory damages;
>
> Exemplary damages up to two times the amount of the damages for willful and malicious misappropriation; and
>
> Reasonable attorneys' fees for the prevailing party for certain bad faith conduct.

The UTSA addresses the issue of injunctions in section two,[34] and damages in section three[35] which notes:

> Damages: (a) Except to the extent that a material and prejudicial change of position prior to acquiring knowledge or reason to know of misappropriation renders a monetary recovery inequitable, a complainant is entitled to recover damages for misappropriation. Damages can include both the actual loss caused by misappropriation and the unjust enrichment caused by misappropriation that is not taken into account in computing actual loss. In lieu of damages measured by any other methods, the damages caused by misappropriation may be measured by imposition of liability for a reasonable royalty for a misappropriator's unauthorized disclosure or use of a trade secret…

French law is similar. As noted in the Trade Code[36] Article L152-3:

---

[33] 18 U.S.C. Section 1836(b)(3).

[34] UTSA Section 2, 14 U.L.A. 437 (amended 1985).

[35] UTSA Section 3, 14 U.L.A. 437 (amended 1985).

[36] Code de commerce version in force on May 3, 2023.

I. In the context of an action relating to the prevention or cessation of an attack on a trade secret, the court may, without prejudice to the award of damages, prescribe, including under penalty, any proportionate measure likely to prevent or put an end to such interference. It may in particular:
   1. Prohibit the performance or continuation of acts of use or disclosure of a trade secret;
   2. Prohibit the acts of production, offer, placing on the market, or use of products significantly resulting from the breach of business secrecy or the import, export, or storage of such products at these purposes;
   3. Order the total or partial destruction of any document, object, material, substance, or digital file containing the business secret concerned or from which it can be deduced or, as the case may be, order their total or partial handing over to the applicant.

II. The court may also order that the products resulting significantly from the breach of business secrecy be recalled from commercial channels, permanently removed from these channels, modified in order to remove the breach of trade secrecy, destroyed or, as the case may be, confiscated for the benefit of the injured party.

III. When the court limits the duration of the measures mentioned in 1 and 2 of I, the fixed duration must be sufficient to eliminate any commercial or economic advantage that the perpetrator of the breach of trade secrecy could have derived from unlawful acquisition, use, or disclosure of trade secrets.

IV. Except in special circumstances and without prejudice to any damages that may be claimed, the measures mentioned in I to III are ordered at the expense of the infringer.

It may be terminated at the request of the infringer when the information concerned can no longer be qualified as a business secret within the meaning of Article L. 151-1 for reasons that do not depend, directly or indirectly, on him.

French law also provides for civil penalties. Article L152-5 notes,

Without prejudice to Article L. 152-6, the court may order at the request of the perpetrator of the infringement, the payment of compensation to the injured party instead of the measures mentioned in I to III of Article L. Article L. 152-3 when the following conditions are met:

> 1. At the time of the use or disclosure of the trade secret, the perpetrator of the infringement did not know, nor could he have known in view of the circumstances, that the trade secret had been obtained from another person who used or disclosed it unlawfully;
> 2. The execution of the measures mentioned in I to III of Article L. 152-3 would cause the perpetrator disproportionate damage;
> 3. The payment of compensation to the injured party seems reasonably satisfactory.
>
> When the payment of this indemnity is ordered instead of the measures provided for in 1. and 2. of I of the same article L. 152-3, this indemnity cannot be set at a sum greater than the amount of the duties that would have been due if the infringer had requested authorization to use said trade secret for the period during which the use of the trade secret could have been prohibited.

And Article L152-6 specifies the method to calculate the damages:

> To set the damages due in compensation for the harm actually suffered, the court takes into consideration separately:
>
> 1. The negative economic consequences of the breach of business secrecy, including the loss of profit and the loss suffered by the injured party, including loss of chance;
> 2. The moral prejudice caused to the injured party;
> 3. The profits made by the perpetrator of the breach of trade secrecy, including the savings in intellectual, material and promotional investments that he has withdrawn from the breach.
>
> The court may, as an alternative and at the request of the injured party, award as damages a lump sum which takes into account in particular the rights which would have been due if the author of the infringement had requested authorization to use the trade secret in question. This sum is not exclusive of compensation for the moral damage caused to the injured party.

In summary, in the case of actual disclosure the typical remedy is damages. This may understate the extent of the recovery since, once the information is publicly available, it ceases to be a trade secret, with a potentially significant economic loss to the owner. For threatened misappropriation the appropriate remedy is an injunction to prevent disclosure or use.

Confidentiality and Non-Competition Agreements in Employment

Discovery in Civil Litigation

"As a general rule, 'confidentiality agreements will not stand as a barrier to discovery between two parties in litigation.' (Citations omitted). ('Confidential' does not necessarily mean 'privileged'.) There certainly may be instances where information that happens to be covered by a non-disclosure agreement — such as trade secrets — is privileged and thereby protected from discovery. However, the non-disclosure agreement itself does not confer a legal privilege from discovery on any documents that were not already privileged."[37]

Not all states permit non-competition agreements. California Business & Professions Code Section 16600 notes:

> Except as provided in this chapter, every contract by which anyone is restrained from engaging in a lawful profession, trade, or business of any kind is to that extent void.

Even in the absence of a law such as California's, such agreements are not without controversy. While non-disclosure agreements are typical, there are limitations. If, for instance, a company restricts post-employment use of publicly available information, a court may strictly analyze the agreement in a way that more closely resembles the attention paid to non-competition agreements. And although California's outright hostility to non-competition agreements is well known, recently a California court held that Section 16600 does not apply during the term of employment since an employee's duty of loyalty justifies such a restriction.[38]

---

[37] *Shvartser v. Lekser*, 270 F.Supp.3d 96 (2017).

[38] *Techno Lite, Inc. v. EMCOD, LLC,* 44 Cal. App. 5th, 462 (2020).

Unless forbidden by law, any such agreements must generally be "reasonable" and "narrowly tailored."[39] The courts look at several issues. First, in order to be narrowly tailored, the covenant must protect a legitimate interest of the employer. And second, in order to be reasonable, the covenant must be reasonable in duration, subject matter, and geographic coverage.

At issue in *Foster Cable Svs., Inc. v. Deville*[40] was an exceptionally broad confidentiality agreement that, in summary, purported to make any information exchanged between the parties as trade secret and confidential. In refusing to enforce the agreement the court noted, "Plaintiff did not tailor the Agreement in a way that explicitly protected information related to its customers or pricing, but instead drafted it to cover 'all information provided by either party [to the other].' Therefore, the Court finds that the Agreement is not reasonably drawn, as it not only bars Defendant Deville from disclosing any trade secrets learned during his employment, but also prevents him from disclosing any information, including his experience and knowledge gained during that time. Moreover, the fact that the Agreement does not state a time limitation, but instead applies forever, further supports a finding that it is unenforceable."

In summary, when it comes to such agreements, one size does not fit all and each agreement must be tailored to the specific employee. Thus, while high-ranking employees in a company are generally subject to an agreement with a longer term, the duration must be no longer than what is required to protect the interests of the employer while recognizing the potential hardship to the employee. As part of that, a court may be unlikely to enforce a nationwide restriction on employment opportunities since it may impose an undue hardship on an employee by requiring them to move to another country. And the covenant must be specific to the employee's work responsibilities.

---

[39] Confidentiality and noncompetition agreements are not limited to the United States. See, for instance, Article L. 1222-1 of the French Labor Code that requires "good faith" in the execution of an employment contract.

[40] 368 F.Supp.3d 1265 (2019).

Inevitable Disclosure

Inevitable Disclosure Doctrine (IDD) Defined

"[W]here an employee's work for a new employer substantially overlaps with work for a former employer, based on the same role, industry, and geographic region, a...court may conclude that th[e] employee would likely use confidential information to the former employer's detriment."[41] In that situation, the inevitable disclosure doctrine may allow a "... court to enjoin a former employee from working at a competitor of the employer, even if the former employee never entered into a non-competition agreement, if the court finds that such employment would inevitably lead to a disclosure of the trade secret."[42]

While courts traditionally relied on the law of equity in this situation, the UTSA Section 2(a) provides that "... threatened misappropriation may be enjoined." Although the remedy may be the same, inevitable disclosure is different from threatened disclosure.

Pepsico v. Redmond, 54 F.3d. 1262 (1995)

> William Redmond worked for PepsiCo in its Pepsi-Cola North America division ("PCNA") from 1984 to 1994. Redmond became the General Manager of the Northern California Business Unit in June 1993, and was promoted one year later to General Manager of the business unit covering all of California, a unit having annual revenues of more than 500 million dollars and representing twenty percent of PCNA's profit for all of the United States.
>
> Redmond's relatively high-level position at PCNA gave him access to inside information and trade secrets. Redmond, like other PepsiCo management employees signed a confidentiality agreement with PepsiCo that stated in relevant part that he w[ould] not disclose at any time, to anyone other than officers or employees of [PepsiCo], or make use of, confidential information relating to the business of [PepsiCo] ... obtained while in the employ of [PepsiCo], which shall not be generally known or available to the public or recognized as standard practices.

---

[41] *Jazz Pharms., Inc. v. Snchrony Grp.*, LLC 343 F.Supp.3d 434 (2018).

[42] *Architext, Inc. v. Kikuchi*, 2005 WL 2864244, at *3 (2005).

Donald Uzzi, who left PepsiCo in the beginning of 1994 to become the head of Quaker's Gatorade division, began courting Redmond for Quaker in May, 1994. Redmond met in Chicago with Quaker officers in August, 1994, and on October 20, 1994, Quaker, through Uzzi, offered Redmond the position of Vice President — On Premise Sales for Gatorade. Redmond did not then accept the offer but continued to negotiate for more money. Throughout this time, Redmond kept his dealings with Quaker secret from his employers at PCNA.

On November 8, 1994, Uzzi extended Redmond a written offer for the position of Vice President–Field Operations for Gatorade and Redmond accepted. Later that same day, Redmond called William Bensyl, the Senior Vice President of Human Resources for PCNA, and told him that he had an offer from Quaker to become the Chief Operating Officer of the combined Gatorade and Snapple company but had not yet accepted it. Redmond also asked whether he should, in light of the offer, carry out his plans to make calls upon certain PCNA customers. Bensyl told Redmond to make the visits.

Redmond also misstated his situation to a number of his PCNA colleagues, including Craig Weatherup, PCNA's President and Chief Executive Officer, and Brenda Barnes, PCNA's Chief Operating Officer and Redmond's immediate superior. As with Bensyl, Redmond told them that he had been offered the position of Chief Operating Officer at Gatorade and that he was leaning "60/40" in favor of accepting the new position.

On November 10, 1994, Redmond met with Barnes and told her that he had decided to accept the Quaker offer and was resigning from PCNA. Barnes immediately took Redmond to Bensyl, who told Redmond that PepsiCo was considering legal action against him.

… PepsiCo filed this diversity suit on November 16, 1994, seeking a temporary restraining order to enjoin Redmond from assuming his duties at Quaker and to prevent him from disclosing trade secrets or confidential information to his new employer. The district court granted PepsiCo's request that same day but dissolved the order *sua sponte* two days later, after determining that PepsiCo had failed to meet its burden of establishing that it would suffer irreparable harm. The court found that PepsiCo's fears about Redmond were based upon a mistaken understanding of his new position at Quaker and that the likelihood that Redmond would improperly reveal any confidential information did not 'rise above mere speculation'.

From November 23, 1994, to December 1, 1994, the district court conducted a preliminary injunction hearing on the same matter. At the hearing, PepsiCo offered evidence of a number of trade secrets and confidential information it desired protected and to which Redmond was privy.

Having shown Redmond's intimate knowledge of PCNA's plans for 1995, PepsiCo argued that Redmond would inevitably disclose that information to Quaker in his new position, at which he would have substantial input as to Gatorade and Snapple pricing, costs, margins, distribution systems, products, packaging and marketing, and could give Quaker an unfair advantage in its upcoming skirmishes with PepsiCo.

On December 15, 1994, the district court issued an order enjoining Redmond from assuming his position at Quaker through May 1995, and permanently from using or disclosing any PCNA trade secrets or confidential information...The court, which completely adopted PepsiCo's position, found that Redmond's new job posed a clear threat of misappropriation of trade secrets and confidential information that could be enjoined under Illinois statutory and common law. The court also emphasized Redmond's lack of forthrightness both in his activities before accepting his job with Quaker and in his testimony as factors leading the court to believe the threat of misappropriation was real. This appeal followed.

The question of threatened or inevitable misappropriation in this case lies at the heart of a basic tension in trade secret law. Trade secret law serves to protect "standards of commercial morality" and "encourage [] invention and innovation" while maintaining "the public interest in having free and open competition in the manufacture and sale of unpatented goods." (Citation omitted). Yet that same law should not prevent workers from pursuing their livelihoods when they leave their current positions. (Citation omitted)...

This tension is particularly exacerbated when a plaintiff sues to prevent not the actual misappropriation of trade secrets but the mere threat that it will occur. While the ITSA plainly permits a court to enjoin the threat of misappropriation of trade secrets, there is little law in Illinois or in this circuit establishing what constitutes threatened or inevitable misappropriation. Indeed, there are only two cases in this circuit that address the issue...

PepsiCo presented substantial evidence at the preliminary injunction hearing that Redmond possessed extensive and intimate knowledge about PCNA's strategic goals for 1995 in sports drinks and new age drinks. The district court concluded on the basis of that presentation that unless

Redmond possessed an uncanny ability to compartmentalize information, he would necessarily be making decisions about Gatorade and Snapple by relying on his knowledge of PCNA trade secrets. It is not the "general skills and knowledge acquired during his tenure with PepsiCo that PepsiCo seeks to keep from falling into Quaker's hands, but rather "the particularized plans or processes developed by [PCNA] and disclosed to him while the employer-employee relationship existed, which are unknown to others in the industry and which give the employer an advantage over his competitors." (Citation omitted).

Admittedly, PepsiCo has not brought a traditional trade secret case, in which a former employee has knowledge of a special manufacturing process or customer list and can give a competitor an unfair advantage by transferring the technology or customers to that competitor. (Citations omitted). PepsiCo has not contended that Quaker has stolen the All Sport formula or its list of distributors. Rather PepsiCo has asserted that Redmond cannot help but rely on PCNA trade secrets as he helps plot Gatorade and Snapple's new course, and that these secrets will enable Quaker to achieve a substantial advantage by knowing exactly how PCNA will price, distribute, and market its sports drinks and new age drinks and being able to respond strategically. (Citation omitted). This type of trade secret problem may arise less often, but it nevertheless falls within the realm of trade secret protection under the present circumstances.

Quaker and Redmond assert that they have not and do not intend to use whatever confidential information Redmond has by virtue of his former employment. They point out that Redmond has already signed an agreement with Quaker not to disclose any trade secrets or confidential information gleaned from his earlier employment. They also note with regard to distribution systems that even if Quaker wanted to steal information about PCNA's distribution plans, they would be completely useless in attempting to integrate the Gatorade and Snapple beverage lines.

The defendants' arguments fall somewhat short of the mark. Again, the danger of misappropriation in the present case is not that Quaker threatens to use PCNA's secrets to create distribution systems or co-opt PCNA's advertising and marketing ideas. Rather, PepsiCo believes that Quaker, unfairly armed with knowledge of PCNA's plans, will be able to anticipate its distribution, packaging, pricing, and marketing moves. Redmond and Quaker even concede that Redmond might be faced with a decision that could be influenced by certain confidential information that he obtained while at PepsiCo. In other words, PepsiCo finds itself in the position of a coach, one of whose players has left, playbook in hand, to join the opposing team before the big game. Quaker and Redmond's protestations that their distribution systems and plans are entirely different from PCNA's are thus not really responsive.

The district court also concluded from the evidence that Uzzi's actions in hiring Redmond and Redmond's actions in pursuing and accepting his new job demonstrated a lack of candor on their part and proof of their willingness to misuse PCNA trade secrets, findings Quaker and Redmond vigorously challenge. The court expressly found that:

> Redmond's lack of forthrightness on some occasions, and out and out lies on others, in the period between the time he accepted the position with defendant Quaker and when he informed plaintiff that he had accepted that position leads the court to conclude that defendant Redmond could not be trusted to act with the necessary sensitivity and good faith under the circumstances in which the only practical verification that he was not using plaintiff's secrets would be defendant Redmond's word to that effect.

Thus, when we couple the demonstrated inevitability that Redmond would rely on PCNA trade secrets in his new job at Quaker with the district court's reluctance to believe that Redmond would refrain from disclosing these secrets in his new position (or that Quaker would ensure Redmond did not disclose them), we conclude that the district court correctly decided that PepsiCo demonstrated a likelihood of success on its statutory claim of trade secret misappropriation.

In conclusion, the court affirmed the district court's order enjoining Redmond from assuming his responsibilities at Quaker through May 1995 and preventing him from ever disclosing PCNA trade secrets and confidential information.

French law is similar and Article L623-27 of the Intellectual Property Code notes,

> Any person with standing to sue for infringement may apply for interim measures to the competent civil court in order to have ordered, if necessary, under penalty, against the alleged infringer or the intermediaries whose services he uses, any measure intended to prevent an imminent infringement to the rights conferred by the title or to prevent the prosecution of alleged acts of infringement. The competent civil court may also order any urgent measures on request when the circumstances

require that these measures not be taken jointly, in particular when any delay would be likely to cause irreparable harm to the plaintiff. Referred to in summary proceedings or on request, the court may only order the measures requested if the evidence, reasonably accessible to the applicant, makes it likely that his rights are being infringed or that such infringement is imminent.

The court may prohibit the prosecution of the alleged acts of infringement, make it subject to the constitution of guarantees intended to ensure the possible compensation of the plaintiff or order the seizure or delivery into the hands of a third party of the products suspected of infringing the rights conferred by the title, to prevent their introduction or circulation in commercial circuits. If the claimant proves circumstances likely to compromise the recovery of damages, the court may order the precautionary seizure of the movable and immovable property of the alleged infringer, including the blocking of his bank accounts and other assets, in accordance with common law. To determine the assets likely to be subject to seizure, it may order the communication of banking, financial, accounting or commercial documents or access to relevant information.

It can also grant the plaintiff a provision when the existence of his prejudice is not seriously contestable.

Seised in summary proceedings or on request, the court may make the execution of the measures it orders subject to the provision by the plaintiff of guarantees intended to ensure the possible compensation of the defendant if the infringement action is subsequently deemed to be unfounded or the measures cancelled.

When the measures taken to put an end to an infringement of the rights are ordered before the initiation of an action on the merits, the plaintiff must, within a time limit fixed by regulatory means, either appeal by civil or criminal means, or file a complaint with the public prosecutor. Failing this, at the request of the defendant and without the latter having to justify his request, the measures ordered are cancelled, without prejudice to any damages that may be claimed.

Summary

Whether in the United States or France, the subject of trade secrets is difficult and will likely involve the services of an attorney. The primary issue is likely to start with whether the information in question constitutes a trade secret. That will be followed by whether the owner took "reasonable steps" to protect the trade secret. Any such analysis may also involve issues regarding the First Amendment, in the United States, as well as the equivalent protection that is specified in French law.[43]

[43]Adding to the complexity will be additional considerations in both the United States and France, involving such diverse issues as tort liability, breach of contract, as well as employment law, and criminal law possibly among others.

Index

www.ingramcontent.com/pod-product-compliance
Lightning Source LLC
LaVergne TN
LVHW011656200926
848484LV00004B/955
* 9 7 8 9 8 1 1 2 7 6 9 0 3 *